THE ACTS OF THE WITNESSES

G.V.Cassel sculp

Lodowick Muggleton
Dyed the 14 of March 169⅞: then Aged 88 years
7 months: & 14 Dayes.

THE
ACTS OF
THE WITNESSES

*The Autobiography of Lodowick Muggleton
and Other Early Muggletonian Writings*

Edited by
T. L. Underwood

New York   Oxford
Oxford University Press
1999

Oxford University Press

Oxford   New York

Athens   Auckland   Bangkok   Bogotá   Buenos Aires   Calcutta
Cape Town   Chennai   Dar es Salaam   Delhi   Florence   Hong Kong   Istanbul
Karachi   Kuala Lumpur   Madrid   Melbourne   Mexico City   Mumbai
Nairobi   Paris   São Paulo   Singapore   Taipei   Tokyo   Toronto   Warsaw

and associated companies in
Berlin   Ibadan

Copyright © 1999 by T. L. Underwood

Published by Oxford University Press, Inc.
198 Madison Avenue, New York, New York 10016

Oxford is a registered trademark of Oxford University Press

Frontispiece: Engraved portrait of Lodowick Muggleton from *The Acts of the Witnesses* (1699).
By permission of the British Library, shelfmark 699.f.9. (1.).

Library of Congress Cataloging-in-Publication Data
The acts of the witnesses : the autobiography of Lodowick Muggleton and other
early Muggletonian writings / edited by T.L. Underwood.
p.   cm.
Includes bibliographical references and indexes.
ISBN 0-19-512074-4
1. Muggletonians   2. Muggleton, Lodowick, 1609–1698.
3. Muggletonians—Biography.   I. Muggleton, Lodowick, 1609–1698.
II. Underwood, T. L. (Ted L.)
BX8698.A37   1999
289.9—dc21   98-49217

1 3 5 7 9 8 6 4 2

Printed in the United States of America
on acid-free paper

To
Christopher Hill
and
the memory of
E. P. Thompson

Preface

The Acts of the Witnesses, our short-title and the title of Muggleton's autobiography, refers to the prophetic efforts of John Reeve and Lodowick
Muggleton, the central figures of a remarkable sect that arose in mid-
seventeenth-century England and that eventually took the latter's name. Of
the radical religious movements born in those tumultuous middle decades,
only Quakers and Muggletonians survived much beyond that period, but
not until the 1980s was it generally known in scholarly circles that Muggletonianism had continued on into the late twentieth century. The story of the
identification of Philip Noakes of Matfield, Kent, as the last Muggletonian
and the discovery of the archive of Muggletonian materials later acquired
from him by the British Library shortly before his death in 1979 is told in
Christopher Hill, Barry Reay, and William Lamont's collection of essays,
The World of the Muggletonians (London: Temple Smith, 1983) and in E. P.
Thompson's *Witness against the Beast* (Cambridge: Cambridge University
Press, 1993). Although perhaps not yet in its final arrangement, the Muggletonian Archive comprises Additional Manuscripts 60168–60256: eighty-
nine volumes of letters, treatises, verses, accounts, and printed works. This
treasury of sources awaits the further examination of enterprising scholars,
for although the above writers have provided fine introductions to the sect,
much more remains to be done, ranging from a general history of the movement (especially the post-seventeenth-century period) to detailed analyses of
specific beliefs and practices with their contextual connections. Such studies

should tell us a good deal more about the milieu of radical ideas of the time and shed further light on what Hill has called "a strange religious underworld, as yet barely explored, to which the Muggletonians relate."[1] In providing this volume of early Muggletonian writings, it is my hope not only to make these materials more accessible but also to attract and encourage such scholarship and to commemorate the tercentenaries of Muggleton's death in 1698 and the publication of his autobiography in 1699.[2]

My work has been generously supported by the University of Minnesota Graduate School Faculty Research Grant Program. It has also benefited from the assistance and advice of Sylvia Carlyle, Juleen Eichinger, Valerie Hart, Terri Hawkinson, Clive Hurst, Neil Keeble, Josef Keith, Margaret Von Hellwig, Elizabeth Johnson, Alice Laird, Ardath Larson, Elizabeth Norman, Geoffrey F. Nuttall, David Savela, Nicholas Smith, Alison Sproston, Yvonne Storck, Charlotte Syverson, Christopher Sheppard, Ann W. Upton, C. J. Wright, and David Wuolu. In addition, I extend my thanks for the service provided by the libraries and staffs noted in the introduction; for the encouragement of Edith Farrell, Thomas and Belinda Keeley, Christine and Peter Stevens, Michael and Ann Jones, Dimitra Giannuli, Eleanor Keeley, Vera and John Stevens, Michael and Anne Wakelin, H. Larry Ingle, Bryony Jones, and Michael Stevens; and for the interest of my many faculty colleagues and students who were first attracted by the name of the sect and then intrigued by its characteristics. Also lending their support were the following University of Minnesota, Morris, administrators: Chancellor David Johnson, Vice Chancellor for Academic Affairs Samuel Schuman, and Social Sciences Division Chair Jooinn Lee. I am especially endebted to Christopher Hill, Stephen Brachlow, Dewey D. Wallace, and Richard Greaves for their strong interest in the project; additionally to Richard Greaves for his critique of an early version of the introduction; and to Linda Elias, the professional legal secretary who, in returning to the university to complete her B.A., served as my project assistant for a year under the Morris Academic Partners program. In addition, I wish to record my gratitude for the steady and good-humored support of my immediate family: Judith, Tamara, Mark, James, Elizabeth, and Charlotte.

Finally, this volume is dedicated to Christopher Hill and the memory of E. P. Thompson, who have done so much to enlighten us about the "underclass" and the "radicals" in English history.

Morris, Minnesota   T. L. U.
July 1998

Contents

Abbreviations

Acts   Lodowick Muggleton, *The Acts of the Witnesses* (1699).

BDBR   Richard L. Greaves and Robert Zaller, eds., *Biographical Dictionary of British Radicals*, 3 vols. (Brighton: Harvester Press, 1982–84).

DNB   Leslie Stephen and Sidney Lee, eds., *The Dictionaty of National Biography*, 22 vols. (London: Oxford University Press, 1949–50).

OED   *Oxford English Dictionary*

Transcendent   John Reeve and Lodowick Muggleton, *A Transcendent Spiritual Treatise* (1652).

Wing   Donald Wing, *Short-title Catalogue of Books . . . 1641–1700*, 2d ed., 3 vols. (New York: Modern Language Association of America, 1972–88).

World   Christopher Hill, Barry Reay, and William Lamont, *The World of the Muggletonians* (London: Temple Smith, 1983).

THE ACTS OF THE WITNESSES

ONE

Editor's Introduction

The Setting

The collapse of government, civil war, the execution of the king, the aboli-
tion of monarchy, and the establishment of a republic marked the period
1640–60 in English history. During these tumultuous years, the grip of the
ruling elite was sufficiently loosened that radical ideas—political, social, economic, and religious—could be advocated openly and even acted out in
England's otherwise hierarchical and deferential society. Levellers, for example, urged the extension of the franchise; Diggers called for land reform
and established agricultural communities on common land; and Fifth Mon-
archists expected the imminent return of King Jesus to rule with his saints
on earth, and some were willing to take up arms to expedite that return.
These two decades also witnessed the expansion of the Baptist sect and the
rise of Seekers, Ranters, and Quakers. In 1652 the experiences of John Reeve
and Lodowick Muggleton led to the beginning of yet another religious movement that eventually took the latter's name and shared the radical end of
the Protestant spectrum with these last four groups. Thus the four—Baptists,
Seekers, Ranters, and Quakers—require our attention by way of introduction.

The first English Baptist church to enjoy historical continuity originated
in 1609 in Amsterdam among English separatists whose minister was John
Smyth. By 1612 some members under the leadership of Thomas Helwys had

returned to establish congregations on English soil. In 1626 there were at least six such congregations, designated General Baptists because of their Arminian theology, which professed a "general atonement" (Christ died for all). A second group of Baptist congregations originated as the result of amicable separations over the issue of infant baptism from an Independent church in London in the late 1630s. These Baptists took with them the Calvinist theology of Independency, which affirmed a "limited atonement" (Christ died only for the elect), and thus were known as Particular Baptists. Seven such congregations existed in London in 1644. By the 1650s, a third but relatively small organization of Seventh-Day Baptists was also present in England, most members having separated from General or Particular Baptist churches. Their observance of Saturday as the Sabbath differentiated them from the other two groups. What set all three of these Baptist associations apart from most Christians was their strong emphasis on emulating the practices of the New Testament church, among which they found no evidence of infant baptism, only believer's baptism. Smyth concluded, "Infants are not to be baptized . . . Because ther is neyther precept nor example in the new Testament. . . . Only they that did confess their sinnes, & confess their Fayth were baptized."[1] However, English Baptists of all varieties were considered radical by most of their contemporaries not only because of their abandonment of the centuries-old practice of infant baptism but also because of their opposition to a national church and religious uniformity, their aversion to a university-educated ministry, the objections of some to tithing and oath taking, and their supposed identity with the Continental Anabaptists, whose atrocities at Münster in 1534 were fearfully remembered. In addition, as members of the parliamentary army, numbers of Baptists fought against the king, and some advocated Leveller or Fifth Monarchist views. Anxiety about this radical sect may have been increased by its rapid expansion in the 1640s and 1650s, from perhaps fifty churches in 1644 to as many as three hundred by 1660 with a total membership of some 25,000.[2]

Whereas Baptists have been "a group curiously neglected by historians," as noted by Barry Reay and J. F. McGregor, at least their actual existence in seventeenth-century England has not been questioned. The latter is not the case with Seekers and Ranters. McGregor himself has persuasively argued that "there was no *sect* of Seekers in Revolutionary England." However, there is evidence that Seekers *did* exist as individuals and in groups, if not as an organized sect. Although Thomas Edwards's accusations should be taken cautiously, this notable heresiographer described and attacked Seeker beliefs and even identified William Erbery, William Walwyn, John Saltmarsh, and Laurence Claxton (Clarkson) as members of this presumed sect. In defending themselves, Erbery, Walwyn, and Saltmarsh related basic Seeker tenets and claimed to be sympathetic with some of them. For his part, Claxton admitted that, having been influenced by Erbery, he became a Seeker and then circulated among Seekers in London, Kent, and Hertfordshire. Richard Baxter also described Seeker beliefs and even distinguished among several different types of Seekers. In addition, John Jackson, who explained and defended Seeker views in *A Sober Word to a Serious People* (1651), was considered by Baxter to be "the most rational and modest that hath wrote for this way." Further, although the traditional view that early Quaker membership drew significantly from Seeker communities in northwest England was probably an exaggeration, Friends such as John Tomkins and Thomas Taylor remembered a time when there *were* groups of Seekers from which conversions were made. And in 1654 the Quaker Edward Burrough wrote to the "mother of Quakerism," Margaret Fell, that Quaker evangelists had spoken to a meeting of "Waiters" or Seekers in London, and in 1657 William Caton informed Fell of several Seekers in Sussex. Thus we have a number of descriptions of Seekers and their beliefs written by Seekers and Seeker sympathizers as well as detractors. In brief, Seekers, maintaining that the church was in a state of apostasy, took a highly skeptical approach to current Christian faith and practice. In their view the true church, ministry, and worship were "lost" and Christians were to wait for God to restore them.[3]

Another problem of historicity has been raised with regard to Ranters. J. C. Davis has claimed that Ranters were probably an invention of seventeenth-century Royalists, Presbyterians, and sectaries, assisted by modern historians anxious to demonstrate a radical tradition in English history. Jerome Friedman, however, has not only accepted the existence of Ranters but also placed them in several categories, including philosophical Ranters and sexual libertines. "Ranter" was a term used loosely and pejoratively to refer to a variety of persons. For example, Captain Robert Norwood and the minister John Pordage, both morally upright, were accused of Ranterism primarily because of alleged theological aberrations. At the other extreme were: Abiezer Coppe, who declared, "I can if it be my will, kisse and hug Ladies and love my neighbours wife as my selfe, without sin"; Thomas Tany, who took the name Theaurau John and who claimed to come from the Jewish tribe of Reuben and to be the high priest of God as well as the rightful heir to the throne of Charles I; and John Robins, whose followers were said to believe he was God and thus also the father of Jesus Christ, who was then in his wife's womb. Ranter beliefs were normally characterized by antinomianism and mystical pantheism. Claiming they were part of the new age of the Spirit, Ranters usually appealed to an inner spiritual authority and sometimes denied that the spiritual person actually sinned in the commission of outward carnal acts. As a result, "they spake most hideous Words of Blasphemy, and many of them committed whoredoms commonly," Baxter claimed.[4]

Unlike Seekers and Ranters, Quakers have not had their historical existence questioned. However, interpretations of their origins and development have changed significantly. A watershed was reached in 1946 with the publication of Geoffrey F. Nuttall's *The Holy Spirit in Puritan Faith and Experience*. Nuttall argued that Quakers should no longer be viewed against an essentially continental background of anabaptism, spiritualism, and mysticism but, rather, in an English context as a group that repeated and extended the English Puritan characteristic of movement toward "direct com-

munion with God through His Holy Spirit." More recently, I have shown
that the element linking Quakerism with the Puritan and Nonconformist
tradition was *primitivism*, the emphasis in faith and practice on the first,
earliest pattern or form as described in the New Testament (this entailed
efforts to recreate or imitate such forms in the present). I have argued that,
just as this emphasis moved Baptists beyond Presbyterians and Independents,
so its even more radical application took Quakers yet further, to adopt several beliefs and practices that seemed heretical to many Christians of their
time. In recent years historians have also brought into clearer focus the radical components of early Quakerism and the serious threat contemporaries
thought the movement posed to the established order. The claim that the
inner light in all people was superior in authority to the Bible, the elimina-
tion of the outward sacraments, the refusal to pay tithes and church rates
or take oaths, the preaching of the uneducated and of women, opposition
to a national church and religious uniformity, and cases of extravagant behavior (such as "going naked as a sign" and James Nayler's entry into Bristol
in 1654 in the manner of Christ's triumphal entry into Jerusalem), resulted
in the imprisonment and punishment of many Quakers. Nevertheless, members probably numbered 35,000 by 1660. Following the Restoration, however, various attempts were made from within the movement to curb extreme behavior and to impose organization and discipline in order to render
Quakerism more socially acceptable. Indeed, H. Larry Ingle has argued that
George Fox's most enduring contribution to the development of Quakerism
was not theological (his doctrine of the universal inner light) but organiza-
tional in that he circumscribed the movement's early radical individualism
by developing an institutional structure to provide the discipline and unity
needed for survival in Restoration England.[5]

In those contentious times, it is not surprising that some members of the
above movements engaged in quarrelsome exchanges with each other. The
Baptist John Bunyan, for example, condemned Quakers as "fond Hypocrites," George Fox denounced Bunyan's "Lies and Slanders," Margaret Fell
rebuked Ranters for their swearing and drunkenness, and the Ranter Abiezer
Coppe criticized Baptists for censuring everyone who was not a member of
their sect. The Quaker Edward Burrough accused Seekers of not following
the *true* light, whereas the Seeker John Jackson asked whether the devil
might be using Quakers as he had Eve. Fox thought the divine voice of
commissioning that Reeve supposedly heard was in fact "a whispering of
Satan," and Muggleton reportedly declared of the Quaker William Penn, "I
care not a Fart for Him, nor his Friends." To this last dispute between
Quakers and Muggletonians we will give further attention later.[6]

The Prophets

In this milieu of radical religion, John Reeve and Lodowick Muggleton
emerged as leaders of an unusual group. Reeve (1608–58) was born in

Wiltshire. His father, Walter Reeve, was said to have been a clerk to a Lord Deputy of Ireland. When his father's financial status declined, he was apprenticed to a tailor in London. Reeve's cousin, Lodowick Muggleton (1609–98), was born in London, the son of a farrier from Northamptonshire. He, too, was apprenticed as a tailor. By the early 1650s the two men were in contact with each other and with communities of religious radicals that included the Ranters' John Robins and Thomas Tany, whom Reeve and Muggleton later denounced following their own reputed divine commission as the two witnesses of Revelation 11:3. It was to Reeve that this commission first came in 1652 as described in the earliest Muggletonian tract, *A Transcendent Spiritual Treatise* [1652]:

> *February* the 3, 4 and 5. 1651[2]. three mornings together, much about an houre, the Lord Jesus, the only wise God, whose glorious person is resident above or beyond the stars, I declare from the spirit of truth, that this Jesus from the throne of his glory, by voice of words, spake unto me *John Reeve*, saying; I have given thee understanding of my mind in the Scriptures, above all men in the world. The next words the Lord spake unto me, were these, saying; Look into thy own body, there thou shalt see the Kingdom of Heaven, and the Kingdom of Hell: the Lord spake these words unto me twice together. Again, the Lord spake unto me these words, saying; I have chosen thee my last messenger for a great work, unto this bloudy unbleeving world. And I have given thee *Lodowick Muggleton* to be thy mouth: at that very moment the holy spirit brought to my mind that Scripture of *Aaron* given unto *Moses*. Again, the Lord spake unto me these words, saying; I have put the two-edged sword of my spirit into thy mouth, that whoever I pronounce blessed, through thy mouth, is blessed to eternity; and whoever I pronounce cursed through thy mouth, is cursed to eternity.

Reeve's reference to Moses and Aaron in describing the divinely appointed relationship between him and Muggleton raises a difficult issue, for Aaron's position was clearly inferior to that of Moses, who was told "he shall be to thee instead of a mouth, and thou shalt be to him instead of God" (Exodus 4:16). Later, when Miriam and Aaron criticized Moses, denying that God spoke only through him and claiming that the Almighty had also communicated through them, God made clear Moses' superiority and punished Miriam with leprosy. The two then repented, Aaron admitting to Moses that they had been foolish and sinful (Numbers 12:1–15). Was such a superior/subordinate relationship between Reeve and Muggleton the intended or actual one? Christopher Hill has cogently argued that Reeve was the central leader and thinker in the movement until his death in 1658, following which Muggleton "deliberately set out to appropriate Reeve's legacy." Using eighteenth-century editions himself and noting that Donald Wing's *Short-title Catalogue* attributes the works published during Reeve's lifetime only to Reeve, Hill has strongly implied that Muggleton added his own name to subsequent editions and has also speculated that the original edition of *Transcendent* had "Aaron obedient *to* Moses" rather than "Aaron obedient *with* Moses," as in later editions. Hill's skepticism in these matters is justified. *Transcendent* was written by Reeve in the first person ("my Commission," "I declare by Revelation from the Holy Spirit"), and Reeve was referred to on the title page as God's "own Prophet, being his last Messenger, and Witness." In 1653 an independent source, *Mercurius Politicus*, reported that the two men were London tailors, "but only one of them works and that is *Muggleton;* the other (they say) writes Prophecies." In 1661 Muggleton *did* revise *A Divine Looking-Glass* (1656), for which he was later criticized by some members of the movement.[7] In his autobiography, *The Acts of the Witnesses*, Muggleton claimed to have had revelations that gave him such strong interpretive powers of scripture that Reeve sought and received similar revelations and powers for himself—all this *before* Reeve's commissioning experience of February 1652. Muggleton further claimed to have disagreed with Reeve when he was alive and to have later corrected Reeve's views on "immediate notice." In addition, in *Acts* (pt. 4, chap. 10, sects. 15 and 16), Muggleton asserted that "God did not chuse *John Reeve* Singuler, but God chose us two Joyntly, so that there could be no seperation but by Death, and seeing God hath Honoured me to be the longer Liver, he hath given me a double Power, . . . So that God hath seated and established the Commission wholy upon me, so that the Prophet now alive doth stand in God's place."

There is also evidence to be considered on the other side of this issue, however. For example, contrary to Hill's speculation, the title page and preface of the two versions of *Transcendent* (see the textual notes in "The Writings" below) bear the names of *both* men, referring to them as God's *two* last true witnesses and prophets. Part 9 includes references to last messengers and *our* commission, and Aaron is said to be obedient *with* (not *to*) Moses. Also, because the year date, perhaps suspiciously, is not printed on either version of the work, it should be noted that the above cited "independent source," *Mercurius Politicus* of 1653, referred to the two men's claim to be the "two last witnesses and Prophets of the *Lord Jesus*" and the "two last spirituall Witnesses and alone true Prophets." Further, in the second edition (1655) of his *A View of all the Religions in the World* (first ed. 1653), Alexander Ross added a section referring both to *Transcendent* and the two men's claim to be the two last witnesses and prophets. In addition, other works printed in Reeve's lifetime, *A Remonstrance* (1653) and *Joyful News from Heaven* (1658), contain title-page references to both men, calling them the two last witnesses and prophets. Finally, rather than trying to usurp authorship of *Transcendent*, in *Acts* Muggleton clearly ascribed the book to Reeve and provided the year date of 1652, and in a printed work of 1662 he said that *The Divine Looking-Glass* (1656), "written by *John Reeve*, hath contained in it (if truly understood) the deepest hidden mysteries that ever was spoken or penned by man."[8] Although both men were searching for religious truth, and Muggleton may have been given interpretive powers before Reeve, the latter was clearly the first to receive the last commission and the one who took the initiative in their early writing activities. Reeve may have considered himself, or been considered by others, to be the divinely appointed occupant of a position superior to that of Muggleton. If so, it seems that from a very early point Muggleton was more than a mere mouthpiece for Reeve, as Aaron was for Moses. There were, after all, *two* witnesses in Revelation 11:3 on which the commission was based, and in this Scripture their relative status was undifferentiated. However, this is one of several issues that deserves further attention from scholars.

Like Bunyan, Fox, and many other contemporaries, Muggleton had experienced a difficult spiritual struggle accompanied by doubt and melancholy concerning the eternal state of his soul. Eventually, however, the pre-1652 revelation observed earlier gave him assurance and peacefulness in his religious faith. He resolved to be "quiet and still" and not to meddle any more in religious affairs but rather let people go on in their own ways. Reeve, he said, reached the same state. However, the 1652 commission, which both men were reluctant to accept, had the opposite effect, for the two prophets felt compelled to send a letter to numbers of London ministers informing them that they were not properly commissioned by God and that if they did not relinquish their ministerial positions they would be cursed for all eternity. It is not surprising that the two witnesses soon found themselves sentenced to six months' imprisonment in Bridewell. Reeve, but not Muggleton, would avoid further incarcerations. In this conflict with authorities, Reeve, exercising the power of the commission, cursed to eternal damnation the London Lord Mayor, John Fowke, in whose court the two were tried. Cursing was, of course, one of the few weapons the underclass had in disputes with the wealthy and powerful. Reeve and Muggleton did not claim arbitrary authority in this regard but rather that God determined and revealed to them who was to be blessed and who cursed (see letter 11). It was perhaps no coincidence, however, that people who opposed their message or authority fell into the latter category, or that Muggleton, at least, seemed sometimes to enjoy the exercise. In the 1860s, looking through the works of the two prophets, Alexander Gordon counted the names of forty-six persons they had assured of eternal blessedness and 103 who were promised the opposite. Muggleton himself estimated that they had cursed about a thousand people in the first ten years of the movement. In *Acts* he recounted the subsequent sufferings of some of those cursed, including the deaths of two prominent Quakers.[9] Their followers could also curse and bless, but subject to the review of the two prophets.

In spite of the notoriety gained in these early months of their commission, the delivery of their message was relatively restrained. The two men remained remarkably "quiet and still," at least by comparison to Bunyan, who traveled in several counties and preached widely and effectively. Fox traveled even more extensively in Britain and also journeyed to America to "proclaim Truth." Quaker evangelists carried out their mission by "speaking to large companies in crowded rooms, in barns, in the open air, conversing more closely and familiarly with single individuals or with groups, disputing with 'priests,' [and] facing the fury of the mob."[10] But Reeve and Muggleton were not preachers or evangelists, nor were their followers. The above letter to London ministers and the title page of *Transcendent* invited people interested in speaking with them to enquire at a chandler's shop in Great Trinity Lane.[11] Through their conversations, discussions, and books the two witnesses gladly communicated their message, but in general people had to seek them out, for, as we will see, hearing that message was not necessary for salvation. Nevertheless, they eventually attracted a following in several counties as well as in the German states, Ireland, the Caribbean, and North America. Barry Reay has estimated that their numbers probably never exceeded several hundred, in contrast to the thousands attracted by the more evangelistic Baptists and Quakers. He has also provided a map of their geographical distribution in England in the seventeenth century, showing them concentrated mostly in the Midlands and the South, and he has charted their occupations and status as being largely that of wholesale and retail traders and artisans. Among those converts whose activities we will encounter in this volume are Alexander Delamaine of London, Thomas Tomkinson of Staffordshire, John Saddington of Leicestershire, Ellen Sudbury of Nottinghamshire, and William Wood of Essex.[12]

Again in contrast to the evangelists among Baptists and Quakers, Reeve and Muggleton were reluctant to undertake the hardships of travel and risks of arrest. Muggleton's journeys into Essex, Kent, Cambridgeshire, Derbyshire, Leicestershire, and Nottinghamshire to visit the faithful, as related in *Acts*, were infrequent. Rather, his letters constituted a major means of pastoral care, as did Reeve's (see especially letters 4, 7, 11, and 12, in which Reeve outlines the basic tenets of the faith and Muggleton chastises a wayward believer, comforts a dying child, and disparages belief in witchcraft). To the benefit of subsequent generations, Delamaine (a former Quaker) and others collected and copied many such letters. In some of these, as well as in his autobiography, Muggleton, for the edification of others, occasionally shares intimate details of his own family experiences with wives (he was married three times) and children. He also illustrates further the risks of travel, telling us in *Acts* that when in 1656 Reeve journeyed into Kent, he so weakened himself in attempting to escape arrest that he spent the last two years of his life in "a sick, wasting condition." In letters 1 and 2 Reeve himself describes the death of his wife and his own deteriorating health. Toward the end he moved into the home of three sisters who cared for him until his death in late July 1658. He was buried in Bethlehem Churchyard, which was in the vicinity of the present Liverpool Street Railway Station but has long since disappeared.

Soon after Reeve's death Claxton challenged Muggleton for the leadership of the movement. In 1671 Muggleton was again provoked, this time by Walter Bohanan (Buchanan) and William Medgate for departing from Reeve's teachings. I will discuss both of these controversies later but note at this point only that he survived both conflicts and continued to "stand in God's place." However, the remaining prophet nearly did not survive his

1677 encounter with legal authorities. In 1663 he had been held in Derby jail to await trial for blasphemy, but the charge was apparently dropped and he was released. In 1670 he had some of his books confiscated by agents from the Stationers' Company but escaped a worse fate by hiding with friends. However, Stationers' Company wardens eventually caught up with him, and in 1677 he was tried in London and found guilty of writing a blasphemous book, *The Neck of the Quakers Broken*. Fined five hundred pounds, he was pilloried at three separate locations. Muggleton reported in *Acts* how he was bruised and battered by mobs that pelted him with stones and other objects and that his life was preserved only by divine providence. He was released on 19 July, a date that, along with those of the commission, would be commemorated by followers for years to come (see song 8 and the dinner expense record of 1682).[13] With this account of his liberation and the divine vengeance subsequently suffered by his enemies, the autobiography came to an end. According to Thomas Tomkinson's "The White Divell Uncased," Muggleton's "memory much failed him" in his later years, yet "he was sencable to the last." The same writer's dedicatory epistle to *Acts* described the prophet's death on 14 March 1698, "being about 88 Years of Age," and his interment in Bethlehem Churchyard with 248 persons in attendance, "Buried by his Fellow-Witness, which was according to his own appointment."[14]

Given the movement's aversion to evangelism, it is perhaps remarkable that it should have continued to exist for nearly three centuries beyond Muggleton's death. After 1698 there was further printing of some of the prophets' works, but membership declined and virtually no scholarly attention was afforded Muggletonians until Alexander Gordon published two papers in *Proceedings of the Literary and Philosophical Society of Liverpool* (1869–70). In these he described his experience as a guest at the annual February dinners commemorating the prophets' commission and presented information on the lives and beliefs of Reeve and Muggleton based on his access to the organization's archive of printed and manuscript materials. Even then, an 1874 *Chambers Encyclopedia* entry noted that the movement was assumed to be completely extinct, evoking a strong response from Thomas Robinson, a member for more than forty-eight years, in which he affirmed that they *did* still exist in England, America, and Australia and that they had a private library and meeting place at 7 New Street, Bishopsgate (formerly known as Walnut Tree Yard, Muggleton's birthplace). Robinson's correction appeared in the 1888–92 edition as "A few Muggletonians lingered in England well into the 19th century."[15] In 1974–75 Christopher Hill's "Milton the Radical," printed in the *Times Literary Supplement*, evoked several letters to the editor dealing mostly with Muggletonianism. One from E. P. Thompson raised the hope that the materials used by Gordon might still exist and averred that their "recovery and preservation in a national collection would be of real importance." As a result of this publicity, Philip Noakes of Matfield, Kent, was soon identified as a Muggletonian and the archive's keeper. On 26 February 1979, only a few months after the British Library acquired these materials from Noakes, he died. He was most likely the last Muggletonian.[16]

The Prophecy and Practice

Christopher Hill has appropriately pointed out that a number of religious views held by Reeve and Muggleton were not unique. The mortality of the soul, anti-trinitarianism, and the eternal nature of matter (earth and water), for example, were among the tenets also held by some of their radical con-temporaries. But this should not surprise us. Just as the two rejected the notion of the creation of the world ex nihilo, there should be no unrealistic expectation that their doctrines should have come ex nihilo. Nevertheless, two Muggletonian doctrines dramatically set them apart from other move-ments of their time and place: the belief that ultimate earthly authority rested in the two prophets and the belief that God was literally a man.[17]

The general framework for Muggletonian beliefs and practices was pro-vided by a particular view of history, the origins of which are often asso-ciated with the work of Joachim of Fiore (ca. A.D. 1135–1202), a monk affiliated with the abbey of St. John of Fiore in Italy. His biblical studies led him to conclude that history was divided into three epochs, each associated with a member of the Trinity. That of the Father was described in the Old Testament and reached from Adam to Christ. The second, that of Christ, was described in the New Testament, and between the two testaments were to be found parallels or "concordances," such as the twelve tribes and the twelve apostles. Although apparently building upon the earlier work of Ti-chonius and St. Augustine, Joachim went beyond them by claiming that the third epoch was yet to come (albeit soon) and would be one in which the Holy Spirit completed the teachings of Christ and revealed special under-standing of the Scripture. Joachim's teachings were of interest in medieval England. Similar views were also held by the German Lutheran shoemaker and mystical writer Jacob Boehme (1575–1624), who in 1600 experienced a brief, sudden transformation in which he thought he saw into the core of reality. His works, some of which were translated and circulated in England in the 1640s and 1650s, included a vision of history rounded out by the belief in a final "Age of the Spirit" in which a spirit of prophecy would prevail, "an age coinciding with the restoration of an ancient knowledge which would clarify the letter of the Gospel and resolve all conflicts over its meaning."[18]

Related to this tradition were the centuries-old interest in millenarianism in general and the notion of the two witnesses of Revelation 11:3 in partic-ular. Rodney L. Petersen has traced this latter concern from earliest times. Interpreters such as Tertullian thought the two witnesses were Enoch and Elijah, whereas others such as Tichonius considered them to be not two individuals but rather the pure church "prophesying and preaching through the two testaments." At the time of the Protestant Reformation, Heinrich Bullinger's influential sermons on the Book of Revelation depicted the two witnesses as the ministry of the true church struggling against the errors of Rome. In seventeenth-century England considerable millenarian interest was kindled by the publication of Thomas Brightman's *A Revelation of the Revelation* (1615) and Joseph Mede's *The Key of the Revelation* (1642), which had previously been published in Latin in 1609 and 1627, respectively. Brightman identified the two witnesses as the Holy Scriptures and the assemblies of the faithful. Mede described them as the prophets who decried sin and preached the gospel faithfully.[19]

In seventeenth-century England, then, the traditions of the three ages and the two witnesses of the final age were present and sufficiently familiar for Muggleton to express awareness of differing interpretations and for him and Reeve to employ for their own purposes. But they were not the first to do so. Two London weavers claimed to be the last witnesses several years before the commission came to our two London tailors. In 1636 Richard Farnham and John Bull declared that they had been given this role, the knowledge of all things to come, and the power to open and shut the heavens and to inflict plagues on humankind. They were imprisoned and, ironically, died of the plague in 1642, although there was an expectation among some followers that Farnham "should be king on David's throne" and Bull "should be priest in Aarons seat" and that they might be resurrected to this end.[20] There is no evidence, however, that Reeve and Muggleton were ever aware of this earlier episode. It appears that the two pairs of witnesses independently based their claims to authority and power on the previously described traditions and the scriptural role assigned them: "And I will give power unto my two witnesses, . . . And if any man will hurt them, fire proceedeth out of their mouth, and devoureth their enemies: . . . These have power to shut heaven, that it rain not in the days of their prophecy: and have power over waters to turn them to blood, and to smite the earth with all plagues as often as they will" (Authorized Version). In Reeve's case there was also God's declaration of 3 February: "I have given thee understanding of my mind in the Scriptures, above all men in the world." All of this resulted in the elevation of Reeve and Muggleton to the position of supreme religious authorities on earth. In the introductory epistle to their first printed doctrinal treatise, *Transcendent*, they declared that anyone, king or beggar, who rejected or spoke evil about the treatise thereby committed the unpardonable sin against the Holy Spirit and would be pronounced cursed for eternity. Among religious radicals such authority contrasted markedly with the Baptist emphasis on the outward Scriptures and with that of Seekers, Ranters, and Quakers on the authority of the inward spirit or light. Many, of course, strongly rejected the authority asserted by the two witnesses. William Penn, for example, denounced such claims as "most arrogant and false," and Fox protested that Muggleton had "made himself [into] a Pope." Accordingly, Muggleton cursed both men to eternal damnation and several other Quakers as well.[21]

Some of Muggleton's strong assertions of authority, such as "You all ought to bee taught of mee, . . . else you cannot bee taught of God," and "The Prophet now alive doth stand in God's place," were evoked by challenges to his authority from inside the movement. In *Acts* he told of his dispute with Claxton (1615–67), who had been successively a Presbyterian, Independent, Baptist, Seeker, and Ranter before his association with Reeve and Muggleton. Following Reeve's death, Muggleton strongly rebuked Claxton for trying to usurp the two prophets' authority, forbade him to write or speak any more on behalf of the movement, and cut off his financial support (see letter 6). The two were eventually reconciled, but with Claxton accepting a subordinate position. In 1671 Muggleton's authority was again challenged, this time by Bohanan, Medgate, and others who charged that he was arbitrarily exercising his authority within the movement and that he had contradicted Reeve's teaching on the subject of "immediate notice." In *Acts* and in his lengthy epistle to Bohanan (letter 9) he responded to the "Nine Assertions" against him, affirmed his original equality with Reeve and his sole authority since Reeve's death, and claimed that although Reeve had been infallible in his interpretation of Scripture and in the doctrine of the Six Principles, his judgment that God took immediate notice of every person's activities or behavior was an error. The law written originally by God in human hearts served as "God's Watchman," Muggleton argued. Perhaps the material nature and specific location of God contributed to this view, but it was a position that also enhanced the prophet's authority and power, since any direct appeal to God by a follower would not be heard. That this dispute had not been resolved by the time of Muggleton's death is probably demonstrated by Tomkinson's statement in his dedicatory epistle to *Acts* that Reeve himself recognized Muggleton's equal authority and there would be no salvation for people who rejected Muggleton or his writings, "*altho' they pretend to own* John Reeve."[22]

Tension over differences between the two witnesses also surfaced in the eighteenth and nineteenth centuries and may have been related to the third edition (1719) and the fourth edition (1760) of *A Divine Looking-Glass*, both of which claimed to be reprintings of the original 1656 version. Apparently no copies of the first edition (1656) have survived, and the two "reprints" are not identical, so some uncertainty about the first edition's contents remains. What seems clear is that following the Restoration, Muggleton issued a revised version (1661) in which he deleted sections supportive of Oliver Cromwell (see Appendix B). These were restored in the third and fourth editions. Within a few years of the printing of the 1760 edition, John Birch and others defected from the "mainstream" in support of, among other things, Reeve's view of immediate notice.

Further problems were evident in the nineteenth century. In 1832 the works of Reeve and Muggleton were published by private subscription in three volumes edited by Joseph and Isaac Frost. In the front of volume 1 of the set presented to the British Library is a letter dated 24 February 1853 to the principal librarian from Joseph Frost asking that a printed letter to readers be appended which explained that of the 1656, 1661, and 1760 editions in Frost's collection, the 1760 edition rather than the 1661 edition had inadvertently been included in volume 1 of the set.[23] Appended to this printed letter is one addressed by Frost to the church criticizing the divisive spirit of those who published the 1760 unauthorized edition and those who continued in the same spirit. William Lamont has argued that the parties in these disputes recognized the portions excised by Muggleton as having theological meaning, for they implied that God was an interventionist who *did* take immediate notice of human actions and thus the excisions were pertinent to that doctrinal disagreement. However, it should be noted that the controversy over immediate notice did not erupt until a decade after the 1661 revision appeared, and Frost himself, who had both the 1656 and 1661 editions, concluded that Reeve's doctrinal tenets were retained by Muggleton in the revised edition of 1661. An alternative to Lamont's view was provided in an 1857 letter to Frost from Thomas Robinson, who acknowledged the arguments over immediate notice but contended that "the case in dispute now, is the History of the Book in connexion with the Times." He argued that after the Restoration Muggleton deleted the Cromwell sections for political reasons, that by 1719 this political "necessity" had long passed, that the work was reprinted in its original form probably by some of the same people who had associated with Muggleton just two decades earlier (perhaps including his widow, who died in 1718), and that such reprinting should not cause disunity in the movement. Nevertheless, the controversies over immediate notice may have made "Reevonians" all the more determined to reject any revisions by Muggleton of Reeve's works whatever the former's motives may have been.[24]

The second Muggletonian belief that contrasted sharply with those of other contemporary movements was their doctrine of God, who as Creator was said to have been from eternity "a spiritual body or person in the form of a man having all parts in Immortalitie as man hath in mortality." Reeve and Muggleton claimed that the Creator entered into the womb of the Virgin Mary, purified her nature, then died and shed his own immortality, quickened himself in pure mortality, and brought himself forth as the first born son of God. Thus God the Father, who had been a spiritual man, became a physical, mortal man, Jesus Christ, in order to become temporarily like his creatures and ultimately to save them and exalt them to his own nature. Moses and Elijah (the two witnesses also used the forms Eliah and Elias) who had been taken up bodily to heaven were God's representatives there in his absence, and it was to them that he cried out from the cross. With the crucifixion he died, both physically and spiritually, but then took on immortality again, yet with the same flesh and spirit. The Father and Son as one person (contrary to trinitarian belief) then ascended into heaven some six miles above the earth. There, the two witnesses declared, God now ruled in the form of a man, Jesus Christ, between five and six feet tall.[25]

This doctrine of God, like some other Muggletonian beliefs, evoked strongly negative reactions from Quakers. The latter, who believed God to be an infinite spirit and emphasized the divine nature of Christ so strongly that their critics concluded they did not believe in Christ's humanity at all, scoffed at the Muggletonian notion that God was in human, bodily form. Muggleton told one such scoffer, William Penn, that the Quakers' infinite formless spirit without a body was incapable of revoking Muggleton's curse on Penn for his blasphemous words against the belief that God was in the form of a man (letter 10). Indeed, it seems that Muggletonians engaged in more hostile exchanges with Quakers than with members of any other group. Joseph Smith's *Bibliotheca Anti-Quakeriana* lists most Reeve and Muggleton works and identifies eleven Quaker "answers to Muggleton and Reeve." Douglas Greene has traced this controversy in England, describing it as "one of the most bitter pamphlet wars of the later seventeenth century." Kenneth Carroll has provided a similar study of the two groups' interaction in Ireland. The intensity of the conflict may be attributed partly to the fact that a few Quakers defected to Muggletonianism and that in their early history both groups had connections with Ranters, for which they later denounced each other and from which they tried to distance themselves. Some Quaker critics, however, believed Quakers had in fact adopted a number of Ranter beliefs but disavowed their immoral behavior. According to the learned Richard Baxter, for example, Quakers "were but the *Ranters* turned from horrid Profaneness and Blasphemy, to a Life of extream Austerity on the other side. Their Doctrines were mostly the same with the Ranters." Muggleton thought so too. But whereas Quaker beliefs may have continued to reflect some of the emphases of Ranters, Reeve and Muggleton, having severed their relationship with John Robins and Thomas Tany and denounced the former as an Antichrist, took a dramatically different theological direction. Thus, Muggletonians and Quakers disagreed on a number of issues, but perhaps none so profoundly as the nature of God. This rift may be seen in the explanations given by two protagonists for the extensiveness of their controversy. On the one hand the Quaker Isaac Penington thought "the reason he [Muggleton] reviles us above all others [is] because we stand most in his way . . . because we have received the true Light, the true Spirit." Muggleton, on the other hand, thought it was because Quakers "are more Antichristian, and Enemies to the true God than any others."[26]

The doctrine of God was the first of the Muggletonian "Six Principles" (see letter 4) that encapsulated several of their basic doctrines. The remainder were the nature of the angels, the character of the devils, the creation and fall of Adam, the qualities of heaven and glory, and the constitution of hell and eternal death. Variations of the six would appear later, including the substitution of the mortality of the soul for Adam's creation and fall.[27] According to the two witnesses, God created the angels from the eternal substances of earth and water. These beings were spiritual, male creatures who enjoyed spiritual, heavenly pleasures. But God withheld the revelation of wisdom from one angel, who therefore eventually thought himself superior to all creatures and even to God himself. Thus the Creator cast him down to earth where he became known variously as the Serpent, Dragon, Devil, or Satan. God also created Adam with all of his own divine virtues—in his own image—except that Adam was mortal. When the cast-down angel as Serpent tempted Eve, he entered into her womb, died in his spirituality, and quickened in her the natural lust, wickedness, and unclean reason of which Adam later partook. The Devil, then, came to exist only within the bodies of men or women as unclean reason, cursed imagination, and lust. The souls of both the damned and the believers were said to die along with their bodies until the resurrection, at which time unbelievers would find their spirits to be fiery devils, their bodies to be the kingdom of hell, and their place of eternal torment to be on earth. Believers, however, would be given glorious bodies like that of God himself and would see his face and dwell eternally with him and the angels in heaven.

These beliefs were among those sketched out in John Saddington's "The Articles of True Faith" and treated in more detail in *Transcendent* and *A Divine Looking-Glass*. However, there is another important, if problematic, tenet that also was weaved into these materials—the doctrine of the two seeds. The seed of the Serpent was said to have resided in Eve, borne Cain, and been passed on through the generations as the unclean reason noted above. By contrast, the seed of faith came from Adam and Eve through Abel and on through the generations. Both seeds resided in all people and resulted in the inner tension between reason and faith, bad behavior and good. Those who had more of the seed of faith than reason were the "elect." Further, in *Transcendent*, part 3 and elsewhere, the two prophets wrote of God creating some people to live in light and joy and others in darkness and misery.[28] But describing the Muggletonian position as "the sect's acceptance of Calvin's theory of predestination . . . [in which] one was either among the elect or was damned to an eternity of torment, and there was nothing that could be done about it" or the doctrine of the two seeds as a "genetic predestination" or "predestination in its most rigorous form" casts the view too simply and rigidly. Indeed, over the past quarter-century historians have disagreed over the meaning as well as the relative extent and influence of Calvinism and Arminianism in the religious life of the early Stuart period. Peter White, in challenging the widely accepted conceptual dichotomy between Calvinism and Arminianism, has usefully reminded us of the fluidity of definition and redefinition as well as the broad spectrum of views within the notion of predestination itself. E. P. Thompson has provided the most sensitive treatment of the issue for our purposes, arguing that Muggletonianism, like other predestinarian creeds, allowed for both a voluntarist and a determinist vocabulary. As a result, on the one hand, the doctrine of the two seeds may be viewed as a great spiritual struggle within the uncommitted or backsliders or, on the other, as "inexorably predestinarian."[29] Thus, for example, the inner struggle between the two seeds appears to have resulted sometimes in such significantly changed behavior in individuals that the two prophets were led to reverse earlier curses or blessings. However, in the epistle dedicatory to *Acts* Tomkinson argued that God still controlled all of this, occasionally letting some of the predestined saints fall, then pardoning them again so as to raise them up to even greater heights of grace, wisdom, and humility. Further complicating the issue was the belief that those who heard the Muggletonian message and rejected it would be damned but that salvation did not require hearing it (see Saddington's creed, articles 46–48, and the conclusion of Tomkinson's "The White Devill Uncased"). Muggleton thought that in the end about half the world would be saved, including all persons dying in childhood.[30]

Several additional Muggletonian beliefs and practices require our attention. Like Seekers, Ranters, and Quakers, followers of the two witnesses thought the church had so long been in a state of apostasy that its worship and belief were invalid and had to be abandoned. Muggletonians met in homes or alehouses for eating, drinking, singing their own compositions to popular tunes, and discussing doctrines and issues. But there was no formal worship. A convert to Quakerism, John Gratton, disclosed that when he was associated with Muggletonians, "they had no Worship at all, nor when we met together . . . we were not for either waiting upon God, or for any other Exercise at all of either Preaching, Praying, or Reading holy Scriptures: No, we had no more to do, but to believe *Muggleton*, and be saved." They also held celebratory dinners to commemorate Reeve's 1652 commission and Muggleton's 1677 release from prison. Item 12 of the songs and miscellaneous materials lists the expenses of one such celebration in 1682 in which the largest single expenditure was for wine. But there is no evidence that Muggletonians imbibed excessively. The expense record further shows that Muggleton and his wife were guests of the members and that they came by coach, also apparently paid for by the attendees. Both Reeve and Muggleton received financial support and gifts from the membership as well as income from the sale of their books (see letters 1, 2, and 14). Although Muggleton opposed most oaths and believers did not normally attend parish church services, occasional conformity and even bribery were acceptable if necessary to avoid punishment by ecclesiastical or civil authorities. Indeed, as in some other radical groups, there was considerable animosity toward magistrates, lawyers, the clergy, the medical profession, and the university educated. Although the two prophets ridiculed those who thought Christ would come to rule with his Elect on earth, there was early in the movement an expectation of the imminent end of the world. With the collapse of the good old cause and the restoration of the monarchy, that expectation faded. However, it cannot be said that Muggletonian pacifism resulted from this reversal, for as early as 1652, nearly a decade before Quakers officially promulgated their "Peace Testimony," in *Transcendent* the two witnesses rejected the "use of the sword of steel to slay men." It is ironic that these two groups whose members waged against each other "one of the most bitter pamphlet wars of the later seventeenth century" should have agreed on the principle of pacifism.[31]

The Writings

The Acts of the Witnesses

This work was printed in the year after Muggleton's death and was reprinted in 1764. The texts of all the copies collated are identical except for those at the Bodleian and the Library of the Religious Society of Friends, which have a variant unsigned version of the epistle dedicatory. Also, the title page of the latter copy reads "Recited by *Fox* in his *Book* of Marters. *pag.* 707" instead of simply "*Fox* in his *Book* of *Marters.*" as in other copies. This alternate version of the epistle dedicatory is reproduced in Appendix A. Prefixed to the copies in the British Library Department of Printed Books, the Brotherton Library at the University of Leeds, and the Lambeth Palace Library is an engraved portrait of the author. The one from the British Library is used as our frontispiece. The one in the Lambeth Palace copy has penned beneath it: "He had yellow hair, & a ruddie complexion." The copperplate engraving, by G. V. Casseel, was based on a cast of Muggleton's features made after his death. The copper plate is to be found in Add. MSS 60256.[32] There is another engraving of Muggleton in Add. MSS 60170/136 and 137 based on a live portrait (now in the National Gallery) done by William Wood of Braintree, Essex, and engraved by J. Kennerley. This portrait is included in *The Works of John Reeve and Lodowick Muggleton* (3 vols., London, 1832) edited by Joseph and Isaac Frost, and both portraits are found in Reeve's *Sacred Remains* 1706.[33]

> *Title page*: THE | Acts of the Witnesses | OF THE | SPIRIT. | [rule] | In Five Parts. | By *LODOWICK MUGGLETON*: | [rule] | One of the | Two Witnesses, and True | Prophets of the only High, Immor- | tal, Glorious God, *Christ Jesus.* | [rule] | Left by him to be publish'd after's death. | [rule] | *In the latter days two Bright Stars shall arise, raising up men | being dead in their sins, which shall resist the Beast, and the | Waters of the Dragon, testifying and preaching the Law of the | Lamb, and the Destruction of Antichrist, and shall diminish | his Waters; but they shall be weakened in the Bread of Afflicti- | on, and they shall rise again in stronger force; and after Truth | shall be revealed, and the Lamb shall be known: After this shall | be but a small Space.* | [rule] | *Fox* in his *Book* of *Marters.* | [rule] | *LONDON*: | Printed in the Year of our Lord God, 1699.
>
> *Collation*: 4°; A1–A4, B1–Z4; pp. [i–viii] + 179 (+ 1) = 188. Signatures A1 and Z2 are not printed; otherwise signatures are printed on the first two leaves (the letters "J" and "U" are not used). The first printed page number is 1. Page number 61 is misprinted 16; 109 is not printed; and 130–136 are misprinted 230–236.
>
> *Contents*: A1ʳ title page; A1ᵛ blank; A2ʳ–4 epistle dedicatory; A4ᵛ errata; B1ʳ–Z2ʳ text. The end of the text is followed by a rule, *"FINIS,"* and another rule.

Catchwords (selected): B1ʳ it, E4ᵛ der-, H1ᵛ 23. So, L1ʳ and, P2ʳ could, T4ʳ CHAP., Y3ᵛ Eter-.

Running Titles: The Epistle Dedicatory: "The EPISTLE | DEDICA-TORY" beginning on A2ᵛ. Text: "The Acts of the Witnesses, | Of the Spirit." Punctuation varies.

Copies collated: British Library, Department of Western Manuscripts (Add. MSS 60248); Bodleian Library, Oxford University; Lambeth Palace Library, London; Library of the Religious Society of Friends, London; Trinity College, Cambridge; Brotherton Library, Leeds University; Haverford College, Pennsylvania; Huntington Library, San Marino, California; Beinecke Library, Yale University.

Our text is based on the British Library copy in the Department of Printed Books.

A Transcendent Spiritual Treatise

There are two versions of this work, neither of which is dated. The version reproduced here is entered as R683 in Wing and was probably printed in 1652. The copy at St. Paul's Cathedral Library and one of the copies (H8698/1.1) at the Lambeth Palace Library have opposite the title page and on the back of the title page, respectively, the notation apparently by the same hand, that they were seized at Muggleton's house by the wardens Samuel Marne and Richard Clarke on 30 August 1676. For Muggleton's account of this episode, see part 5, chapter 1 of *Acts*. The other version of *Transcendent* is designated R683A and as "Anr. ed.," "1653?" with "59 pp." in Wing. I have examined the copies of this second version in the collections of the Beinecke Library, Yale University; Christ Church, Oxford; and Worcester College, Oxford. The three are identical to each other and are the same in content as Wing R683, differing only in such things as font, capitalization, and punctuation. *Transcendent* was reprinted in 1711, 1756, and 1822. British Library Add. MSS 60184 is a manuscript said to be in Muggleton's own hand in which folios 26–33 are replaced by pages 25–40 of the printed Wing R683. One might at first assume that the printed pages were substituted for the missing folios in an originally complete manuscript. In fact, it is clear from the spacing of the manuscript lines preceding and following the printed section that the manuscript was fashioned to fit around the printed portion and thus, apparently, to substitute for missing printed pages. Differences between the manuscript portion and Wing R683 consist of punctuation, capitalization, and a few instances of a missing word or a slightly different arrangement of words. It is a curious document that perhaps deserves futher attention.

Title page: A Transcendent | Spiritual Treatise | Upon several heavenly Doctrines, from the holy | spirit of the man Jesus, the only true God, sent | unto all his elect as a token of his eternal love | unto them,

by the hand of his own Prophet, be- | ing his last Messenger, and Wit-
ness, and forerun- | ner of the visible appearing of the distinct perso- |
nal God in power and great glory, in the clouds | of Heaven, with his
ten thousands of personal | Saints, to separate between the elect world,
and | the reprobate world, to all Eternity: Contain- | ing those several
Heads set down in the next Page following. | John Reeve *and* Lodo-
wick Muggleton, *the two last Witnesses | and the Prophets of the man
Jesus, the only Lord of Life and | Glory, sent by his holy Spirit to seal
the foreheads of the Elect, | and the foreheads of the reprobate with the
eternal Seals of Life | and Death, and suddenly after we have delivered
this dreadful | Message, this God the man Jesus, will visibly appear to
bear | witness whether he sent us or not: ye that are the blessed shall |
patiently wait for the truth of this thing.* | If any of the Elect desire to
speak with us concerning any | thing written in this Treatise, they may
hear of us in *Great | Trinity Lane,* at a Chandlers Shop, against one
Mr. *Millis,* | a Brown Baker, near the lower end of *Bow-Lane.* | *Printed
for the Authors; and are to sold by them at the place above named.*

Collation: 4°: A1–F4; pp. 48. Signatures A1, B3, and E3 are not
printed; otherwise signatures are printed on the first three leaves. The
first printed page number is 3 (on A2^r). Page number 12 is misprinted
11, page number 13 is misprinted 12, and page numbers 46 and 47 are
reversed.

Contents: A1^r title page; A1^v blank; A2^r table of contents; A2^v epistle
to the reader; B3^r–F4^v text. A long row of ornaments appears at the top
of pages 3, 4, and 5. The end of the text is followed by *"FINIS."*

Catchwords (selected): A2^r *An*; C3^v *into*; E1^r *and*, F2^v *the.*

Running Titles: None.

Copies Collated: British Library, Department of Western Manu-
scripts (two copies: Add. MSS 60246, Add. MSS 60250/1); Cambridge
University Library; Lambeth Palace Library, London (two copies:
H8698/1.1, H8698/2.1); St. Paul's Cathedral Library, London; Harvard
University Library; Newberry Library, Chicago.

Our text is based on the British Library copy in the Department of Printed
Books.

The Articles of True Faith

John Saddington (1634?–79) was born in Arnesby, Leicestershire. He was
engaged in the sugar trade in London where he joined with Reeve and Muggleton early in their ministry. In 1675 he wrote "The Articles of True Faith,"
which became a standard statement of Muggletonian beliefs. It is said to
have been printed in 1830, although I have yet to locate a copy.

Title: The Articles of True Faith Depending upon the Commission of
the Spirit Drawne up into XLVII heads by John Saddington an Ancient

Beleiver for the benefit of other Beleivers, that now are, or hereafter
shall come to beleive And to confound and disprove All Despisers that
say wee know not what wee Believe. Anno M.DC.LXXV.

Our text is based on Add. MSS 60203 in the British Library Department of
Western Manuscripts. The manuscript consists of seven folios.

The White Divell Uncased

Thomas Tomkinson (1631–1710?) was born in Ilam, Staffordshire. He became a Muggletonian about 1662. He made frequent trips to London and
eventually settled there in the 1680s. As previously observed, Muggleton
gave him the responsibility of printing his *Acts*, for which he wrote the
signed dedicatory epistle. Tomkinson wrote several works himself, a few of
which were printed. A number are still only in manuscript in the Muggle-
tonan Archive. Of these, Add. MSS 60196, "The White Divell Uncased"
(1704) is in Tomkinson's own hand. (It is not to be confused with Add.
MSS 60197 with the same title, which is a different work.) It is a polemical
tract written in response to *Muggleton Unmasked* by James Steward or
Scott. I have been unable to locate a copy or identify its author. However,
Tomkinson cites Scott's criticisms, which he then answers, and thus the tract
provides a useful example of a Muggletonian polemical encounter with an
adversary outside radical religious circles.

Title: The White Divell Uncased.

Our text is based on Add. MSS 60196 in the British Library Department of
Western Manuscripts. The manuscript consists of six folios.

Letters

Most of the letters in the archive are copies. Alexander Delamaine and Tobiah Terry copied many of the letters of Reeve and Muggleton that are part
of Add. MSS 60171. (A mystery that may attract the attention of future
scholars arises from the fact that in Add. MSS 60171 one leaf after folio
13, two after folio 392, and 16 after folio 430 have been deliberately torn
out; see folios 13ᵛ, 392ᵛ, and 430ᵛ.) These and other letters by the two
prophets were printed in *Sacred Remains* (1706), *A Volume of Spiritual
Epistles (Verae Fidei)* (1755), *A Stream from the Tree of Life* (1758), *Supplement to the Book of Letters* (1831), and eventually in the three-volume
Works of 1832. The letters reproduced below include some by persons other
than the two witnesses. All are based on the manuscript materials in the
archive and a few on originals rather than copies. They were selected to
illustrate the prophetic and pastoral work of Reeve and Muggleton and the
interests and activities of other members of the movement.

1. Copy, John Reeve to Christopher Hill of Maidstone, Kent, 11 June 1656. Add. MSS 6071/10.
2. Copy, John Reeve to Christopher Hill, 1656. Add. MSS 60171/11.
3. Copy, John Reeve to Christopher Hill, no date. Add. MSS 60171/12.
4. Copy, John Reeve to Mrs. Alice Webb, 15 August 1656. Add. MSS 60171/13.
5. Copy, Lodowick Muggleton to Mrs. Elizabeth Dickinson of Cambridge, 20 August 1658. Add. MSS 60171/21.
6. Copy, Lodowick Muggleton to Larennce Claxton [Laurence Clarkson], 25 December 1660. Add. MSS 60168/6–7.
7. Copy, Lodowick Muggleton to William Cleve, near Cambridge, 1665. Add. MSS 60171/73.
8. Original, Lodowick Muggleton to Mr. [John?] Martain, minister of Orwell in Cambridgeshire, 19 January 1666/7. Add. MSS 60168/10.
9. Copy, Lodowick Muggleton to Walter Bohanan, 23 January 1671/2. Add. MSS 60181A/21–26
10. Copy, Lodowick Muggleton to William Penn, 23 January 1673/4. Add. MSS 60171/182
11. Copy, Lodowick Muggleton to Elizabeth Dickinson, Jun.[ior], 6 March 1674/5. Add. MSS 60171/134.
12. Copy, Lodowick Muggleton to Mrs. Hampson of Cambridge, 11 June 1674. Add. MSS 60171/173.
13. Copy, Mrs. Ellen Sudbury to Mr. Thomas Tomkinson, 10 August 1664. Add. MSS 60182/14
14. Original, Thomas Dudson to Lodowick Muggleton, 2 March 1668/9. Add. MSS 60168/9.
15. Copy, Alexander Delamain[e] to Mr. George Gamble, merchant in Cork, 14 August 1677. Add. MSS 60180/6–18.
16. Original, William Wood, painter, to Lodowick Muggleton, 9 February 1691/2. Add. MSS 60168/41.

Songs and Miscellaneous

The singing of religious songs was a disputed issue in some sects. Most General Baptists, for example, allowed unaltered psalms to be sung by a solo voice but objected to their being sung conjointly and in rhyme and meter because of the formalism it allegedly introduced into worship. Psalm singing was more acceptable among Particular Baptists. However, when the Particilar Baptist Benjamin Keach introduced the congregational singing of hymns of human composition, controversy among both groups of Baptists was the result. Quakers sometimes also objected to singing psalms in rhyme and meter because of the alteration of the originals and the belief they were often sung without the spiritual power that David enjoyed. Singing induced by the Holy Spirit, on the other hand, was approved by Fox, and early Friends sang psalms and hymns in their meetings and elsewhere. In the 1670s, however, there was a sharp decline of this practice, apparently the result of its inappropriate use by some members and its association with the practice of Ranters who allegedly sang bawdy verses to hymn tunes and sometimes sang and danced naked.[34]

Muggletonians seem not to have had such reservations. Numbers of them wrote religious verses intended to be sung. Some were generic in content while others were specific to the Muggletonian experience. Like the above letters, they were often copied by hand, sometimes as part of collections. According to Smith's *Bibliotheca Anti-Quakeriana* (p. 320) such a collection was printed as *Songs of Grateful Praise* (1790? extant?). Another collection, *Divine Songs of the Muggletonians*, was printed in 1829. However, all of the songs below as well as the two miscellaneous items are based on the manuscripts in the Muggletonian archive.

1. Song by Nathaniel Powell. Add. MSS 60208/23–26.
2. Song by William Wood. Add. MSS 60208/10–12.
3. Song by Thomas Tomkinson. Add. MSS 60219/31–32.
4. Song by Thomas Turner. Add. MSS 60208/27–28.
5. Song by John Ladd. Add. MSS 60220/17–18.
6. Song by Alexander Delamain[e]. Add. MSS 60220/16.
7. Song by William Wood. Add. MSS 60215/19–20.
8. Song by John Ladd. Add. MSS 60223/128–29.
9. Song by William Wood. Add. MSS 60227/52.
10. Song by Thomas Tomkinson. Add. MSS 60208/112–13.
11. An Acrostic by Tobit [Tobiah] Terry. Add. MSS 60210/2–3.
12. Expense Record, Dinner, 19 July 1682. Add. MSS 60232/1.

TWO

LODOWICK MUGGLETON

The Acts of the Witnesses

The Epistle Dedicatory

To all True Christian People that do or shall hereafter come to believe in this Third and Last Spiritual Commission, is this ensuing Treatise *directed, with love and peace to you be multiplied: It being a Legacy left you by the Lords last True Prophet, for your further establishment in Truth: As also it is left for a Convincement of the Seed of Reason, when he is in the dust; that by these* Acts *they may see how he hath been slandered, reproached, and belied, persecuted and imprisoned without a Cause.*

For how many Lying Reports hath been not only flung upon them, but also upon the True Believers of them; saying, That we own neither God nor Devil, Heaven or Hell; *and all because they see us use no outward glittering shew in fruitless Forms of Worship; whilst we worship an invisible Spiritual, yet personal God, in Spirit and Truth, which the World knows nothing of.*

For this we know and affirm, that the Doctrine of this Commission of the Spirit is of as great purity and power, as to Godliness, as ever any was, and as they were themselves, ever kept innocent from the breach of the Morrall Law, as to Act; Even so the Fruits of their Doctrine is of the like efficacy in the knowing seed of Faith, by which they have dominion over Sin, as in respect of Act.

And altho' this last Prophet in his Answer to the Nine Assertions, hath shewed his great mercy and clemency to some corrupt Natures, yet it is but to such who act not so; for as the breach of the Morral Law; *as to borrow Money, and not to pay it again; or to be passionate and hasty natur'd, overcome with Strong Drink, or the like, and tho' these are evil, yet reach but to the Borders of the Law, being Frailties in Nature, which disturb the peace of the Mind, for in such things, as the Apostle* James *saith,* We offend all: *But where there is true Faith, it prevents the Act; as this Prophet saith in one place, among many his Words are these,* Faith, *saith he,* overcomes all Sin, Death and Hell, within a man's self, and that none but such shall be admitted into the Kingdom of Heaven. *And the Prophet* Reeve's *Doctrine is thus, saying,* All those that are led by the Voice of the holy Spirit of *Jesus,* do work Righteousness in their bodies whereby they die unto Sin. *Again, saith he, in another place,* The Light of Christ in man doth convert from the Ruling Power of Sin. *And in a Third Place, which is not yet printed saith,* That they that are led by the Spirit of Faith, are kept from the commiting of sin: I do not say, *saith he,* that they have no Motion to sin, but the Spirit of Faith purifies their hearts, giving them power against those Motions, that they commit not the Act; and from hence it is, that all that are born of God, know the Voice of God, and hath this Power over Sin, as I have declar'd, *said he.*

These Doctrines of the Prophets are absolute and possitive, and do give great light into several Scriptures, *as* Matt. Chap. 5. ver. 28. I John chap. 3. ver. 9 *and* ver. 15. *in these places we are to distinguish between the Motion and the Action of Sin: This may also give light into* Rom. chap. 7. *how that* Paul *spake there as to his state by Nature, as also of the strife and struggle between the two Seeds of* Faith *and* Reason, *until the Law of* Faith *was quickened, and power by it attain'd, and then had he dominion over Sin, as* Chap. 8. *and so came to have peace with God, and with his own Conscience, and Assurance of Eternal Life.*

And from hence comes the Grounds of true Worship, and flows forth all spiritual Praise, *as* David *said,* O how sweet is thy Law: *This sweet Law is the Law of Faith; and he or she that is truly possessed hereof, can seal to those words of the Prophet* Reeve, *which saith,* That he that is born of God, his Language and Practice is such as speaks forth the Power of Godliness, *to the confounding of all glittering Tongue Hipocrites, and Faithless Formalists.*

Now let all True Believers know, that under every Commission this is made the ordinary way of life and salvation; yet to prevent an objection, this is confessed by us: That tho' there is this power in Faith, as aforesaid, yet the Lord for the Tryal of His Creature, may suffer some of his Chosen Ones to fall in the time of a Commission; and for the praise of his Free Grace may grant them one Repentance, or second Free pardon; for thus writes the Prophet Reeve in a Writing not yet printed.

The Lord, saith he, leaves some to their own strength, through which he rebels against the Light that is in him, to the wounding of his own Soul; to the end that he may learn, that the power, by which he is preserved from the Act of Sin, and so from eternal ruin, is not in himself, but in the Living

God that made him. Therefore the Scripture here and there pointeth forth one that the Lord hath left for a season to manifest his Prerogative Power over his Creatures, and afterwards doth his God-head Spirit move him to a second Free Pardon, wherein he raiseth that Soul to a higher and greater measure of Grace, Wisdom and Humility than it had before; which fulfils that Saying of Paul, Where Sin abounded, there Grace did superabound. *And this was fulfilled both by* David *and* Paul.

Here we see that if an Elect Vessel should once fall after his knowledge and belief in Truth, that his second Pardon doth raise him to a higher degree of Grace, Wisdom and Humility then he had before: This by the Prophet is made a true tryal to know whether a repentance or conversion from the Act of Sin committed be real or fained; as also that a second fall or relapse will prove dangerous; because it is rare to find a Third Pardon, and a Third increase of Grace to that Pardon.

Thus it is made clear that the Doctrine of this Commission of the Spirit hath power of Purity in it, and none that is truly born of God can dispute against it, but rather fear to offend, as the Prophet Reeve *saith, That a true born Saint is afraid of his own evil thoughts, much more of evil words or deeds against God or man.*

Again we see by this Book of the Acts, that these two Prophets were jointly chosen by God, and made equal in Power and Authority; for the Prophet Reeve *saith, That his Fellow Witness had as great power as he had himself. And further said, That he was the Lords last High-Priest: If this be granted, then it must follow, that there can be no Salvation to such as shall reject him, or his Writings, altho' they pretend to own* John Reeve.

Moreover the mighty sufferings that these Prophets have undergone for their Testimony sake are admirable; yet notwithstanding all opposition, providence preserv'd them so, as that they both died in their Beds in peace; and not only so, but this last Prophet liv'd to see the downfall of many of his great Enemies, and of his Persecutors and Judges.

Now to come to a conclusion of this Epistle: *When the Prophet had wrote this Book of the Acts, he kept it by him, not letting any to see it; but about two Weeks before he died, it was put into the hands of one of us, that was his true Friend, and ancient Acquaintance; in order to be printed after his death: Which now with the assistance of some Friends, through providence it is perfected, and is recommended to the whole* household of Faith, *which I doubt not, but it will be accepted of being a true Copy from the Original, there being nothing here printed but what is really his own; only you are to know that there are some things omited that are of a Temporal accompt, as a dispute with* Mr. Leader *concerning Eclipses and the hight of the Visible Heavens; with some other particulars which, things are left out, because of the greatness of the Charge, for all cannot be Printed that is Writen, for it is evident that altho there is above a Hundred Sheets of theirs in print, yet is it not past a Third part of what is Writen by them two Witnesses, for in the Year 1682* Mr. Delamaine *did Transcribe so many of their Works and bound up in a Book as contained 1052 pages in Folio, in which Book, and in what is printed almost all the Scripture hath been Interpreted that are of concernment to Salvation. But whether it may enter into the Heart of any that are Rich to be stirred up to Print the same, or whether the Powers of the Nation may permit it We leave to Providence.*

But before I conclude, it is Requisite to give you an Acompt of the Prophets Death and Burial which was thus upon the First of March, 1697[8], the Prophet was taken with an Illness and Weakness, upon which he said these Words, Now hath God sent Death unto me: *And presently after was helped to bed, and tho' he kept his Bed, yet we could not perceive that he was sick, only weak and he lay as if he slept, but in such quietness, as if he was nothing concerned with either Pain or Sickness.*

So that it was mear Age that took him away, which was the 14th day of March, *he then departed this Life with as much peace and quietness as ever any man did, being about 88 Years of Age, so that he had that Blessing, to come to the Grave in a full Age, like as a Shock of Corn cometh in at its Season. Upon the 16th day his Corps was remov'd to* Larsimus Hall, *and on the 17th day was from thence honourably Attended with two hundred forty eight Friends accompanying him to* Bethlehem Church-Yard, *where he was Buried by his Fellow-Witness, which was according to his own appointment.*

And thus was the Lord's Last Prophet brought to his Grave in peace, without noise, or without tumult, though thousands of Spectators beheld it, and there they are both to remain until the coming of their Lord, their King, and their Redeemer the Lord Jesus Christ, the High and Mighty God, and our God, and blessed are they that know their Voice, and wait for that day, and are offended with these things. Farewel.

T. T.

THE FIRST PART.

CHAP. I.

The Prophet sheweth first, That Moses *and the Prophets did record strange and wonderful things; As also their* Revelations, *which we are bound to believe.*

1. There is, and hath been Recorded many and several wonderful strange Things and Deeds of the righteous Fathers, as, *Noah, Lott, Abraham, Isaack,* and *Jacob,* and of their Faith in God.

2. And also, how wonderfully God did appear unto them, and strengthen them in their time, when they were upon the Eearth. These things are Recorded by the *Revelation* of *Moses,* as God revealed it to him.

3. Also *Moses* declared his own Birth, and how he was preserv'd from being drown'd: These things did he declare, and how God appeared unto

him and chose him and *Aron* for that great Work, to lead that great People through the *Wilderness*, and to be a Law-giver.

4. Which was the first visible appearance of God upon Earth, that is Recorded, for all Generations to come. For tho God did appear in a wonderful manner unto *Enock, Noah, Abraham, Isaack* and *Jacob*, and several other righteous Men, yet we could never have known it, had not *Moses*, by his *Revelation*, left it upon Record.

5. How could the Generations to come have known any thing of the Creation of the World, and how God made Man in his own Image and Likeness.

6. Or that there ever was the Man *Adam*, or *Cain*, that slew his Brother *Abel*, or that the World was ever drowned, except eight Persons, if it had not been revealed by *Moses*.

7. So that we have nothing but *Moses's* bare Word for it; for we did not live in his time, to see the Wonders he wrought, nor hear him speak.

8. Yet we are bound to believe his Record, and *Revelation*, and Acts he did: And blessed and happy were all those that did believe him when he was upon Earth, when they saw his Acts, and heard him speak.

9. And more blessed are these now, that understand and believe, which have not seen his Wonders he wrought in his time, nor heard him speak forth those *Revelations* God revealed unto him concerning the Creation of the World as aforesaid.

10. Also we read in Scripture of many wonderful Acts that was wrought and done by the Prophets, in the time of the Law, after *Moses*.

11. As *Samuel, Isaiah, Jeremiah, Elijah, Elisha*, and several other Prophets, in the time of the Law; their wonderful Acts are recorded in Scripture.

12. Besides the *Revelation* they declared as from God, which the Ages following did not see nor hear, yet many did truly believe, and doth truly belive, and are by Faith satisfied, as those that did both hear and see.

13. So that the Scriptures Record, is a Record of spiritual and heavenly Things, and of some of those wonderful and powerful Acts of *Moses*, and the Prophets, and the righteous Fathers, manifesting their great Faith in God and being in favour with God.

14. Which I, by Faith, have found their Record true, and so have many more of the seed of Faith found their Record and *Revelations* to be true.

CHAP. II.

The Prophet makes a Rehearsal of the Acts of the Apostles in the New Testament, and of the Lord Christ, and how that they were writen for the Comfort of the Seed of Faith: After which he enters upon the third Record, and shows the cause of his writing some of the most principal Acts of the Witness of the Spirit under this third Record.

1. Also we find written in the New Testament many wonderful Acts and Miracles, acted by the Lord Christ, and his Apostles; as *Matthew, Mark,*

Luke and *John* doth declare concerning Christ; that if all the things Christ spake and Acts he did were written, the World would not contain the Volume.

2. That is, the verge of a Man's understanding could not retain the particulars, so as to tell it to his Friend, the particulars would be so many.

3. So likewise, the *Acts of the Apostles*, that Book hath little else in it, but wonderful Acts wrought by the power of Faith in the Apostles.

4. And these things were written for the seed of Faith, that they might have Comfort in believing the Record that is given of the Apostles, how God strengthned them in Faith and power, as by the power of Faith to work Miracles.

5. Because they were chosen of God to bear Record on Earth, to the Blood of the New Testament, or, New Covenant.

6. Thus did the Apostles bear Record on Earth to the Flood, as the Prophets did bear Record on Earth to the Water, which signifies the Law of *Moses*, and the Blood signifies the Gospel of Jesus Christ.

7. The Scriptures are a Record, that sheweth many wonderful Acts that Christ and his Apostles did when on Earth, besides the heavenly Revelation.

8. And it is very comfortable to the Seed of Faith, true Belivers, to read of the Acts of the Prophets, and of the Apostles, as it is of their Doctrin, Revelation, Prophesies, Interpretations; or Epistles.

9. These things, I having experience of, and seeing it hath been the Practice of some of the Prophets and Apostles to leave a Record behind them, for after Ages to peruse, of some of the most remarkable Acts, done by them when they were upon Earth, as a remarkable Remembrance to their Prophesies and Epistles.

10. So, likewise I being one of the two last Prophets and Witnesses of the Spirit, being the Third and last Record from God on Earth.

11. I thought it convenient and expedient to leave some Record on Earth, behind me, of some of the most remarkable Acts and Passages that hath been done and acted by us, and to us, the Witnesses of the Spirit, since we were chosen of God in the Year 1651[2].

12. That I may leave it as a Legasy to the Seed of Faith after me, who shall happen to Read and Believe those Writings of ours after I am gon.

13. They may know by the Doctrin therein declared, who, and what we were, and what God we believed in.

14. Also I thought it necessary to write of those Acts my self, rather then any other, being acted in my sight and perfect knowledge, as other Profits have done before me, as *Moses* and others.

CHAP. III.

Of the Birth, Parentage, and Trade, of the two Witnesses, and how the Profits Nature led them forth to all Sobriety, hateing Drunkeness, and of their inclining to the Principles of those Call'd Puritans, and of their being perswaded from judging Cases of Concience before they new the truth.

1. But before I write of the Acts, I shall give the Reader a little to understand what we were before God did chuse us two, to be his last two Prophets and Witnesses of the Spirit.

2. And of some Experince I had, and Working within me before I was Chosen of God, little expecting God would have chosen me for such a great Work.

3. As for *John Reeve*, he was born in *Wiltshire*, his Father was Clerk to a *Deputy* of *Ireland*, a Gentleman as we call them by his place, but fell to decay.

4. So he put *John Reeve* Apprentice here at *London*, to a *Taylor* by Trade. He was out of his Apprentiship before I came acquainted with him, he was of an Honest, Just Nature, and Harmless.

5. But a Man of no great Natural Witt, or Wisdom, no Subtilty, or Pollicy was in him, nor no great store of Religeon he had, but what was Traditional, only of an Innocent Life.

6. I knew him many years before God spake to him by Voice of Words to the hearing of the Ear, three Mornings together, as is declar'd in the Commission Book, call'd a *Trancesendant Spiritual Treatise*, the first Book he writ.

7. And I *Lodowick Muggleton* was born in *Bishop gate-street*, near the *Earl of Devonshire's*[1] House, at the corner House call'd *Walnut-Tree-Yard*.

8. My Father's name was *John Muggleton*, he was a *Smith* by Trade, that is a *Farrier*, or *Horse-Doctor*, he was in great Respect with the *Post-Master* in King *Jame's* time, he had three Children by my Mother, two Sons and one Daughter, I was the youngest and my Mother lov'd me.

9. But after my Mother dy'd, I being but young, my Father took another Wife, so I being young was Expos'd to live with Strangers in the Country, at a distance from all my Kindred: I was a Stranger to my Fathers House after my Mother was dead.

10. But it came to pass when I was grown to 15 or 16 Years of age, I was put Apprentice to one *John Quick*, a Taylor, he made Livery Gowns, and all sorts of Gowns for Men, he made Gowns for several Aldermen, and Livery Men of their Company in *London*.

11. And he lived in this *Walnut-Tree-Yard*, and knew my Father and Mother very well; he was a quiet peaceable Man, not crewel to Servants, which liked me very well.

12. For my Nature was always against Cruelty, I could never indure it, neither in my self, nor in others, living peaceably in my Apprentiship.

13. I took my Trade well, and pleased my Master better then any of his other Servants, for they were bad Husbands, and given to Drunkenness, but my Nature was inclin'd to be sober, hating Drunkenness and Lust in the time of my Youth.

14. But when my time of Service was pretty far expired, I grew to more

understanding, and hearing in those days a great talk amongst the vulger People, and especially, amongst Youth, Boys, and young Maids, of a people called *Puritans;* some of these *Puritans* came to talk and discourse with my Master, though he was no Religious Man.

15. But I being ignorant, did perceive they pleaded more for Righteousness, and were better versed in the Scriptures then he was, so that I liked in my self their Discourse upon the Scriptures, and pleaded for a Holy keeping of the Sabbath day, which my Master did not do, nor I his Servant.

16. But I not knowing my Right Hand from my Left in Religion at that time; yet, methoughts I had a Love for those People call'd *Puritans,* and could not endure my Companions should speak Evil of them.

17. And when young Boys as I was, and young Maids would speak Evil, and lay many Slanders upon those People call'd *Puritans,* as if they had been the wickedest People in the World, with many Scoffs and Jears.

18. Yet all this while my Heart did not close with their Reproaches, but rather was inclin'd to love those People, and to think the better of them, thinking in my self, Oh! that I might be so happy as them, yet I knew not what Happiness was, nor what Condemnation was, for I knew nothing by my self, why I should be Condemned.

19. But the Seed of God lay hidden in my Heart, which kept me from speaking Evil of things I knew not, even from my Childhood, which many others of my Age did.

20. Like unto those Children that mocked the Prophet *Elisha,* which two she Bares did tare in pieces; so many of these mockers of Religion, in that my time did come to great Poverty and Destruction in this World, but the God of Truth preserved me, though I knew him not.

21. Also I was smitten with the Plague[2] in that great sickness after King *James* dyed; it was not extream tedious to me, for the sore broke, and I recovered quickly, and hath not had half a days sickness since, not this forty Years and more.

22. I never bestowed Six-pence in Physick in my Life for my self, but what the Kitchen would afford, as Water-gruel, Broth or such like, and I have had my Health, and hath been as perfect in Nature from all Distempers and Diseases, as any Man in the World ever since.

CHAP. IV.

How the secret providence of God prevented the Expectation of the Prophet in his choice of a Wife, and in his desire of Riches, of the Prophet's Zeal for the Law, and a Righteous Life.

1. After this it came to pass my time of Service grew near out, and my Nature had a great desire to be rich in this World, that I might no more be Servant to any Man, and I thought the Trade of a Taylor would not gain much Riches, I having little to begin with; and withal, I thought I should be

too much subject to the humours of People to please them, which I had experience of in my Apprentiship.

2. So I went to work in a Brokers Shop in *Hownsditch*, who made Cloaths to sell, and did lend Money upon Pawns, called a Pawn-broker, and the Brokers Wife had one Daughter alive; and after I had been there a while, the Mother saw that I was a good Husband, and knew how to manage that way, being a Workman better than they, and that I was a civil and sober young Man, not given to Drunkenness nor to Debauchery.

3. She was willing to give her Daughter unto me to Wife, and I lov'd the Maid well, and thought my self too inferiour for her, because she had something to take too, and the Onely Child; and I having nothing, yet the Mother being well perswaded of my good natural Temper, and of my good Husbandry, and that I had no poor Kindred came after me to be any Charge or Burthen to her Daughter.

4. Those things consider'd, she thought I might be a convenient Match for her Daughter; so she seeing there was some kind of Affection between her Daughter and me, she proposed unto me, that she would give me a Hundred Pound with her to set up, which thing I axcepted on in my Mind, but told I was not yet a Free-man of *London*.[3]

5. So she urged me to be made Free as soon as I could, also she urged me to be made sure to her Daughter before the Father-in-law and her self.

6. So the Maid and I were made sure by Promise before her Mother and Father-in-law, and before I was made Free; and I was resolved to have the Maid to Wife, and to keep a Brokers Shop, and lend Money upon Pawns, and grow Rich as others did.

7. And the Maids Mother had Five Hundred Pounds more then what she promised me, which her Husband knew not of, for he was a kind of a Distracted Hare-brain'd Man; his Name was *Richardson*, there is many alive at this Day that knew them; but for the Daughter I should have had to Wife, she is alive at this Day, and is worth Seven Hundred Pound a Year.

8. But the secret Providence of God prevented my expectation and desire of being Rich in this World, in an unlawful way against the Checks of my own Conscience.

9. But it came to pass in the 22d. Year of my Life, not being quite out of my Apprenticeship, yet sure to the Maid, I went to work as a Journeyman, and happened to work with a *Puritan* in *Thomas Apostle London*. His name was *William Reeve, John Reeves's* brother.

10. He was a very zealous *Puritan* at that time, and many others of that Religion came to him, and disputed with me about the unlawfulness of lending Money upon Pawns, because they pleaded it was Usury and Extortion, and did alledge many places of Scripture against it.

11. And I used all the Arguments of Reason I could for it, because I had a great desire to be Rich, and considered I was ingaged to this Maid, and that her Mother would not let me have her to Wife, except I would keep a Brokers Shop and lend Money, so that I was in great strait, and much perplexed in Mind.

12. For I lov'd the Maid, and desired to be Rich, but these *Puritan* People being well versed in the Scripture words, and zealous for Righteousness, threatened great Judgments, and danger of Damnation hereafter.

13. They overpowered my Natural Knowledge and civil Practices in me, and made me afraid of eternal Damnation, and they pressed the Scriptures so hard upon me, which exceedingly perplexed my Mind, reasoning in my self, that if I did lend Mony upon Usury and Extortion, I should be damned, and if I would not, then I should not have the Maid to Wife.

14. So that the love of the Maid, and the fear of the loss of my Soul did struggle within me, and dispute within me like two distinct Spirits, even as a Woman in Travail with two natural Sons in the Womb, so that I was in a great strait which I should cleave unto.

15. So after much dispute and reasoning in my self, it came to this result, I considered the Riches of this World, and the Love I had to the Maid, and I weighed it in my Mind, and was loath to forsake it.

16. Then I consider'd my Soul was of more value, and what would it avail me to be rich in this World for a Moment, and to loose my Soul, for I was extreamly fearful of eternal Damnation, thinking my Soul might go into Hell Fire without a body, as all People did at that time.

17. And after much strugling in my Mind, I came to this resolution in my self, that rather then I would loose my Soul, or be damned to Eternity, I would loose the Maid. And that way that would have made me Rich, and that I would be zealous of the Law of God, as afterwards I was.

18. Here the two Seeds of Faith and Reason did work in me, but I knew them not by Name nor Nature at that time, nor many Years after.

19. But as I did fear it, it came to pass, for the Maids Mother seeing my Mind so changed, and so zealous of the Laws of the Scriptures, and that I would not keep that way, as I thought to do before.

20. She would not let her Daughter have me to her Husband, so the Maid was perswaded by her Mother.

21. And my Zeal to save my Soul, perswaded my Mind to let her go, so we parted.

22. Thus I forsook the World and a Wife, which I lov'd in the days of my ignorance, for zeal to the Law of God, which I thought to be Truth, and the true way, and so it was.

23. But I did not know it till many years after; but the Lord God of Truth had respect unto my Person and Zeal at that time, and prevented me from falling into that Snare of being rich in this World.

CHAP. V.

The Prophet shews his Care, his Fear, and Zeal in the Law of God, and of the working of his Thoughts, and heighth of the Puritan Religion.

1. So after I had parted with the Maid, and that way that did offend my

Conscience, I was resolved to live so upright to the Law of God, and so just between Man and Man, that I thought in time I might procure favour with God, and to attain assurance of my Salvation.

2. For I was fully possest that there was really Salvation to be attained unto by my Righteousness, and that there was a real Damnation to all those that were unrighteous, or did not demean themselves so strictly as I did.

3. For I was exceeding fearful of Hell and eternal Damnation: The very Thoughts of it made my Spirit many times fail within me.

4. But by Prayer and my Righteous Practices, I did many times recover some Hope and Peace again.

5. All this while I did suppose my Soul might go into Hell without a Body, and that Millions of Souls were in Hell Fire without Bodies; and that the Devil being a Bodily Spirit did torment those Souls that came there, and that the Devil had liberty to come out of Hell to Tempt People here on Earth, and go there again, but no Soul that he had gotten there could come out of Hell more.

6. These things wrought in my Mind exceeding great Fear, and stir'd me up to a more exceeding Righteousness of Life, thinking thereby that my Righteous Life would have cast out those tormenting Fears, but it did not.

7. Yet, notwithstanding, I did continue in my Zeal and was earnest in the *Puritan* Religion and Practice; neither did I know how to find Rest any where else; neither did I hear any Preach in those Days but the *Puritan* Ministers, whose Hair was cut short.

8. For if a Man with long Hair had gone into the Pulpit to preach, I would have gone out of the Church again, tho he might preach better than the other.

9. But we *Puritans* being Pharisaically minded were zealous of outward Appearance, and of outward Behaviour, for we minded that more than their Doctrin.

10. For we took it for granted, that God was a Spirit without a Body, and that Christ Jesus his Son had a Body in form like Man, and that he did mediate to God his Father, who was a Spirit without a Body, and that for Christ's sake, this Spirit without a Body, did hear us, and speak Peace unto us.

11. Also I believed that the Devil was a Spirit without a Body, and could assend out of Hell, when God did give him leave, and sugest evil Thoughts of Lust, Theft, Murther, and Blasphemy against God; not thinking that these Thoughts and Motions did arise out of Man's own Heart, but from a Divel, a Spirit without a Body, without Man.

12. Also I thought, those Souls which God did Save were carried up to Heaven without Bodies, and should be with God, who was a Spirit without a Body, and that we should see Christ Jesus in Heaven, with his Body, with our Spirits that were Saved without Bodies, till the Resurrection, and then Body and Soul should be United together again.

13. Also we did believe, that the wicked Spirits should be cast into Hell Fire, without Bodies, where the Devil and his Angels, being Spirits without

Bodies, should Torment the Souls of the Wicked till the Day of Resurrection; and then those Wicked Souls should be United to their Bodies again, and be Tormented Body and Soul together, with the Devil and his Angels, who were Spirits without Bodies in Hell Fire for ever and ever.

14. And we did believe that the Angels of God were Ministring Spirits without Bodies, as God was a Spirit without a Body, so were they, and could minister Comforts unto Men without Bodies.

15. And we did believe our own Souls to be Immortal, and could not Die, but did subsist the good Spirits with God in Heaven without Bodies, and the wicked Souls did subsist in Hell without Bodies.

16. These were some of the Fundamental Principles of Faith and Religion, we Zealous *Puritans* did believe and practice; and there is no better Faith in the World to this day in the generality of Professors of Religion.

17. These Things was I very well versed in, and I grew in great Experience and Knowledge in the Letter of the Scriptures, and had a good Gift of Prayer, and was very strong in Disputes, because my Mind was extreamly perplexed with the fear of Hell, notwithstanding my exact life to the Letter of the Law.

18. But the fear of Hell wrought in me much Experience, so that I did exceed several other Men in that Knowledge which was in those days; and tho' I was judged a very godly knowing Man, and a happy Man by others, yet I could not judge so of my self, but the fear of Hell was oft rising up in me.

19. For I never Conceited well of my own Knowledge, but thought the Knowledge of other Men did far exceed me, because they seemed to be better satisfied in their Minds than I was.

20. Yet I thought in my self, that in time, by my Prayers and Righteousness, and exact Walking and hearing of Preaching, that I might heal that Wound in my Soul which was made, and I knew not for what.

21. For I never had committed any Sin that I knew of that did trouble my Conscience.

22. Yet the fear of Hell produced many deep Sighs and Groans even from the bottom of my Heart, for fear God had made me a Reprobate before I was Born, because he did not answer my Prayers, nor speak Peace to my Soul; notwithstanding my earnest Desires and Zeal for him I knew not at that time.

23. Yet many times I had great Refreshments of Soul, and as I thought, Communion with God, whereby my Hope was increased for a Season, but it was quickly lost again; so that the Troubles of my Mind did continue still many years.

24. Yet at some times I had Elevations in my Mind, and Raptures of Joy, that I thought I should never be moved again.

25. But a while after all was lost again, and Doubting took place in my Soul; but since, I saw the cause of those Raptures and fears of Hell were both groundless.

CHAP. VI.

After the Prophet hath given a Description of his Marriage, of his Wives, and of his Children, from the Twenty sixth year of his Life to the Thirty Eighth, he then shews the alteration of the Religion in the Puritan People, and of the Confusion that was amongst them.

1. After this, it came to pass in the Twenty sixth year of my Life, I took a Wife that was of my own Mind and Religion. She was a Virgin of about 19 years of Age, and I had by her Three Daughters in three years and an half's time.

2. The first Daughter I had by her was named *Sarah*, after her Mother's Name: She is yet alive, and is become the most experimental and knowing'st Women in Spiritual Things of that Sex in *London*; but I shall say no more of her here, because I shall have occasion to speak of her hereafter.

3. Also my youngest Daughter *Elizabeth*, which I had by my Wife *Sarah*, is now living, but the second Daughter died; when three years and an half was expired my Wife *Sarah* died also.

4. After this, my Children being young, I put them forth to Nurse in the Country, and lived a single Life, and followed my Trade, and lived very well.

5. Only the Spirit of fear of Hell was still upon me, but not so extream as it was the year before.

6. After this, in the Thirty second year of my Life, I took another Virgin to Wife; Her Name was *Mary*, she was about nineteen years old, and I had by her three Children, two Sons and one Daughter; the eldest died at three years old, and the youngest was a Daughter and she died three days after she was born, and my Wife *Mary* died five days after.

7. I had only one Son living by her, and I had her to Wife a matter of six years; and that Son lived until *John Reeve* and I was chosen of God; and about a year and an half afterwards, being about nine years old, he died; so all the Children of my second Wife died.

8. After my Wife *Mary* died, I was then about Thirty eight years old; but at the time when I was Married to my Wife *Mary*, about six years before, there was Raising of Arms by the Parliament against the King.

9. And generally the *Puritans* were all for the Parliament, and most of my Society and Acquaintance in Religion did fall away from that way we did use, and declined in Love one towards another, and every one got a new Judgment, and new Acquaintance, and New Discipline.

10. Some of them turned to *Presbytery*, and would have Elders; and some turned *Independants*, and would not let none work to them but their own People that was in Church Fellowship; others fell to be *Ranters*, and some fell to be meer *Atheists*.

11. So that our *Puritan* People were so divided and scattered in our Religion, that I knew not which to take too, or which to cleave unto, for I was altogether at a loss, for all the Zeal we formerly had was quite worn out.

12. And to joyn with any of these new Disciplines I could not, except I would play the Hypocrite for a Livelihood, which my Heart always hated, notwithstanding my Kindred by my first Wife *Sarah*, were all *Puritans* and Zealous in Religion.

13. And I had a great stroke of Work of them, and they were a great Generation of them, and most of them pritty Rich in this World; and most of them went into Church Fellowship, so that I lost several of them because I could not joyn in Church Fellowship.

14. For thought I, there is no more satisfaction to be found in Church Fellowship than before, for none could serve God and be more Zealous for God and for Righteousness than we were before.

15. So that going into Church Fellowship would not satisfie my Soul, as to my Salvation, no more than before.

16. For satisfaction of Mind, as to another Life, was always my Aim and End that I strove after, but could not attain to it as yet.

17. So I being at a great loss in my Mind, what to do, I had lost my Friends and Relations because I could not follow them in Church Fellowship, and I had no freedom in my self so to do.

18. For I had seen the utmost Perfection and Satisfaction that could be found in that way, except I would do it for Loaves, but Loaves was never my aim, but a real rest in my Mind I always sought after, but could find it no where.

CHAP. VII.

The Prophet shews his great dissatisfaction and loss in Religion, even almost to Dispair, yet in the Conclusion, resolves to hold his Integrity, to do Justly, and keep from actual Sin, but mind Religion no more, but left Happiness and Misery to Gods disposal.

1. So I seeing these *Puritans* of my Acquaintance they had no Comfort nor Peace of Mind, as to a Life to Come, that were in Church Fellowship than before, nor so much.

2. Then I saw several of them that were Zealous before towards God, and Righteousness towards Man; and now they had left that Zeal, and turned Ranters, not only in Judgment but in Practice, to the Destruction both of Soul and Body.

3. When I saw this, that neither the Righteous could find Peace in the Days of their Righteousness, but were afraid of Hell, nor those that turned from their Righteousness to actual Wickedness, I thought must needs go to Hell.

4. Yet they said all was well and quiet with them, so that I was as *David* was, almost like to have slept, and to have said in my Heart, *sure there is no God*: But all things comes by Nature, because the Righteous could find no Peace in their Righteousness, as I could not, nor the Wicked were not troubled for their Sins.

5. But when I went into the Sanctuary of my Mind, I considered the visible things of Nature, I could not conceive how this vast Element we see could make it self; or, how the Sun, Moon, and Stars could give Being to themselves.

6. How could the Beasts of the Field, the Fouls of the Aire, and Fish of the Sea: I could not imagine how these things could give Being to themselves, nor how they should come by Nature, nor how they should Create one another. Then thought I, Man might as well Create himself, and come by Nature as those Things.

7. So I thought there must needs be some Original Cause, or, supreme Power, that gave Being to these Things, and hath placed a Law of Order in all Things, sutable to its Nature.

8. This supreme Power that made those Things; That Power that is the Cause of Causes we call God; but what he is in himself I knew not at that time; But these Thoughts preserved me from saying in my Heart, as the Fool doth, *there is no God.* Many of my Acquaintance did say in their Hearts, and Tongues both, *That there is no God, but Nature only.*

9. But notwithstanding I did not know that God that made all things, and Man in his own Image and Likeness, yet I considered that innocency of Heart, and a just upright Spirit, was good in it self, if there were no God to Reward it.

10. And that Unrighteousness and Lust after his Neighbours Wife, and not to be of an upright Spirit, it was Wickedness in it self, if there were no God to punish it.

11. Therefore I was loth to let go my Integrity, but kept close to it; for as I had been Innocent from my Childhood to this Day, I was resolved to keep to it to the end, if there were nothing after Death; yet would I keep my Heart upright, and would do nothing to wound my Conscience.

12. For I never had no Guilt of actual Sin that did ever trouble me.

13. So with this Resolution I did resolve to live in, to do just between Man and Man, and to keep from all actual Sin, as I ever had been, and not to mind any Religion more, for I saw all profession of Religion in all Men was vain and unsatisfactory to all Men, as it was to me.

14. So I gave over all publick Prayer, and Hearing and Discourse about Religion; and lived an honest and just natural Life: And I found more Peace here then in all my Religion, and if there were anything, either of Happiness or Misery after Death, I left it to God, which I knew not, to do what he would with me.

15. But I was in good Hope at that time, that there was nothing after Death, but all Happiness and Punishment was in this Life: For I saw a temporal Punishment follow Wickedness in this Life to many.

16. And I saw Prosperity to those that were Righteous, even in this Life; so that I was in good Hopes all Punishments and Happiness would end in this Life.

17. So I was resolved to keep myself as I always had done, unspotted of the World, and not to defile my Conscience: And I had a great deal of peace

of Mind in this Condition. And in this Condition did I continue some three Years, until I was about forty years old, and in the year 1650.

CHAP. VIII.

The Prophet gives a Discription of John Tannye *and* John Robins, *being counted greater than Prophets, and sets forth their Appearance and wonderful Actions.*

1. After this it came to pass, in the year 1650. I heard of several Prophets and Prophetess that were about the Streets, and declared the Day of the Lord, and many other wonderful Things, as from the Lord.

2. Also, at the same time I heard of two other Men that were counted greater than Prophets, to wit, *John Tannye,* and *John Robins.*

3. *John Tannye,* he declared himself to be the Lord's High-Priest, and that he was to act over the Law of *Moses* again: Therefore he Circumcised himself according to the Law.

4. Also he declared that he was to gather the *Jews* out of all Nations, and lead them to *Mount Olives* to *Jerusalem;* and that he was King of Seven Nations: With many other strange and wonderful Things.

5. And as for *John Robins,* he declared himself to be God Almighty, and that he was the Judge of the Quick and of the Dead, and that he was that first *Adam* that was in that innocent State, and that his Body had been Dead this Five Thousand, Six Hundred and odd Years, and now he was risen again from the Dead; And that he was that *Adam Melchisadick* that met *Abraham* in the Way, and received Tithes of them.

6. Also he said, he had raised from the Dead that same *Cain* that killed *Abel;* and that he had raised that same *Judas* that betrayed *Christ;* and now they were Redeem'd to be happy.

7. Also he said he had raised several of the Prophets, as *Jeremiah,* and others, and that he had raised the same *Benjamin, Jacob's* Son, that had been Dead so many Thousand Years, now he was raised again.

8. I saw all those that was said to be raised by *John Robins,* and they owned themselves to be the very same Persons that had been Dead for so long time.

9. Also I saw several others of the Prophets that was said to be raised by him, and they did own they were the same; for I have had Nine or Tenn of them at my House at a time, of those that were said to be raised from the Dead.

10. For I do not speak this from Hearsay from others, but from a perfect Knowledge, which I have seen and heard from themselves.

11. Also they declared unto me, That their God *John Robins* was to gather out of *England* and else where, an Hundred and Forty Four Thousand Men and Women, and lead them to *Jerusalem* to *Mount Olives,* and there to make them happy: And that he would feed them with *Manna* from

Heaven: And that he would divide the Red Sea, and that they should go through upon dry Land.

12. Also he said, that those Prophets he had raised should be their Leaders, and on *Joshua's* Garment should be the *Moses* Man that should be chief under his God *John Robins*. And that all the Leaders should have Power by the clap of their Hands, and a stamp of their Foot to destroy any that did oppose them.

13. Also I have seen one of his Prophets, that should have this Power, to kneel down and pray to *John Robins*, as unto God Almighty, which such high and Heavenly Expressions which was marvellous unto me to hear.

14. Those Things, and many more lying Signes and Wonders did he shew to some, as presenting the appearance of Angels, burning shining Lights, Half-Moons and Stars in Chambers and thick Darkness, where it was Light to the Phantasies of People, when they covered their Faces in the Bed.

15. They said he presented Serpents, Dragons, and his Head in a flame of Fire, and his Person rideing upon the Wings of the Wind.

16. Also his Prophets had Power from him to damn any that did oppose, or speak evil of him, they not knowing he was neither false nor true, for this Rule he went by.

17. That he, or, she that would speak evil of Things they knew not, they would as soon speak evil of a true Prophet as a false Prophet.

18. So his Prophets gave Sentence of Damnation upon many, to my Knowledge, for speaking evil of him, they not knowing him, whether he was true or false.

19. And I saw afterwards that his Sentence was true upon them, for they would have said as much to the true *Christ* as they did to him: So I saw his Sentance was true and efectual upon those he condemned, notwithstanding he himself was false.

20. For this was observed, that the Elect Seed would be preserved from speaking Evil of things they knew not. That belongs only to the Seed of the Serpent to speak Evil of things he doth not know: For who upon Earth did know, at that time whether he was False or True: I say none, not one.

CHAP. IX.

Of the Prophets Application concerning these wonderful things, and of his Qualification.

1. Now this *John Robins's* knowledge in the Scriptures was more at that time than any Man in the World.

2. These things had I perfect Knowledge of, yet was I quiet and still, and heard what was said and done, and spake against nothing that was said or done.

3. But shewed Kindness and Mercy to all of them, Marvelling in myself what the Ephect of these things would be.

4. And one of his Prophets came to my House very oft, and he told me all things that was done amongst them; and he had a very high Language, and very knowing in the Scriptures, and spake as an Angel of God.

5. And my natural Temper was always merciful to Strangers; and this place of Scripture run much in my Mind: *Forget not to entertain Strangers, for some in entertaining of Strangers have entertained Angels.* So I never let him go without Eating and Drinking.

6. And if I had nothing in the House to Eat, if I had but Eighteen Pence I would give him one Shilling of it; and if I had but Twelve Pence, I would give him Six Pence of it.

7. This I did many times, though I had need enough myself, for I had Three Children to maintain at that time: Two Daughters by my Wife *Sarah*, and one Son by my Second Wife *Mary*, then alive.

8. All these things never moved me to rejoyce, in any Hope of any Happiness or Deliverance to any better Condition then I was then in, or to be in any worse Condition after Death, then I was in at present.

9. But I kept close to my Integrity of Heart: That is, I would do nothing that should condemn by Conscience, but would do what I could to justify my Conscience.

10. Tho I looked for no Reward hereafter, yet I would do well, that Sin might not ly at the Door of my Conscience.

11. And these things working in my Mind kept me from actual Sin, and from the Pollutions of the Flesh.

12. Yet all this while was I as one without God in this World, as to my knowledge of him; I had none that was true.

13. But the Lord God of Truth, had Respect unto my Person, and to the upriteness of my Heart, but I knew it not all that time; as will more plainly appear in the following Discourse.

CHAP. X.

The Prophet here showes of a Melancholy that came upon him, and after-wards of Two Motions arising in him, and speak as Two living Voices.

1. After this, in the beginning of the Year 1651. and in the Year of my Life 41. and better.

2. In the beginning of the year it came to pass upon a Day in the Month called *April*, I being silent, all alone, my Children being all abroad, there fell upon me a great Melancholy upon my Spirit, and I knew not for what; yet I was pressed exceedingly in my Heart with Fear.

3. So I began to cast about in my Mind, what I had done that I should thus fear: So I called to mind all my former Righteousness and Zeal which I had left thinking in myself that might be the Cause of this Fear.

4. Reasoning in myself whether I had best turn again to my former Practice of Religion, or not.

5. There did arise in me an Answer to that; and said, *No, For thou*

*knowest when thou did'st worship in that Zeal thou had'st no Peace, but
was oft tormented with fear of Hell, so to no purpose to turn or go back
to Ægipt again.*

6. Then did two Motions arise in me, and speak in me, as two lively
Voices; as if two Spirits had been speaking in me, one answering the other,
as if they were not my own Spirit.

7. But I knew afterwards they were the two Seeds strove in me for mas-
tery.

8. So my old Fears of Hell rose in me, as it did formerly, when a *Puritan.*

9. So I began to reason in myself, what I should do to escape being
damn'd to Eternity, for I dreaded the Thoughts of Eternity; for I did not so
much mind to be saved, as I did to escape being damn'd.

10. For I thought, if I could but ly still in the Earth for ever, it would be
as well with me, as it would be if I were in eternal Happiness; for I believed
the Soul was mortal many years before, which Belief yielded me much Peace
of Mind: And was in hope God would never raise me again.

11. For I did not care whether I was Happy, so I might not be Miserable.
I car'd not for Heaven so I might not go to Hell, but I could not be sure I
should go to Heaven, nor certain I should escape Hell which was a great
perplexity to my Mind, not knowing which way to help myself out of Gods
Hands.

12. Now this place of Scripture of *Paul* in the *Romans* pressed hard upon
me, *What if God willingly make thee a Vessel of Wrath, fired for Destruction*: And that saying, *What are thou; O Man! that replyest against God?*

13. *Shall the thing that is formed, say unto him that formed it, why hast
thou made me thus*: And that saying, *Shall not the Potter have Power over
the Clay, of the same Lump, to make one Vessel to Honour, and another
to Dishonour.*

14. These things pressed hard upon my Soul, even to the wounding of
it. Then I replyed against this, and said in my Heart, that God did seem to
be more cruel than Man, for Man made Vessels of Honour and Dishonour
of dead senceless Clay, that is neither capable of Honour nor Dishonour,
nor capable of Pain, nor of Misery; nor of Joy or Happiness, Oh! that I had
been as the Clay I tread upon, rather than a living Man.

15. But God made Vessels of Wrath, to bear eternal Torments, of living
sensible Creatures, not giving any reason why; but it was his prerogative
Will so to do, and who shall hinder him.

16. The apprehension of this sunk deep into my Heart, and brought forth
deep Sighs and Groans.

17. And it was answered me again; saying, that God hath a Prerogative
Power above and over all Life because he gave Life to Man and all Creatures
else. And as a Man hath a prerogative Power over dead Clay, so hath God
a prerogative Power over all Life, to make what Life he will a Vessel of
Wrath for the manifestation of his own Power and Glory.

18. For if all Life were made to be happy, or all Mankind sav'd, then
where would Gods Honour appear, But because the greatest part of Man-

kind are made Vessels of Wrath to bear eternal Torments, therefore it is that God's Redeemed ones shall praise him.

19. So that there is a perticular People to be sav'd, but my Fear was that I was none of the Redeem'd.

20. And it was said within me, dost thou consider the nature of a prerogative Power, that is above all Law; who shall dispute with a prerogative power that is above all Law, and can do what it will with living Creatures, even as the Potter doth what he will with the dead Clay.

CHAP. XI.

The Prophets further Reasoning in himself how hardly God delt with him; and of his Reasoning against Adam: *And shews how a contrary Seed; or, Voice in him repeld his Arguments.*

1. When I consider'd this, I wished in myself I had never been born, then had I not been sensible neither of Joy nor Sorrow: I did not so much seek after Heaven as to be freed from Hell.

2. Again, I Reasoned in myself wishing that I had dyed in my Infancy: I thought, if I were a Vessel of Wrath, my Torments would be the less, than now I am grown to maturity of Age.

3. But the Answer said to this, Though thy Torment be less than others, yet it is Eternal: This Eternity struck a deep Fear in me, which made me almost despair.

4. Again I reasoned in myself, saying in my Thoughts, *That God dealt somthing hardly with me, that he should save* Adam, *which brought me, and all Mankind into this Condemnation; so that I must be damned for original Sin, which I received from my first Parents.*

5. *And that God should save him that brought me into this Condition, and Condemn me that could no way avoid it, neither by Prayer towards God, nor by Righteousness towards Man.*

6. So that right or wrong, I must be damn'd by God's prerogative Will, and which way to help myself I could not tell.

7. Then I reasoned in my Heart with Anger against *Adam,* saying within myself, God *made him upright, and gave him Power to stand, but he did not, but did fall from that Innocency and Uprightness, and so corrupted his Seed: And so by this means do I come to be damned.*

8. Then was I answered in myself, as it were with a Voice without me, saying, *How wilt thou help thyself if God will save Adam and condemn thee; shall not a prerogative Power do what he will?*

9. Than was brought to my Mind that saying, Jacob *have I loved, and* Esau *have I hated:* Before the Children had done either Good or Evil, that the Purpose of God, according to Election might stand: So that it is not of him that willeth, nor him that runeth, but God that sheweth Mercy on whom he will have Mercy, and whom he will he hardeneth.

10. In this I saw that a prerogative Power and Will of God is not to be contended with.

11. These Scriptures and Arguments upon them, come so powerfully upon my Spirit, that my Heart failed me, and my Hope begun to turn to Dispair.

CHAP. XII.

The Prophet raiseth Arguments more, to give him some Hope that he might escape Hell; but another moshional Voice gave Answer, which quite frustrated all his Hopes again.

1. After a while I recovered another Argument or two, which I thought might give me some Hope to escape Hell: Which was this, I said in my Heart, *There can be no Hell till the Day of Judgment, and except God doth raise me and others again I cannot be damned;* hoping there would be no Resurrection at all, then should I ly still in the Earth for ever.

2. Then Answer was made me to this: *Dost thou think that God would be so unrighteous as to deceave* Abraham, Isaack *and* Jacob, Moses *and the Prophets, and Apostles, and all righteous Men that believed and put their Trust in God in hope of the Resurrection? And if God doth not raise them again, then God hath made them suffer great Sufferings, and loss of the Lives of many of them, in hope of the Life to come, and of the Reward hereafter; which if there be no Resurrection of the Dead after this natural Death.*

3. And if God doth not raise them again they cannot enjoy any such thing as eternal Happiness. Then to what purpose did God spake those Words, and make such glorious Promises to *Abraham, Isaack* and *Jacob,* and to the Prophets and Apostles.

4. That he would be the God of *Abraham,* the God of *Isaack,* and the God of *Jacob;* for God is not the God of the Dead but of the Living, for all live unto him.

5. For said I, in my Heart, if God do not raise *Abraham, Isaack* and *Jacob* again in the Resurrection, then perhaps God may not raise me; which would have gladed my Heart that I could have been sure God would never have raised the Dead.

6. But the Answer said to me, *That God is powerful and hath Power to fulfil his Promise he hath made unto Man, in that he can and will raise* Abraham, Isaack *and* Jacob,*and the rest, at the last Day, and will give them the Inheritance he promised them in this Life. Consider,* said the motional Voice, *what an infinite prerogative Power can do.*

7. *Because God doth not raise the Dead daily as he doth other visible Wonders: And in this visible Creation thou doth think that God cannot raise the Dead when they are turn'd to Dust, because thou never didst read he did.*

8. *But this know, That God can do that which he never did, when his time appointed is come: For there is a necessity that God should raise the Dead; and that there is a Day; or, Time prefix'd in God's Will, which none knoweth; no, not the Angels in Heaven, but himself only.*

9. *Also the Resurrection of the Dead is the last great Work God hath to do: And he hath power to do this his last Work, to put an End to this World, as he had power to Create this World, and make a Beginning of it.*

10. *So that God will perform his Promise in the Resurrection to all the Righteous, in that he will give them everlasting Life in another Kingdom above the Stars, and he will execute that Damnation upon the Seed of the Serpent, wicked unbelieving persecuting Reprobates, here upon this Earth, where they acted all their Wicknedness, to Eternity.*

11. *And that none that have lost their Lives for his Promise sake; but it shall be given them Life everlasting that day: Which if God do not raise them again, then is he the God of the Dead, and not of the Living.*

12. *Then was* Abraham, Isaack *and* Jacob *their Faith vain: The Prophets and the Apostles Faith vain, and their Condision, in believing God would raise them again, and he doth it not, their Condision is worse than the Wicked*: Which thing I was afraid to think of.

13. Also I was afraid to question, or doubt of Gods Prerogative Power in raising the Dead at the last Day, or performing his Promise to *Abraham, Isaack*, and *Jacob*, and the rest of the Seed of the Lord: But I could have been glad if there had been no Resurrection at all, neither of the Righteous nor Unrighteous.

14. But thought I, what is that to me, if I be raised to Hell-Fire. Then I reasoned in myself, saying, It is above Five Thousand Years since the Creation of this World, and perhaps it may last Five Thousand Years more; then shall I ly still in the Earth a great while before I am raised: So that I shall escape the Torments of Hell for a long time, thinking to have Hope in this Argument.

15. But I was thrown out here immediately, and my Hope cut-off; for the Answer said, *What if it should be Five Thousand Years before thou art raised again, consider it will not be a quarter of an Hours time before thou art raised again*

16. *For there is no time to the Dead, all time is to the Living; for it will not be thought a quarter of an Hour by* Adam *the first Man, when he is raised from the Dead; he shall not think he hath been in the Grave one quarter of an Hour.*

17. Then I conceived if a Man slept a sound Sleep three Days, that is no time to him; Time is known to him that was awake that three Days.

18. So this yielded me no Comfort, but increased my Fears of Hell the more.

19. One Argument more I had arising in me, thinking to have got some Ease and Hope here: Thought I, this World hath been so many Thousand Years already, and may be as many more, for ought I know.

20. And there hath been many Millions of People since the Creation,

more than can be numbered, and more than be numbered hath been drowned in the Sea and other places.

21. Sure, said I in myself, God cannot remember every perticular Person since the Creation thereof: Thought I, perhaps God may forget me, and not raise me again, then shall I ly still and be quiet, and be as happy, never to be as those that are raised to eternal Joys.

22. But the Answer to this speak, with a strong motional Voice, saying, *How wilt thou know whether any is missing when God doth raise the Dead? How canst thou tell whether any perticular Person is wanting by Sea or Land that is not raised.*

23. *But however,* said the Voice, *if there be any wanting that is not raised, God will be sure to raise thee.*

24. Then I had no more to say, nor to plead for myself, but must yield and submit to the prerogative Will of God; if he would save me he might, if he would damn me he might, I could no ways prevent his Will.

25. And this was my Resolution, seeing the Case in matter of Salvation so with me, that it lay in God's prerogative Will only, I was resolved to seek after him in Forms of Worship no more.

26. But as I had been always kept innocent and upright in Heart towards that God I knew not, and Just between Man and Man, and never had committed any deadly Sin to trouble my Conscience, so I was resolved to keep myself free from Sin to the end of my Life.

27. Thinking that if I were damned meerly by Gods prerogative Will, my Torment would be the more easy.

28. Here a secret Voice said, *Tho thy torment may be easier than others, yet it is eternal.*

29. This Word Eternity caused my Heart to fail within me, yet I resolved in myself to live justly, and get as good a Livelyhood as I could in this World, and let God do what he would with me after Death.

30. All this Dispute which I have written before, and a great deal more, it was in one Day.

CHAP. XIII.

The Prophet submitting to Gods prerogative Power, immediately wrought in him Peace and Quietness of Mind, even to all admission in Wisdom and ravishing Excellencies.

1. In the next place I shall give the Reader a little account of the Ephects of this Dispute, as follows.

2. When I had done this I was quiet and still in my Mind, but very Melancholy, and faint and sickly with the Trouble of my all Day in this Dispute which was in my Mind.

3. Neither could I quiet my Thoughts untill I did submit to God's prerogative Power.

4. There was abundance more of motional Voices spake in me that Day,

besides what I have here set down, but these were the most remarkable to be taken notice of by the Reader; yet it was a blessed Day to me, as it will appear hereafter by that which followeth.

5. After this, that very same Night the Windows of Heaven were opened to me, and the Fountains of the Water in Heaven were broken up, and the Water of Life run down from Heaven upon me.

6. And the Spirit of Faith in Heart here on Earth did arise up with sweet Waters of Peace, so that I said in myself, as *Peter* did in another Case, *It is good for me to be here* for I was in the Paradice of Heaven, within Man upon Earth; neither could I desire any better Heaven.

7. Then was the Scriptures opened unto me, so swiftly and more swiftly than my Understanding could receive it; and the Water of Life run down from the understanding of the Scriptures abundantly: And the knowledge of the Scriptures flowed in upon my Understanding faster than I could receive it, and yet I thought my Mind was very swift.

8. Then was no saying of Scripture too hard for me to understand: Then I saw that the assurance of eternal Life, here on this side of Death: it lay in understanding the Scriptures.

9. Then I marvelled no longer at the Fathers of Old, in their expressing their Faith in God, and depending upon Gods Promises to them.

10. Also I saw the Excellency of the Prophets Prophesies; Neither did I wonder any more at *Paul's* Expressions, when he was wrapt up into the third Heaven, and saw things unutterable.

11. Neither could I utter the Revelations of the Scriptures as was poured upon me at that time, nor the Joy and Peace I received from the Revelation of the Scriptures.

12. For it brought unto my Mind all my Experience I had formerly, and shewed what did uphold me at that time, even a single upright Heart before God and Man.

13. Then the assurance of eternal Life cast out all Doubts and Fears of Condemnation; neither did I ever doubt of that more after that day.

14. Then I praised the Scriptures highly, which I had laid aside several years before.

15. Then did I see it was not in vain to submit to Gods prerogative Will, and to wait in patience.

16. Here was that saying of Scripture fulfilled in me, *Isaiah* 42. 16. *And I will bring the Blind by a Way that they knew not; I will lead them in Paths they have not known; I will make Darkness Light before them.* Though this Scripture was fulfilled in Christ's time, yet it was fulfilled in me now.

17. For I was led by a Faith now, which I did not know: That was by the Revelation of Faith. This was a Path I did not know: for I never knew what Revelation was before.

18. Also this Revelation of Faith, it made that Darkness of the immagination of Reason be light before me, to see the Truth of those Sayings of Scripture, *Matt.* 4. 16. *The People that sat in Darkness saw great Light; and*

to them which sat in the Region and Shadow of Darkness Light is sprung up.

19. This Scripture also was fulfilled in me at that time, for I sat in Darkness, and in the Shadow of Death but the Day before.

20. But in the Evening the Light of Faith sprung up in my Soul, and the Revelation of it took me, as it were, by the Hand, from place to place in Scripture, and shewed me the meaning of it.

21. And it led me to that place of Scripture, *Luke* 1.79. *He gave Light to them that sat in Darkness, and to guide our Feet into the way of Peace.*

22. Here did I see that the Day before I sat in Darkness and in the Shadow of Death, but now the Light of Life is risen in me, and gave me Revelation to guide my Feet in the Path of Peace, where no Fear nor Doubt should ly in my way, never to stumble more.

23. These, and many more, places of Scripture was set before me, and the Light of them shined clear about my Understanding, and gave me the Interpretation of all Scripture, and all Questions in Spiritual Things that could arise out of the Heart of Man, was easy to me to answer.

CHAP. XIV.

Of the time of the Prophets Revelation, his Satisfaction in it, and his Resolution to sit still now, and be quiet from Disputes about Religion. Yet shews that Providence order'd it otherways. Of the Prophet Reeve's *Revelation of the Raven and Dove.*

1. This Revelation aforesaid was upon me Six Hours; it began about nine of the Clock at Night, and about twelve of the Clock I got a little Sleep, 'till three of the Clock in the Morning; then it came upon me again, and lasted 'till six of the Clock in the Morning: And so it did in like manner for four Nights together, six Hours in a Night.

2. And I never was without motional Voices opening the Scriptures all Day long, when I was alone, for a long time after.

3. So that I was so well satisfied in my Mind as to my eternal Happiness, so that I was resolved now to be quiet and still, and not to medle no more with Religion; but to let every one go on in their own way, for I looked at no Bodys Peace and Happiness but my own.

4. So now I thought to get as good a Living as I could in this World, and live as comfortably as I could here, for I knew all things would be well with me hereafter: Thinking that this Revelation should have been benificial to no body but myself.

5. For I lov'd for to be private and still, for my Nature could never indure to be publick. So I thought all was well now I had attained my Desire.

6. But when I thought to be most Secure and most Private; in a little time after, it made me the most publick. I not thinking that this Revelation was a Preparation for God to chuse me to be a Commissioner of the Spirit, to declare the Mistery of the true God, and the Interpretation of the Scrip-

tures, which is Life and Salvation unto Men; whereby I was made the most publick Man in the World in spiritual Things.

7. This Revelation continued with me all one from *April* to *January* in the Year 1651[-2], and in the year of my Life 41. And in the same year *John Reeve* came often to my House.

8. And he hearing me speak such high Revelation, and giving such Interpretation of Scripture, he was so taken with my Language that his Desires were extream earnest unto God, which he knew not at that time, that he might have the same Revelation as I had.

9. His Desires were so great, that he was troublesome unto me, for I could not follow my Business quietly for his asking me Questions, for if I went out of one Room into another, he would follow me to talk to me.

10. So that I was weary of his Company, yet I was loath to tell him so, because I knew he did it out of Innocency of his Heart, and Love to the Things which I spoke.

11. Thus, as aforesaid, *John Reeve* continued, and came almost every Day to my House most part of that Summer and Winter. And in the Month of *January* 1651[2], about the middle of the Month, *John Reeve* had the Revelation of the Scriptures in a large measure.

12. So he came to me very joyful the next Morning, and said *Cousin* Lodowick, *now*, saith he, *I know what Revelation of Scripture is as well as thee.* Said I, *Let me hear what Scripture is opened unto you.*

13. He answered and said, as he was thinking of several things, *there fell a quiet stillness upon his Mind, and immediately there was presented to his Understanding this place of Scripture,* Genesis, viii. 7, 8, 9, 10, 11 verses; Concerning *Noah's* Ark with the *Raven* and *Dove*.

14. Of which Scripture this was the Interpretation.

15. *This* Raven *and* Dove *which* Noah *sent forth of the Ark*, saith he, *was a Tipe of the Two Seeds in every Man, and the Ark was a Tipe of the Body of Man.*

16. *For there is two Motions always speaking in Man. Now*, saith he, *the Body of Man signifies the Ark of God; or, the Ark of* Noah.

17. *The Raven that is sent forth of the Ark signifies the Motions of Reason in Man; for the Motions of Reason goeth out of Man, walking through dry Places, seeking Rest but can find none.*

18. *Also it was the Reason of Man that took Christ, when on Earth, up into an exceeding high Mountain, and shewed him all the Kingdoms of the World.*

19. *This Reason in Man is that* Raven *that goeth forth of the Ark, the Body of Man, to and fro, and taketh Comfort in nothing but earthly Things.*

20. *For as soon as ever the Tops of the Mountains of the Earth did appear, the natural* Raven *never return'd into the Ark again, as you may see in the 5th Verse.*

21. *So it is with the Reason of Man; That* Raven *when it goeth forth by its motions out of Body of Man the Ark: It goeth to and fro the Earth.*

22. *For the Reason of Man cannot indure to be inclosed or confined, but*

will be flying upon the Mountains of the Earth, or in the Air. Therefore it is called the Prince of the Air, which ruleth in the Hearts of the Children of Disobedience.

23. *Now what Ruleth in the Children of Disobedience Hearts but the Spirit of Reason, the* Raven, *which goeth out of the Ark, the Body of Man, and liveth upon the Mountains of earthly Things.*

24. *Also the* Dove *that* Noah *sent forth of the Ark signified the Seed of Faith.*

25. *And when Faith sends forth her motions out of the Ark, her Body, they are innocent as a* Dove, *humble, meek and low.*

26. *And when she findeth the Flood, and Waters of Trouble of Persecution upon the Face of the Earth, the Dove entreth into her Ark, her Body, again, and is quiet and still till the Waters of Trouble be abated.*

27. *For the Dove cannot fly upon the top of the Mountains of earthly things, as Reason the* Raven *can.*

28. *The Seed of Faith, the* Dove *can find no Rest there but when the Waters of Trouble are abated, and the dry Land appeareth, and the Olive Trees of Joy and Gladness are to be seen.*

29. *Then the* Dove, *the Seed of Faith, can go out of its Body, the Ark, and fetch an Olive-Branch of Peace and Joy in its Mouth, and return into its Body the Ark again, and there remain until it is turned out of the Ark by Death.*

CHAP. XV.

Shewing how John Reeve's *Revelation gave him Satisfaction, and full Resolution to sit still and be quiet, never medling about Religion more; But contrary to the Resolutions of them both, a little while after, where made the greatest medlers of Religion of all the World.*

1. To this purpose, as aforesaid, did *John Reeve* declare his first Revelation, with a many more Expressions which he uttered at that time with great Joy of Heart, he not thinking in the least, nor I neither, that it was a Preparation for God to chuse him, nor me neither, to be his two last Prophets and Witnesses of the Spirit.

2. *For,* said he unto me at that time, Cousin *Lodowick, now I am satisfied in my Mind, and know what Revelation is, I am resolved now to medle no more with Religion, nor go forth after any upon that account.*

3. *But to get as good a Livelyhood as I can in this World, and let God alone with what shall be hereafter.*

4. Now he had been with *John Robins* not many Weeks before he knew, or had Revelation himself.

5. For *John Robins* Knowledge and Language overpowerd *John Reeve,* before he had this Revelation: Therefore he said, *now he would not go forth after any, upon that account, no more.*

6. Thus, when he thought to be most quiet, and not to medle with any

about Religion; and so was I also then, a little while after we were made the greatest Medlers in Religion of all Men in the World.

7. Because our Faces were against all Mens Religion in the World, what Sex or Opinion soever, as will appear hereafter, by our Writings and Speakings.

8. *John Reeve*, nor I, little thought at that time that this Revelation we had given us did prepare us for a greater Work than for the Peace of our own Minds.

9. But it prov'd that God prepared us for a Commission, and that he did intend to chuse us two to be his last Prophets and Witnesses of the Spirit, as will be seen, as followeth.

10. For after *John Reeve* had this first Revelation aforementioned, it did continue and increase exceedingly, that it grew very high in him for two Weeks together.

11. And at the two Weeks end God speak unto him by Voice of Words, to the hearing of the Ear, three Mornings together, as is more largely set down in his first Book he wrote, Called *A Trancendant Spiritual Treatis*.

12. Where the Words of God, as he spoke to him, are set down plainly, as they were spoken to him, the *3d. 4th.* and *5th*. Days of *February* 1651[2], and in the year of *John Reeve's* Life 42. and in the year of my Life 41.

13. Thus I have given the Reader a little hint, whereby he may see the ground of things, and the rise how these wonderful things came to pass.

14. Also what we were at first, and how we were acted out in the time of our Lives, and of the Experience I had in the Days of my Ignorance, and of my Dispute with God and my own Soul.

15. And of that great Revelation I had before *John Reeve* had any; and of the Revelation *John Reeve* had, before God spake to him in the year 1651[2].

16. And now in the Treatis following I shall only speak of some of the most remarkable Acts and Passages which hath been acted and dun by us since we received our Commission from God.

17. That after Ages may see some of the Acts of the two Witnesses of the Spirit, as well as their Writings and their Doctrin now in this last Age. As they have read of some of the wonderful Acts of *Moses* and the Prophets, and the Acts of the Apostles. So there will be some remarkable Acts of the Witnesses of the Spirit left upon Record: Which is as followeth.

THE END OF THE FIRST PART.

THE SECOND PART.

CHAP. I.

Of the Commission given the Prophet Mugleton's *Children, blessed by the Prophet* Reeve; *the great Wisdom given unto* Sarah Mugleton.

1. The first Morning God spake to *John Reeve*, he came to my House, and said Cousin *Lodowick*, God hath given thee unto me for ever: And the Tears ran down both sides his Cheeks amain.

2. So I asked him what was the matter, for he looked like one that had been rissen out of the Grave; he being a fresh couloured Man the day before: And the Tears ran down his Cheeks apace.

3. So he told me the same Words as is written in his first Book; and said unto me, *That God had given him a Commission and that he had given* Lodowick Mugleton *to be his Mouth*: And said, at the same time was brought to his Mind that saying, that *Aaron* was given to be *Moses's* Mouth.

4. But, said he, *what my Message is, he could not tell: But,* said he, *if God do not speak unto me the next Morning, I will come no more at thee.*

5. Which I was in good Hopes he would not, for I was willing to be quiet.

6. Also he said at the same time, Cousin *Lodowick, Thy Children are all blessed, but especially thy Daughter* Sarah, *she shall be the Teacher of all the Women in* London.

7. She heard him say these Words, as she stood upon the Stairs, for she was afraid of him, that he would rather have condemned her, because he never did love her so well as he did the youngest Daughter.

8. But he spake not then for Affection, but as the Revelation moved him.

9. And she was the first Person he blessed to Eternity, after God spake to him the first Morning.

10. It was the more marvelous, because it was never heard this many Ages, that a poor Man should have that Power to Bless and Curs Men and Women to Eternity.

11. And she believed him, and did grow exceedingly in Experience, and in Disputes with Religious People; and they marvelled that one so young should have such Knowledg and Wisdom to answer Questions: So that she did afterwards indeed become the Teacher of all Women in *London*, in matters of Faith and Religion.

12. And she was imployed by *John Reeve*, at the first, to carry Letters to any that he did send unto.

13. And there were several Persons came afterwards to my House, more to discourse with her than us.

14. She was at that time about fourteen Years of Age, when this Blessing was given her by *John Reeve*: And this was the first Morning.

15. But I was in good hopes God would not speak to him no more, for I was loath to be publick: I would gladly have sat still and be quiet, and not to contend with People about Religion.

16. But the second Morning God spake unto him, and told him what he should do, as is set down in the Book aforesaid.

17. *John Reeve* said unto me the second Morning, *If thou wilt not obey to go along with me, I must pronounce thee Cursed to Eternity, as God did me, had not I obeyed him.*

18. Then said I, *In case they will not obey me when I speak unto them, I have no Power to curse them, if they will not go along with me or you.*

19. *Yea*, said he, *but you have, as much Power as I have, for you are given to be my Mouth, as* Aaron *was given to be* Moses's *Mouth.*

20. So I went with him to one *Thomas Turner* his House, and said unto him, *Mr.* Turner, *you must go with us to* John Tauny, *else you must be cursed to Eternity.*

21. But *Thomas Turner* was willing to go with us, but his Wife was exceeding Wrath and Fearful, that her Husband would be brought into Trouble by it.

22. And she said, if *John Reeve* came again to her Husband, *That she would run a Spit in his Guts*, so *John Reeve* cursed her to Eternity.

23. For she looked with Wrath and fear, as if she had newly risen out of the Grave.

CHAP. II.

The Transactions of the second Morning, and how Thomas Turner *went with the Prophets to* John Tauny's *and of* John Reeve's *Message to him; and how* John Tauny *and his Design perished and came to nothing.*

1. But *Thomas Turner* went with us to *John Tauny*, and *John Reeve* delivered his Message to him to this ephect. Said he,

2. *God hath not chosen you to be the Lord's high Priest, as you declared your self to be; neither is the Law of* Moses *to be acted over again, as you pretend to do, notwithstanding you have circumcised your self to fit you for that Work.*

3. *Neither are you, being of the Tribe of* Rubin, *ever to be chosen high Priest, for your Father* Rubin *lost that Birthright of the Priesthood, by going up to his Father's Couch.*

4. *But the Priesthood was confirmed upon the Tribe of* Levy, *and to his Seed for ever.*

5. *And here is my fellow Witness of the Tribe of* Levy; *which you know your self he is of that Tribe, and God hath chosen him high Priest in the last Age, and the last that God will ever choose to the end of the World.*

6. *And as* Aaron *was the first high Priest that God chose to be* Moses's *mouth, so* Lodowick Mugleton *is the last high Priest that God hath chose to be my mouth, by Voice of Words to the hearing of the Ear.*

7. *Besides*, said he, *you are not fit to be the Lord's high Priest, because you stuter, or stamer in your Speech.*

8. *Which God never chose none to be high Priest but perfect men in Nature, which you are not.*

9. *Also he said, You pretend to be King of seven Nations, and to gather the Jews, in all parts of the Earth, together, and to lead them to* Jerusalem, *and to mount* Olivet, *and to make them Kings of all the Earth: And that you must follow* John Robins *with Sword and Spear.*

10. These, and several other things did he speak to *John Tauny;* and told him that there should never any such things come to pass, as he pretended unto; and charged him to lay all these things down, upon the pain of eternal Damnation, and gave him about a Months time to lay it down.

11. But he did not, but afterwards went further on to prosecute that Design, and made Tents for every Tribe, and the Figures of every Tribe upon the Tent, that every Tribe might know their own Tent.

12. So *John Reeve* seeing this, he wrote the Sentance of eternal Damnation upon *John Tauny* for his Disobedience of the Lord's Commission, and left it at his Lodging; for he would not be spoken with at that time.

13. Because he had shut himself up for nine Days, and he would speak with none for that time: But he received it afterwards of the Man where he lodged; and after a while he and his great Matters perished in the Sea.

14. For he made a little Bote to carry him to *Jerusalem,* and going to *Holland,* to call the Jews there, he and one Captain *James* were cast away and drowned; so all his Power came to nothing.

CHAP. III.

Of the Transactions of the Third Morning, and of the Message of the Prophet Reeve *to* John Robins.

1. The Third Morning God spake to *John Reeve,* as it is written in that Book aforesaid; where it is said, *Go thou to* Lodowick Mugleton, *and he shall bring thee to such a Woman, namely* Dorcas Boose, *and she shall bring you to* John Robins, *Prisoner in* New Bridewell, *and deliver my Message when thou comest there.*

2. So we went to this *Dorcas Boose,* and said unto her, *You must go with us to* New Bridewell, *for we have a Message from God to declare to* John Robins: She was willing to go, but her Husband made a little Demur: Then said I to her Husband, *If you will not let her go, I must pronounce you cursed to Eternity.*

3. So he was willing to let her go, for he was some Kin by Marriage to *John Reeve* and me both: The Woman was a true Beleiver of this Commission afterwards.

4. So we Three went to *New Bridewell,* and asked for *John Robins;* and the Keeper opened the Gate, and said, *Who would you speak with? John Reeve* said, with *John Robins.*

5. The Keeper said, *You shall not speak with him.*

6. Then said *John Reeve* to the Keeper, *Thou shalt never be at Peace.*

7. So he shut the little Gate upon us; and as we stood a little while without the Gate there came a Woman, a Disciple of *John Robins* to come out: Saith the Keeper to the Woman, *There is two or three without would speak with your Lord, show them the other Way.*

8. So the Keeper let the Woman out, and the Woman said unto *John Reeve, Would you speak with my Lord? Yea,* saith he, *I would speak with*

thy Lord: Saith the Woman, *He is the same, and will be the same for ever. Thou saith right*, said he, *he is the same, and will be the same for ever.* Meaning the same false Christ for ever.

9. So the Woman went and shewed us the place where *John Robins* was: And she said, *Knock at that Window, and my Lord will look out.*

10. So the Woman parted from us; then *John Robins* put by a Borde of the Window and looked out; and *John Reeve* put off his Hat, and held it under his Arm, and said, *Art thou* John Robins? He said to *John Reeve, Put on your Hat.* He said, *I put it not off to thee, but to him that sent me.*

11. *Stand thou still, and hear the Message of the Lord to thee*: He answer'd and said, *I will not, except you put on your Hat.* This he said three times. Said *John Reeve* the third time.

12. *I put not my Hat off to thee, but to him that sent me. Therefore I charge thee to stand still, and hear the Message of the Lord to thee.* After the third time, *John Robins* said, *speak on.*

13. Then *John Reeve* spake, and said, *Thou maist remember, I was with thee about Six or Eight Months ago, and thou didst declare unto me, That thou wert* Adam Melchisadick *that met* Abraham *in the way, that received the Tithes of the Spoil, and that gave* Abraham *Bread and Wine.*

14. *Also thou saidst to me, that thou wast the first* Adam *in state, and that thou wert the God and Father of the Lord Jesus Christ; and that thou knewest the Names of all Angels, and their Natures: And that thou hadst Power over all Voices: And that thou wast the Judge of the Quick and the Dead: And that Christ was a weak and imperfect Saviour, and afraid to dy, but thou wast not afraid to dy.*

15. *Also thou didst deceave many People, in that thou madest them bring in their Estates, and then gavest them leave to abstain by degrees from all kind of Food, that should have preserved and strengthed their Natures: But thou didst feed them with windy things, as Aples, and other Fruit that was windy; and they drank nothing but Water.*

16. *So that thou hadst full Power over their Bodies, Souls and Estates; and some were starved under thy Dyet and dyed. Therefore look what measure thou hath measured to others must be measur'd again to thee.*

17. *That Body of thine, which was thy Heaven, must be thy Hell; and that proud Spirit of thine, which said was God, must be thy Devil.*

18. *The one shall be as Fire, and the other as Brimstone, burning together to all Eternity: This is the Message of the Lord unto thee.*

19. *John Robins* pulled his Hands off the Grates, and laid them together, and said, *It is finished, the Lord's Will be done.* These were all the Words he spake, I was both an Eye-Witness and Ear-Witness of it.

20. After this it came to pass, that about two Months after, *John Robins* did write a Letter of Recantation of all his great matters unto General *Cromwell*, and so obtained his Liberty out of Prison.

21. And one of our Acquaintance went to him, and asking him how he could do so: And he answered and said, *That after those two Men had passed Sentence upon him, he had a burning in his Throat, as if he should*

be burn'd to Ashes; and that he had a Voice within him, which bid him deny those things he had declared of himself before, and he should have his Liberty.

22. And said afterwards, he should come forth with a greater Power; but he never came forth more with any Power at all, to his dying Day.

23. Thus these two great Heads, *John Tauny* was the Head of that Mistery *Babel*, the atheistical Ranters and Quaquers Principle: And *John Robins* was the Head of all false Christs, false Prophets, and false Prophetesses, that were in the World at that Day; and there were many.

24. Now *John Robins* was that Man of Sin spoken of in *Thesalonians*: Neither will there come any so high after him to the end of the World.

25. Thus the Reader may see that these two Powers were brought down in these two days Messages from the Lord.

CHAP. IV.

When the transcendant Treatis was wrote many People more offended with the Doctrin than the Commission. Of the Letter sent to the Ministers, and when: How the Children mocked John Reeve, *called him Prophet, Prophet, and followed him flinging Stones at him; and how a Woman hearing this followed the Prophet to his House, and was converted to the Faith. Of Sentence given upon one* Penson, *and its Effects.*

1. After this there came a many People to Discourse with us, and asked Questions about many things, in matters of Religion, and we answered them to all Questions whatsoever could arise out of the Heart of Men; and some few were satisfied and beleived.

2. And many dispised it, calling it Blasphemy, Delusion, and Lys; and we gave the Sentance of eternal Damnation upon all those that blasphemed against the Holy Ghost.

3. After this, in the year 1652. *John Reeve* wrote that Book called, *A transcendant spiritual Treatis*, wherein is declared the Words God spake unto him three mornings together, to the hearing of the Ear, and his Message to *John Tauny* and to *John Robins*: Which is more largely set down, with several Interpretations of Scripture, concerning the true God, and right Devil.

4. Never so clearly made manifest by any, as now in that Treatis.

5. Many People were more offended at the Doctrine therein than at the Commission.

6. After this *John* wrote a letter to several Ministers in *London*, and about *London;* which was afterwards printed,[1] forbiding them to preach any more after the receipt of this Epistle, upon pain of Damnation to Eternity.

7. These Epistles were given to the most eminent Presbiterian and Independant Ministers in *London*, and about *London*: For they were in Power at that time.

8. After this it came to pass in the same year, that as *John Reeve* was going through *Pauls-Church-Yard*, one that he had given the Sentence of

Damnation upon, said unto some Boys, *There goes the Prophet that damns People.*

9. The Boys hearing this run after him, calling him, Prophet, Prophet, and threw Gravel and little Stones at him; so he made hast into *Pauls*, and the Boys left him. And a Woman, named *Elizabeth More*, seeing the Boys cast Stones at him, and calling him Prophet, she followed him into Pauls, keeping a distance from him, to see where he would go: So she followed him, and he came to my House in great *Trinity*-Lane, *London*.

10. And she desired to speak with him, being a Prophet, for she had a great respect for Prophets: So she told those things she had seen, and she became a true Beleiver of this Commission of the Spirit.

11. After this, it came to pass in the same year, that I *Lodowick Mugleton* having occasion to go into *Houds-Ditch* to see my Master's Son where I was Prentice, as I went through the *Minories, London;* there I met with one *Morgan Guilliam*, a Man that had been Prentice with my Master.

12. And he would needs have me drink with him, that he might have some talk with me, for he said, he heard strange Things of me: So I went in with him into the Alehouse to drink, and there followed, of his Acquaintance, a Neighbour of his, a Gentleman, as we call them: His Name was *Penson*, and he sat down in our Company.

13. So *Morgan* began to tell me, that he heard that *John Reeve* and your self do say, That you have Power to Bless and Curse Men, that do oppose you, to eternity? He desired me to tell him whether these things were true or no.

14. So I told him the Words that God spake to *John Reeve*, three Mornings together, as is set down in that Book aforesaid: But I repeated those Words, *I have put the two edged Sword of my Spirit into thy Mouth, that whoever I pronounce blessed through thy Mouth, is blessed to eternity; and whoever I pronounce cursed through thy Mouth, is cursed to eternity.*

15. Then did he begin to fear, and said, for God's sake, *Lodowick* do not say so: Upon that, this Mr. *Penson* said it was Blasphemy, and that it was the Devil that spok those Words.

16. Whereupon I did pronounce this *Penson* cursed, and damned both in Soul and Body, from the Presence of God, elect Men and Angels, to eternity.

17. Whereupon, this *Penson*, his Spirit was struck into his Body, so that he could not speak for a Season.

18. And the Woman of the House hearing me give this Sentence upon him, and seeing him in that Condition, she was troubled in her Spirit and grew sick, and went up to Bed: And an old Man her Father, being there, and seeing this, he railed exceedingly at me, and grinded his Teeth at me.

19. So in a little Season after this *Penson* had recover'd himself again, and said unto me, *Wilt thou say I am damn'd to eternity?* Yea, said I, *thou art.* Then he rose up, and with both his Fists smote upon my Head; and after I had receiv'd a few Blows, my Friend *Morgan* stood between us, and bare off the Blows.

20. And said, *For God's sake.* Lodowick, *let us be gon, else we shall be killed:* So he paid for the Drink, and we departed out of the House, and went to another a little distance off.

21. And immediately after came in the Woman's Husband, and finding her not well, he asked what was the matter, and they told him all that was don: He asked where the Man was? They answered, They went down that way.

22. So he found *Morgan* and I together: The Man knowing him, asked If he knew me, *Morgan* answered, He did know me, and said, *He did not speak ever a Word to your Wife, or to her Father; but that which he spake, it was to Mr.* Penson, *which did abuse him, and smote him on the Head with his Fists, and your Father kicked at him with his Feet, and he did nothing to them again.*

23. So the Man went away quiet and satisfied, and comforted his Wife, that the Man said nothing against her to be troubled.

24. But it came to pass that this *Penson* was sick immediately after, and in a Week; or Ten Days after he dyed, much troubled in his Mind, and tormented.

25. Insomuch that his Friends and Relations sought to apprehend me for a Witch, he being a rich Man; but they could not tell how to state the matter, so they let it fall.

CHAP. V.

Of one Jeremiah Maunte, *a great Friend to this Commission: And of a damn'd Man and his Fury; and how* John Reeve *intreated the People that he might ly down and expose himself to his Fury, with the ephects of that Submission: And of one* James Barker *his Hipocricy to get the Blessing of* John Reeve; *and how he was cursed by* Lodowick Mugleton, *with the Ephects of that Curse.*

1. Also thus it came to pass in the same year, that one *Jeremiah Maunte,* a young Gentleman, hearing that God had spoke to *John Reeve,* and that he had damn'd several of his Acquaintance, he came to us to discourse about those things; and when he had hear'd an Answer to all his Objections he submitted unto us, and did belive the Voice that God spake to *John Reeve,* that it was the Voice of God, and that the Lord Jesus Christ was the true God.

2. Also there was one Captain *Clark* of his Acquaintance that did truly beleive in this Commission of the Spirit.

3. Also this *Jeremiah Maunte* was the greatest Friend to this Commission, and shewed the greatest Love to it of any all the days of *John Reeve's* Life.

4. But he and Captain *Clark,* their Acquaintance many of them were of the Ranters People; who were at that time very high in Imagination, like *Capernahum,* exalted in their Knowledge up to Heaven, as they thought;

but this Commission of the Spirit brought them down to Hell in a short time.[2]

5. These Ranters were the most Company we had at that time, and they to have discourse with us, did use to club their Twelve Pence every Week, that they might have Discourse with us.

6. And it came to pass that one of those Ranters kept a Victualing House, and sold Drink in the *Minories, London*: And they would spend their Mony there.

7. So *John Reeve*, and myself came there, to discourse with them, but there came in many more than was apointed, to discourse with us; and many of them dispised our Declaration, and the Voice of God to *John Reeve*, calling it Blasphemy, the Voice of the Devil, and such like.

8. So *John Reeve* gave Sentence of eternal Damnation upon many of them, for this their Blasphemy against the Holy Ghost; we being the Witnesses of the Holy Spirit that sent us.

9. But one of them being more offended at his Damnation than all the rest, he was moved with such Wrath and Fury, that he would be revenged of *John Reeve*, and would fall upon him to beat him, so that five or six Men could hardly keep him off, his Fury was so hot.

10. Then *John Reeve* said unto the People standing by: *Friends*, said he, I pray you stand still on both sides the Room, and let there be a space in the middle.

11. And I will lay down my Head upon the Ground, and let this furious Man tread upon my Head, and do what he will unto me.

12. Our Friends, and the rest, were loath to venter, lest this furious Man should tread upon his Head and spoil him: But *John Reeve* intreated the People to let it be so.

13. And the People were perswaded, and did stand of a Row on both sides, and a vacant Place in the middle.

14. So *John Reeve* pulled off his Hat, and laid his Face flat to the Ground, and the People stood still; and *John Reeve*, said, with his Face to the Ground, *Now let the Man do what he will unto me.*

15. So the Man came runing with great Fury, and when he came near him, lifting up his Foot to tread on his Neck, the Man started back again, and said, No, I scorne to tread upon a Man that lyeth down to me. And the People all marvelled at this thing.

16. After this it came to pass, in the same place in the *Minories, London*, that several Ranters and Astrologers did come to talk with us: And one Astrologer being more knowing in that Art than the rest, would fain himself to be humble, and desirous to be saved, and would endeavor to get the Blessing of *John Reeve*.

17. The Mans name was *James Barker;* he was a Gun-Smith, by Trade, but very skillful in the art of Astrology: There were many more People talking with *John Reeve* at that time.

18. So this *James Barker* came near to him, and desired him to tell him what it was that God spake unto him three Mornings together: *For*, said he,

I have heard much of you by others, but now he was glad he had that opertunity to speak with him himself.

19. So *John Reeve* related to him all the words God spake: And when this *Barker* had heard it, he said, He did verily believe it was the Voice of God that spake unto him: And further said, that he did desire him to give him the Blessing.

20. *John Reeve* answered, and said, *If thou dost truly believe it was the Voice of God that gave me this Power*: He said, he did believe it. Whereupon *John Reeve* did pronounce him one of the blessed of the Lord, both in Soul and Body to eternity.

21. Immediately after he had got the Blessing he departed from him into another Chamber, and said unto some of the Company: *I have got the Blessing of* John Reeve, *but if any of you will lay a quart of Sack with me, I will go to* John Reeve *again, and call him a false Prophet, and say, it was the Devil that spake to him three Mornings together, and see if he will curse me again.*

22. There were several Men that heard him, said unto him, *That he dar'd not do it*: He said, *But he would, if any one of them would lay with him.*

23. So one Captain *Clark*, a Friend of ours, was afraid to lay with him without my concent; so he came to me, which sat at a distance from *John Reeve*, (and knew nothing of it,) and whispered me in the Ear, telling me what *Barker* had said; then, said I, *Do you lay a quart of Sack with him to prove him.*

24. And when *Barker* saw that he would lay with him indeed, he began to repent, and was loath to stand to his word: But the Company seeing him begin to flinch, they scoffed and geer'd him, and said, *We thought you durst as well be hang'd as do it.*

25. Yet rather than he would be geer'd for not performing his Words, and loosing a quart of Sack besides, He said, *he would do it.*

26. So he, with the Company, came towards *John Reeve*: (And *Barker* came with his Hat off, and put it under his Arm) saying these Words, Mr. Reeve, *you have declared me one of the Blessed of the Lord, both in Soul and Body to eternity:* But said he, *I do verily believe that you are a false Prophet, and that it was the Devil that spake unto you three Mornings together, that gave you that Power to bless and curse Men to eternity.* These were all the Words he spake.

27. So I came to him, and said, *Barker, Thou hast acted the part of a Hipocrite, both with God and with Man, and with thy own Soul.*

28. *Thou lyedst against thy own Heart, when thou saidst to* John Reeve *thou didst believe it was the Voice of God that spake to him, and that he had Power to give a Blessing to whoever beleived*; whereupon thou didst ask him to bless thee? He said, *If thou dost truly beleive what I have said*; thou replyedst, *Thou didst beleive*, and said, *else why should I ask a Blessing of you.*

29. Whereupon he gave this Blessing both of Soul and Body to eternity: And this I say, though thou out of thy Dissemulation and Hiprocricy of thy

Heart hath got the Blessing of *John Reeve*, so that he cannot curse thee again.

30. But I gave not my Consent unto it. Therefore for this thy Hipocricy of thy Heart, I do pronounce thee, *Cursed and Damn'd both in Soul and Body, from the Presence of God, elect Men and Angels, to eternity.*

31. And not only so, *But thou art cursed in thy Estate in this World*; For Sins of this nature are to be punished with a double Curse.

32. He was exceeding wrath and angry at me, more for cursing his Estate than for his eternal Damnation, he was so mad at that: So that he knew not whether he had best fight me, or take the Law of me as a Witch, if he did not prosper.

33. But my Words and Curse came to pass upon him, even in this Life, as many can witness; even a poor miserable beggarly Fellow.

34. Notwithstanding he was as cunning a subtil Serpent as most Men in the World: But at last a Lawyer which he had cheated followed the Law so close upon him, that he seaised upon all his Goods, and took them away, and put him into Prison besides; and there he lay some years, and dyed there miserably poor: Which was the last End of him.

35. Thus I saw the Ephects of that Curse upon him, even in this Life; and in the Life to come, I am sure he shall indure those eternal Torments for that Act of Hipocrisy.

CHAP. VI.

What the Ranters God was: And how them and their God was damn'd by this Commission: And of the Resolution of Three of the most desperatest to Curse the Prophet Reeve and Mugleton's God.

1. After this, it came to pass, at another Meeting of the Ranters in *Aldersgate-street, London.*

2. There was many Ranters that heard what was done by *James Barker*; so they consulted among themselves why they might not damn us as we did them.

3. Now those that were to damn us, were three of the most desperatest atheistical Ranters, that had ever been in our Company as yet.

4. And they thought nothing too hard for them; but two of those Ranters which had been often in our Company, and had seen the Passages that passed with, and upon those we had condemned: That their God they worshiped was damn'd with them; for they had no other God but a Spirit without a Body, which they said was the Life of every thing.

5. So that the Life of a *Dog, Cat, Toad*, or any venomous Beast, was the Life of God: Nay, That God was in a Table Chair, or Stool.

6. This was the Ranters God, and they thought there was no better God at all.

7. This God did we damn with their Persons, these two Men that had

seen many condemn'd by us: The one his Name was *Proudlove*, a notable Ranter, the other his Name was *Remington*.

8. So this *Proudlove* he consulted with those three desperate Men which knew nothing of us: So they asked him what they must do, he said, this you must do.

9. *You must curse them and their God, and perhaps you may bring down their Powers.*

10. They said they were willing to do that, and that was but a small matter to curse them and their God: They made nothing of that.

11. So the Time appointed came, and there was prepared a good Dinner of Pork, and the three came ready prepared to curse us and our God.

12. So *Proudlove* and *Remington* went from us to those Men, and *Remington* said unto them, *If you Three will go up and curse them and their God you shall have a good Dinner of Porke.*

13. Then one, the stoutest of the Three, said unto him, pray tell me what is their God that we must curse?

14. *Remington* answered and said, *That the Lord Jesus Christ is their God, and they own no other Father or God but he:* And now if you will go in, they be there, and curse them and the Lord Jesus Christ, their God, you shall have a good Dinner of Porke.

15. When they heard this, the most stoutest Man of them smote his Hand on his Breast, and said; *If that be their God, I will never do it, if I might gain the whole World*: And said, *That he was sorry and troubled that he should conceive such a thing in his Heart.* So said the other Two, *We will do no such Wickedness.* So they departed without their Dinner of Porke.

16. But he that repented himself could not be at quiet in his Mind until such time he had asked us Forgiveness.

17. So we forgave him his Sin for that, and he remained very kind to *John Reeve* all his days, tho he did not beleive that we were the two last Prophets and Witnesses of the Spirit.

18. Also this *Remington* was called to an account by *John Reeve*, as one in this Plot; and he told the truth, how *Proudlove* laid the Plot, and that he did but go with him, being an old Acquaintance: So we forgave *Remington*, and gave *Proudlove* the Sentence of Condemnation to Eternity.

CHAP. VII.

Of the Dispute with Mr. Leader, *a* New England *Merchant*; *and of the* Prophet's *convincing him how that God had a Body; and how God is worshiped in Spirit and Truth with Bodys, and that there is no Spirit without a Body.*

1. After this in the Year 1653, there came a certain Man, a Merchant, and a great Travellor into many parts of the World; and he was a religious Man, but had somwhat declined the outward Forms of Worship, because he could find no Rest there.

2. So he applied his Heart more to Philosophy and the knowledg of Nature more than Religion, for he thought he had seen the utmost of Religion, and that there was nothing in it.

3. Indeed he was a great Philosopher, and a very wise Man in the things of Nature: His Name was *Richard Leader.*

4. It came to pass when he came out of *New-England*, being persecuted there, because he could not submit to their forms of Worship; and when he came into *Old-England* again, he heard there were two Prophets now risen up, who called themselves, *The two Witnesses, &c.*

5. So he enquired where he might speak with these Prophets; so he was brought unto us, and he was very sober in his talk, and he propounded his Questions with great Moderation.

6. The first Question was concerning God: *Whether God that created all things could admit of being any Form of himself.*

7. We answered, and said, *That God made Man in his own Image and Likeness*: And if Man have a form, then God must needs have a Form himself, even in the form of Man, else them Words of *Moses* are not true, that *God made Man in his own Image, and breathed into him the Breath of Life, and he became a living Soul.*

8. Mind, the Form of Man was the Image and Likeness of God, before God breathed into him the Breath of Life.

9. Therefore God must needs be in the form of a Man from Eternity: Therefore it was that God said, *Let us make Man after our own Image and Likeness.* This was the true Sense and Meaning of *Moses*, and it is dangerous for any Man to deny it.

10. *Besides,* said we, *there is no Spirit can have any Being without a Body, neither God, Angels, nor Man*: And, further, *that God that is a Spirit without a Body is no God at all.*

11. *For we that are men that have Bodies, have power over all Spirits whatsoever that have no Bodies: For it is the dark Imagination of Reason in man that hath created to it self Spirits without Bodies, which is none of God's Creation.*

12. When he heard this he considered the things of Nature, that no Spirit could have any being without its Body.

13. Then he marvelled, and said, Where have we been all this while, that took God for a Spirit without a Body: Oh! how have we been in the dark.

14. But, said he, doth not Christ say, *God is a Spirit, and God will be worshiped in spirit and truth*: And Christ said, *His Words were Spirit and Life.*

15. We answered, and said, Can a Man worship God in Spirit and Truth without a Body? He said, *No.* Then said I, neither can God accept of any Mans worship except he hath a Body of his own: For God hath a Body of his own, as Man hath a Body of his own; only God's body is spiritual and heavenly clear as Christial, brighter than the Sun, swifter than Thought, yet a body.

16. For Man's body is earthly, and made of the Earth, in the image and

likeness of God's own body, only Man's body is of the Earth earthly, and God's body is the Lord from Heaven heavenly: Yet Man's body is the image of God as well as his Soul as *Moses* did truly mean as he spake.

17. For this I say, that if Man's Body and Soul had been spiritual in its Creation, then when Man's Thoughts do assend up to Heaven, his body would assend with it, in the twinkling of an Eye.

18. For the Thoughts of Man are swift; and if his body, which is earthly, do but put on Immortality, then his body would assend with his Thoughts up into the Aire, and so to Heaven.

19. These immortal bodies can do, and at the last day these vile bodies of ours that doth truly beleive, shall be made like unto his own glorious body.

20. For now our bodies are natural bodies, but when these natural bodies shall rise spiritual bodies, then shall Immortality take place; and these vile bodies of ours, that are now mortal, yet made in the image of God's own glorious body, shall be spiritual and heavenly bodies, even like unto his glorious body.

21. And because God's body is spiritual and heavenly, and cannot be seen by the natural sight of the Eye, therefore it was that Christ said, *God is a Spirit, and will be worshiped in Spirit and truth.*

22. Observe, For as a Man cannot worship in spirit and truth without a body, neither is that any God at all that hath no body of its own; neither is a Spirit without a body of its own any Object of Faith or Worship, for a Spirit without a body hath no substance: And as for those words of Christ being Spirit and Life, consider they were spoken from a body.

23. For this I say, no words whatsoever can be spoken of any Spirit that hath no body: For those words God spoke to *Moses* and the Prophets, they were from the body of God: And those words Christ spoke, that was spirit and life, was from his body when on Earth: And those words he spoke to *Paul* after he was assended up to Heaven, it was from his own body.

24. So that, without Controversy, no Spirit can speak at all, or hath any being without a body: And this is the very Cause that Men find so little Comfort in worshiping and beleiving in such a God that is a spirit without a body.

25. Also we declared unto him the nature of God, shewing that there can be no form without a nature, for it is the nature that gives the form.

26. Also we shewed unto him the Person and Nature of Angels, and the Person and Nature of the right Divel, and the rice of the two Seeds, and the secret Misteries how God became Flesh, and how the Divel became Flesh, and many other things which satisfied his mind.

27. So that he became a true Beleiver of this Commission of the Spirit, and shewed Kindness unto *John Reeve* all the days of his Life, likewise his Brother *George Leader* became a true beleiver.

28. This Mr. *Richard Leader* grew very mighty in Wisdom and Knowledge, both in natural and spiritual Wisdom, so that every great Man of his Acquaintance did submit unto his Wisdom, and lov'd him for his Knowl-

edge; so he continued in it all his Life, but about a year or two after *John Reeve* dyed he dyed at *Barbadoes*.

CHAP. VIII.

Of one Mr. Cooper, a great Disputant, and how convinced: And how a true Ministry is known from a false. Of his Conversion: And how he passed Sentance of Damnation upon Fifteen of his Companions: And of his trouble for so doing without Commission: And of a Minister's censoring him to be bewitched.

1. After this, in the same year, it came to pass that a certain man, a Silk-Weaver, his name was *Cooper*: He being acquainted with one Mrs. *White*, who was a beleiver of this Commission of the Spirit: She lived in *Duning hill-Ally* near *More-fields*.

2. This Man was very desirous that she would tell him how he might speak with these two Prophets; for he had a great desire to see us, and speak with us; so she directed him where.

3. So when the Man came and found us both together, the Man desired to drink with us, thinking in himself that he would talk and discourse better over a Cup of Drink than otherway, because it was his Custom so to do.

4. For he thought himself very strangly armed with Questions, thinking it impossible for us to answer, because he could finde none that ever he had talked withal, Ministers, nor other to do it,

5. So we went with him to drink, and he propounded his Questions concerning the true God, and the right Devil, and how the Devil came to be; and how a Man may know the History of the Scripture to be true, seeing they did contradict themselves in many places, with several other things.

6. Unto which we gave him a full Answer unto whatsoever he asked, so that he could not make any Reply against anything we said.

7. Also we showed him the power of the Commission of *Moses*, and the power of the Commission of Christ and his Apostles, and the power of our Commission in this Age.

8. And that every Commission had power to bless and curs Men to eternity, and that he was no true Minister of Christ which had not power to bless and curs.

9. For if a Man pretend to be a Minister of the Gospel, and cannot say to him that beleiveth in him to be a true Minister, and the Doctrine he preacheth to be true, *is blessed to eternity*.

10. And say to that Person as dispiseth and persecuteth the Person of this Minister, and his Doctrine, *is cursed Soul and Body to eternity*: If he have not Power to do this, he is no true Minister of Christ, neither did Christ send him to preach unto the People.

11. These things stuck upon the Mans Mind exceedingly, and he was much affected in Love towards us: and he was elevated in his Mind, as if he would get up to Heaven immediately.

12. And he thought himself so strong now that he could drive all People before him.

13. So he departed from us, elevated in his Mind: He went among his own Company, and those of his own Trade, and he talked amongst them of things he had heard, and that he had been with the two Prophets.

14. But his Company laughed him to scorn: But he in his elevation and zeal to what he had heard, gave Sentance of Damnation to eternity upon fifteen of his Companions.

15. Some were angry at him and some laughed and scoffed at him, and said he was bewitched.

16. It came to pass that the next Day after he had given Sentance upon those fifteen Persons he fell sick, yet he held to what he had said the Day before.

17. So that his Wife, and some of them he had damned said, the Man was bewitched, and would needs send for the Minister of the Parish to pray with him, and give his Judgment whether he was bewitched, or no.

18. But when the Minister came, the Man would not let him pray for him.

19. So the Minister gave his Judgment, that the Man was absolutely bewitched: But after three or four days the Man got up, and was well again, and told us what the Minister had said, and confessed that he damned fifteen Men, which was the cause of that Trouble in his Mind.

20. Because he did it without a Commission, not but that I do beleive they will be all damned as I said; but my Trouble was for giving Sentance without a Commission.

21. For at that time no Beleiver gave Sentance upon any Dispiser, but us two only: But in that he confessed his Fault he was forgiven by us.

CHAP. IX.

Of one Captain Stasy, a Friend to the two Witnesses, and of their Dispute with a Minister, proving that God was in the form of a Man: And of the Minister's Blasphemy, and John Reeve's *passing the Sentance upon him, and that he should never see any other God but that Sentance: And how* John Reeve *was threaten'd with a Warrant from* Cromwell, *or the Councel of State: And how* John *replyed, that if they dispised as the Priest had done, that he would pronounce them damn'd.*

1. After this it came to pass in the year 1653. there was one Captain *Stasy* in the Parliament's Service, that came to talk with us; he was a wise and moderate Man, able to hear and bear Words, but did not beleive what we said.

2. But he heard us gladly, and liked many things which we spake, insomuch that he invited us to Dinner at the Inn where he quartered.

3. So we went, there was of his Acquaintance a Minister, as they are called, a *Cambridge* Schollar, and with him an Excise Man; his Name was

Ebb, and the Priest's Name was *Goslin*,[3] and there was with them two Souldiers.

4. These Men being at Dinner with us, Captain *Stasy* put the Priest upon Discourse and Dispute with us.

5. So we disputed with him concerning God; and when we came to prove by Scripture, that God was a form like Man, according to those Words in *Geneses, God made Man in his own Image and Likeness* the Priest pleaded, that was Holiness and Righteousness.

6. We showed him that Holiness and Righteousness had no Form nor Image without a Body, nay it is nothing at all in it self, but as it is acted forth by a Body.

7. For it is a Body that acteth holy good and righteous Things, therefore it is we call such a Man a Holy Man, a good Man, a righteous Man: Now if God made Man in his own Image an holy upright Man, could he be said to be Man except he had a Body.

8. Neither could them Words be proper to say, God made Man in his own Image and Likeness, if Man was made with a Body to act holy and righteous Things, and God that made him had never a Body himself.

9. How then could Man be said to be made in the Image and Likeness of God, whereas there is no likeness at all between them, for the one hath a Person, Form and Body, and the other hath none.

10. And if you say Holiness and Righteousness is the Image and Likeness of God, we pray will you show us the Form and Likeness of the Image of Holiness and Righteousness distinct of it self from a Body.

11. Then where ever we see Holiness and Righteousness distinct of it self, then we shall know God, and that Holiness and Righteousness is the Image and Likeness of God without a Body.

12. And when we see this we will worship Holiness and Righteousness for God without a Body; if you can show us the form of it by it self.

13. Then the Priest grew angry, and called it Blasphemy, to say God was a Form or Person, and said we were Deceavers; with many other railing Speeches.

14. Whereupon *John Reeve* pronounced him cursed and damn'd both Soul and Body, from the Presence of God, elect Men and Angels, to eternity.

15. And further said, that he should never see any other God in the Life to come, but the Sentance he had passed upon him.

16. Then the two Souldiers were very angry to see the Priest damn'd, and they would have fallen upon us to beat us, and one of them took up a great Stoole to knock *John Reeve* on the Head.

17. But Captain *Stasy* held him, and perswaded him; then they said they would have a Warrant for us, either from General *Cromwell*, or the Councel of State, or from the Parliament.

18. *John Reeve* answered, and if General *Cromwell*, the Councel of State, or Parliament should dispise those things we declare as you have done, and as this Priest hath done, I would pronounce them damn'd as I do you.

19. So with a great many words more, at that time, between them and us, and Threatnings wherewith they threatned us, we parted.

20. And Captain *Stasy* seemed to be sorry that they were no more Civil; but he was glad the Priest was damn'd, because he was a great Enemy to the Clergy.

THE END OF THE SECOND PART

THE THIRD PART.
FROM THE YEAR 1653 TO THE YEAR 1665.

CHAP. I.

Shewing how five Men got a Warrant from the Lord Maior and brought the two Witnesses before him: Of their Accusation: Of their Examination: And of their Answer to it with boldness:

1. But a little while after this, as is aforesaid, it came to pass that these Men did get a Warrant from the Lord Maior of *London*,[1] because we lived in the City of *London*, it was under his Jurisdiction.

2. So this Priest and the two Souldiers, and *Ebb* the Exciseman, and another Salseman, his Name was *Chandler*, a damn'd Man, he lived near me in great *Trinity Lane*.

3. These five joyn'd all together to prosecute us, and having a Warrant from my Lord Maior they came to my House, and they brought the Marshal of the Citty of *London* and his Men to apprehend us and bring us before the Lord Maior.

4. And they came up to the Chamber where *John Reeve* and I was, and the Marshal and his Men took us before the Lord Maior to be examined.

5. And when we came before him there were several Accusations against us, besides what these five Men did accuse us of.

6. First, that Book intituled, *A Transcendant Spiritual Treatis*; the Lord Maior had this Book in his Hand. Secondly there was a Pamphlet by one *Needham*, sent to the Lord Maior of his own Damnation.[2]

7. And several Letters we had sent to the *Presbyterian* Ministers in *London* and about *London*, to lay down their Preaching, (because they had no Commission from God to preach) upon the receipt of this Letter, upon pain of eternal Damnation. These Letters were in the Lord Maiors Hands also.

8. And there came one Minister forty Miles to accuse us before the Lord Maior, he came rideing all Night, and came in great Fury and Rage, at the very time the Lord Maior called for us to examin us.

9. But the Lord Maior did not mind this rageing Priest at all, notwithstanding his great Jorny.

10. But he minded these five Men that Joyned in the Warrant, and set them together by themselves, and us two by our selves.

11. The Lord Maiors Examination of us the two Witnesses, and our Answer to him, as follows.

12. He asked the Accusars what they had to say against these two Men; one of them answered and said, that *John Reeve* did say, *That he was their God.*

13. The Lord Maior said to *John Reeve, Did you say so?* He answered and said, *No. What did you say?* said the Lord Maior.

14. Said *John Reeve. These Men desired to have Discourse with us about Spiritual Matters, and when I declared the Truth to them, they called it Blasphemy, Delusion, and Lyes.*

15. *Whereupon I did pronounce the Sentance of eternal Damnation upon them, in that they had sinned against the Holy Ghost, which the Scriptures saith,* shall never be forgiven, in this World, nor in the World to come.

16. *And that they should see no other God in the World to come, but that Sentance which I had passed upon them;* This I did say, and this his Clerke set down.

17. Another of the Accusers said that *John Reeve* should say, *That General* Cromwell, *the Counsel of State, and the Parliament were all damn'd.*

18. *Did you say so?* said the Lord Maior, No, said John Reeve.

19. *What did you say?* said the Lord Maior.

20. *John Reeve* answered, *that we were in a place where one Captain Stasy invited us, and these Men, being Strangers to us, they would needs propound Questions to us, concerning God and the Scriptures, because this Minister was among them; and he was the greatest Blasphemer of Truth of all of them.*

21. *Whereupon I pronounced him, for his Blasphemy against the Holy Ghost, and for Preaching without a Commission from God, cursed and damn'd, both in Soul and Body, from the Presence of God, elect Men, and Angels, to eternity.*

22. *Upon this he and the rest of them said,* They would fetch a Warrant from General *Cromwell,* the Counsel of State, or from the Parliament, to prosecute us.

23. And I said, *That if General* Cromwell, *the Counsel of State, or the Parliament, should dispise those things we have declared, and sin against the Holy Ghost, as these Men did, That General Cromwell, the Counsel of State, and the Parliament, would be all damn'd as you are?* This I did say.

24. This was set down by the Clerke.

25. Then said the Maior, *You are accused for denying the Three Persons in the Trinity: You say there is but one Person, Christ Jesus, you deny the Father.*

26. *No, said* John Reeve, *we owne the Trinity more than any Men, both Father, Son, and Spirit, are all but one Person and one God Christ Jesus, as is declared in that Book in your Hand.*

27. Then the Maior said, *Here is several Notes from the godly Ministers which you have forbid to preach the Gospel, upon pain of Damnation.*

28. Said *John, We do own these Notes sent unto them, and if any of them Ministers we sent these Letters unto have preached publickly since receipt of them, they are damn'd to eternity, because they preach and are not sent of God: Neither do they know the true God, nor can they preach the Truth unto the People.*

29. These Words were set down by the Clerke.

30. Then said the Lord Maior unto *John Reeve, What was it that God* spake unto you?

31. *John* related the Words God spake unto him three Mornings together; *the same Words that are written in that Book in your Hand.*

CHAP. II.

Shewing John Reeve's *Answer to the Lord Maior's Questions, and* John Reeve's *Question to the Maior, what his God was, with the Maior's Answer*: And John's *Replycation to it. Of the two Witnesses Commitment to Newgate.*

1. The Lord Maior answered *John Reeve*, and said, *He did beleive it was the Devil that spake to him.*

2. Then to this I answered and said, *Sir, you have sin'd against the Holy Ghost, and will be damn'd.*

3. The Maior clapt his Hand upon his Brest and said, *God forbid.*

4. *Yea*, said I, *but you have*, then said *John Reeve* to the Maior, *Sir*, you say you do beleive it was the Devil that spake unto me; I pray Sir tell me what your God is.

5. The Lord Maior lift up himself, and laid his Hand on his Brest: *Oh!* saith he, *my God is an infininite incomprehensible Spirit.*

6. *What*, said I, *without a Body or Person?*

7. Said the Maior, *God hath no Body or Person at all.*

8. *Why*, said I, *hath God that made man in his own Image, who hath a Body and Person, and hath made all other Creatures with Persons; and shall he that made them have no Body or Person of his own?*

9. *Doth not the Scriptures say, That Christ was the express Image and Brightness of his Father's Person; and had not Christ a Body or Person in form like Man, Sin excepted?*

10. Then said the Maior unto me, *must I beleive you?*

11. *Yea*, said I, *That you must, or you will be damn'd.*

12. Then there was a Gentlewoman in the Court called out, and said, Mr. *Reeve, pray tell me what the Devil is?*

13. *John* answered with a loud Voice, and said, *Thy own Soul is the Devil.*

14. Then one of the Officers said unto the Woman, *I think he hath met with you now.*

15. Then the Lord Maior asked the Accusers if they would be bound in 40 *l.* Band a piece to prosecute against these two Men, they said, *They would;* so the Clark bound them to prosecute.

16. Then the Lord Maior called for the Act of Parliament, which was newly made against Blasphemy:[3] So the Maior read this Passage in it, *That if any man should say that he is God, and that God is no where else, shall be guilty of Blasphemy, and shall suffer six months Imprisonment, without Bail or mean prise.*

17. Then said I unto him; Sir, *What have you to do with this Act, you are a temporal Magistrate, and ought to judg of temporal Things between man and man.*

18. And you are to do Justice between Man and Man, in all moral and temporal Affairs, which concerns you to be the Judge of, and you will do well to keep there, for you are not to Judge of Blasphemy against God; nor those that made this act neither.

19. *Why,* said the Maior, *must I beleive you?*

20. *Yea,* said I, *That you must, else you will be damn'd.*

21. For God hath chosen us two to be the Judge of Blasphemy against God, and hath given us power to pronounce Sentance of Damnation upon all those that do Blaspheme against that God, which is a Person, which you do deny.

22. *Why,* said he again, *must I beleive you?*

23. *Yea,* said I, *else you will be damn'd.*

24. Many things more than what is here written was spoke at that time, but these were of most concernment to take notice of.

25. And when this Dispute and Examination was ended, the Lord Maior asked if we would put in Bail? and we said No.

26. So he gave order to his Clark to make our Mittimus, and send us to *Newgate;* and he went away out of the Court into another Chamber, and the Clark carried the Mittimus into him to set his hand to it: So that he came no more into the Court.

27. For *John Reeve* intended to give the Sentance of eternal Damnation upon him, both Body and Soul, in the open Court, it being full of People.

28. But he came no more out until we were led away by the Marshal and his Men to *Newgate,* there to remain Prisoners till the next Sessions.

29. This Commitment was the fifteenth Day of *September,* 1653.

CHAP. III.

Shewing how the Prisoners brought Irons: Required Mony of the two Witnesses, they having none, took one of their Cloaks for a Pledg. How long they were Prisoners: The Bordes were their Bed. And of the Wickedness of some of the Prisoners, which had a Design to have hanged them; and how Providence preserved them.

1. Now we being Prisoners in *Newgate* Goal, I shall speak of some Passages that hapend there.

2. As soon as ever the Keeper had put us in, and shut the Gate upon us, the Prisoners brought to each of us a pair of Irons to put on our Leggs, except we would lay them down three Shillings and Six Pence a piece.

3. Also they said, they must have Mony for Garnish, which did amount to five Shillings a piece in all.

4. I said we have no Money about us, but however, if they pleas'd, they might put the Irons upon our Legs, and I held out my Leg for them to be put on: I was very free to wear them for Truths Sake, though it was a thing unusual; for it was the first time that ever I was in Prison before in all my Life.

5. The Prisoners seeing us so willing, they said they would trust us for Tenn Shillings, upon this condition, that we would give them one of our Cloaks for a Pledge; we said do, take which you will.

6. So they looked on *John Reeve's* Cloak, and said it was not worth Tenn Shillings: Then they looked upon my Cloak, and took it off my back, and said, *This wilt do, this is a good Cloak, it is good fine Cloath*; said they, *We will keep this Cloak till you pay Tenn Shillings.*

7. And in Five Days after my Daughter *Sarah* brought Tenn Shillings, and I gave it them, and sent my Cloak home by my Daughter; for I durst not keep it there, for fear I should loose it; though I had need enough of it, for the Weather was cold at that time, for it was the 15*th.* of *September* 1653 we were commited, and we were there Prisoners until the 17*th. of October.*

8. And the Bordes was our Bed; we had no Sheets, only a poor Flock-Bead upon the Ground, and one thin Blancket at top; and we paid seven Groats[4] a Week for this Lodging, and thought our selves very well used in a Prison, which thing we was never acquainted with before.

9. But we were more perplex'd with the Prisoners within, than with the Imprisonment it self.

10. For there were three Highway-Men, and they were very malitious against us, especially one of them, that if I went to the Grate when any came to speak with us, he would lay his Leg in the dark for me to stumble at, and strike me in the Neck with his Fists, thinking to throw me down.

11. And if I were but walking in the Hall he would come and drive me out, and strike at me, and say, *You Rogue, you damn'd Folks*: And so it was with the Boys that were Prisoners: that when I went to the Grates to speak with any, they would snatch off my Hat, and paun it for half a Duzen of Drink: So the Boys did.

12. And I gave them Six-pence every time they did it, to please them.

13. So that other Prisoners said it was not fit I should be so abused, and wished me to complain to the Keeper, and he would punish them.

14. *No*, said I, *It is not for Prisoners to complain of prisoners.*

15. And when these three notable Thieves saw they could not provoke me, no ways, so much as to say why do you so?

16. Then they thought upon another way, and wrote a Letter to *John Reeve* with the Sentance of Damnation to us both; thinking to have provoked *John Reeve* to have given Sentance of Damnation to Eternity upon them, that they might have had wherewith to have done him a Mischief.

17. But he gave them no Answer at all.

18. When they saw this would not do, they came into our Room where we lay, with a Rope in their Hands, to measure how high the beam was, that they might hang *John Reeve* in the Room.

19. And as it happened there was four condemn'd Men in *Newgate* at that time, and these Men were our greatest Friends to protect us from the Violence of other Prisoners.

20. And these two that lay in our Room, they pulled out those Men by Head and Sholders, that came to measure the beam: Those condemned Men had great Respect for us, because we gave them many times Victuals and Money.

21. Also we gave seven Prisoners, at one time, twelve Pence a piece, so that we found Favor in their Eyes for the Loves sake.

22. There was one Prisoner that begged at the Grate, and when he was drunk, he would trouble *John Reeve* to bless him: So one day, when he was very drunk, he broke into *John Reeve*, and kneeled down upon his Knees before him, and held his Hands together and said, *for Jesus Christ sake* John Reeve *bless me, for I am a wicked Sinner.*

23. And *John* went from him, and prayed him to be quiet, but he was so much the more earnest for him to bless him.

24. He was so troublesom to *John Reeve* that he could not tell how to be delivered from him, 'till one of them that lay in our Room came and pulled him out by Head and Shoulders, and turned him down Stairs.

25. Those convicted and condemned Men were made under Keepers, which did help the uper Keeper to shut up the Prisoners every Night: These were the Preservers of us from the Violence of the Prisoners all the while we were in *Newgate*.

26. And while we were in *Newgate*, *John Reeve* wrote a Letter to the Lord Maior, Alderman *Fooke*, who commited us to Prison: And one *Jeremiah Mount*, a Friend to us, got it Printed, at his own Charge, against the Day of Tryal.

27. There was in it, the Sentance of Damnation upon the Lord Maior; and they were given to the Recorder *Steele*,[5] and several other Officers in the Court: That Letter was Printed in the year 1653.[6] and in the Third year of our Commission.

28. There is many Beleivers of this Commission of the Spirit that hath them Letters in Print at this Day; but none will part with them at any Rate, not now.

CHAP. IV.

Of the Two Witnesses being brought to their Tryal: How John Reeve *would not suffer the Maior, a damn'd Man, to speak: How the Jury brought them in guilty; and of the Recorder's Sentence upon them. And of several other Transactions.*

1. And when the day of Tryal came, we were brought before the Court, and the Accusers stood all Five before us; but the Court asked the Accusars not one Question, neither did the Accusars speak one Word before the Court.

2. But when the Lord Maior, the chief Judge of that Court, began to speak against us.

3. *John Reeve* said, with a loud Voice, *That he would not hear a damn'd Man speak, neither will answer to anything; But,* Mr. Recorder, we will hear *you.*

4. So the Lord Maior sat down, and said never a word more.

5. Then *John Reeve* called to the Recorder for our Examination before the Lord Maior, for that will shew all things, and that we will stand to.

6. But there was no Examination could be produced by the Lord Maior, notwithstanding *John Reeve* called for it three times, but they gave no Answer at all; therefore no need for the Witnesses to accuse us, for the Examination answered to all that the Accusars could say against us.

7. But the Court waved them, and tryed us only by that book *John Reeve* first printed; in which book Christ is proved to be the only God: So they judged it Blasphemy to deny the Trinity of Persons.

8. Therefore the Recorder asked *John Reeve* what Father it was that Christ prayed unto in his Agony?

9. *John Reeve* answered, and said, *It was to his representitive Power in Moses and* Elias *that he prayed unto; as you may see,* said he, *when he said* Ely, Ely, Lama sabatheny; *my God, my God, why hast thou forsaken me.* You may see that the Jews knew the Hebrew Language; for the Jews said he called for *Elias, let him come and save him if he will have him.*

10. So that it is clear, that Christ prayed in his Agony, to the representitive Power in *Elias.*

11. Then said the Recorder, *Mr. Reeve, Mr. Reeve, You have spoke enough; let* Aaron *speak.*

12. Said *John Reeve, Scoff on* Mr. Recorder.

13. *Truly Friend,* said the Recorder, *I do not scoff.*

14. Then said I, *I can say no more to that one Question than he hath said before, but if you have anything else to aske I will answer you.*

15. But he asked never a Question more, nor spake a word more, because the Examination which they would not produce in the open Court had fully answered to all things they could object against us.

16. But commanded us to withdraw; and the Jury laid their Heads a little together and brought us in guilty of Blasphemy and execrable Opinions.

17. So the Recorder gave Sentance upon us, That we should be sent to *Old Bridewell,* and be kept Prisoners there for six Months, without Bail or maine Prise.

18. So there we remained full six Months.

19. And while we were Prisoners in *Old Bridewell, Jeremiah Mount* got that Epistle to the Ministers printed, which are yet to be seen, and will be to the end of the World by some.

20. After this, while we were Prisoners there, we wrote a Remonstrance of all the Transactions that had passed, that was remarkable, from the day of our Commission 1651[2] to this our time of being Committed Prisoners in *Old Bridewell.*

21. And this Remonstrance was directed to General *Cromwell,* and *Jeremiah Mount* got that printed at his own Charge also.[7] This Remonstrance is yet to be seen with some, and will remain in the hands of some to the end of the World.

22. This *Jeremiah Mount* was a great Friend to us in the time of our Imprisonment, and so was *John Brunte* and his Wife, and one *Richard Russell*: There was very few Beleivers of us at that time, this was in the year 1653. It was a year of great and many Troubles to us both, but especially to me.

23. And about the Month of *April,* in the year 1654. after our seven Months Imprisonment we came forth of Prison.

24. And after this *John Reeve* wrote Letters to several Men; as to Esquire *Penington, William Sedgwick,* Minister,[8] and to the Earle of *Pembrooke.*[9]

25. And some of them sent Answers to him again; but none of these Letters are in print.

26. Also *John* wrote that Spiritual and heavenly Treatis, Intituled, *A divine Lookinglass*: And he got it printed in the Year 1656. *Jeremiah Mount* was at the greatest part of that Charge.

27. But the Printer being knavish and covetous, quite spoiled it in the Press; he hudled it up so close together, for want of more Paper, that no body had any Delight to read it through, so that it never yielded the Mony it cost printing.

CHAP. V.

Of John Reeve's travelling to Maidstone *in* Kent, *where he met with Enemies, and gave them the Sentance, upon which they got a Warrant against him: Of the Notice he had and departed. Of his Treatis, Called,* Joyful News from Heaven: *After the writing of which he died.*

1. After this *John Reeve* went to *Maidstone* in *Kent,* to see some Friends there.

2. There was but Four Beleivers in that Country at that time.

3. And he going to visit them, having never been in that Country before; after he had been three days there he met with Enemies enough.

4. But they falling in Discourse with him, they dispised his Doctrin and Commission; so he gave Sentance of Damnation to eternity upon one or two of them.

5. And they stur'd up others to persecute him, so they got a Constable to apprehend him, but having notice of it, he departed out of those Coasts in hast, and over heated his Blood with traveling to the Waterside, which was Sixteen Miles: And he went upon the Water at *Gravesend*, at Night, when he was all in a Sweat, and cooled himself too soon.

6. So he surfited his Blood, and drove him into a Consumption, which killed him: He lived almost two Years afterwards, but in a sick wasting Condition.

7. That surfit he got then, was absolutely the Cause of his Death, else he might have lived many years longer.

8. Yet, notwithstanding his Sickness, he wrote that excellent Piece, a Book called *Joyful News from Heaven; or, The Mortality of the Soul.*

9. This he did in the time of his Sickness; and just as it was in the Press, to be printed, he saw the first Sheet printed, but his Eyes were dim that he could not see the print, not to read, for he died in two days after.

10. There was at that time three Sisters that were true Beleivers, which he did oft resort unto: The one was Mrs. *Frances*, the eldest, the second Mrs. *Roberts*, the third Mrs. *Boner*.

11. This Mrs. *Frances* closed up his Eyes; for he said unto her, *Frances*, close up mine Eyes, lest my Enemies say, *I died, A staring Prophet*.

12. And she did so, and he gave up the Ghost, and said not one word more.

13. And she took and cut one Lock of his Hair to keep, for a Memorial of one of the two last Prophets that God will ever send while his World endureth.

14. He had a fine Head of Hair, it was black, waveing over his Shoulders.

15. So he was buried in *Bethlahem Church-Yard*.

16. He dyed about the latter end of *July*, in the year 1658 in the seventh year of our Commission, and in the Forty Ninth year of his Life.

17. Thus I have given a true Account, to be upon Record of some of the most remarkable Acts and Passages, and Sufferings, which we the Witnesses of the Spirit hath acted and suffered in this Seven Years of our Commission.

18. Only for God's Cause, in Obedience unto the Voice of God, that spake to *John Reeve* the Third, Forth, and Fifth days of *February*, in the year 1651[2].

CHAP. VI.

Of Laurance Claxton, *what Books he wrote of his exalted Pride: The Be-leivers complain of him: The Prophet forbad him for writing any more: How he humbled himself: The Prophet forgave him: And of his Death.*

1. After *John Reeve* was dead, there was one *Laurence Claxton* who had

been a Preacher of the Ranters that came to beleive this Doctrin and Commission of the Spirit.

2. And he owned it some little time before *John Reeve* dyed, and afterwards he asked me to give him leave to write in the vindication and justification of this Commission of the Spirit.

3. And I gave my Consent, whereby several of his Acquaintance in
Cambridge-shire, were brought to the Faith of this Commission.

4. The first Book he wrote, the Title of it is, *Look about you, for the
Devil that you fear is in you.* It is in print at this Day.

5. The second Book he wrote, the Title is called, *The Quakers Downfall*:
Which is in print at this Day.

6. The third Book he wrote, the Title is called, *A Dialogue between Faith
and Reason*: Which is in print at this Day.

7. The forth Book he wrote, is called, *A Wonder of Wonders*: Which is
in print at this Day.

8. After this he grew so Proud, and Lording over the Beleivers, saying,
That no body could write in the vindication of this Commission, now John
Reeve *was dead, but he*: And to that purpose he wrote another Book Intit-
uled, *The lost Sheep found*:[10] It is in print to this Day.

9. Wherein he had proudly exalted himself into *John Reeve's* Chair, exalting *John Reeve* and himself, but quite excluded me in all the Book.

10. So many of the Beleivers complained to me of his lording over them,
and that he had excluded me quite in this last Book.

11. Whereupon I read the Book over, and found the Report was true.

12. Whereupon I put him down, for ever writing any more, and I wrote
to the Beleivers in *Cambridge-shier*, and else where, that he was put down
for his Pride and Covetousness, for ever writing any more upon that account.

13. And the Beleivers did obey my Voice every where.

14. He continued thus, four Years after John Reeve dyed, until the year
1661. and in a while after *Laurance Claxton* humbled himself to me, and
acknowledged his Fault, and I forgave him, and took him into my Favour,
but ty'd him not to write any more.

15. So he continued several years afterwards, justifying his Faith and
Confidence, in this Commission of the Spirit.

16. But it came to pass, when the Fire destroy'd the Citty of *London* he,
to get a Livelyhood, did ingage to help Persons of Quality to borrow Mony,
to build their Houses again.

17. But the Persons that had the Mony did run away, and left *Claxton*
in the Lurch; the Debt was one hundred Pounds.

18. So he only was Arrested, and put in *Ludgate* Goal, for this Mony:
He lay there a whole year, and dyed there.

19. But he gave a very good Testimony of his Faith in the true God, and
in this Commission of the Spirit, and of that full assurance of eternal Happiness he should enjoy, to eternity after his Death.

20. Insomuch that all the Prisoners marvelled, and were sorry they had
opposed him so when he was alive.

CHAP. VII.

Shewing how the Prophet caused, The Divine Looking Glass *to be Reprinted: Of the Prophets printing a Book of the Interpretation of the 11th. of the Revelations:*[11] And, The Quakers Neck broken:[12] *Of his Travels to* Nottingham; *and the Transactions that passed there: And then to* Chesterfield.

1. The first thing I did after *Claxton* was put down, I caused the *Divine Looking-Glass* to be new printed 1661. Which was done very handsomly, and is now to be seen.

2. After this I wrote a Book containing Twenty four Sheets of Paper; Intituled, *The Interpretation of the 11th. Chapter of the Revelations by St. John,* and got it printed in the same year 1662. Which is yet to be seen: Never was such a thing extant in the World before.

3. After this I wrote a Book called, *The Neck of the Quakers broken,* containing Tenn Sheets of Paper; and got it printed in the same year 1663. Which is yet to be seen.

4. After this it came to pass, that several in the North Country, hearing and seeing these Books, had a great desire to see me, and especially one *Ellin Sudbury* at *Notingham,* and one *Dorothy Carter of Chesterfield* in *Darbyshier.*

5. These and others were very desirous to see me, but they could not tell how, for they thought it would be too much Charge and Labour for them to come to *London* to me so far; for they were loath to put me to so much Charge to come to them; yet *Ellin Sudbury,* her desiers were so strong, that she could not be satisfied except she did see me: So she wrote a Letter unto me, that I would come into those Parts; and that the Society should bare the Charge.

6. Now I marvelled what that Society should be, but it was the Beamonists mix'd with the Quakers; as I found afterwards: But this being in the Winter, I sent word I would come and see her in Summer.

7. And accordingly it came to pass, that one *Thomas Hudson,* a Friend of ours at *London,* had occasion to see his own Relations in *Lancashire,* and *Notingham,* and *Chesterfield* being in his way, he was willing to travel with me, to see those Friends we had never seen before.

8. And when we came to *Notingham, Elin Sudbury* was glad to see us, and so was her Husband also, but at that time he was upon the *Beamonist* score; so there came several of the *Beamonists* People to discourse with me, and some of the Speakers of them, and Mr. *Sudbury* he thought they would be able to dispute with me, though he could not.

9. But he saw they were more weak than himself, to maintain their Principles of Religion; so that he disliked them, and said, *That their was no true knowledge of the Scriptures amongst them:* Also he heard me pass the Sentence of Damnation to eternity, on four of them.

10. And one of these was very much troubled, and asked *Elin Sudbury, whether she did beleive he was damn'd, because I had passed Sentence upon*

him, only to insnare her, she being but weak, and had never heard such a thing before.

11. But I, to free her from that Bondage in her Minde, for I knew she had not Confidence enough, at that time to say she did beleive he was damn'd: And if she should say no, then she would loose the assurance of her own Happiness, in beleiving me to be a Prophet of the Lord, and had Power to give Sentance of Blessedness to one, and Cursedness to the other; So I knew the Woman was in a strait what to say, and he urged her for an Answer.

12. But I said, *she shall not give you her Judgment at all, to insnare her Mind: I have passed the Sentence upon you, and I do beleive without doubting, That you are the Seed of the Serpent, and will be damn'd to eternity, and it matters not if all the People in the World, should beleive to the contrary, yet my Faith shall be stronger than all to keep you down.*

13. Then they grew angree, and threatned to prosecute me, but could not tell how to state a ground of Prosecution.

14. After *Thomas Hudson* and I went from thence to *Chesterfield*, which was Twenty Miles further, to *Dorothy Carter's* House, a Widdow; she had one Daughter, her Name was *Elizabeth*, that was a true Beleiver; and a young Maid that was Servant to *Dorothy Carter*, her Name was *Elizabeth Smith*, a true Beleiver also.

15. And there was in that Town, a Man, his Name was *Edward Fewterer*, a Chirurgeon, that was a true Beleiver also: These Four were glad to see me, for they had never seen me before.

16. But the Professors of Religion, in that Town, hearing of me, there came several to dispute with me; but some of them blasphemed, and dispised what I said, whereupon I pronounced the Sentence, of eternal damnation upon Four, or Five Men there.

17. And they being inraged at it, they thought to prosecute us both; and they went to the Maior and Aldermen of the Town, to see what could be done unto us.

18. And the Maior and Alderman said, they could not tell what to do in it, seeing there was no Law against any Man for saying a Man is damn'd; but if you bring them before the Maior, and if they cannot give a good Account where there Habitation is, they may be set in the Stocks for Vagabonds if they stay in the Town any more than so many days: But we did not know this till afterwards.

19. And while they were ploting this Mischief; we not thinking of it, *Thomas Hudson* was to go Fifty Miles further, so *Edward Fewterer* and I took Horse, and went a matter of Fifteen Miles, on the Way with Mr. *Hudson*: Upon this, the Quakers reported, that I fled away from *Chesterfield*, to *Bakewell*, for fear of a whiping, when as we did not know there was any Mischief intended against us.

20. Besides *Edward Fewterer* and I, came back again to *Chesterfield* the same Night; but none sought after me as I heard of, and in two days afterwards, I departed from *Chesterfield* to *Notingham* again.

21. And as I stay'd there Three days more, there was a Conspiracy amongst those I had passed Sentance of Damnation upon, how to apprehend me.

22. For every place in the Country, where I had any that beleived, and that was a Friend to me, there was a many Enemies that sought to do me harm, only they had no Law on their side; but I being of Mr. *Sudbury's* Acquaintance, and at his House, the Maior or Sheriffs would do nothing in it.

23. And it came to pass afterwards, that the Sheriff's Wife came to be a true Beleiver unto this day, her Name is *Mary Barker*.

24. So after Three days, I departed for *Notingham* to *London*, to my own House: This was in the Year 1663.

CHAP. VIII.

The Prophet travels into Cambridgeshare *and* Kent: *And of his marriage to his Third Wife, and of his Second Jorney into* Darby-shire; *and of his being brought before the Maior of* Chesterfield: *Of his Examination by the Priest, and of his Commitment.*

1. After this I travelled into *Cambridge-shire*, to see several Friends there, and they were very joyful to see me at *Cambridge*, and the Countries round about, for there were a many of Beleivers in that Country.

2. I stayed there but a matter of Three Weeks, and then returned to *London* again: And a little while after, I travelled into *Kent* to visit some Friends.

3. And there was one *John Martine*, a Tanner, at *East-Malin* in *Kent* which did truly beleive in this Commission of the Spirit, and so did his Wife: He had Two Sons and one Daughter; his eldest Son *Thomas* did not beleive, but his youngest Son *John*, and his Daughter *Mary* were both true Beleivers; and his Daughter *Mary* was very zealous and strong in the beleif of it.

4. And it came to pass, a while after this *John Martin* dyed, and I going thither again afterwards, I took his Daughter *Mary* to Wife with her Mothers Consent, and I married her according to the Law of *England*, as I did my other two Wives before.

5. I had been a Widdower Sixteen years, before I took this Maid to Wife, she was Twenty Five years of Age when I married her, and I was about Fifty Three years old when I took her to Wife: She was of a good meek innocent and just Nature, besides the strong Faith and Zeal she had in this Commission of the Spirit; so that she was very sutable, both in spiritual and temporal Qualifications unto my Nature.

6. After this, it came to pass, the same year that I was married, great Troubles did befal me, both upon a Spiritual and Temporal Account, as may be understood in the following Relation.

7. It came to pass, that one *Richard Hutter*, a true Beleiver, had some Business at Law, at the Assizes at *Yorke*: He had a mind to go by *Notingham*

and *Chesterfield*, to see those Friends there; and if I would go with him, he would bear me Company so far.

8. Now these Friends, had greatly desired me to come down into the Country to see them; so I was glad of his Company, and we jornyed together; but Mr. *Hatter* stay'd but one Night at *Notingham*, and went his way and left me there at Mr. *Sudbury's*, and I stayed there a few days: And in that time there came several Quakers, Beamonites, and Indipendants, religious Men and Women, to discourse and dispute with me.

9. But several of them dispised, and blasphemed against what I said, whereby I gave Sentance of eternal Damnation, in that they had sinn'd against the Holy Ghost, a Sin which God will not forgive: Which made them very angry, and spead it abroad the Country, where ever I was known. And after a few days I went form *Notingham* to *Chesterfield*.

10. And in the middle of the way, there is a Market Town, called *Mansfield*, and there I used to bait my Horse and myself, and that Town is full of *Quakers;* and when I did Inn there, the *Quakers* and others, they would press into the Room where I was, to see me and talk with me: And they being an obstinate, and stiffnecked People against a personal God, many of them came under the Sentence of Damnation at *Mansfield*, and they reported it at *Chesterfield*, before I could come there.

11. And when I came to *Dorothy Carter's* House; after I had been two or three days there, came several Persons to speak with me in that Town, being a Market Town; and they were wicked Dispisers of a personal God.

12. And several of them were damn'd, at *Mansfield* and *Chesterfield*, and about twelve: But these at *Chesterfield* were most of them *Independants*, and they consulted with the Priest of the Parish, with the Maior and Aldermen of the Town to persecute me; and the *Quakers* were glad, the *Independant* People did so.

13. So the Priest being a more subtil Serpent than all the Beasts of the Feild, he consulted the Maior and Aldermen, to send a Constable for me, before them, and he would examin me, and see what Words he could get out of me, to have Matter to accuse me of, For, said he, we can do nothing to him for saying a Man is damn'd.

14. So the Constable was commanded to fetch me before the Maior, and he came where I was, and said I must go before the Maior.

15. I asked him if he had any Warrant for me; he said, *No*, then I said, *I will not go*: Said he, *I can command Aide*; then he commanded the Man of the House, where my Horse was at grass, but the Man was loth to do it, but he commanded him in the Kings Name to aide him.

16. So the Man took hold of one Arm, and the Constable by the other, and led me to the Hall, where the high Priest sat, for he was one of the Commissioners of the *Ecclesiastical Court*, with the Maior and Aldermen of the Town, and the Town Clarke, and all the Officers of the Town, were gathered together against me.

17. My Examination before them was as follows; the Priest's Name was *John Cupe*,[13] the Maiors Name *John Allwood*, the Recorders Name was

Needham, and the Constables Name was *Slater,* and the Aldermen, one was *Clarke,* and another his Name was *Pinder;* the rest I did not know their Names.

18. The first thing the Priest asked was, *what I came into that Country for.*

19. I said, *I came to visit some Friends at* Notingham, *and* Chesterfield, *and that I was sent for*: He asked me where I lived. I said at *London,* and what Trade I was of, I said, a *Tailor by Trade, and that I lived in* Trinity Lane, *and had fined for most Offices in the Parish were I lived.*

20. Then he waved that, because he thought I was no Housekeeper, but a Lodger, that hath no certain abiding place, but as a Vagabond that goeth to and fro and hath abideing every where, So when he saw he could do nothing here then he asked me whether I did beleive the Three Persons in the Trinity, Father, Son, and Holy Ghost.

21. I answered, *No, I did beleive there was three Names, or Titles, of Father, Son, and Holy Ghost, but one Person, the Lord Jesus Christ.*

22. He rejoyced at this before the Maior, and said, *this was enough,* and caused the Recorder to set it down, the same words.

23. Then he asked me if I was one of the Two Witnesses spoken of in the 11*th.* of the *Revelations.*

24. I answered and said, *I was one of those Two Witnesses of the Spirit, spoken of in the 11th. of the* Revelations; then he commanded the Recorder to set these words down.

25. Again, he asked me, if I had power to damn and to save.

26. I answered, and said, *I had power to give Sentence of Damnation upon those that dispised my Doctrin that I declare, and to pronounce the Sentence of Salvation upon those that truly beleive it.*

27. And that you may know that I have Power, I do pronounce you *Cursed and Damn'd both Soul and Body from the presence of God, elect Men and Angels to eternity.*

28. Then was the Priest struck dumb for a season, and when he had recovered himself to his Sences again, he said to the Recorder, set that down, but did not mention a word that the Priest was damn'd.

29. Then said the Maior, Mr. *Mugleton, we do not beleive you, we do beleive the Apostles.*

30. I answered, and said, *That will do you but little good now.*

31. Those words the Recorder was commanded to set down.

32. There were many more Words and Circumstances in the Examination, but these were the main things they made a Charge against me.

CHAP. IX.

Shewing that the Prophet proved before the Priest, Maior, and Aldermen, that Christ was the only God. The Priest made no Replycation against it, but fauning upon him with fine Words, to insnare him against the Government: The Prophet's Wisdom discover'd it. Of his Commitment.

1. But this I observed, that after I had given the Sentance of Damnation upon the Priest, he was very meek and moderate, and asked me Questions in the Scriptures concerning Christ being the only God.

2. And I opened unto him the First of *John, In the beginning was the Word, and the Word was with God, and the Word was God, and the Word became Flesh, and dwelt amongst us.*

3. *Now,* said I, *was not Christ the Word become Flesh, and that Word that became Flesh was God: And did any other God dwell among Men but Christ.*

4. And is it not said in Scripture, *That in him all the fulness of the Godhead dwelt bodily,* Not a part, or a piece of the Godhead, but all the fulness dwelt bodily in him.

5. Again, doth not the Scripture say, *Great is the Mistery of Godliness, God manifest in the Flesh, justified in the Spirit, seen of Angels, beleived on in the World, received up into Glory.*

6. Now was not this Christ manifest in the Flesh? Was not he preached unto the Gentles, and beleived on in the World? And was not he received up into Glory? So that Christ must needs be God become Flesh, and God manifest in Flesh.

7. Also, was not this Jesus Christ that *Alpha* and *Omega,* the *First* and the *Last,* the *Begining* and the *End,* he that was Dead and is Alive for ever more.

8. Here you see the *Alpha* and *Omega* was dead; And was not the *Alpha* and *Omega* God? And you see by the Scripture that the *Alpha* and *Omega* was dead: And was there any *Alpha* and *Omega* that dyed but Jesus Christ? And was there any *Alph*a and *Omega* that quickened out of Death to Life again, but Christ? Therefore he is said to be a quickening Spirit.

9. Therefore it must needs be, that Christ is God become Flesh, and manifest in Flesh; and he it was that dwelt among Men; and he was in the Person of a Man, in all things like unto Man, Sin excepted.

10. So that God is but one Person in Form, like a Man, and not Three Persons, as Men do vainly imagine.

11. But when he heard these sayings of mine, he replyed nothing against it, but seemed to faun upon me, and speak softly unto me, tempting me, And asked me secretly what I thought of this present Power, that he might have had some what to accuse me of, that the Law would have taken hold of.

12. But I answered him, and said, That I never was concerned with no temporal Powers, neither did I meddle with them at all.

13. So when the Priest saw he could get nothing out of me, concerning the Government of the Nation, then he applied to the things before mentioned.

14. And he caused the Recorder to read over the Examination before the Maior; the things were but few.

15. First, denying the Three Persons in the Trinity: Secondly, That I said I was one of those two Witnesses spoken of in the 11*th*. of the *Revelations*.

16. Thirdly, That I said I had power to damn and save: And Fourthly, that I said their beleiving the Scriptures would do them little good now.

17. Those were the chief things I was charged with. Then the Priest asked me if I would be Prisoner that Night at the Constables House, at my own charge, or at the Town charge.

18. If I had said at the Town charge, then I must have lain in the Cage all Night; but I answered and said, *At my own Charge*.

19. But I said to the Maior, Do you not take Bail in these cases? The Maior said, *Yes*: But the Priest, before the Maior had perfectly spoken, said, *if you can put in Bail that are not excommunicated Persons*.

20. Then *Dorothy Carter*, my Friend, being a Widdow, would have been Bail, with one of her Sons, and she pressed at the Door to come in, but the Priest thrust her out, and said, *She was an excommunicated Person, neither should the Maior accept of her*.

21. And I had never a Friend more in that Town, but one *Edward Fewterer*, but he was not in the way at that present, so could not procure Bail.

22. But was committed into the Constables Hands that Night; and as soon as ever I was committed Prisoner into his hands, to be sent to *Darby* Goale the next Morning, being Sixteen long Miles from *Chesterfield*.

23. Then the Baylies of the Town seezed upon my Horse for the Lord of the Mannor, and sent me to the Goal upon their own Horse.

24. But I was more troubled for the Horse than for myself, because my Friend *John Brante* at *London*, was ingaged for the Horse, else pay four Pounds.

25. But my Friend *Dorothy Carter*, she went to the Earle of *Newcastle*,[14] he being Lord of the Mannor; and she told him what these Baylies had done.

26. So the Earle sent for them, and was angry with them, and did reprove them, and said; *Will you take away a Man's Horse before he be Convicted and Condemn'd? I charge you*, said he, *that the Horse be put to Grass, and that no Saddle be put upon his Back, and let the Owner pay for his Meat, if he be quit, or otherwise*.

27. So it was done, according to his Command.

CHAP. X.

The Priest gave that Character of the Prophet, of a wise and sober Man the Prophet, gave the like Character on Pendor. *Of a Dispute between the Prophet, and two of the Officers of the Town and the Keeper of the Person, and the Sheriff's Men. The Prophet proves Three Records on Earth to answer the Three Records in Heaven: All this in the Goal.*

1. Now I shall speak of something of my Imprisonment in *Darby* Goal, which is as follows.

2. For all the Priest's Malice towards me, yet he could say to the Alder-

men, when I was gone, That this Man was the soberest, wisest Man of a Phanatick that ever he talked with; for he thought I had been like the Quakers.

3. This did one of the Aldermen tell me, for he was as *Nicodemas*, his Name was *Pendor;* he came to me by Night, for he had a great desire to talk with me alone, so that Night I was in the Constables House he had his desired Oppertunity.

4. And when I was Prisoner in *Darby* Goal, there came the Sheriff's Men, and Two of the Officers of the Town, and the Keeper of the Prison, to talk with me.

5. The Officers of the Town came to me, thinking themselves wise and knowing enough in the Scriptures, especially one of them, for to talke and dispute with me.

6. But the Sheriff's Men came on purpose to insnare me, if they could, so one of them, the most surly angriest Man of them, asked me, saying, *Have you taken the Oath of Allegance and Supremacy.*

7. I answered and said, *That Prophets do not use to swear:* Did you ever read in Scripture *that Kings have been subject to Prophets Words, and those Kings were happy that were obedient to the voice of Prophets.*

8. Why, said he, *are you a Prophet?*

9. Yea, said I, *that I am a Prophet.*

10. Then said he, *do you go to Church to hear our Ministers.* At that time there was a Law to persecute Men that did not come to Church, which caused him to ask that Question.

11. I answered him, and said, *That it is not the practice of Prophets to go to Church to learn of your Ministers, the Ministers ought to hear Prophets and learn of them.*

12. *For Prophets were always above Bishops and Ministers.*

13. When he heard me answer him so confidently, and with Authority as from Heaven, he said no more.

14. And when the Officers of that Town heard me answer him so positive, they were the more afraid to enter into a Dispute with me.

15. Yet one of them being more Atheistical, being of the Saduce Spirit, upon whose Wisdom and Knowledge they all depended upon; he was a moderate Man, and asked his Questiens moderately, as you shall hear.

16. Saith he, Mr. *Mugleton*, you say there is Three Commissions, or Records to be acted upon this Earth, and you say your Commission is the Commission of the Spirit, and the last: Now, saith he, if you could prove this by Scripture, I should be satisfied.

17. I answered, and said unto him, will you beleive me, if I do prove it by Scripture, here before these People.

18. Then said he, *truly, I think I shall beleive you, if you prove it by Scripture.*

19. Then the Keeper, and all the Men, were silent, and speak not a word, none but he and I.

20. Then said I, you shall not be troubled with any more Scriptures than

that in the Epistle of *John*, the 5*th*. Chapter, and such Scriptures as do allude to the same purpose; where it is said, *There is Three that bare Record in Heaven, the Father, Word, and Spirit, and these Three are one: And there are Three that bare Record on Earth, the Water, Blood, and Spirit, and these Three agree in one.*

21. Said I, here you see that there is Three Records to be upon Earth, answerable to the Three Records in Heaven; and as the Three Records in Heaven were but one God, though called Father, Word, and Spirit.

22. So likewise the Three Records on Earth, of Water, Blood, and Spirit, are said yet to agree in one, as the Scipture faith, do you beleive this?

23. He answered, and said, *he did*, and so they said all.

24. Then, said I, you see this one God in Heaven is called Father, Word, and Spirit, yet but one God; yet said to be Three that bare Record in Heaven, yet but one God.

25. Said I, how will you interpret this Scipture.

26. He answered and said, *he knew not how*, but desired me to unfold it.

27. Then said I, these Three that bare Record in Heaven, it was spoken in relation to the Three Records on Earth.

28. For this one God bearing Three Records in Heaven, would have signified but little unto Mankind, had there not been Three Records on this Earth given unto Men, to declare unto Men the Three Records in Heaven.

29. That Men might understand that one true God that is in Heaven, demonstrated by Three Titles, of Father, Word, and Spirit.

30. Which God cannot be known, but by the Three Records on Earth, and those Three Records on Earth must be acted by Men, that Men and Women may come to know that one true God in Heaven, which is distinguished by Father, Word, and Spirit, and be saved.

31. For it is Life eternal to know the true God, and he is to be known no other way, but by these Three Records on Earth, of Water, Blood, and Spirit; and these Three Records on Earth are acted by Men, *be they not*, said I. He said, *yea*.

CHAP. XI.

Shewing the Interpretations of the Two past Records on Earth, of Water and Blood, being undeniably unfolded.

1. Then, said I, will you interprit who those Men were and are, that have acted the Records of Water and Blood and Spirit upon Earth?

2. He answered and said, *No, he could not*, but desired me to interprit it.

3. Then, said I, the Interpretation is thus; the Record of Water upon the Earth it was *Moses* and the Prophets under the Law.

4. They worshiped God with divers Ceremonies of Tipes and Offerings of Bulls and Goates, and sprinkled upon the Alter their Blood, and upon the

Flesh of the Leapers, and other distempered Persons that were unclean, and much Washings and Purifyings with clear Water, was used under the Worship of the Law.

5. Which was the Record of *Moses* and the Prophets, it being set up by *Moses* and practiced by the People of the *Jews* many Generations: And this Record of *Moses* upon Earth is that Record of Water, answering and bearing Testimony to that one God the Father and Creator of all things both in Heaven and Earth.

6. This is the Interpretation of the Record of Water upon Earth, and this agreeth with the Record of God the Father in Heaven.

7. Now you must understand that the Record of Water upon Earth, it was acted by Men, as *Moses* and the Prophets, and the high Priests, in the time of the Law: They all cryed with one accord, *This is Truth.*

8. The Interpretation of the Record of the Blood upon Earth, it was Jesus Christ and his Apostles; In that Christ came to fulfil the Law, and he is said to be the end of the Law to every one that beleives, and to lay down his Life for many.

9. Now, in laying down his Life, is understood that he shed his own precious Blood: Therefore it is said, *his Soul was heavy unto Death and he power'd out his Soul unto Death; and except you eat my Flesh and drink my Blood you have no Life in you.*

10. That is, no Man hath the Assurance of eternal Life, abideing in him, except he doth truly beleive that Flesh of Christ that was Crucified upon the Cross, to be the Flesh of God.

11. That is, the Word became Flesh and dwelt amongst Men, and that Blood of Christ that was power'd out unto Death, to be the Blood of God: Except this be beleived there can be no eternal Life abideing in Man.

12. For this Blood of Christ doth purge the Conscience from dead Works, to serve the living God: So that Christ which is manifest in Flesh, as the Scripture saith, did pass through Blood.

13. And his Apostles, after he had given them a Commission, as in the Second of the *Acts*, they bare Testimony and Record on the Earth, that Jesus was the Christ.

14. And they did witness, that he shed his Blood, and was put to Death by the *Jews*, and did rise again and assend up into Heaven, in that same Body he suffered Death in.

15. For which Record of theirs they were put to Death, and their Blood was shed, and so were many Beleivers in their Commission put to Death, and passed through Blood, for bearing Record to this Jesus which they had crusified, to be the Son of God.

16. And this Record on Earth was acted by Men, who lost their Lives for their Record; therefore it is called the Record of Blood upon Earth.

17. Answerable to the Record in Heaven, in that the Word became Flesh; and Christ is that Word that bare Record in Heaven, and became Flesh, and shed his Blood: And those that bare Record unto him, their Blood was shed also.

18. So that the Blood of Christ, and the Blood of the Apostles, and the Blood of Saints, is that Record of Blood on Earth: And this Record of Blood on Earth, it was acted by Men, by Christ, his Apostles, and Saints.

19. This is the true Interpretation of the Second Record of Blood here upon Earth, is it not said I.

20. They all rejoyced, and said it was true so far, and that they never hear'd the like.

21. Now the Interpretation of the Third Record of the Spirit upon Earth: You see, said I, that there is to be Three Records upon Earth, as there is Three in Heaven: Now you see there is but Two acted upon Earth as yet, to wit, Water and Blood.

22. Now the Water Record was to witness to God the Father, the Blood Record witnessed to Christ the Son, and you see they were Men like your selves, that did bear these Records on Earth, of Water and Blood.

23. Likewise, you see, that these Two Records on Earth, they did witness to one God in Heaven: *Did they not?* said I. He answered, and said, *They did.* Yet, said I, you see they differ one from the other in point of Worship, notwithstanding they did agree to bear Record to one God in Heaven.

24. Now, said I, as these Two Records of Water and Blood were acted upon Earth by Men, so likewise must the Record of the Spirit upon Earth he acted by Men also.

25. And not as People do vainly imagiin, That the Two former Records were acted by *Moses* and the Prophets, and the High Priests, which were Men: And the Record of the Blood was acted upon this Earth by Christ and his Apostles and Saints, which were Men.

26. But you cannot conceive the Record of the Spirit upon Earth is to be acted by Men, as the other Two were: But you conceive that God doth act this Record upon Earth himself, only by inspiring his Spirit into every Mans Heart secretly giving the Knowledge of himself.

27. Two answered, and said, *Indeed this was their Beleif.*

28. But, said I, the Record of the Spirit upon Earth must be acted by Men, as the other Two were, else them Words be not true, *That there is Three that bare Record on Earth.*

29. For if God which is in Heaven doth act the Record of the Spirit himself, and Men acted the other Two, then there is but Two Records on Earth, and Four Records in Heaven.

30. When they heard this, they rejoyced, and said to the Man that disputed with me, Mr. *Benet, We think you have met with one that is two harde for you now.*

CHAP. XII.

The Interpretation of the Third Record on Earth, the Record of the Spirit, and who it is acted by.

1. Then, said I, The Record of the Spirit upon Earth must be acted by

Men, as the other Two were. Now, said I, there must be Witnesses of the Spirit upon Earth, as there was Witnesses of Water and Blood.

2. And some Men must be the chief Teachers or Commissioners, as he did *Moses* and the Prophets, Christ and the Apostles; these were chosen of God, and happy was it for those that beleived them in their time.

3. Now, said I, God chose *John Reeve* and myself by Voice of Words, to the hearing of the Ear, to be his Two last Prophets and Witnesses of the Spirit, and he gave us Understanding of his Mind in the Scriptures above all the Men in the World at this Day.

4. And this I know to be true, and many that can witness the same: I spake not this out of any Pride of Heart, but out of perfect Knowledge, for true Knowledge is never proud.

5. For I would make nothing of the greatest learned Man that is upon the Earth, if he will dispute of the Scripture in the *English Tongue*: And not persecute with a *Sword of Steel*, to overthrow him by the Scriptures, that there is but one true God in the person of a Man, who made Man in his own *Image* and likeness, as the Scriptures saith; And not Three Persons, and one God, as all Profesers of Religion do own at this Day.

6. Also we being the third Record of the Spirit upon Earth, we use no outward visible Forms of Worship, But do Worship God in Spirit, and Truth, as Christ said.

7. So that every Record on Earth, doth differ, one from another, in Point of Worship.

8. For it is not proper, for every Record, to Act one and the same thing, over and over again: And as there is a difference in the Three Titles called Three Records in Heaven, of *Father, Word, and Spirit*; Now these are Three Distinct Titles, yet but one God.

9. So it is with the Three Records on Earth, of *Water, Blood, and Spirit*: These be Three distinct Records, And Three distinct Persons; the head of these Three distinct Records. And there is Three distinct differences, in there visible Worships; yet they all Three agree in one.

10. In witnessing to that one, Jesus Christ to be the very true *God*, and *Saviour* of all those that beleive in that the Word was God, And God was that Word, And the Word became Flesh, and Dwelt among Men: He that is called the *Alpha and Omega*, the *First and the Last*; The Beginning and the End: He that was Dead and is Alive for Evermore.

11. This one God, doth all the Three Records agree, to witness unto this one God, though differing all of them in their Several dispensations, of outward Worship as aforesaid.

12. For every Record Acts his part upon this Earth, suitable to the Three Titles in Heaven; *Moses* and the Prophets, their parts in the dispensation of Water, as being under the Title of God the Father and Creatour of all things.

13. Christ and the Apostles, Acted their Commission of the Blood, under the Title of a Redeemer by his own Blood, And he was that Word made Flesh, and Dwelt among Men.

14. And now we the *Witnesses of the Spirit*, do Act a Spiritual Record on Earth, which is to Worship God in *Spirit, and Truth*, Answerable to the Title of Spirit in Heaven.

15. In Witnessing to that one *Personal God*, though Three Titles, of Father, Word, and Spirit; yet but one Personal God.

16. So that the Three Records on Earth, do agree in one, though they differ in their outward dispensations of worship as aforesaid; so that we the Witnesses do Act our part on Earth under the Title of the *Holy Spirit in Heaven*; therefore our Worship is Spiritual, and Invisible in the Heart only.

17. And now you see, I have prov'd by Scripture; that the Commission of the Spirit is now Extant upon the Earth; and Acted by Men like yourselves, even by *John Reeve, And myself*; and those that beleive our Doctrin.

18. Said I, do you beleive me now, I have prov'd by Scripture, that I am one of the Two last Prophets, and Witnesses of the Spirit or last Record on Earth.

19. He answered and said, *that he could not gain say any thing that I had spoken, but did aprove, of what I had said better than of any that ever be heard in his life, but said he could not venture his Salvation upon my Words.*

20. Then said the Sheriffs Men, and the Keeper of the Prison, *Now Mr. Benet, you have met with your Match, One that hath Answered you all things.*

21. Then said Mr. Benet, *suffer me to ask you one question more.*

22. What is that said I.

23. Why saith he; *I have been a long time of the Oppinion, that the Soul of Man is mortal and doth dye, But I cannot satisfie myself in it.*

24. I answered and said; your Oppinion was true, for the Soul of Man is Mortal and doth Dye, For nothing doth Live, but the Soul, for it is the Soul that Eats and Drinks, and Walks, and Talkes; And the Soul that Lives and Dyes, For nothing can be said to Dye but Life, for if the Body be Dead, the Soul or Life is Dead also: For the Body and Soul is all one being: And if one be Alive, both are Alive, And if one be Dead, both are Dead.

25. For both Body and Soul, came into the World together, For the Soul is begotten by Generation, as well as the Body; so that they go both Body and Soul, out of the World together; For that Life that is begot by Procuration must Dye, which all Souls are; and not by Infusion from God, but by that very Law that said Encrease and Multiply.

26. Therefore the Soul or Life of Man, and all things else, that is begotten by Generation must Dye as well as their Bodies.

27. When he heard this, He was very much taken with my answer, and seem'd very Respective to me, and so did the Sheriffs Men; they show'd themselves very Civil.

28. This dispute was upon the Sunday before the Assizes: For that began on the Monday following, a matter of Four Hours in the Afternoon, this dispute was.

CHAP. XIII.

The Prophets Arraignment. And Examin'd by the Judge: And he Required
of the Judge to take Bail, the Judge granted it: The Maior, Aldermen and
Recorder that Committed him, saw their Folly and Madness, and were as-
ham'd of themselves: How the Prophet had the Love of all the Prisoners.
Of his Printing of the whole Book of the Revelation, &c.

1. After this dispute aforesaid, upon the *Wednesday* following being the
last Day of the Assizes, I was call'd before the Bar: And when I came before
the Bar.

2. The Judge asked me, *if I would be Try'd by this Note of Examination.*

3. I answered no, and said, I thought your Honour would have excepted
of Bail for my appearance the next Assizes; For Mrs. *Carter* had delivered
the Judge a writing, to that purpose, of mine, the Day before; and the Judge,
his Name was *Terral.*

4. The Judge, answered and said; *that he would take Bail,* but had said
to her, he would see the Man: So when I asked him at the Bar to take Bail,
the Judge said, *he would;* and asked me who they were.

5. And I said, one is *Richard Sudbury;* He asked *where he Liv'd;* I said
at *Notingham;* he asked *what Trade;* I said an Iron-monger. Then *Richard*
Sudbury was call'd, and the Judge asked him, *whether he would be bound*
for my Appearance the next Assizes; He said, *he would;* then the Judge
Commanded him to be set down for one.

6. Then said the Judge; *There must be another,* then said, I, there is one
Edward Fewterer; where Liveth he, said the Judge, I said at *Chesterfield;*
what Trade, said the Judge, I said a Surgeion, then the Judge Commanded
Edward Fewterer to be called, then the Judge asked him, *whither he would*
be bound in two Hundred Pound Bond, for this Man's appearance, He said,
he would.

7. Then speak one of the Aldermen of the Town; *If it shall please your*
Honour; Mr. Fewterer *is not Capable to be his Bail; why* said the Judge;
said he, *Because he is an Excommunicated Person;* said the Judge, *What*
was he Excommunicated for; said he, *For not coming to Church.* Said the
Judge, *How long hath he been Excommunicated:* He said, *but last Sunday;*
Push, said the Judge, *that Signifies nothing, Except it was for the cause of*
Adultry; set him down to be Bail.

8. Then the Maior, Recorder, and Aldermen, all of them were Ashamed
and vexed, they could do me no further Mischeif, than Imprisonment.

9. And when I was Bail'd out of Prison, the Maior and Constable, and
the rest were afraid I would trouble them.

10. The Maior for Committing me to Prison, without any Accusers, and
denying to take Bail for me, and for not binding some over for to Prosecute
against me, which things he did not, but was in danger to pay Five Pound
a Day for false Imprisonment.

11. And the Constable, was like to suffer for Apprehending me, without
a Warrant.

12. I was Councelled to sue them at the Law; and so I would, if they had put in any Indictment against me, but they were afraid; And did nothing but let it fall.

13. So I was quit, only it put me to a great deal of Charge, but seeing they put no Indictment against me, I let is pass, and fall.

14. *Dorothy Carter*, and Mr. *Sudbury*, were great Friends in this business, both in Purss and Person; because I was taken at her House, and she brought me from *Darby Goal*, to her own House again on Horse back, which is 16 long Miles.

15. I had the Love of all the Prisoners, on that side I was put, and they said, *they thought themselves Blessed for my sake.*

16. For they were every one of them, that were with me, free'd without any punishment, only the Fees of the Prison. I was in Prison in *Darby Goal* but nine Days, but this falling out so quickly after I was Married to my Wife *Mary*, it was some greif to her, but being delivered so quickly, she was pacified the better.

17. This was a Year of great Trouble to me, both upon a Spiritual Account, as afore Written; and upon a Temporal, which I shall not mention.

18. This was in the 13*th*. year of my Commission, and in the 54 year of my Life, and in the year of the Lord 1664.

19. After this, I Wrote a Book, containing 32 sheets of Paper, Called the *Interpritation of the whole Book of the Revelations of Saint* John, the bigest volum of all the Books that were written by us.[15]

20. Also, I wrote a Letter after that to *Thomas Taylor*, a Quaker, Containing two sheets of Paper; And in the year 1665, I got them both Printed; they are yet to be seen by many.[16]

THE END OF THE THIRD PART.

THE FOURTH PART.
FROM THE YEAR 1665 TO THE YEAR 1670.

CHAP. I.

The Prophets Travels into Kent: *Of Judge* Twisden; *and of the Prophet's Letter to him. Of the increase of Beleivers,*

1. After this I travelled into *Kent*, to see my Wife's Friends, and there I had like to have been apprehended by the Judge of the Town, his Name was *Twisden*:[1] But I having intilligence of his wicked Intent, I escaped away out of his Coasts.

2. And I wrote a Letter to him, forbiding him for persecuting any Man for his Conscience: For tho' he was made a Judge of the Law in temporal Matters, yet he was not the Judge of Conscience, nor of Spiritual Matters.

3. Therefore I advised him to meddle with those Things he knows, as the Laws of the Land, and not with those Things that belongs to God, as the Conscience doth.

4. For God only is the Judge of spiritual Things, and them whom he doth chuse, least you bring your self under the Sentance of eternal Damnation: This Letter is large, but not in Print, but is yet to be seen in Writing.

5. He was netled in his Mind at it, but knew not how to help himself; so he brought the Letter in his Hand to my Wife's Mother's House, and asked her, if she thought he should be ever the worse, if he did persecute me; on purpose to insnare her, because she did not go to Church, and was under his Power; for he was the cruelest Devil to all Prophessors of Religion, that did not conform to Worship as he did, that was in all that Country: Also he would have had a Book of her, that he might have done me the more Mischief; but I charged her, before, to let him have none, nor none in that Town should let him have one.

6. Also, I told him, in the Letter, that if he would send to me at *London*, and send Money, I would let him have half a Dozen of Books, several, but without Money he should have none, for they cost a great deal of Monies Printing: But he never sent for any, but threatned my Mother, that if ever I came there any more to deceave People, as he called it, that he would do great Matters to me: So he went his way, and never came there more, as I hear'd of.

7. Now by this time there was many Men and Women that did beleive in this Commission of the Spirit; and the Doctrin of the true personal God was received by several Persons of Quality, so that many were aded to the Faith: Some I shall name.

8. *First*, One Mrs. *Feild*, who lived in *Wales*; she was counted a Lady in that Country; and one Mrs. *Sharte*, a Draper's Wife in *Cannon-street*: This *Sarah Sharte*, she sent for me several times, to speak with her, but the Messenger missed of me so oft, that she thought herself forsaken of God, that she could not speak with me.

9. For she had kept her House several years of a Weakness she had in her Body, so that she could not go forth, nor come to me herself: So she seeing none of them she sent could meet with me, she grew out of patience, and could not sleep 'till she had seen me.

10. So she desired her Husband, to go himself in the Morning betimes, before I was gon out; so he did, and he ingaged me to come to his Wife about Two of the Clock in the Afternoon, the same Day, for she had a great Desire to speak with me.

11. So at the time appointed I went, and she was glad to see me, who had desired it a long time: And when she had seen me, and had discoursed with me about spiritual and heavenly Things, concerning God, his Form, and Nature: The right Devil, his Form and Nature: The Person and Nature of Angels: The Place and Nature of Hell: The Place and Nature of Heaven: The Rice of the Two Seeds, and of the Fall of *Adam*.

12. And how every Man came to have two Voices; or Motions, speaking

in Man: These were all heavenly Secrets, and hiden from the World, which I declared unto her, so that she was very well satisfyed in her Mind; and she desired that I would come often to her, which I did always when she sent for me, not else: And she was a true Beleiver afterwards, and lived in the full Assurance of her eternal Happiness after Death, all the Days of her Life.

13. And she had a Kinswoman, a Virgin, that waited upon her, by reading of the Books her Aunt had of mine by stelth; she became a true Beleiver, her Name was *Ann Loe*; and in process of time this *Ann Loe* married one *William Hall*, a true Beleiver of this Commission of the Spirit.

14. And she did grow in Wisdom and Knowledge, in spiritual and heavenly Knowledge and Experience, and strong in Faith, more than her Aunt before her; and she was a great preserver of me, from the Hands of my Enemies, when the King's Messengers sought after me; as will more appear hereafter.

CHAP. II.

Of one Captain Wildye, *an honourable Man: And of one Mrs.* Cowlye, *of her Faith, and Obedience of her Husband, and of her Son, a University Scholar; and of his Convincement by the Prophet, both as to the Ministry, Law, and Phisick.*

1. Also there was one Captain *Wildye*, he was one of the Masters of *Trinity-House*, an honourable Place: For that *Trinity-House* is a Court for the ordering of Shiping, and Seamen: This Captain *Wildye* became a very true Beleiver of this Commission of the Spirit, and he shewed a great deal of Charity to several poor Beleivers of this Faith, more than any perticular Person in his time.

2. Also he was the occasion of bringing to this Faith one *Ann Cowlye*, a Gentlewoman at *Mile-End-Green*. She was carried through several Principles of Religion, as *Independant, Quaker*, and *Virgin-Life-People*: She was zealous in all things she clave unto, being very desirous to be saved, and afraid to be damn'd.

3. She was in the Principle of a *Virgin-Life*, and would not let her Husband know her in Twelve years before she saw me, notwithstanding she had born several Children by this Man, and had one Son and one Daughter living by him.

4. But after she came to be acquainted with me, I convinced her both by Scripture and Reason, of the unlawfullness of a married Wife, to live a *Virgin-Life*, and that she could not possibly have Peace as to another Life in that Practice: And I advised her to give herself up to her Husband, else I could not give Judgment of Blessedness upon her to Eternity.

5. She being troubled at this saying of mine, was forced to yield to her Husband, which thing, she thought an Angel from Heaven could not have perswaded her to do.

6. But the Words of a Prophet was of great Power, whose Word she could not resist, but obeyed his Voice, and had Peace of Minde, and the Blessing of eternal Life in her Self; and she grew very zealous for the Commission of the Spirit, and contended for the Faith very much; and this thing wrought upon her by the Word of a Prophet.

7. This caused her Husband to beleive also; and he was a very Wise and Prudent Man of the *Independant* People, who had been a Preacher among them; he became a very knowing Man in the Faith, also his Son and his Daughter became both true Beleivers of this Commission of the Spirit.

8. His son, *John Cowlye*[2] was well bread, he was brought up at the University of *Cambridge*, his Learning cost his Father many hundred Pounds, and when he was to receave some Benefit or Livelyhood for the future, for all the cost past, the Benefice was, to be ordain'd a Minister, or a Doctor of Phisick, or Lawyer: These Three be the most honourable Things in the World.

9. But when he came to speak with me I convinced him of the Unlawfullness of all the Three, for any Saint, or Gods Elect to undertake that Practice.

10. The Seed of the Serpent were the fitest Men to take them Practices upon them, because all the Kingdoms of this World is given into the Hands of the Seed of the Serpent, as the Devil said to Christ.

11. And these Three sorts of Men are reputed by the Seed of the Serpent, the most honourable Men of all, and are reverenced and subjected unto, both by Princes and common People, yet the greatest Cheats that is in this World, as will appear.

12. First, I shewed him how dangerous a thing it was to take upon him to be a Minister of Christ, without a Commission from God, it would be counted by him spiritual High Treason: For Ministers are in more Danger of eternal Damnation than any other Men, for going to Preach, and are not sent of God.

13. For when they shall say in the Conscience at that Day, *Lord, we have preached in thy Name, and prayed in thy Name, and cast out Devils in thy Name.*

14. The Answer of God in the Conscience, will say, *Depart from me you workers of Iniquity, I know you not*: And why did not God know them, because he did not send them. So that preaching and praying as a Minister, without a Commission from Christ, is counted but a Work of Iniquity.

15. And as for the Doctors of Phisick, they are the greatest Cheats, upon a natural Account, that is in the World: They cheat the People of their Money, and of their Health; for they are in the original, but atheistical Witches; and it would be good if there were never a Doctor of Phisick in the World, People would live longer, and live better in Health.

16. For God never appointed any Doctor of Phisick, but he appointed Nature to preserve Nature.

17. But through the wicked intemperate Life of Man it hath brought a necessity of Doctors of Phisick.

18. But those People that go to a Doctor of Phisick to get Health, he goeth to a Witch to seek his Health, even as a Man that is troubled in Mind seeketh unto a Witch that hath a Familier Spirit for satisfaction, as did King Saul.

19. But when the Conscience of the Doctor of Phisick shall be opened at the last Day, he shall say, *Lord, we did not think that there were any God at all, but Nature only; therefore our Minds fed upon Gold and Silver that groweth in the Earth, that we might Cloath our selves in rich Apparel, that might make us honourable among great Men of the Earth, and reverenced by the Poor; not thinking, in the least, that there was any better Heaven hereafter, or any Punishment after Death for practiseing this Cheat, that is Autherised by the Powers of the Nations.*

20. *And tho' we have done a great deal of Hurt, yet, Lord, we have done some good; we have cast out many Devils in Drunkards and Whoremasters, and Whores, who by their Wickedness have procured that Pox which no righteous Man could cure; we have made them leave off that Practice by our Medicines and Advice, and from Drunkenness, and have lived a sober Life afterwards, and many divilish Diseases have we cast out by our Spirits of Witchcraft, which we have given them to drink.*

21. But the Answer in the Conscience will say, *Inasmuch as you forsake me, the living God and creator of all things, and said, in your Hearts, There is no God, then you gave your selves up to natural Witchcraft, diving into the nature of the Planits and Stars, and into the Spirit of the Herbs of the Field, so that you became absolute Witches your selves, and you have caused Thousands of Men and Women to be bewitched by you, both in their Bodies, Souls and Estates.*

22. *Therefore depart from me you atheistical workers of Iniquity, into utter Darkness, where is weeping and knashing of Teeth for evermore.*

23. And as for the Lawyers, they keep the Keys of the Knowledge of the Law, and will neither enter into Truth and Honesty themselves, nor suffer others to enter in that would.

24. For no Man can do anything in his own Cause, but as his Lawyer instructs him; for he is sworn when he enters into that Practice, he hath a Commission to keep the knowledge of the Law from his Clyant, so that the Clyant being ignorant how to proceed in Law, Step by Step, the innocent Clyant his Clause is many times put off and neglected by his Lawyer, to the great Discontent and further Charge of the innocent and just Cause.

25. And as for the Poor, they can have no Law at all, tho his Cause be ever so just, no Judge will hear him, nor no Lawyer will give him any Councel, except he hath Monies in his Hand; nor no Judge will do the Poor any Justice, except he go in the way of the Law, and that the Poor cannot do.

26. So that if the Birthright of the Poor be ever so great, or just, it must be lost, for want of Monies to fee Lawyers; Besides, where Monies is to be had, let a Man's Cause be never so unjust, yet Lawyers will undertake it, though they know certainly that their Clyant will be overthrown, before

they took it in hand: This is Wickedness in a high degree, so contrary to the Law writen in Man's Heart. *To do as he would be done unto.*

27. But the Government of this World hath brought a necessity of the use of Lawyers; but it is not expedient that any Saint should take that Practice upon them, there is enough of them in the World, it being the Devil's Kingdom.

28. But when the Book of Conscience, the Law writen in the Lawyer's Heart, is opened, at the last Day, what can they plead for themselves.

29. They will say, *Lord, we thought, because it was the Government of the Nation, and that learning of the Knowledge of the Law it made us rich and honourable among Men; it made us Companions for the wise and great Men of the World; the Knowledge of the Law, it made us Atornies, Councellors and Sarjants at Law; honourable Places, and by degrees we came to be Judges of the Land.*

30. *So that Kings and Princes have asked Councel at our Lips, we have Cloathed our selves with fine Scarlet and white Robes, signifying Justice and Mercy to the People: We have been as Gods upon the Earth, and we have done justice to some in all our Degrees, tho we have failed in others, therefore hope for Mercy.*

31. But the Answer in the Conscience will say, *In as much as you have fed upon Riches and Honour all your Days, and have not walked by the Law written in your Hearts, To do as you would have been done unto, had you been in their Condition, and they in yours; but you have the Penny of this World, Riches and Honour, your Hearts Delight: Therefore depart you wicked Lawyers, workers of Iniquity, into utter Darkness, where is weeping and gnashing of Teeth for ever more.*

32. This I know will come to pass in these Three sorts of Men, in that Day when God shall raise the Dead.

33. When the young Man heard these Things, he left all Preferment that way, for Truths sake, and became a stedfast and true Beleiver, and he being a Scholar was mighty able to oppose the Learned.

34. Also there was one *Robert Phare*, he was Governor of the City of *Corke* in *Ireland*, he was inclineable to be a *Quaker*; but after he saw me, and had read our Writings, he became a true Beleiver of this Commission of the Spirit, and so did the Lady his Wife: She became the chief Champion in this Faith of all the Women in that Nation.

35. Also he had Four Sons and Daughters that were true Beleivers: He was the cause of many Persons of Value in that Kingdom of *Ireland*, that did truly Beleive, as one Captain *Moss* and his Wife, and Doctor *Moss*, his Son; and Captain *Gaill*, and Major *Denson*, and *George Gamble*, and Mr. *Rogers*, Merchant. And several more, which I omit to name, because it would be too tedious, that were true Beleievers in that Kingdom of *Ireland*.

36. After this it came to pass that I wrote a Book in answer to *George Fox*, Quaker;[3] containing Twelve sheets and a half of Paper, and got it Printed in the Year 1668 and in the Seventeenth year of my Commission, and in the year of my Life 58.

37. This Book caused the *Quakers* to be exceedingly angry at me, and several Speakers of them to write cursed Letters unto me, and some of them came to discourse with me, and a woful Ephect did befal some of them a little while after, as is expressed in the Writing following.

The Coppy of *Thomas Loe*,[4] a Quaker's Letter,
Dated *London* 16*th*. of the 7*th*. Month 1668.

Lodowick Muggleton, *having seen some of thy Writings, more especially thy Book Intituled* A Lookinglass, *which I have looked in, and do clearly see thy wicked, abominable, and anti-christian Spirit; and can do no less than cry, Oh! thou Blasphemer, thou Enemy of God, and of all Righteousness; thou Son of Perdition and Child of the Devil, how hast thou Laboured to pervert the right Way of God, in speaking of the blessed Truth.*

And, Oh! thou Seed of the Serpent, and old Sorcerer, how hast thou belyed, slandered, wickedly and falsly accused and condemned the just? And now, be it known unto thee, That thy false Judgment, and wicked Envy, both in speaking and writing against the Servants of the living God, is returned back upon thy own Head; and thee, with it, will God in his Fury and Indignation sink in the Pit of Darkness, from whence it hath risen: And in the great and mighty Power of God and Christ, I Reprove, Judge, and Condemn thee, which shall stand upon thy Head; and thy Power, thou boasteth so of shall not reverse it: Oh! ignorant Sot, how canst thou consider thy Blasphemies, and not be ashamed This is a Testimony in the Power and Spirit of God, against thee, and all thy Wickedness, by a Servant of Jesus Christ, who am a Witness of the Spirit and Power of God, with many others.

CHAP. III.

The Prophets Answer to Thomas Loe's *Letter: His Sentance, with the Ephects of it. The Prophet's Dispute with* George Whitehead *and* Josiah Cole:[5] *With his Sentance passed upon them both.*

1. Who ever may read this Letter, let them understand thus much, that I never saw the Man, nor he me; but he reading the Book aforesaid, he was moved by the Light within him to send this cursed Letter unto me: Whereupon, after I had read it, I sent him an Answer to it, with the Sentance of eternale Damnation for his cursed Blasphemy. The Bearer staid for it 'till it was writen, he being a Quaker, would not go without it.

2. But it came to pass that the same Night that this *Thomas Loe* received his Sentance, in answer to his cursed Letter, he went to Bed sick, and never did rise more till he was carried to the Grave, which was almost Three Weeks after. Which is a clear Testimony that the Curse of God, the Man Christ Jesus, by his Messenger doth take hold of the Quakers People, and more especially of their Ministry.

3. Because they are the absolute Spirit of Antichrist in this last Age, which

teacheth the People to deny both Father and Son to become Flesh, and that the Father, nor the Son hath no Person of his own distinct from Man, but denyeth a personal God in form like Man, his own Image.

4. For which Cause hath the Wrath of this God overtaken several of these desperate Quakers, even of their Ministers or Preachers hath been cut off this Earth, that they might not deceive People no more, nor incumber the Earth with their wicked Antichristian Spirit, which defieth the living God, who is in the form of Man, who made Man in his own Image.

Lodowick Muggleton.

5. Upon the Sickness and Death of this *Thomas Loe*, Quaker, after the Sentance sent him, it caused several to discourse with me about it, therefore I shall relate some of the most remarkable Passages, and the Persons I discoursed with upon the 17th. Day of *October* 1668. The Persons discoursed withal were *George Whitehead* and *Josiah Cole*, both Speakers of the Quakers.

6. First, the Words *Cole* spoke unto me are these (saith he) *Thou sayest God is in form of a Man, and thou sayest his Hand is not much biger than thine or mine, and thou seest what a little this Hand will hold: Yet* (saith he) *God is said to have measured the Waters in the hollow of his Hand, and behold the Nations are as a drop of a Bucket.*

7. I answered, and said, *Do you beleive God to be so big to hold the Waters in the hollow of his Hand?* This is spoken in Relation to his great Wisdom, Power, and Dominion, as he is a Creator, not relating to the bigness of his Hand, but to the greatness of his Power, being infinite.

8. An earthly King may be said to be King of many Kingdoms, and that he hath brought the People of those Kingdoms to Obedience to his Law: By the strength of his own Arm, for Power, or Strength is the right Hand of an earthly King.

9. Yet the King doth not hold all the People under his Arm, nor in the hollow of his Hand, but People may be said to be under his Hand, and that he holds them in the hollow of his Hand, because his Power and Laws doth protect them, and keep them within Bounds, for a prerogative Power is great, but the Hand of a King is no biger than the Hand of another Man, that hath no Power at all.

10. So it is Gods prerogative Power that is above all Law, in seting Bounds to the Waters, and keeping the Waters within Bounds in the deep Places of the Earth; and so may be said, that God doth hold the Waters in the hollow of his Hand, that is, they are confined to a little place of his Power in his Creation.

11. Also I said, that I that am but a mortal Man hath Power over such a great God whose Hand is so big; for that God, whose Hand is much biger than thine or mine, I have Power to Condemn. This was passed by, and no Reply made by them.

12. Then spake *Whitehead*, and said, He did hear that I had cursed a Man, and he changing his Aparel, came afterwards and did procure a Bless-

ing, and that this Man, or some other, did smite a Pewter Pot upon my Head.

13. This, I said, was false, for never did any Man strike me over the Head with a Pot, in all *my Life*; it was that reprobate *Pope*, that damd'd Devil, *that hath* reported that he was Blessed after he was Cursed: It is a false Report, and he hath reported it several times amongst the Ranters and Quakers,

14. This *Pope* was a Ranter then, when he was Cursed, which was about fifteen Years ago, in *John Reeve's* time, and he is a worse Ranter now than he was then, and that you Quakers know very well, and what a wicked lustful Life he liveth now in, and yet you will rather beleieve the damn'd Devil, and wicked lustful Person than beleive me, who have been kept innocent from the breach of any Law, from my Childhood to this Day.

15. But I know, you Quakers, being of the same Nature and Seed of the Serpent, as those Jews were in Christ's time, who desired of *Pilate*, that a Thief and a Murtherer should be delivered from Death rather than Jesus, the Saviour of all them that beleive in him.

16. So is it with you for you had rather beleive this *Pope*, this notable Sinner, than to beleive me, who am the Prophet of the most High God, the Man Christ Jesus in Glory, and have Power given of God, as *Moses* had, to set Life and Death before you; but I know you do say in your Hearts, tho not with your Lips, as those Jews did by Christ, *Away with this* Muggleton, *let us have* Pope, *that wicked lustful Man, that we might hear and inquire of him.*

17. Then said *Josiah Cole, Thou saist thou art an Embassador in God's steed, and thou standest in his stead*; said he, *I would willingly do anything that I might be saved.*

18. Then I answered him, and said, *I will tell thee what I will say unto thee, if thou wilt but deny, and forsake the Quakers Principles, and beleive me, I will assure thee thou shalt as certainly be saved as ever any Prophet or Apostle ever was.*

19. Then *Cole* fell into a Fit, and waited upon his own Thoughts, what to answer, and I waited for his Answer.

20. But *George Whitehead* perceived that *Cole* was in a strait, he came unto me, and spied a Knot of Ribon upon my Coat Sleeve, and said unto me, *Why dost thou wear this Vanity*, and touched the Ribon with his Fingers.

21. I answered and said, *I know a piece of Ribon is a great Sin in a Quaker's Eye*; But, said I, *Why dost thou wear silk Buttons on both thy Coats?* He said, *they were necessary.* I said, *No, thou mightest wear Hooks and Eyes, Clapses or Eyletholes*: That was past by.

22. But then I will tell thee why I do wear Ribon, it is on purpose that I might not be taken, or thought to be a Quaker, for I do hate the Quakers Principle.

23. With that *Whitehead* said, *Thou hatest all Righteousness*; and spake as if he himself, *Cole* and *Fox*, and others of the Quakers were writing a

Book against me, to make me manifest, which in a little time after it was set forth by *William Pen*, a Quaker:[6] And further said, *that they would post me up*, and he slighted my Power and my God, and said, *he would trample my God and my Power under his Feet as Dirt*, and taped his Foot upon the Ground.

24. Whereupon I did pronounce *George Whitehead* cursed and damn'd Soul and Body, to Eternity, and that God within him, which he trusted in, was cursed also; and so I ceased Discourse with him.

25. All this while *Cole* was in his Fit, and said not one word, but immediately after he uttered these words, saith he, *I have heard of several thou hast cursed*; but said he, *I did not beleieve, had I not heard or seen, I could not have beleived that a Man could have spoken so presumptiously.*

26. Then said I, *I dare you say that I speak presumptiously*, to *George Whitehead*; he said, *he did beleive it was Presumption.*

27. Then said I, on the contrary, *I do beleive that thou art the Seed of the Serpent and wilt be damn'd; and now see whose Faith will be strongest, yours or mine; for my Faith shall keep you down for ever.*

28. *Under what?* said *Cole.*

29. *Under eternal Damnation*, said I.

30. Then said he, *Doth thou ground thy Sentance upon my Belief?*

31. *Yea*, said I, *I do*, for you beleive I speak presumptiously, and I do beleive you to be the Seed of the Serpent, and will be damn'd to eternity.

32. Then said he, *Dost thou judge this to be a final Sentance upon me?* said I, *Yea, what should it else be?*

33. With that *Josiah Cole* rose up with great zeal for his God within him, and said, *I told thee before that I would try thee and thy God*, saying that they were seting forth a Writing against me, and withal *Cole* pronounced many Curses upon me, with his Eyes dazled with the Witchcraft Power in him, being disturbed with my Words, it got up into his Head.

34. So that *Whitehead* and he both came near me with great Threatnings and Judgments upon me, being both so full of Curses: *Cole* cursed me into utter Darkness, Pit of Darkness, Chains of Darkness, blackness of Darkness; and that he would trample that God of mine, that was in the form of Man, under his Feet, as Dirt, and stamp'd his Foot upon the Ground, as the other Devil did: *Cole's* Curses were much what like *Thomas Loe*, his Curses in his Letter to me.

35. But when *Cole* had done cursing, I said these Words unto him, *That this Sentance that I had passed upon him should stick by him for ever, and that he should never put it out of his Mind, neither should he grow Mad nor Distracted to forget it, but should be sensible all the Days of his Life.*

36. *And when my God, whom you trampled under your Feet, shall raise you again at the last Day, which will not seem to you a quarter of an Hours time, you shall remember afresh my Words, what I said unto you in this Life to eternity.*

37. Many more Words was between us at that time, but these were the

Words and Passages of most concernment at that time, and a final Judgment and Sentance of eternal Damnation that I gave that Day upon *Josiah Cole*, and *George Whitehead*, Speakers of the Quakers.

CHAP. IV.

Of Cole's *being sick unto Death immediately after the Sentence of his Testimony against the Prophet: Of his Death: The Quakers God described; with the nature of Reason, and the Law that is writen in it. Of* William Pen's *blasphemous Letter to the Prophet.*

1. Now in some Four or Five Days time after our Dispute, I heard that *Josiah Cole* was sick, and going out of the Body: For the Quakers do not beleieve that their Souls do die, but slips out of the Body.

2. This caused the Quakers People to visit him very much, to know of him, whether *Muggleton's* Words had taken place in him, wondering that he should go out of the Body so sudenly after *Muggleton's* Sentance, as *Thomas Loe* did after his Sentance. But he denyed very stifly that my Words had no Power over him, but that he had left me in Chains of Darkness.

3. Nevertheless he grew worse and worse, so that the Quakers were not satisfied except he would go to the *Peal* in St. *John's Street* at their Meetingplace,[7] and give his Testimony against *Muggleton* before the People, to satisfy the ignorant Quakers, else they would judge that his Power in *Loe* and him was greater than the Ministry of the Quakers.

4. So they led him by the Arms to the place aforesaid, and *Josiah Cole* wrote his Testimony, as followeth, exactly word for word.

For as much as I have been informed that Lodowick Muggleton *hath vaunted concerning my departure out of the Body, because of his pretended Sentance of Damnation given against me, I am mov'd to leave this Testimony concerning him behind me; namely, that he is a Son of Darkness, and Coe-worker with the Prince of the bottomless Pit, in which his Inheritance shall be for ever, and the Judgment I passed on him when present with him, stands sealed by the Spirit of the Lord, by which I then declared to him, that in the Name of that God who spans out the Heavens with his Span, and measures the Waters with the hollow of his Hand, I bind thee hear on Earth, and thou art bound in Heaven, and in the Chain under Darkness, to the judgment of the great Day thou shalt be reserved: And thy Faith and Strength thou bosteth of, I defy and trample under Foot. And I do hereby further declare the said* Lodowick *to be a false Prophet, in what he said to me at that time, who told me, that from thenceforth I should be always in fear of Damnation, which should be a Sign to me that I was damn'd; which Fear I was never in, so that his Sign given by himself did not follow his Prophecy, which sufficiently declares him to be a false Prophet.*

Josiah Cole.

5. This was given forth word for word by *Josiah Cole*, about Three Hours before his departure out of the Body, the Fifteenth of the Eleventh Month 68[9].

6. Whoever doth read this last Testimony of *Josiah Cole*, may easily see that the Curse I pronounced upon him by Commission, received from the Man Christ Jesus, the only wise God, blessed for ever, in the form of a Man, whom he dispised and trampled under his Feet as Dirt.

7. For this very Sin, did this Curse of this God pronounced by me take Ephect upon him and *Thomas Loe*, immediately after their cursed Blasphemy against the true God.

8. I was zealous in giving Sentence upon them, in that I heard the true God was trampled under their Foot as Dirt.

9. As for their Reproaches, Lyes, Slanders, and Judgments threatned against me, I did not matter: For this I know the Quakers do beleieve, that *Loe* and *Cole's* Souls is not dead, but slipt out of their Bodies, and gon you know not where, and into a Power you know not what.

10. But I said their Souls is where you laid their Bodies, they both came into this World together, they both dispised the Truth together, they, both Bodies and Souls received Judgment and Condemnation together, and both dyed together, and were both Soul, and Bodies buried together, and shall both rise again spiritual dark Bodies and Souls together.

11. Every Seed its own Body; that Seed of Reason which was their Life, which they thought was the divine Nature of God, but it was the Nature of the Devil and Serpent.

12. And the Law writen in their Hearts, which you Quakers call the Light of Christ, or Christ in you; which is no other Christ or Light but the Law writen in your Hearts. And the Light of the Law, which doth accuse and excuse the Conscience of every Man, you call the Light of Christ, yea Christ himself.

13. For this Light of the Law writen in your Hearts, is that which doth cause your Thoughts to accuse when you do evil, and to excuse when you do well: And when God shall raise them again, that Seed of Reason shall rise and bring a spiritual dark Body with it: And that Law which was writen in their Hearts here in this Life, shall quicken again in that new dark spiritual Body.

14. And then shall they and you, dispisers of a personal God, know that your own Souls, which you thought was the Life of God, but it was the Life of the Devil, and that your selves were Devils, and that Law writen in your Hearts, which you in this Life called the Light of Christ, and that was no other God or Christ but this Light within you.

15. But when this Law doth quicken again, as I said before, it will prove the only and alone Devil to torment you to eternity; because you made the Light of this Law in your Hearts to be your only God; and by this Light of the Law you do fight against the true personal God, who created Man in his own Image and Likeness, and hath trampled him under your Feet as Dirt.

16. These things may seem strange, and as a Riddle unto you, and as a thing impossible, but with God all things is possible, which his own Will moves him unto.

17. And this I say, as it was possible for God to write the Law in the Angels Natures, and by his secret Determination suffer one of these Angels to become very Man, and so the Angels Seed and Nature having conjunction with the Seed and Nature of *Eve*, which was of *Adams* Nature, and so by Generation the Law comes to be writen in every Man's Heart; in that ever Men and Woman that is born into this World is partaker of the Angel's Nature of Reason, and so comes to have this Law writen in every Man's Heart.

18. Man finds it there accusing of him, but knows not how it came writen there.

19. So it is as strange for you Quakers to beleive, that God will raise your Souls again that were dead, how they should quicken out of Death, by the Power of that God that made all Souls to live at the first: In as much as he made all things by the power of his word in the Beginning.

20. So by the same power of his word he shall quicken the Souls of Men and Women again, out of Death to Life again at the last day; and the Law that was writen in them shall quicken also, and be alive again in you, to torment you to eternity.

21. For the Law and your Souls shall never part one from the other; for as the Law is secretly writen in your Hearts, but originally in the Reprobate: So by Gods secret Decree, and Power he will revive that Law again in that Reprobate Seed of Reason, as in *Thomas Loe, Josiah Cole, George White-head, William Pen*, and many of you Speakers of the Quakers, and others of your Bretheren, who are under the Judgment and Sentance of this Commission of the Spirit: You shall find my words to be true upon you, and over you, to eternity; neither shall you be delivered from it.

22. For if I had but any thought of Compassion towards you in my Mind, it was answered me, That there is a necessity, that there should be Enmity between the Seed of the Woman and the Seed of the Serpent, which hardened my Heart against all Dispisers of a personal God in the form of Man.

Lodowick Muggleton.

23. After this, in the same year, came another thundering Letter, from a Lyon like Quaker, being a learned Man brought up at the University; his Name is *William Pen:* Here is the Copy of it *verbatim.*

Lodowick Muggleton, having had *a deep and serious Sence of thy insulting Spirit, over the Death of that valiant and painful Servant of the most high God,* Josiah Cole, *as if it were the ephect of thy solely Curse; who, alas, for these Twelve Years, hath in these Nations and Iles abroad, in all Straits, Difficulties, and hard Sufferings, been an incessant Labourer for the Lord, and so impared his Health, that within these Twelve Months, or little more, have I known him Five times sick, and Three even unto*

Death, before he had ever seen thy Face: I say being sensible of thy Vaunts. And it now being laid upon me.

Therefore once more I come in the Name, and Authority of that dreadful Majesty, which fils Heaven and Earth, to speak on this wise; Boast not, thou Enemy of God, thou Son of Perdition, and Confederate with the unclean croking Spirits reserved under Chains to eternal Darkness, for in the everlasting glorious Light thou dispisest thou art seen Araigned, Tryed, Condemned and Sentanced for a lying Spirit, and false Prophet, who having counterfited the Commission and Seal of that God whom the Heaven cannot contain, hath bewitched a few poor silly Souls: But their Blood, Oh! Muggleton, lies at thy Door, and the Wrath of the Almighty is kindled against thee, and his eternal Power in his Servants the Quakers came, whom thou hast past thy envious Curse, shall suddenly grind thee to Powder, and as formerly, so again, on the behalf of the God of the Quakers whom I worship.

I boldly challinge thee, with thy Six foot God, and all the Host of Incepherian Spirits, with all your Commissions, Curses, and Sentances, to touch or hurt me; practice your Skill and Power, behold I stand in a holy Defiance of all your Enmity and Strength: And this know, Oh Muggleton, with thy God art chained, by the Spirit of the Lord, and on you I trample in his everlasting Dominion; and to the bottomless Pit are you sentanced, from whence you came, and where the endless Worm shall knaw and torture your imaginary Soul to eternity.

Written, Signed, and Seal'd by Commission receiv'd about the First Hour of the Eleventh Morning of the Twelfth Month 1668[9]. from the glorious Majesty of the most high God, who fils Heaven and Earth, that lives in his Servant.

William Pen, junior.

CHAP. V.

The Answer of *Lodowick Muggleton* to *William Pen*, Quaker, his proud presumptious and blasphemous Letter.

1. William Pen, *I have perused your proud, presumptious, blasphemous Letter against the true God; how hath your Learning lifted up your Heart with Pride, to fight against the true God, and to bid him Defiance to his Face, and let him stand forth and see, if he can deliver himself from your bodiless God, that gave you a Commission, as you say.*

2. *You know that Reeve and myself have declared in all our Writings, that the Lord Jesus Christ is our God, and that the Worlds were made by him, and that nothing was made in the Beginning, but what was made by him, as the Scripture saith.*

3. *This Man Christ Jesus was in the form of Man, a spiritual, heavenly and glorious Body, before this World was.*

4. *And in the Beginning this glorious, spiritual Body made Man in his own Image and Likeness, the Form of Man, else Moses's Words were not true; do you disprove it if you can.*

5. *Only the Man* Adam, *his Body was earthly, and made of the Earth, but God's Body was spiritual and heavenly, yet in Form like* Adam: *And* Adam *was a Man, which none can deny that owns the Scriptures.*

6. *And in process of time this God became Flesh, and dwelt among Men, and that he took upon him the Form of a Servant, and was in all things like unto Man, Sin excepted, and made himself capable to be put to Death, by the Seed of the Serpent, his own Creatures; his Blood was poured out unto Death, for the Redemption of the Seed of* Adam, *to make good that Promise to* Adam *in Paradice,* That the Seed of the Woman should break the Serpent's Head: *Which was fulfilled when he suffered Death upon the Cross.*

7. *And when he quickened out of Death into Life again, then was that Saying fulfilled,* Oh Death, I will be thy Death, Oh Grave, I will be thy Victory: *And that other Saying,* I am Alpha and Omega, the First and the Last, he that was dead, and behold I am alive for ever more.

8. *This* Alpha *and* Omega *was Christ, and he was God; and this Christ was the Lord from Heaven, a quickening Spirit: And was there any other God, or* Alpha *and* Omega *that dyed but Christ, and did any quicken out of Death to Life again but he; and did any God become Flesh and dwell with Man but Christ.*

9. *And was not Christ in the form of Man, when on Earth did not he retain the same form when he assended up to Heaven, and doth retain the same Form now he is glorified; and is in the same Glory which he had before this World was.*

10. *Oh Pen! How is it that you cannot understand that Eternity did become Time, and Time is become Eternity again: That is, that spiritual and glorious immortal Body of God that was eternal before Man was made; but in the fulness of time this glorious immortal Body became a pure mortal Body, even Jesus Christ, capable to dye, so eternity became Time: And in that he quickened out of Death into Life again, Mortality became Immortal again, and Time became Eternity again.*

11. *This great Mistory,* That God became Flesh *is hid from the Eyes of the Seed of the Serpent, such as* William Pen *the Quaker is, and revealed unto us unlearned Men.*

12. *And this is that God that* Reeve *and* Muggleton *hath declared in our Writings, and this God we received our Commission from, and that Power to Bless and Curse to Eternity.*

13. *This God you have proudly and blasphemously defied and trampled under your Feet as Dirt; also you have boldly challenged the true and living God, that is in the form of Man, to touch or hurt you, and stand in a holy Defiance of me and my God's Strength, and that me and my God is chained, and on me and my God you trample, and to the bottomless Pit you have sentenced us both, me and my God: And if this be not high Blasphemy, Pride and Presumption against the living God, there never was any.*

14. *Oh Pen! did you never read how* Goliath *defyed the living God, the God of* Israel; *and how* David *flung a Stone into his Forehead, and slew him, for defying the living God, the God of* Israel: *For* David *knew the God of* Israel *was in the form of a Man, but* Goliath *his God was the same God as the Quakers God is, a bodiless God, so vast and so bigg*

that he cannot be confined, neither to the vast Heavens above, nor in this vast Earth below, but he must fill the Aire also, and all Places at one and the same time. This is the Heathens God, and the Quakers God also.

15. *Did you never read of Corath[8] and his Company, Captains of Rebellion and Conspiracy against Moses and Aaron, and against God that chose them to teach the People; neither would God suffer any other Men to do it but them he chose; therefore it was the Earth clave and swallowed them all up alive.*

16. *Now, you Pen, and many of you Quakers have practiced the same thing against Reeve and Muggleton, whom the God of Heaven hath chosen in perticular, and no other Man upon Earth at this Day, to set Life and Death before Men.*

17. *Now hath not you, and your Captain Teachers of the Quakers, Railed, Reviled, Reproached, and Condemned Reeve and Muggleton, and our God the Man Christ Jesus in Glory, because we had our Commission from him to open Hels Mouth, and swallow up such Rebels as you are, into those eternal Torments, where the Worm of Conscience shall never dye, nor the Fire of Hell never go out, for your dispising the living God in the form of a Man; which you Quakers have done, and are more guilty than any People in the World.*

18. *Neither are you sensible of the great Ephects that this Commission God gave to Reeve and Muggleton hath wrought: How many of your valiant Captains, and mighty Men of War have fallen by the two edged Sword of the Spirit put into my Mouth, even the Commission God put upon me.*

19. *Do not you miss many of your Captains and Leaders of the Quakers? What is become of William Smith, Samuel Hutton, Thomas Taylor, Richard Farnesworth,[9] and many more I could name here of late Years: Do you not miss Thomas Loe, and Josiah Cole? These were valiant Men, like your self, to reproach and defy the living God.*

20. *Are you not sensible how the Curse of God took hold of them sudainly after they had defyed the living God in the form of a Man.*

21. *And now, last of all, you come like Goliath the Philistian, with a Commission from a great bodiless God, that can neither be found, neither in Heaven, nor in Earth, nor no place else, signed and sealed, to defy the living God that made Man in his own Image and Likeness.*

22. *As, first, you have proudly challenged me and my six foote God, with our Commissions, to touch or hurt you. Secondly, You say you stand in a holy Defiance of all our Strength. And Thirdly, You say, Know, Oh. Muggleton with thy God art chained, and on you I trample, and to the bottomless Pit are you sentanced, where the endless Worm shall knaw and torture your Soul to eternity.*

23. *For those wicked, proud, presumptious, blasphemous Speeches, not only against me, but against the living God, as your two Brethren did before you: Therefore in obedience to my Commission from the true God, I do pronounce William Pen, Quaker, cursed and damn'd, both Soul and Body, from the presence of God, elect Men and Angels, to eternity.*

24. *I thought good to leave this upon Record, that the Age to come may be instructed, and take heed how they dispise Prophets, and that God that sent him.*

Written by Lodowick Muggleton, *one of the two last Prophets and Witnesses of the Spirit, unto the high and mighty God, the Man Christ Jesus in Glory*, March *the* 16th. 1668[9].

CHAP. VI.

Of the Prophets Travels into Cambridge, Leicester, Notingham, *and* Darbyshire, *to visit Friends there.*

1. After this it came to pass, in the Year 1669. and in the year 1670. In these two years I had a great deal of trouble, both upon a spiritual and a temporal Account, but in the beginning of the year 1669. in the Month of *April*, before my Troubles began, I had a desire to travel into several Countries to visit Friends there.

2. And there was one *James Whitehead* who lived in *Brantry* in *Essex*, a true Beleiver, and a Man of an Estate in this World; he was of the Independant People before he came to beleive in this Commission of the Spirit, he had a desire to visit Friends of this Faith in other Countries, because he had never seen them, so he was willing to bear me company.

3. I went this Jorny in secret, and let no Beleiver in *London* know of it, but my Wife only.

4. I appointed *James Whitehead* to meet me at *Ware*, and so he did, and we went from thence to *Cambridge*, and we stayed there Three Days with Friends at *William Dickinson's* House, for I had many Friends in that Town and Country about, and they were very glad to see us, and intreated us kindly.

5. So we departed after three Days from thence to *Leicestershire*, which was forty Miles from *Cambridge*, and in two days we came to some Friends in *Leicestershire*, where were several Beleivers which I had never seen before.

6. And we lodged at one *John Hall's* House, a Farmer, where was kind Entertainment, both for our selves and our Horses; and the Mother of this *John Hall* was a true Beleiver and she had three Sons that were true Beleivers of this Commission of the Spirit; but they knew nothing of my Jorny beforehand.

7. But they intreated us exceeding kindly, and was exceedingly rejoyced to see us, because they had never seen us before, though much desired; and coming upon them unawares, they having no Inteligence, it did amuse them the more.

8. Also there was one *John Sadington*, a true Beleiver, had a Sister hard by there, named *Lidiah Brooks*, that did truly beleive, and she rejoyced to see me, because she never saw me before, nor none of them there, tho they had heard of me, by the hearing of the Ear, the Towns name was *Arnsby* in *Leicestershire*.

9. We stayed there but two Days and departed, and jornyed towards *Notingham*, there we came unawares to Mr. *Sudbury's* and his Wife, and

Mary Parker, a Sheriff's Wife of that Town: There were but those three Beleivers in that Town, and they kindly received us with much affection.

10. And *James Whitehead* departed from thence in two Days, and left me there, for to meet him at *Chesterfield* in *Darbyshire*, which was twenty Miles from *Notingham*, because he was to go forty Miles further about other business, and was to call at *Chesterfield* as he came back.

11. Likewise he was to see if he could enquire in his Jorny for one *Thomas Tomkinson*, a true Beleiver, and a great Writer in the vindication of this Faith; he lived at *Sladehouse* in *Staffordshire*.

12. He did in his Jorny enquire for *Sladehouse*, and the Name of our Friend, but could not hear, neither of the place, nor of the Man, nor could not hear that any knew *Sladehouse*, or *Thomas Tomkinson*, he not travelling within twelve Miles of the place.

13. So he missed of him, which was a greet Trouble to us all when he came back to *Chesterfield*, and told it to us, we were much troubled.

14. For I did fully expect he had found him, because he stayed two Days longer than was intended.

15. But it was an exceeding great Trouble to him that he should miss of the Sight of us, being so near; and many more in that Country had an earnest Desire to see me, for I had not then ever been in that Country.

16. And when it was too late, he did hear by one *Alexander Delamaine*, a true Friend at *London*, and a great writer in vindication of this Commission of the Spirit, for as soon as ever he heard that I had stolen away out of *London* into the Country, and none in *London* knew of it; for it was above a Week afterwards before he heard I was gone, for he heard from some in the Country where we had been.

17. So he sent *Thomas Tomkinson* word by the Post, that I and my Friend were some where in those parts of the Country; so *Tomkinson* went immediately to *Bakewell*, a Market Town, where one of our Friends saw me at *Chesterfield*, his Name was *William Newcome*, a Bookseller, who lived at *Darby*, but was every *Saturday* at *Chesterfield* Market, and at *Bakewell* Market on the *Monday*.

18. And he told our Friend *Tomkinson*, that I and my Friend Mr. *Whitehead* departed from *Chesterfield* that *Monday* morning, and that he saw us take leave of Mrs. *Carter* and her Daughter, as also *Elizabeth Smith*, and other Friends at *Chesterfield*, for to go by *Notingham*, and from thence, on *Tuesday*, they said they would go for *London*, the same way they came, and call of the same Friends.

19. And when our Friend *Tomkinson* heard this, and that it was too late to meet with us, neither at *Chesterfield* nor *Notingham* neither, he was exceedingly troubled, and lift up his Voice and wept, and could not tell who to be angry with, himself, or with us.

20. So that he could not be passified in his own Mind, 'till Patience had possest his Soul, until he heard from me the Cause of that Misfortune.

21. For I depended wholy that Mr. *Whitehead* would have found him out; but it was such a cross Rode that no Letter could be sent unto him but

from *London*, except it were on purpose, so that I made no question but my Friend would have brought him along with him to *Chesterfield*, for he enquired, but could not hear of the Place nor of the Man.

22. So all Intents were frustrated, which caused trouble of Mind to us all, for no People have greater Love to one another than those of this Faith.

23. We were in this jorny, going and coming, and at Friends Houses about five Weeks.

CHAP. VII.

The Prophet's House searched for Books: The Sercher's Civility: The Prophet acknowledges their Kindness, and after sent them a Gratuity. A second search for Books, where several were taken. Of a great Rebellion that hapened upon the Prophet's Absence.

1. After this, in the same year 1669. I wrote two Books, the one of them was an Answer to Esq; *Penington*, a Quaker,[10] who wrote a Book against me: And the other Book was the Interpretation of the Witch of *Endor*,[11] and other Witches; and in the Winter I did endeavor to get them printed, and had agreed with two several Printers.

2. But it came to pass that the Answer to *Penington* was taken in the Press, through some Neglect of the Printer, when half a Sheet had been printed; but the Searcher of the Press, he being a violent Man, he made a great adoe about it, and troubled the Printer, and put him to the Charge of Seven Pounds, and me Five Pounds, to pacify the matter; But the Interpretation of the Witch of *Endor* escaped in the other Printer's Hands, and is now in Print, and giveth great Satisfaction to many in that Point.

3. After this, it came to pass, in the year 1670. before *Midsumer*, there came Fourteen Men to search my House, for unlicensed Books; these Men were informed by the Printer, but they would not connfess who sent them: There was Three or Four of the King's Messengers, and the Warden of the Stationer's Company, and Printers and Booksellers.

4. The Warden was very surly, when my Wife asked what he would have: He bid her open the Door, else he would break it open: She said, She would not, unless he would tell his Business: So he made no more adoe, pulled the Hatch, and wrenched open the Spring Lock, and came runing up Stairs so sudainly that no Door in the House could be locked.

5. And being so many of them, they ran into every Room in the House, and they came into the uper Rooms where I was, and there they seized upon Ten Poundsworth of Books, and were binding them up to carry away.

6. I said, *I hope you are civil Gentlemen, there is nothing in the Books that is against King or State, and some of them were printed before the King came into* England; *and if you will be pleased to ask what Mony you will for your Pains and Civility, I will give it you.*

7. Then said one of them, *Do you think we will be bribed?* Then said I, *Who is the chief among you, that I may appeal to him for Relief when you*

have taken them away. Said they, *here is Mr.* White, *the Warden of the* Stationers Company, *he hath the Warrant, and is chief, and he liveth in St.* John's *on* Clarkinwell-Green: Then said I, *take them away*, and I helped them to Strings to ty them fast.

8. And when they saw this, that I was so fair, and gave them goodly Words, not in the least charging them with Folly or Unrighteousness, they went from me into another Room, and whispered among themselves, and said one to another, *These Books are most of them against the Quakers, and some Printed long ago, we had best only take one a piece single; and one bound alltogether, and leave the rest till we have read them over, to see what is in them:* So they agreed thus among themselves

9. Then Mr. *White*, the Warden came to me, and said, *Mr. Muggleton, you shall see that we will be civil; we will only take one of these bound alltogether, and of each single; and let the rest be forthcoming when we shall call for them.*

10. I thanked him for his Civility: So they departed away at that time, only one of them, took one of the Books bound altogether under his Coate, more than was agreed by themselves, and it was well I escaped so: And about Four or Five Days after I sent a Letter to Mr. *White* the Warden, praising him, and the Gentlemen with him, for their Kindness and Civility; and withal I sent him Two Guinea Pieces of Gold by my Wife, to drink with the Gentlemen; and prayed him to accept of them, and if I were a Man of Ability I would have given a great deal more.

11. For civil Kindness ought to be respected, for I know you had Power to have taken them away; and that if you would be pleased to send but one of those Books bound, again by my Wife, that I might know by that you have accepted of that small Token of my Love for your civil Usage.

12. The Letter was more large, but Mr. *White* read the Letter twice, and said to my Wife. *Indeed one of the Men did take a Book under his Coat,* but said, *he shall restore it again, for it is your Husband's; and as for the Two Guinea's,* said he, *let them alone 'till you hear further from me, for it doth not ly altogether in my Power to accept of them;* So he would not receive the Two Guineas.

13. So my Wife brought them again, and I waited, expecting to hear from him, but did not; for I perceived he had turned the Power over to the King's Messengers, as I found afterwards; for I heard, by one that belongs to the Law, that saw my Name in a Warrant in the Office, to take my Person, and to bring me before the Councel of State, so he gave me Intilligence of it.

14. So I went from my own House, and lodged at a Friends House in *Waping* Three Quarters of a Year, and a Week after I was gon came the King's Messenger with his Warrant, but I being not at home, he lost his Labor: He came Three times, and saw he could do no good, he gave over coming for a long time.

15. After this, in the same year; (no sooner out of one Trouble, but into another) about the Month of *October*, a little before the Parliament sate,

there came Eight or Tenn Men of the Stationers, and other Officers to my House, to search for Books.

16. But it hapened that my Wife was newly gon out, else they would have taken away many Books, to a considerable Value; but she being not at home, went away very angry, saying they would take some other Course; but after this I took and got all the Books out of my House: By this means I prevented them from taking away any more for many years.

17. These Troubles, and many more, I went through in the year 1670. and in the year of my Life 60. And in the 19*th*. year of my Commission.

18. And while I was in these Troubles, and absent from my own House, even as a Prisoner, for Three Quarters of a year, there did arise a great Rebellion and Conspiracy amongst the Beleievers, of me, which was like the Conspiracy and Rebellion of *Corah, Dathan*, and *Abiram*, against *Moses* and *Aaron*.

19. The Heads of this Rebellion were these, *William Medgate*, the elder, Scrivner; *Thomas Burton*, a Flax Man; Mr. *Witall*, Brewer; *Walter Bohanan*, Scotchman.

20. These drew a many Beleivers to side with them for a Season: Some of these Rebels, Two of them I did excommunicate, and the other Two I gave Sentance of Damnation to eternity.

21. And gave Charge to all those that sided with them in their Conspiracy, not to Trade, nor Eate, nor Drink with those Men any more, upon the pain of being Excommunicated out of my Presence; which the People did obey, and were setled in Peace again.

22. Likewise one of these Conspirators, namely *Thomas Burton*, came and humbled himself, and acknowledged his Fault, and I forgave him, and received him into my Favour again.

23. There is the whole Relation left upon Record in Writing, in a Volume by it self:[12] Which is as followeth.

24. William Medgate, *in his Rebellion, sent unto me Nine Assertions, as he calls them, being contrary to all Truth, as he saith, and against all sober Reason, being* verbatim, *as follows.*

   1. That God taketh no Notice of his Saints, nor doth not mind them at all.
   2. That you are not to mind God at all, but by the Prophet only.
   3. You must pin your Faith upon the Prophet's Sleeve, or else you can have no true Peace.
   4. Altho the Saints give Sentance against Blasphemy, if the Party comes to the Prophet he can take it off.
   5. Altho a Man have a corrupt Nature, and defraud and deceive all Men, yet if the Prophets Love be in him, he will uphold him.
   6. Tho false Worship be an Idol, yet with the Prophet's Leave he may go to that Worship blameless.
   7. To whom the Prophet gives the Blessing it shall support him, altho his Life and Conversation be wicked.
   8. If the Prophet should disown the Commission of the Spirit, all those that beleives it should be damn'd.

9. And lastly, That after the Blessing is given to any by the Prophet, yet though they walk contrary to the Commission, yet they shall be damn'd but to the Graves Mouth.

William Medate.

CHAP. VIII.

The Three first Assertions Answered.

1. Now these Assertions seemed very strange to many of the Beleivers, as they were laid down together, but being interpreted apart, they became easy to the understanding of all, as may appear: As First, of God's taking no Notice of his Saints.

2. For if God did take Notice of all Actions, there would be a present ephect of Blessing and Cursing, as in times past; neither can either Saint or Devil prove he doth take any Notice of him at all, but as he doth vainly imagin, because his Thoughts doth sometimes accuse him, when he doth evil, and excuse him when he doth well.

3. But thus far I do acknowledge, that God doth take notice and minde particular Saints here on Earth; that is, when God hath any Work to do for a perticular Saint, or any perticular Devil, then God taketh perticular notice of Saint or Devil, if it be one or more, according to the pleasure of his Will.

4. But no Man now upon Earth, can truly say that God hath minded, or taken notice of him, but my self only: Also I do acknowledge that God doth take notice and minde every perticular Saint, and every perticular Devil, in the Original, as will appear thus.

5. God hath written the Law in every Man's Heart, both Saint and Devil, and this Law is God's Watchman, and stands in God's Place and Stead, both to acquit and condemn the Conscience of every Man; and where this Law doth acquit, God doth acquit, and where this Law doth condemn, God condemns, yet God's Person minds it not, but leaveth the whole Power to the Law, to justify or condemn; only God's Power is to be seen, and to be taken notice of, when he shall raise the Man again, and that Law in his Heart shall quicken again by Gods Power, and shall stand as God, to judge, to justify, or condemn the Conscience of every Man.

6. So that if a Man have not true Faith in his Heart to justify his Person in the sight of God, while on Earth, to free him from that Law of Sin and Death writen in his Heart, then in the Resurrection that Law writen in his Heart shall quicken again, and shall stand as God and Judge, to condemn him to eternity.

7. Therefore I may say unto you Rebels, as God did unto *Cain, If thou dost well, shalt not thou be rewarded, and if thou dost Evil Sin lyeth at the Door of thy Conscience;* for the Law said in his Heart, *Thou shalt not kill*: And shall not your Act of Rebellion ly at the Door of your Consciences, as sure as *Cain's* Murther lay at the Door of his Conscience.

8. Therefore it was that *Paul* did thank God, that he was delivered from

the Law of Sin and Death, and so doth every Man that is delivered from that Law writen in his Heart: And *John* saith, *If thy Heart condemn thee not, then hast thou Confidence to the Throne of Grace, but if thy Heart condemn thee, God is greater than thy Heart, and knoweth all things*: That is, if the Law writen in a Man's Heart do condemn a Man worthy of eternal Damnation, God is greater than this Law, and knoweth how to raise you again, and to condemn you to eternal Torments.

9. Thus in the Original, God taketh notice, and mindeth Saints and Devils here on Earth, by the Law writen in their Hearts; and if the Saints grow in Faith, Love and Knowledge of the true God, then is Conscience justified in the Sight of God, because the Prophet and Messenger of God justifies the Saints Faith to be true Faith.

10. But if the Prophet doth not justify a Man's Faith to be a true Faith, nor him to be a true Saint, neither will God do it, and that Man's Heart will condemn him also.

11. For it is a true Prophet, or true Minister that make a Saint, one or more, for a Saint cannot maketh a true Prophet, nor true Minister, but a Prophet may make a wicked Sinnor a glorious Saint, as I have done several: As Christ, he could make simple ignorant Men Apostles, but Apostles could not make him their Christ, so that no Prophet no Saint.

12. They may be elected Vessels, but not Saints, for no Man can possibly be said to be a Saint, except they come actually to beleive in a true Prophet, true Apostle, or true Minister of Christ.

13. And further, I say, whoever doth not stand in Awe, and Fear to offend that Law of Conscience, as if God himself did stand by and take notice of all his Actions, so he doth well, because God's Eye is over him, else not: I say all such a Man's Doings is but Eye Service, and respected of God no more than the cuting of a Doggs Neck, and that Man is in the depth of Darkness; but such a Man, if he doth Evil, then he desires God to take no notice of that, but to blot it out of his Remembrance; as if God were beholding to Man to do well, when as there is a Blessing in Well doing, and a Curse in Evil doing.

14. For this I say, if there were no God to reward the Good, nor punish the Evil, yet could I do no otherways than I do; for I do well, not because I expect any Reward from God, and I refrain from Evil, not for fear God should see me, or seeing me, will punish me, or that his Person doth take notice or mind me in it at all; but I do well, and refrain from Evil, to please the Law writen in my Heart, so that I might not be accused in my own Conscience, by that Law writen in my Heart, as God hath placed for a Watchman, to tell me when I do well, and when I do ill.

15. So I being justified by Faith in my own Conscience, and being not condemned by the Law writen in my Heart, I have Confidence to the Throne of Grace. Neither do I refrain from Evil, for fear God seeing me, and so to punish me, but I refrain from Evil, because the Law in my Heart seeth all my doings, and that Watchman God hath set there to watch me will tell God of all my Doings, and that Law will be the only Accuser of Conscience.

16. So that God needs not to trouble himself to watch over every Man and Woman's Actions himself, but hath placed his Law, a Watchman in every Heart, as above said.

17. Thus in the Original, God taketh Notice by his Law: Not that I do own the Law writen in Man's Heart to be the very God, as the Quakers do, but God is a distinct Person of himself, and distinct from this Law: And no other ways doth God mind or take notice, now at this time, but by this Law.

18. And to that Second Assertion, how the Saints are not to mind God at all, it is plain, and is Truth also, as by Scripture appears, how that he that receiveth a Prophet in God's Name, receiveth him that sent him: And seeing God doth not come to treat with Men himself, he sends his Prophet or Embassador in his stead, and he is impowred by him to make Peace between God and Man, upon such Articles as the Prophet and the People can agree on: And thus.

19. Whoever beleives the Prophet's Report shall be saved, and he that doth not beleive his Prophet's Report shall be damned. Therefore it is said by *Esau*, who hath beleived our Report, and to whom is the Arm of the Lord revealed. So that God hath placed the whole Power in the Prophet, to determin upon Life and Salvation, as if God was present himself, and if the People do not agree with the Prophet while he is in the way, how shall a Man make his Peace with God.

20. For God will say to such that shall think to come to him, and dispise the Prophet; If you would not receive the Prophet whom I sent, you will not receive me, if I should come my self.

21. So that God doth not expect that you should come unto him, but unto the Prophet only; neither doth he own your coming unto him; for he will say, you should have minded my Prophet, and have beleived him, and have made your Peace with him, and then I would have accepted of you; for it will be said to you as it was unto *Dives, They have* Moses *and the Prophets,* &c.

22. So it will be said to you, if you believe not my last Prophet whom I sent; he hath spoken unto you, and hath declared Life and Salvation unto you, and if you will not believe him on Earth, you will not believe if God himself should come from Heaven and speak unto you.

23. So that there is a necessity that Men should believe the Prophet only: These Things are common Practices with the Kings of the Earth: Would a King be well pleased with that Man that rejects his Embassador? For doth not an Embassador stand in the King's place, and what he doth the King doth, &c.

24. Why should you that are Men think it strange to mind the Prophet only: Were not all those People blessed that minded the Prophets only, as *Moses* and *Aaron, Elijah* and *Elisha,* and those that did not mind the Prophets only, were they not cursed.

25. So likewise whoever mindeth the Prophet now alive only, shall have true Peace with God; and whoever doth not, shall never have true Peace

with God, nor perfect Peace in his own Soul; for this is God's way, and that Honour he hath put upon Prophets for all their Sufferings, therefore it is said, *How beautiful are the Feet of such as bring glad Tidings of Peace and Salvation? And whoever receiveth a Prophet shall receive a Prophet's Reward?* Which Reward is no less than the Blessing of everlasting Life; and if so, sure such a Prophet ought to be Received while on Eath, to be minded only, seeing that he that receives him receives God; and in this Sence People ought to mind the Prophet only, and no other ways.

26. And as to the Third Assertion, my Answer is this, *I say it is impossible for any Man or Woman to have true Peace, except they do pin their Faith upon the Prophet's Sleeve.* Why? why because the Prophet represents the place of God, nay God himself; and he that doth believe a Prophet's Report, he believeth in God; for such a one resteth his Soul only upon the Prophet's Words: Now if a Prophets Words be Truth, then a Man that believes rests his Soul upon the Truth; and this is seting the Seal that he is true.

27. And so it may be said, a Man pins his Faith upon the Prophet's Sleeve, that if he be true my Faith is true, if he be false, my Faith is false also; and if he be a false Prophet, then he shall be damn'd, and he that believes him will be damn'd also.

28. For if a Man be saved by pining his Faith upon a true Prophet's Sleeve, so by pining his Faith upon a false Prophet a Man is damn'd; this must and is ventured by some: For this I say, there is no Man upon Earth, that professes the Christian Religion, but he hath either a true Faith, or a false Faith, and he pins his Faith upon either a true Minister, or a false Minister's Sleeve; and he loveth one Teacher better than another, and here he pins his Faith, and hath Peace so long as his Faith holds there.

29. But when his Faith faileth, and Pin looseneth and falleth quite out, so their Faith and that Preacher is parted, and that Peace he had in that Faith is lost, and another Faith sought after; for no Man in the World can live but by a true Faith, or a false Faith, so that all Men in the World doth or must pin their Faith upon some Mans Sleeve or other, or else there can be no Peace at all.

30. But when their Faith faileth, the Peace they had in that Faith is lost, and another Faith sought after, which Faith pitches upon the dead Letter of the Scriptures, which yields no Peace at all without an Interpretor.

31. Thus all Men in the World must and do pin their Faith upon some Man's Sleeve or other, else there can be no Peace at all to the Mind of Man; and in this sence the Saints must pin their Faith upon the Prophets Sleeve, else they can have no true Peace at all.

CHAP. IX.

The Fourth, Fifth and Sixth Assertions answered.

1. To this Fourth Assertion, I say, Who made any of you Saints, but the

Prophet only? For as I said before, no Prophet, no Saint; for though Men and Women be elected in the Seed, in God's electing Power, and may be saved by Election, yet they cannot properly be called Saints, as aforesaid, because he must first come actually to believe in a true Prophet, or true Minister of Christ; for a Saint cannot make a Prophet, but a Prophet can make a wicked Man a Saint, as I have done several.

2. Furthermore, who gave any Saint, in these our Days, power to give Sentance upon any Man for Blasphemy, was it not the Prophet now alive.

3. God gave the Saints no such Power, neither did *John Reeve* give any such Power to any Saint all his Days of his Life, neither did any Saint give Sentance upon any all his Days.

4. Now seeing the Saints receive their Power to give Sentance for Blasphemy, from the Prophet now alive, and not from God; sure then there is a Power in that Prophet to take off that Sentance that any Saint shall give, in case the Party so sentanced comes unto the Prophet, and the Prophet decerns him capable of true Sorrow for his rash Speeches, the Prophet can take off that Sentance that any Saint hath given, and shall have perphect peace of Mind, as if no Sentance at all had been passed upon him.

5. There hath been an Example of this both in *John Reeve's* time, and since; for it came to pass that *John Reeve* had passed the Sentance upon a Man for writing blasphemous Words upon the Marjant of the Commission Book, and when the Man read the Sentance he was exceedingly troubled all that Night, so that no Rest could be found: So that he came in the Morning, with the Sentance in his Hand, and besought us with Tears, upon his Knees, to take this Writing again, for, said he, *I have done foolishly, and spoken rashly before he had considered;* with several other Words of Repentance.

6. So *John Reeve*, seeing his Sorrow for this Sin, he took the Writing from the Man again; and the Man was setled in Peace of Mind, as at first.

7. Now if the Prophet *Reeve* had Power to take off his own Sentance for Blasphemy, then much more can he take off the Sentance that any Saint shall give against Blasphemy.

8. Another Example since it, was so; That *Claxton* gave Sentance of Damnation upon Mrs. *Masson;* and he was, at that time, as knowing a Saint counted by the Beleivers, as ever any of you were; yet when her Husband caused her to apply her self unto the Prophet: I understanding the Cause, I took off that Sentance he had given her; and not only so, but for that and other Things, I took away his Power also, so that no Sentance of his afterwards should be of any Value to any Man.

9. So that Prophets have a prerogative Power, as God, above the Power of Saints; because the Power of a Saint is at the second hand, subordinate to the Power of a Prophet; and therefore a Prophet hath power to take off that Sentance, where and on whom he pleaseth, &c.

10. And as to the Answer of the Fifth Assertion, this I say, Who should uphold a corrupt natured Man but a Prophet, in case a corrupt natured Man do beleive the Prophet, then the Prophet's Faith shall uphold him from the Sensure and Judgments of those that looks upon their own Natures to be

more pure and uncorrupt, as to his Happiness in the Life to come, the Prophets Love being in him, he will uphold him.

11. And whereas you say, *defraud and deceive all Men*, to this I say, I do not uphold no Man to defraud nor deceive any Man; it was always contrary to my Nature to uphold any such Practice in any Saint or Devil, because I never did practice any such Things my self; not in the Days of my Ignorance.

12. But in case some Mens Natures are so corrupt, as to practice such Things, and yet are true Believers, what shall the Prophet do with such Men, shall he cast them out of the Kingdom of Heaven for ever, because his Nature is corrupt, surely no? For this was not the Practice of Christ when on Earth: But this I do allow and tollerate every Saint, that if they cannot freely forgive the Defraud and Deceivings of such natured Men, they may take the Law of them: The Law is open to Right him self that is deceived, or else let them trust such Men no more.

13. But this I say, I think you Fault Finders are the least defrauded, or deceived by those corrupt natured Men of any: Prophets cannot give Men honest Hearts, that are not honest by nature; and if they be honest by nature, Prophets cannot give them Mony to uphold their Honesty.

14. Neither can a Prophet change corrupt Natures, for if the Prophet could I would have changed yours, and have made you more Merciful to forgive the Trespass of your Brother of your own Faith, and not to rake up the Sins of others, and lay them as a Charge against the Prophet, as if he were the cause of their Defraud and Deceit, because I uphold them in Peace of Mind, concerning the Life to come, my Faith being in him it shall uphold him, so that the fear of eternal Death shall not surprize him.

15. Also, if I could have changed your corrupt Nature, I would never have suffered it to have broken forth into Rebellion, as it hath done, but would have upheld you in peace of Mind, and Hope of eternal Life, notwithstanding your Nature is corrupt enough; yet while my Love was in you I did uphold you in Peace of Mind, but now my Love is taken from you, through your Rebellion, your Peace, Hope, and Assurance, will weather and dye in you: And in this Sence will he uphold corrupt natured Men if his Love be in him.

16. The Sixth Assertion answered, which saith, *Tho' false Worship be an Idol, yet with the Prophets Leave he may go to that Worship blameless*: As to this, I never did forbid any Believer of this Commission of the Spirit from going to Church, neither did *John Reeve* in his time, they all went to Church, or to Meetings; *John Reeve*, nor I never laid any Injunction upon any Believer, not to go to Church.

17. But since I wrote the Book of the whole Revelation, I had occasion to write concerning Worship, and the Believers reading of it, their Eyes were opened to see it was Idolatry to worship as the Nation doth, so that many of them refrained from it, and they found much Peace in it; but some could not refrain, because of Persecution; but those that did refrain had much Peace in themselves, and were better beloved with me, than the other which

did go to Church: So that they that did go to Worship, they had Shame and Trouble, and Doubting in themselves; and I let them bear their own Sin, and never reproved them for it.

18. And because I did not advise, nor command them to the contrary, they were the more incouraged; but had not that Peace in themselves as those had that did refrain, not because of my Dislike, but because of their own Peace of Conscience: But having no Command from us to the contrary, some few took leave, that were in high Places, which could no ways uphold their Honour and Livelyhood, except they went sometimes to Church.

19. Now those not being forbid by the Prophet, they were not disobedient to the Prophet, nor to God, but to their own Souls, they brought Guilt upon their Conscience and Fear upon their Mind; yet by the Prophets winking at them as God did the Days of old at there Ignorance, and not accuseing them of Evil, but continueing his Love in them; the Prophet Remembring their former Faith and Love to *John Reeve*: They are blameless as to the fear of Eternal Damnation, and why, because the Prophet did never forbid them, nor never did Condemn them for any thing they had done in that Nature.

20. And in this Sence they are blameless of the Prophet and blameless of God, for a Prophets Power is unlimited as God's Power is: None is to call a Prophet to an Account but God only, for if the Prophet will Wink at the faileings of some upon consideration of the Snares great Men are in, and of other good they do, and the Prophet will not Wink at others that are not under such Snars of this World, nor can do no Good to others of their own Faith, who shall againsay it, none but Rebels.

21. They will undertake to be more Righteous then the Prophet, they would make all the Lords People Holy, if they were in the Prophets place, by Reproving and Exhorting and Judging the People, some for going to worship an Idol, and others for defraud and deceit, but if we were in his place, we would give Righteous Judgment upon all according to demerit, without respect of persons, this is *Corath, Dathan*, and *Abiram* like, the practise of Rebels.

22. And in this Sence those that go to worship an Idol may be said to be blameless of the Prophet, and no other ways.

CHAP. X.

The Seventh, Eighth, and Ninth Assertions Answered.

1. How should Men that do Evil after the Blessing is given be supported, if the Prophet should not support him, suppose some that are under the Blessing may borrow Mony of his Brethren of the same Faith, and never pay them again, others perhaps are passionate, hasty natured, which wounds their own Souls, others may sometimes be drunk, others of a hasty wrathful Nature as you are.

2. Those things are all Evil, the one as well as the other, and perhaps

some of this Faith to whom the Prophet hath given the blessing are guilty of those things; now to whom shall they apply them selves too, to be supported; in the trouble of his Mind he hath borrowed Mony, but cannot pay it again, so his Credit is lost, he can borrow no more there, neither will he forgive him freely, but looks upon him, though he be of his own Faith, but a paltry deceitful Man, and will have no more Dealing with him: This is Punishment enough where an honest Heart is.

3. And where shall such a Man be supported but by the Prophet, for his Brethren will not support him, and the World Condemns him for a base Cheat, and his own Conscience Condemns him and makes him ashamed and where shall he go; he cannot go to God for Relief, but to a Man like him self, a Prophet.

4. And to this Prophet he can appeal unto, and be supported under his Blessing he once gave him, for a Prophets Word is as the Word of God him self, in case the Mans Faith be in it: For who hath need of Support but such, for legal Righteous Men need no Support, neither of God nor of the Prophet; for it hath a Blessing in it self, in the very deed doing.

5. Therefore it is said that Christ did Justify the Ungodly but not the legal Righteous Man, but rather Condemn him, as the Proud *Pharise*, who bosted of his Righteousness, *and did thank God that he was not like the* Publican *who deceiv'd all Men he delt with.*

6. And in this Sence it may be said, that the Prophet doth uphold a Man, though his Life and Conversation be counted Wicked by Rebels, yet his Faith being stedfast shall be upholden by the Prophet.

7. As to the Eighth Assertion, my Answer is, suppose Christ when he was taken and carried before *Pilate*, and when he was examined by him whether he was the Christ, the King of the *Jews*, if Christ for fear of Death should have denyed, and said, *No, I am not the Son of God*, &c. If this should have been said by Christ, then he would have prov'd a False Christ, and his Faith, a False Faith.

8. And so, those that Believed him, their Faith would be False and vain, and the assurance of Eternal Life in them would have perished, for a False Christ will be Damn'd, then all that Believe in that False Christ will be Damn'd also.

9. For it is by Faith that Men are saved; now if a Man's Faith be pitched upon the true Christ, and hold out to the end, he shall be saved, because the Christ he Believed in shall be saved.

10. But if a Man have faith in the true Christ for a while, and afterwards his Faith whither and grow coul'd, and not hold out, this Man may perish to Eternity, yet the Christ saved.

11. Furthermore if the Prophet now alive should disown the Commission of the Spirit; that is, if he should deny and disown that God spoke to *John Reeve*, and that God did not Chuse us two Joyntly to be his Two last Prophets that God will ever send to the end of the World, now if it were possible the Prophet should disown this, but it is not possible, which way then can those that have believed in us possibly be saved, but must be Damn'd.

12. For a False Prophet will be Damn'd: And again, if a true Faith Justify a Man, being pitched upon a true Prophet, then a False Faith pitched upon a False Prophet, it whithers and dies, and Condemns the Heart of Man.

13. If it should be objected, that we believe *John Reeve*, that God spake to him, and we believe his Writings, and that he Dyed in that Faith: But if the Prophet now alive should disown *John Reeve*, that God spake to him, &c. yet we shall be sav'd, by believing in *John Reeve's* Writings now he is Dead.

14. This is just like the Faith of all the World that believeth the Prophets and Apostels that are Dead, many hundred Years before they where Born, but would not have believed them when they where alive: No more then their Fathers did: For it is the Nature of Reason to believe dead Prophets rather then living Prophets, and it is the Nature of Faith to believe live Prophets rather then dead Prophets, for a living Faith believeth a living Man, but a dead Faith believeth a dead Man, and thus the Seed of reason dealeth by me.

15. But to this I say, this Faith will not save you, nor do you little good in the Day of Trouble, why, because God did not chuse *John Reeve* Singuler, but God chose us two Joyntly, so that there could be no seperation but by Death, and seeing God hath Honoured me to be the longer Liver, he hath given me a double Power, as he did to the Prophet *Elisha* when *Ely's* Mantle fell upon him.

16. So that God hath seated and established the Commission wholy upon me, so that the Prophet now alive doth stand in God's place, and doth Represent his Person to make Peace with Men, neither can any Man have true Peace in his Soul but by casting himself by Faith wholy upon the Prophet that is now alive.

17. Now if it were possible for this live Prophet to disown the Commission of the Spirit, (but it is not possible) then should he be found a false Prophet and will be Damned, then all that believes him will be Damned, also this must be ventured by all Men and Women that are saved by Faith in a Commission.

18. But as Christ spake many hard Words which made many forsake him: So likewise the Prophet hath spoken many hard Words as those Assertions where by some that were his Disciples were offended at him, and forsooke the Prophet and followed him no more; this hath been the practice of some in all Commissions.

19. But Woe will be to all that set the Hand of Faith to the Plow of Obedience to the Prophet and look back as *Lots* Wife did, or draw back unto perdition, whose Faith doth not hold out to the end that they might be saved.

20. And in this Sence, if the Prophet should disown the Commission of the Spirit, all those that believed him would be Damned.

21. As to the Ninth Assertion, in answer thereunto, behold the Power of a Prophets blessing, that though a Man walke contrary to the Commission his Faith is in: Yet the Condemnation of his Conscience, it shall not Reach

unto Eternity, but unto the Graves Mouth; why because the Rememberance of the Prophets blessing is in him and doth uphold him, else his Sin might make him despair of Eternal happiness, and fear Eternal Torments.

22. Also the Prophet cannot call back his blessing again though the Man doth walk contrary to the Commission, whereby his own Conscience is Wounded and the Prophet Dishonoured: Yet the Man keeping to the Prophets blessing, not Rebeling against him, the Prophets Faith and Love abideing in him will uphold him so that the fear of Eternal Death shall not surprise him.

23. So that all his Condemnation that he hath in his Conscience, and disgrace he hath received in this World, it shall end in Death, and shall never be remembered in the Resurrection; all his misdeeds shall be buried in the Grave and never rise again and that Faith he had in the Prophets blessing, and the Prophets blessing shall be raised again to the Glorious Estate of Saints and Angels.

24. And there shall be no Remembrance in the Resurrection of any Failings on this side of Death, but the Faith he had in the Prophet's Blessing only, shall uphold him, and free him from eternal Torments; and this is more than any legal righteous Man can attain unto, though his Nature be ever so pure.

25. So that a Prophet's Blessing is of no small weight, nor of any small concernment, but as the Blessing of Almighty God; for whoever receiveth a Prophet that is true, receiveth God, and what is the Blessing of a Prophet but everlasting Life.

26. And shall not this support and uphold a Man above all the Frailties of Nature.

27. And in this Sence, he that keeps the Prophet's Blessing, tho he be subject to many Frailties of Nature, which is contrary to the Commission, yet his Condemnation of Concience shall extend no further than the Graves Mouth.

28. Thus I have given Answer to all those Nine Assertions which *William Medgate* hath drawn up as a Charge against me, saying they are contrary to all Truth and against all Sober Reason.

THE END OF THE FORTH PART.

THE FIFTH PART.

CHAP. I.

Of one Sr. John James's *Opression of Widow* Brunt, *and of her Death: The Prophet left her Executor, and how he would not sell his Birthright, but Arrested Sr.* John James's *Tenants: Of his great Troubles and Tryals.*

1. After this it came to pass, that in the Year 1675, and 1676, that great Troubles did persue me, both upon a Natural and a Spiritual Account, through the Envy of wicked Men, as will appear by what doth follow.

2. There was a certain rich Man, being covetous and cruel, he was a Knight, his Name was called Sr. *John James*;[1] he through his cruelty and covetuosness did take away a matter of 30 Foot long, and 4 Foot broad, and a brick Wall that closed in this parcel of Ground, and a Pump that stood in this Ground, to considerable Vallue; the Woman's Name was *Deborah Brunt*, and this he lett to another Tenant of his, to make his Yarde wider.

3. Also, this Knight did lett another part of his Yarde to a Timber Merchant, and this Tenant of his did stop up the Light of the poor Widow's House with his Timber, insomuch that it was a great Hindrance and Loss to the Widow, in that no Tenant would live in it: This rich Man did, and she could no way deliver herself, but her Right was clearly taken from her for ever, for this rich Man had stated it upon his Two Tenants, and they enjoyed it for a Season.

4. It came to pass, in a while after, this Widow *Brunt* dyed, and I was her Executor; and I performed her Will in every particular, according to the Law of *England*; and I knowing this rich Man had taken away these Things before mentioned, from the poor Widow, that was her Right; which Widow I had been as a Father unto several Years before, and did more for her than her Husband could do for her, had he lived.

5. So that, I thought in myself; I would not, like prophain *Esau*, to sell my Birthright for a Mess of Pottage, but would gain that the poor Widow had lost wrongfully; whereupon, I did, according to Law, arest these two Tenants for Trespass and Damage.

6. The Men I went to Law withal were Three, one was *Denis Swenye*, a notable wicked Devil, the others were *Charles Mall*, and *William Picke*; they were Three inveterate Devils, being incouraged by this rich Man: Yet notwithstanding I proceeded on in the Law, and when they saw they were in danger to be overthrown, they used all ways possible to defer the Cause.

7. And when they Saw that would not do, but that I would bring it to Tryal, They consulted together, and Summon'd me into the *Spiritual Court;* thinking to have me Excommunicated, that I might not have the benefit of the Law against them; But I spent Money in that Court, and kept off their Excommunication, and proceeded in the Common Law towards a Tryal.

8. And when they Saw that would not do, then they Conspired, and Consulted with the *Wardens* of the Company of *Stationers*, to Search my House for Unlicenced Books; upon which the *Wardens*, brought many *Booksellers* and *Printers*, and Three of the *Kings Messingers* with them; and because my Wife denied to let them come up Stairs, they Immediately with a Weapon, they had, broke open Four Doors that were Lock'd and Boulted, Contrary to the Law of *England*, and they took away Four Hundred Books great and small from me, of a considerable Value.

9. After they had done this, they Consulted with the Bishop of *London*,[2]

to put me into the *Spiritual Court*, and Sue me there for *Blasphemy*, and get me Excommunicated, that I might not have the Benefit of the Law against them, neither for breaking upon my House, and Stealing away my Goods.

10. And for that purpose, they got the Lord Chief Justice *Rainsford's*[3] Warrant for to take me; he was a deadly Enemy to me, as will appear in that he would have taken away my Life, if he could, but I defended the *Spiritual Court* from being Excommunicated, and from his Warrant being Executed, or Served upon me, until these two Tryals in the Common Law, against these two Tenants of the rich Man were ended.

11. I was forced to be absent from my own House, for above a Quarter of a Year: I was entertained by that ever honoured, and true Believer, that young Widdow, *Ann Hall*, I was Entertained by her as an *Angel of God*, when other Believers durst not; I was kept at her House in Obscurity from Friends, and Enemyes, not knowing where I was, yet I Employed my Lawyers to manage my Business in both Courts, and in my absence they overthrew my Adversaries, in the two Causes aforementioned, in the Common Law, and I received again, that which the rich Man had taken away, with some of my Charges again.

12. But the *Wardens* of the *Stationers* Company, because they could not catch me, though they hunted after me as Blood-Hounds, but could not find me out to Serve their Warrant upon me; then they pressed hard in the *Spiritual Court* to get me Excommunicated, they fearing I might Overthrow them in the common Law, for breaking open my House, and taking my Goods, for they had committed an absolute Burglary and Fellony, by the Laws of *England*.

13. But I being pressed so hard upon in the *Spiritual Court*, that it came to this Resultation in the Court, that if I did not Personally appear the next Court Day, then I should be Excommunicated, and being advised by him that managed my Business in that Court, to appear, he saying he thought there would be no Danger.

14. Now by his words I was perswaded to appear though against my own Mind, for I did fear I should be Trappan'd, and as I fear'd it came to pass, and it proved of woeful Consequence to me; as will appear by what doth follow.

15. To omit many Circumstances, I shall Record the Heads, and Substance of the whole matter, and as I did appear in the *Spiritual Court*, to prevent my self of being Excommunicated; The Court had little to say unto me, only asked me, *if I did own that Libel*, which they knew I denied by my Procter before.

16. This was only to Deliver me into the Temporal Magistrates Hand; for the *Wardens*, the Lord Mayor, the Lord Chief Justice, together, with the *Spiritual Court*, were agreed together to Proceed against me this way; otherwayes they could never have catched me while they Lived, nor have brought me under their Law.

17. Therefore the *Wardens Merne*, and *Clark* they got the Lord Chief

Justice of *England's* Warrant, with a Constable ready, and as soon as I was Discharged in the *Spiritual Court* at *Docter's Commons*, that curssed Court is meerly to betray People into the Hands of their Enemies, and to ruin the Estates of the Poor People, for it is of no more Consequence for the good of the Nation, then to throw Stones against the Wind.

18. For the Wickedness and Envie of the Ignorant People is such, because they cannot be revenged of the Innocent and Just, by the Temporal Laws of the Land, then they Cite the Innocent, (that cannot Bow Down to their Worship) into the *Spiritual Court*, which I have had great Experience of this curssed Court, which did betray me into the Hands of wicked envious Magistrates, as will appear.

19. For as soon as I was coming out of the Court the Constable served the Lord Justice *Rainsford's* Warrant upon me: Then was I delivered into the Hands of *Satan*, to be plain, into the Hands of *Devils*.

20. And I was led to *Guild Hall* before the Lord Mayor, and Court of *Aldermen*, the Mayors Name was *Thomas Davis*,[4] a Stationer by Trade, a deadly Enemy to me, and to all Moral Justice, and a Man made up more of Mallice, and Ignorance of the Law of the Land, than Natural Wisdom, or Moral Knowledge: And as to Spiritual Knowledge he was as Blind as a *Beetle*.

21. The Constable gave Judge *Rainsford's* Warrant into the Lord Mayor's Hand, and the *Wardens* gave the whole Book bound into his Hands; and the Lord Mayor asked me, *whither I did own this Book;* I said *I did.*

22. Then he commanded me to withdraw into another Room, and I did so with an Officer with me; I stay'd a little while and the same Constable brought my Mittimus from the Lord Mayor, to carry me to the Geoal of *Newgate* until the next Sessions.

23. So I being carried to Prison, I was Bailed out until the 17th of *January*, in the Year 1676[7], then did *Merne* and *Clark*, draw up an Indictment against me, but out of one of those Bookes they stole from me, called, *The Neck of the Quakers Broken.*

CHAP. II.

Of the Bill of Indictment, and of the Cruelty of the Judges.

1. Now followes the Bill of Indictment, as I was Condemn'd for: The Persons or Jury Sworn for our Lord the King; gave in that *Lodowick Muggleton* late of *London* Labourer, being a Man Pernicious, Blasphemous, Seditious, Heritical, and a Monster in his Opinions.

2. Pretending that he the said *Lodowick Muggleton*, is one of the two last Witnesses of *Almighty GOD*, and devising, and intending to Spread Abroad his Pernicious, Blasphemous, Seditious, and Monstrous Opinions, and to disturb the Peace and quiet of this Kingdom of *England*, and dispise and debase the True Religion, Established and Exercised therein.

3. As also to make and Excite discord, between the King and his Subjects, and to bring into Odium and Disgrace, his said Majesty's Kingdom as to Eclesiastical Matters.

4. He the said *Lodowick Muggleton*, on the 30th of *August* in the 23d Year of His Majesty's Reign, in St. *Giles's* Parish, without *Cripplegate London* aforesaid, by force and Armes, did Unlawfully, Wickedly, Maliciously, Scandalously, Blasphemously, Seditiously, Scismatically, and Heritically, Write, Print, and Sell, Utter and Publish, a certain Malicious, Scandalous, Blasphemous, Seditious, and Heritical Book Intituled, *The Neck of the Quakers Broken*.

5. In which Book, Written to *Edward Burne*,⁵ are contained these Unlawful, Blasphemous, Seditious, Heritical, and Scandalous Sentences following, viz. *I Write these Lines unto you*, Edward Burne, *knowing you to be the Seed of the Serpent*.

6. There was repeated out of this Book much more, as Page the 18, 31, and 54. That whosoever Reads that Book, may see those Blasphemies, these Quakers did first Judge me with; so that I had cause enough given me to Pronounce those sad Sentences of Damnation upon them, and those Books was known to the Powers of the Nation many Years before, and the Power of the Nation took no notice of it, because that, and all others were Pardoned by the King, and Act of Parliament, till within three Years, and that Book was Printed 13 Years before.⁶

7. Yet these wicked Judges, and Jury and others, Conspired together to perswade, the Court, that this Book was Antidated 13 Years ago, yet Published this *August* 30th 1676, that it might come within the Act of three Years.

8. Now these words that were taken out of this Book, made some of the Judges Mad with Envie, and grin'd their Teeth, and their Counsel said, *it made his Hair stand on an End, he was so Affrighted*, which caused one of the Judges to belch out of his Mouth, saying, *it was to the great contempt and Scandal of their said Lord the King, of His Crown and Dignity*.

9. When as that Book did not meddle with their Established *Religion* at all, neither was it any dishonour to the King, but rather an honour, if he had but Read it over; but Truth doth alwaies offend the reason of Man, as is seen by what a Multitude of Hellish Expressions, and Palpable lies, uttered in their Indictment, being patch'd up with Reproaches, and Slanders, against the purest Truth that ever was spoken by Prophet, or Apostle.

10. I shall now Record how unjustly Judge *Rainsford* dealt with me before the Tryal: The Sessions before I was Tryed, the Bill of Indictment was Read in Court, and I answered *not Guilty*, and said unto *Davis*, then Lord Mayor, *that I would Traviss the Indictment, and put in Bail to the Indictment*.

11. So *Davis* asked whither I could put in three Sufficient Men, that could Swear they were worth Two Hundred Pounds a Man, he would Accept of Bail, thinking I could not have procured such great Security: And Judge *Rainsford* Sate at the Right-Hand of the Mayor, and I heard Judge

Rainsford, say to the Lord Mayor, *that it was pitty but I should be Burn'd;* I heard by his Words, and saw by his Countenance, that he was, and would be a Deadly Enemy.

12. But the Mayor, could not deny Bail, nor to Traviss the Indictment by the Laws of *England;* so the Men were called, and the Mayor being Envious, asked one of them if they were of my Gang, one of them answered and said thus, *Sr. We do not come here to be Examin'd whose Gang we are of, but we came to be Bail for this Man for Six Hundred Pounds for his Appearance the next Sessions;* The Mayor said no more but Accepted it.

13. And when the time drew near, I did according to Law (with my Lawyer) go to this Judge *Rainsford*, and got his Clerk to draw up a *Sessarary*, which was to remove it out of that Court, into the Court of *Kings-Bench;* and this Envious Judge, being Judge of the *Kings-Bench-Court*, and we could not have a *Sessarary* in any Court else, which he knew well enough, which caused his Envie to act so wickedly and unjustly towards me.

14. For when his Clerk, and my Lawyer had Drawn up the Writing, and had recived their Money, (near Forty Shillings) they went into the Judges Chamber, for him to set his Hand to it, to remove my Cause into his own Court, which was but Law, but he made them answer, and said, *he would not set his Hand to it, but would hear the Tryal himself, at the Sessions.*

15. So I was Cheated of my Money by his Clerk, and he knew it, and he deprived me of it and of the just Law, which is the Birth right of every free born *Man of England.*

16. But now as to the Tryal, I shall in the next place Record some of the most remarkable Words, and Passages of the Judges, and the Counselors, and the Witnesses against me in the Tryal: Upon the 17th of *January* 1676[7], first the Indictment was Read, and the Cryer of the Court, said, *Are you Guilty or not Guilty.*

17. I answered, *not Guilty*, but desired the Court to let my Counsel Plead the Cause, because I knew they would have taken hold of my Words, and made them a more horrible Crime, then the Book it self; which Judge *Rainsford* readily granted, and asked *Who was my Counsel*, I said Mr. *Gener.*

18. And he received a Breviat of the Cause, shewing the Wrong I had received by their breaking open my House, and taking away my Goods, contrary to the Laws of *England*: Also I gave into my Counsels Hands, the Kings Gracious Act of Pardon; *That whosoever did Sue any Man for what was Pardoned in that Act afterwards, that the Partie so Sued, should Plead the General Issue and should Recover Ten Pound a Man of those his Adversaries.*

19. This Act was given into my Counsels Hands to Plead, and that Book that stated the Indictment out of, was given into his Hand, which Book was Pardoned by that Act, being Printed 13 Years ago, all was Pardon'd till within Three Years.

20. Also their Counsel, (I know not his Name) had one of the Books, with the whole Volumn Bound and Clasp'd, (which they stole from me) in his Hand, I saw the Chief Judges were bent upon Mischief against me.

21. Therefore I was resolved to follow the Practice of Christ, when Examined by the high Priests, Rulers and Counsel, gave them no answer neither before *Pilate;* for he knew they watched to catch Words out of his Mouth, that they might have some what to Accuse him of, to make his Cause worse, then what his Enimies did Accuse him with, as may be Read *Luke* 22.70. where Christ held his Peace, and answer'd nothing.

22. Then said they all, *Art thou the Son of God;* and he said unto them? *Yea say that I am,* and to this they said, *What need we any further Witness, for we our selves have heard out of his own Mouth;* so *Mark* 14. and in verse 62, Jesus answered and said to his question, *I am the Son of God,* &c.

23. Then the high Priests rent their Cloathes, and they all Condemned him to be guilty of Death; so likewise I did perceive that if I had pleaded my self I should have Justified my Commission from GOD, and that he gave *John Reeve,* and my self that Power and Authority to give Sentance of *Damnation,* to all that Blaspheme against the Holy Ghost, as they did, as are Writen in that Book.

24. These Words would have Enraged the Judges, and Jury, and the People more then that Book; so that they would have said by me as the Priests, Scribes and Pharisies said by Christ as aforesaid: The angrey and Malicious Judges, and Envious Jury, and Ignorant Officers and People in the Court, would have rent their Hearts with Madness against me, and said, *What need we to mind this Book, or Indictment, or Witness against him, for you hear his terrible Blasphemy out of his own Mouth, therefore what think you?* so that they all would have Condemned me to greater Torments than they did.

25. Considering this, I held my Peace and speak not one word; which prevented the Expectations of Thousands, which thought to have had a large Relation of the Matter.

26. So that I left the Book that was Pardoned, & Act, and Indictment and Witnesses, for them to Judge and Condemn me by; So they had no farther Matter from me at all, which did frusterate their Expectations and Moderate their Punishment, as the Reader may perceive by what doth follow.

CHAP. III.

The Counsel against the Prophet, Pleads with fear and horrour: The Prophets Counsel Pleads, and through fear, did wrong his Cause.

1. Upon the 17th of *January* 1676[7], after the Indictment was read, my Counsel Pleaded to it, proving that this Book the Indictment was grounded upon, it was Pardoned by the Kings Gracious *Act,* being Printed 13 Years ago; neither was this Book Published, nor Sold in any Shop, or to any Person in publick; as can be proved, but were locked up in *Cheasts,* &c. This with many other Words, according to the Laws of *England*: This my Counsel pleaded, and my Counsel Sate under Judge *Atkins.*[7]

2. And their Counsel Sate under Judge *Rainsford,* and he did hold up

the Book in open Court, which Book was the whole Volumn Bound and Clasped: He held one of the Claspes between his Finger and his Thumb up in the open Court, in oppossition to my Counsel.

3. And he expressed these Words, and said with a loud Voice, *That he did Read one Leaf of this Book, and turn'd over another.* But said he, *it was so full of Horrible Blasphemy, that he durst not Read any further, for the Blasphemy was so great, that it made his Hair stand on end, and his Heart to tremble;* with other Expressions of Dread and Fear.

4. As if the very Reading of it would have caused God to have parted the Heavens assunder, and have Rained down Vengance upon him for Reading it, if he had Read any further: For said he, *It was impossible for any Man to Write such a Horrible Blasphemous Book, in Assuming the place of God upon him,* Except *he went to the bottom of Hell,* for said he, *it is so cunningly contrived, that it confounds all the Reason in Man,* with many other hedious expressions, which I cannot remember.

5. He spoke truth, but knew it not, for the Spirit of Revelation doth descend to the bottom of Hell, else we could not tell others where it is, and prevent others from falling into it; and as Christ himself Descended into Hell, and quickened again out of it, so hath the Spirit of Revelation in me descended into the bottom of Hell a Thousand times, and hath quickened out of it again, and hath forewarned many from going into that Place; but I know this Counseler shall go into Hell, that hath no bottom, called a Bottomless Pitt, and he shall never come from thence, to Eternity.

6. Likewise indeed the Revelation of Faith in me, hath confounded all the Reason in Man, as to Spiritual and Heavenly matters.

7. After this my Counsel pleaded again to the same purpose; as he did before, but he through extream Fearfulness did wrong my cause, in two things: First in that he made no mention of the Wardens breaking open four Doors, contrary to the Laws of *England;* which was by the Law absolute Burglary, and the taking away the Books, was absolute Fellony.

8. This was in the Forefront of his *Breviat,* and I had reposed the Business to him, because I would not plead my self, but he like a deceitful Knave, and fearfull Fool; did not speak one Word of it before the Court; which if he had, it would have put these Envious Judges, and Jury to a Nonplush, how they could have brought me in Guilty; so he spoyld my Cause.

9. For after he had Pleaded the Kings *Act* of Grace, as aforesaid, he said these Words, that he had Pleaded so far as the Law would bear him out, but as for the Words, and cause of Indictment, he was ashamed of it.

10. Upon these Words, did Judge *Rainsford* say unto the Jury, *You see that his own Counsel is ashamed of his Cause.*

11. Here the Reader may see those Words verified, as I have Read, for my Counsel did do at my Tryal those things which he ought not to have done, and he left undone those things which he ought to have done; for he ought to have Pleaded the Breaking open of so many Doors, but he left that undone, and to say he was ashamed of my Cause, he ought to have left

those Speeches undone, and not to have spoken them, being not forced by the Court.

12. And for a Man to take Forty Shillings to Plead a Man's Cause, and to say he is ashamed of his Clyants Cause; what Man that hath but Moral Reason, and Sense in him, but will say such a Counseler hath no Truth in him.

13. But Judge *Atkins* siting over my Counsel, might see the *Breviat* in my Counsels Hand, which caused him to ask one of the Witnesses (his name was *Garat) how did he come by those Books*, he answered, *that he did Seize them, as they use to do*, the Judge asked *how many there were of them*, he said *a Porters Load;* the Judge asked him where the Books were, he answered, *at the Bishop of* Londons *House.*

14. The Judge asked him again, *if they were all of a sort, or all of a bigness*, he answered *no, some were great ones, and some lesser, some three or four bound together, and some single*: He was asked how many of them great Books that were in the Court, he answered *Six* of them; he was asked what was the Price that great Book was sold for; He answered *Twelve or Fourteen Shillings.*

15. Now when the two Counsels had done Pleading, and the Witnesses Examin'd, the aforesaid Judge *Atkins* stood up and said, *Gentlemen of the Jury, you see that the Book which the Indictment was grounded upon, was Printed* 13 *Years ago, and is Pardon'd by the Kings Gracious* Act. *Therefore said he, I cannot see by the Lawes of* England, *how you can possibly bring this Man in Guilty, therefore Jury look to it.*

16. Then stood up Judge *Rainsford* and said, *That if it was not Law, we will make it Law*, and further said, *who knoweth but this Raskal might Antidate the Book* 13 *Years ago, and Publish it this* 30th *of* August *last past.*

17. The Envy of this wicked Judge, made him speak against his own Conscience, for he knew it was impossible for me to do such a thing as to get it Printed so lately, for he knew it were those that Stole my Books, published them.

18. And further this *Rainsford* vented his Envy exceeding high and called me *Incorrigable Rogue, that should Assume to himself to be in Gods place, a Man Pernicious, Blasphemous, Seditious, Heritical, and a monster in his Opinions; Pretending himself one of the Two Witnesses of Almighty God, to the great Scandal and Contempt of our Lord the King, his Crown and Dignity, as also the Religion of this Kingdom rightly Established*: And further said, *he was Sorry that the Laws of* England *were so unprovided to Punish Crimes of this Nature.*

19. And further he goeth on in his Rage against me and faith; *Gentlemen of the Jury, if you do not bring this Man in Guilty, you will be pertakers with him in all his Horrible Blasphemy, and grand Apostisie.*

20. Many more hateful Words, with the Fire of Hell, that proceeded from his Heart, and did appear in his Face; his Zeal was great to have me Pun-

ished, Nay he thought in his Heart, that Hanging was too good a Death for me, for said he, *This Crime of horrid Blasphemy* (as he accounted it) *was worse than Murder, Fellony, or Treason; and was Sorry that the Laws was so unprovided to punish such Crimes.*

21. I was so moved in my mind, to hear this Cursed Devil to Blaspheme against the Holy Spirit that sent me, and gave me Power to give Sentence of Eternal Damnation upon such Blaspheming Devils. That I could have wished, that God would have Executed some vissible Vengeance from Heaven upon this Blasphemous Judge, to have smote him with a natural Blindness, for I knew he was Spiritually Blind, for I had done wrong to no Man.

22. Only I had Executed the Commission of God faithfully in giving Sentence upon all dispising Devils, who sinned againg the *Holy Ghost*: This was that Sin the high Priests and Elders committed in Christ's time against him, in that they said he cast out Devils by *Belsebub* the *Prince* of *Devils*.

23. I know this, that Judge *Rainsford* would have said the same to Christ himself, had he been in my place, for his Blasphemy was great, not only against me, but against God that sent me, which God he knew not.

24. Therefore my Anger was kindled against him, and desired an immediate vissible Vengeance from Heaven upon him, that might have been a vissible Witness, whither God did own him or me.

25. But there was a secret Voice within me said, thy Commission is Spiritual, and hath to do with the Spiritual and Eternal Estate of Mankind; and that all such Persons are the Seed of the Serpent, and are to receive for their Blasphemy against the *Holy Ghost*, their Punishment in the Life to come, even Eternal Damnation, which is the second Death, where the Worm of Conscience shall never Dye, nor the Fire of Hell shall never be quenched to Eternity.

26. Then I was quiet and willing to bear all they could do unto me, even to the loss of my Life.

CHAP. IV.

The Prophet is brought in Guilty of his Sentence and Judgment; with the nature of his Sufferings.

1. After that Judge *Rainsford* had made his Speech to the Jury, then was the Goler commanded to take me away from the Bar and put into a little Room for a season, and after a little space I was called for to the Bar again, and *Jefferies*[8] being then in the Recorders place, that Bawling Devil, was to give Sentence, and Judgment upon me.

2. And when I did appear before him, a great Fire was between us, where they did Burn those in the Hand which were Condemn'd to that Punishment, but all that was over before I did appear.

3. And this *Jefferies* Sate in the Judgment Seat, as *Pilate* did against *Christ*, and I stood a Prisoner at his Bar; and when he saw my Face, the

first Words he speak, he called me Impudent Rogue, because my Countenance did not change, nor look sad, nor asked any Favour of the Court, and said nothing to all their Threats, Revilings, and Reproaches, whereby they Reproached me.

4. Then he asked the Jury, *Is Muggleton Guilty, or not Guilty*, They stay'd a little space before they speak; *Jefferies* asked again, *is Muggleton Guilty, or not Guilty*, the Jury *said Guilty*.

5. Then he Proceeded in Judgment and said, *the Court is sorry the Laws of* England *are so unprovided to punish Crimes of this Nature, therefore the Court hath thought Fit, to give you but an Easie, Easie, Easie, Punishment.*

6. You shall be committed, and put to stand upon the Pillory in three of the most Eminent Places in the Citty: That is one Day in *Cornhil*, near the *Exchange, London;* Another Day in *Fleet-street*, near the end of *Chancery lane;* and the Third Day, (being on the Market Day) to Stand in *West-Smith-Field, London,* from the Hours of Eleven in the Forenoon, until one in the Afternoon.

7. *On which said several Days, a Writing Paper shewing your Offence, to be put upon your Breast, and also your Blasphemous Books, in three Parts, to be devided, and with Fire before your Face, near the Pillory aforesaid, by the Common Hangman, then and there to be Burn'd.*

8. *And then to be returned into* Newgate *in safe Custody, until your Fine of Five Hundred Pound be paid, and then to put in good Security, to be of good Behaviour the time of your Life, but none of your own Gang (as he call'd them) shall be Security for you;* These are the Words of the Sentance that *Jefferies* passed upon me the 17th of *January* 1676[7].

9. The Paper that was tyed to my Brest, every Day I stood upon the Pillory, to shew my Offence, and cause of this Suffering, the Words were as followeth.

10. Lodowick Muggleton, *Standeth hear for Writing, causing to be Printed, Selling, Uttering, and Publishing a Blasphemous Book.*

11. After this Sentence, and Judgment was passed upon me, I shall Record as short as I can, the manner of the Execution of this Sentence; and how I did suffer it, and bear the Curse of their wicked Wills; for they did make that Law, which was not Law, as *Rainsford* said before, and as Judge *Atkins*, when he saw me Condemn'd contrary to Law, he went off the Bench and said, *there were no fair Dealings with me.*

12. This Sentance have I Suffered, in every Tittle in the greatest Rigour that could be inflicted, even beyond their own Law, they made me Ride in a Cart, as a Thief, or a Murtherer, Bareheaded, without Hat or Cap; which never was done in *England* before: I stood bareheaded upon the Pillory, which no Cheat ever did, but were suffered to weare a Cap of Steel under another Cap.

13. I was set as a Mark for every one to Throw a Stone at me.

14. My Books were offered up in Three Burnt offerings *unto the Unknown God*, as Three Sacrifices before my Face, the smoke of them ascended into my Nostrells, which caused me to Cry to Heaven for Vengeance, upon

those Great Men of the Earth, that were the cause of those Burned offerings unto Devils.

15. And my self was Offered up, as a Sacrifice Three times, to the Rude Multitude: For the People came from the Four Winds, or from the Four Quarters of the Citty, and Subburbs round about; they were for Multitude without Number.

16. I was maul'd by the People, some cast Dirt, and Mudd out of the Kennel at me, others Rotten Eggs, and Turnops, and others cast Stones at me, some Stones weighed a Pound, and out of the Windows at the *Exchange*, they cast down Fire Brands, (Pieces of Billits with Fire upon them) at my Head, which if they had lighted upon me, would have done the Work, as they desired.

17. I was Bruised and Battered, and my Innocent Blood was shed, tho' not unto Death, for Gods Cause, for that the Blood of the last True Prophet, and Witness of the Spirit, hath been shed, by this Bloody Citty, for my Testimony to the Commission of God, put upon me.

18. And it was the wonderful Providence of God, my Life was preserved; for I was delivered into the Hands of unreasonable Men, the rude Multitude, by the Hands of *Rainsford, Davis*, and *Jefferies*, Judges of the Law of Reason, and Jury, these were the Men that were Guilty of my Innocent Blood.

19. I was willing to be stoned to Death, by the rude Multitude, and would have gone off the Pillory to be stoned to Death, but the Officers would not let me come down, when this was over, my Wounds and the Blood stanched, I was put into the Cole Cellar again, the same Day at Night, I went Three pair of Stairs high to my Lodging.

20. And the next Day, I would willingly have kept my Bed, but the Keeper said, *If I would not come down into the Cellar in the Afternoon, they would put me in the Common Side;* so I was forced into the Cellar, who had more need to have kept my Bed.

21. But there is no mercy in Prison, therefore it may well be compared to Hell, for in Hell there is no mercy, but Justice only, neither is there any mercy in Prison Keepers at all without profit.

22. After I had suffered these things, I was put into Prison again for the Fine of Five Hundred Pounds that was laid upon me to Pay, but I did lye in Prison Six Months after I had suffered these things aforesaid.

23. And now in my Imprisonment, I considered that my sufferings were much like unto the sufferings of the Prophet *Jeremiah* Chap 11.19. he suffered for his Message from the *Lord of Host, the mighty God of Jacob.*

24. And my sufferings was for my Commission received from the high and mighty God, the Man Christ Jesus, in Glory, the only wise God my King and my Redeemer.

25. And as his Enemies, that caused him to suffer, and would have had him put to Death, were Princes, and great Men of the Earth; so likewise, those my Enemies, were great Men, and as Princes on the Earth; and they sat upon the Thrones, as Gods on Earth, in Judgment against me.

26. And as it was with *Jeremiah*, so it was with me, for I was like a

Lamb, that is brought to the Slaughter, and I knew not that they had devised devices against me, if I had, I could have prevented them. They saying, *Let us destroy the Tree with its Fruite thereof, and cut him off from the Land of the Living, that his Name may be no more Remembered.*

27. That is, *let us destroy this* Muggleton, *the Tree, and the Fruit thereof; his Doctrine of the True God, and Right Devil in his Writings, that none may receive his Writings more, nor believe his Doctrin, or Commission, that he hath Power from God, to Bless, and Curse to Eternity* any more: This Reprobate Men have practiced against me.

28. So that I have had Cause, to make my Complaint unto my God, my King, and my Redeemer the Lord Jesus Christ, as *David* and *Jeremiah* did.

29. *Oh Lord God of Truth, that Judgeth Righteously, that Tryeth the Reins, and the Heart, let me see thy Vengeance on them, for thou knowest I have been Faithful in Executing thy Commission, the Burthen of the Lord, which thou didest lay upon me.*

30. *And thou knowest the unrighteous, unjust Judgments, these wicked unjust Judges gave against me: They were not only Enemies to me, but thy Enemies, Oh God; for they have hated me without a cause, and they have said, let us smite him with the Tongue, with Lyes, Slanders, and Reproaches.*

31. *Therefore give heed, O Lord God of Truth, and harken to the Vioce of these wicked Judges, and Jury, and all those that assented to that Judgment for harm, that contended with me: And let me see thy Vengeance on those thy Enemies, for their Fathers did unto thee when thou was upon Earth, as these do unto me.*

32. *Thou hast saved me from Bloody Men: For they laid wait for my Soul to Kill it, had the Law been provided with Strength, and not for any Transgression of any Law that I had broken, but for thy Commission and Doctrine thou gavest me to declare.*

33. *Therefore Oh Lord God of Truth! be not merciful unto any wicked Transgression, that Persecuteth only for Conscience sake; it being the Sin against the Holy Ghost.*

34. *And God will let me see my desire upon my Enemies, and bring them down, Oh Lord my God.*

35. This was my secret Supplication unto my God, when I was Prisoner in *Newgate*, after I had suffered all those Corporal Punishments, which they Sentanced me to Suffer.

CHAP. V.

Shewing how that the Prophet in a short time, saw his desire (unto God) in part fullfilled.

1. And a little while after these my Sufferings I saw my desire (in part) granted, and several of my Potent Enemies cut off this Earth by Death: As first that certain rich Man that took away poor Widdow Brunt's Ground, as is aforemention'd; he was call'd Sr. *John James.*

2. And notwithstanding I had overthrown his two Tenants in the common Law, yet when he saw that I was in Prison, and Condemn'd for those Books, and had suffered as aforesaid, yet I being Fined Five Hundred Pounds, he thought I could not be delivered out of Prison no more, the Fine was so great.

3. Whereupon he wickedly took advantage upon my sufferings for God's Cause, and sent a Writt of Ejectment to my Tenants, to Eject me out of Possession, so my Atturney Read it and said, *I must answer to it, else he would Eject me out the next Term*, so I was forced to Imploy a Soliciter to answer to it, which wickedness of his, cost me three Pounds.

4. And my Lawyer went to Treat with him, and this Knight was not very well, very Cross, and said, *he had turn'd his Business over to his Atturney*: And his Atturney was so full of Imployment that nothing could be done.

5. So I hearing by my Lawyer that he was Sick, I desired of God, that he might never come down from that Bed of Sickness, whereon he lay; and in a few Days after, it came to pass, that he Dyed.

6. So our Law Suite was ended, I had been a quarter of a Year in Prison then, now I knew this Man was the Seed of the Serpent, a Devil, and will be Damn'd to all Eternity.

7. After this, there was another great Enemy, his Name was *Garret*, he was one of those that broke open my House, and Stole my Books, and was a Witness against me in the Court: He brought the Books to the Court, for the Common Hang Man to Burn, every Day I stood upon the *Pillory*, my Wife *Mary* gave him the Sentance of Damnation to Eternity, and he Dyed Six Weeks after.

8. The third Person, was Judge *Rainsford*, Chief Justice of *England*, he was an Implacable Enemy to me, but in a little time after his Judgment upon me, before I was delivered out of Prison, he was put down from his Seat of Justice, and all his Temporal Power was taken from him by the King; and another put in his Place: And the King would give no Reason for it, but his own will.

9. So that his great Power, Honour and Glory, was departed from him, and he had not so much Power as a common Justice of Peace, he was in the same Condition as King *Saul* was, the good Spirit of Power of giving Righteous Judgment in Temporal Things according to Law was departed from him, and an Evil Spirit of Shame and Disgrace was sent unto him.

10. Which Troubled his Soul, so that in a little time after he Dyed, and went to the same place, as King *Saul* did, that did enquire of a Witch that was rejected of God, and not of his Prophet *Samuel*. And I am sure he shall be rejected of God, even this *Rainsford*, and rejected of me, the last True Prophet of the Lord, and that he will be Damn'd to all Eternity.

11. And he shall Remember in the Resurrection, that his Damnation is the very same which he called horrible Blasphemy, which he Judged me for, and said *he was sorry the Laws of* England *were so unprovided to Punish me no worse than they did.*

12. And as he had no Mercy for me when he was in Power, neither have

I any Mercy for him; and I am sure God will have no Mercy for him, but hath provided a Law to Punish him for his Envy against me, who did him no wrong.

13. And his Blasphemy against the Holy Ghost which God hath said, and made it a Law (never to be altered) that shall never be forgiven in this World, or in the World to come: This is the Law that God hath provided for us, the Two last Prophets and Witnesses of the Spirit to Judge by; so that I know the hottest of Hell Fire will be his Portion, and Reward, for his Sin against the Holy Ghost, to Eternity.

14. The Fourth great Enemy to me was Sr. *Thomas Davis*, then Lord Mayor, he being a Stationer himself, he was Confederate with the whole Company of Stationers, and Booksellers, and Jury: To Fight against the Lord and his Chosen Prophet, and Witness of the Spirit, which did Incense the Court and Jury, that I might Antidate that Book 13 Years ago, and yet Publish it this *August;* even against his own Conscience.

15. Wherein he shewed himself of that wicked reprobate Seed of the Serpent, a Son of the Devil, and I certainly know him to be a Devil, and that he will be Damn'd to all Eternity.

16. And about two Years and a half after he Judged me, he Dyed and passed through this first Death, which is Natural, into the second Death, which is Spiritual, and Eternal.

17. These great Enemies, I have lived to see them cut off from the Land of the Living, with many others more Inferiour Devils, which were my Enemies, have I seen cut off by Death, and some to Poverty.

18. There is one more, that is yet alive, that I desire of God to have Executed some vissible Vengeance at my Tryal; his Name was *Jefferies* Recorder of *London*: He was the Man that sate in the Judgment Seat, and gave Sentence against me; He used several Scurrilous, and Disdainful Expressions, in the Sentence he gave upon me.

19. He was a Man, whose Voice was very lou'd, but he is one of the worst of Devils in Nature, for he is not only an Enemy to God, and all Righteous Men, but an Enemy to all Moral Justice and Equity.

20. For if a Mans Cause be never so just, except he be Imploy'd in it, he will be sure to baffel and make quabbles, and wrangle out the justest Cause that is, and will make that which is unjust it self to be right by Law, were it not for more juster Judges that have a more just Conscience then he hath, else the Innocent would always loose his just right, if he be against him.

21. But that which I have against him is for his Blasphemy against the Holy Spirit that sent me, and his wicked Malice and Envy against me, when he sate in Judgment against me; That he said *he was sorry the Laws of* England *were so unprovided to Punish Crimes of this Nature, he was sorry the Laws could not Impower him to give Sentence of Death upon me*: This I know was the Desire of his Heart.

22. And as he was sorry the Laws of *England* were so unprovided to Punish me, so in like manner, am I glad that the Laws of Heaven is always provided to Punish him with Eternal Torments, which is a Living Death,

and a Dying Life, it is well for me, and all the Elect, that Gods Laws are always provided to give Sentence of Eternal Damnation upon all such dispising persecuting Blaspheming Devils as this *Jefferies*.

23. I knew he was a Reprobate and appointed of God to be Damn'd before: But this Tryal of mine hath given Testimony to me and all that truely believe me, that he is an absolute Devil in Flesh, and his Sin doth cry to Heaven for Vengeance.

24. And look what measure he would have measured unto me, in that he would have slain my Innocent Blood unto Death, the same measure shall be measured to him again, because the Laws of Heaven are always provided, and hath Impowered me to give Sentance, and Judgment upon him, for I know, by Revelation of the Spirit of God, that he is Recorded in the Tables of Heaven for a Reprobate Devil, and he shall be Recorded here on Earth to the end of the World for a Damn'd Devil.

25. For that Body of his, which is now his Heaven, which Cloathed it self in Scarlet, and sat on the Judgment Seat against me, shall be in Hell. And that lofty bauling Spirit of his shall be his Devil, the one shall be as Fire, and the other as Brimstone, Burning together to all Eternity.

26. And he shall remember in the Resurrection, when he is Raised again, that he gave Judgment upon me for Writing this Sentence to others, and I am sure the God of Heaven will not deliver him from those Eternal Torments.

27. There is a Necessity, that these Men of all others, should be Damn'd to Eternity? For there was more Enemies against me then could be Numbered through the Occasion of these Five Men aforementioned.

28. And I could freely forgive the rude Multitude, for they knew not what they did, but there is no forgiveness of these Five Men, nor Jury, nor Judge, nor Officers, that gave their consent to that Judgment that was passed upon me the 27th of *January* 1676[7].

29. Therefore I have left these Five Men upon Record, that the Age to come, may see the wickedness of them; and take heed how they Persecute Innocent Men, that doth not break any Temporal Law? And especially such Men that hath a Commission from God to give Sentance of Eternal Damnation upon them, least they come under the same Condemnation as these Men are under.

30. This I have left upon Record for the Age to come, after my Death, some of the most Remarkable Sufferings which I have passed through in the Year 1676.

CHAP. VI.

Of the Prophets deliverance out of Prison; of the Price and Value that was made of him: The Rewards to the two Seeds at the last Day.

1. Now having given an Account of my Sufferings, it will be necessary to give an Account of my deliverance out of those Troubles.

2. While I was in the *Press-yard*, Prisoner, the Sheriffs did send several times by the Goal keepers to see what I would do about the Fine, but they were at no certainty, what they required: At last the Clerk of *Newgate* said, *they would take the 5th* Part, which was one Hundred Pound.

3. I was unwilling to give so much, I let it alone a quarter of a Year longer, for some Reasons I had in my self, after that time I sent a Letter to Treat with them about the Fine: The Sheriffs Names was one Sr. *John Peak*, Sheriff of *London*, the other was Sr. *Thomas Stamp*, Sheriff of *Middlesex*.[9]

4. But they were very high, and would not abate one Shilling of one Hundred Pound, and the cause why, was because some of the Goal Keepers, had Proffered one Hundred Pound for me, to keep a Prisoner for ever, or else to have a large Summ of Money for my Ransome.

5. I perceive, had not the Shreiffs Honour layn at the stake, I had been Bought and Sold as *Joseph* was in *Egypt* for a Prisoner during Life, or till such Ransome was Paid: It would have been a great Disparragment to the Sheriffs, if they had Sold me, such as was never done in *England* before.

6. But they having an Eye to Credit, and somewhat to Conscience, they would not do such Wickedness; but however it caused them to abate nothing of one Hundred Pound neither would they give any time, but Pay down presently.

7. So We Borrowed an Hundred Pound the next Day, and gave to them, upon the 19th Day of *July* 1677, and the same Day at Night I was Released out of Prison, and many of the Believers do keep that Day as a Feast Day every Year, in Remembrance of my Deliverance out of Prison.

8. For I was Prized at a goodly Price, far Higher than the Lord of Life, when he was on Earth: He was valued at but Thirty Pieces of Silver, the Thirty Pieces of Silver was Thirty Pound, but they valued me at a Hundred Pieces of Silver, for the Thirty Pieces of Silver they valued Christ at, must be so much, else it would not have Bought the Potters Field.

9. Now the cause why they valued me at such a High Price above my Lord and Master, it was because they knew I had some Interest in this World: And many followers of me, therefore they valued me at such a High Price as 100 Pieces of Silver.

10. And as the Thirty Pieces of Silver was the Price of Innocent Blood, therefore not fit to be put into the Treasury, to be Expended upon any Holy use, or to Relieve the Poor and the like; but to Buy a Potters Field to Bury the Stinking Carcasses of strangers, Thieves, and Murderers, insomuch that the Thirty Pieces of Silver was bestowed on the basest way, suitable to the Purchase; being the Price of Innocent Blood.

11. So likewise the Hundred Pieces of Silver they valued me at, it was the Price of Innocent Blood also, tho' not unto Death, as our Lord was a very Goodly Price.

12. And this Money will not be put into the Treasury, to repair Churches, or Relieve the Poor, but will be spent basely in Lust and Drunkenness, and in Volumptiousness suitable to the Purchase of it, being the Price of Innocent Blood.

13. Thus I have left upon Record, the substance of the whole matter, as short as I can, both of my Sufferings and my Deliverance out of all those Troubles that hath happened upon me in the Year 1675, and in the Year 1676, and 1677, and in the Year of my Life 67.

14. This is the 5th part of the Acts of *John Reeve* and *Lodowick Muggleton*, the two last Prophets, and Witnesses of the Spirit, from the Year 1651 to the Year 1677 I have been preserved, and had Experience of the Truth of all these things.

15. And wonderful Revelations, and passages, and Acts, that are Writen in these Five Parts, that I might leave it as a Legacy for the Age to come upon Record, that the unbelieving World may be convinced when I am turned to Dust, as my Father *Adam* is, that I was Slandered, Reproached, Belyed, Persecuted, Imprisoned, and Pilloried, without a Cause.

16. But I shall be raised again, by the Power of that God, the Lord Jesus Christ, in whom I Believed, that he was Dead, even the *Alpha*, and *Omega*, and is Alive for Evermore.

17. And it will not seem a quarter of an Hours time to me from my Death, to my Rising again: For there is no time to the Dead: Time belongs to the Living.

18. And this I know, that as the 12 Apostles in the Resurrection, shall Sit upon Thrones and Judge the 12 Tribes of *Israel;* those that Believed them when they were upon the Earth. They were Judged with an Eternal Blessing of Life Eternal, and those that Dispised, and Persecuted them when on Earth, are Judged by them to be Cursed and Damn'd to Eternity, which is a Second Death which is Eternal.

19. So shall *Reeve* and *Muggleton* in the Resurrection Sit upon Thrones, and Judge all True Believers of our Docterin and Commission of the Spirit, when we were upon Earth, to be Blessed both in Souls and Bodies, that were Mortal when they believed us, but now Immortal to Eternity.

20. And we shall Judge all those Wicked Despisers and Persecutors of us when we were upon Earth with the same Judgment in the Resurrection, as we did here on Earth.

21. That is, they are Cursed in that Soul and Body they shall have in the Resurrection to Eternity; and shall remain in utter Darkness here upon this Earth: Weeping and Gnashing of Teeth for Evermore.

Written by Lodowick Muggleton, *one of the two last Witnesses and Prophets of the Spirit, unto the High and Mighty God, the Man Christ Jesus in Glory.*

FINIS.

THREE

JOHN REEVE AND
LODOWICK MUGGLETON

A Transcendent
Spiritual Treatise

[Contents]

XI. *Of all heathen Magistrates, and their heathen Prophets, false worship or image.*

XII. *Of the mortality of the soule, and how and when it became mortal.*

XIII. *With what bodies the elect and the reprobate shall appear after death.*

XIV. *How the bodies and spirits of the world of the elect believers shall be like unto the glorious body of God their Redeemer, in his glory to eternity.*

XV. *Of some difference between the glory of Men and Angels in glory in the heaven above.*

An Epistle from the holy Spirit of the Lord Jesus Christ the eternal Father, written by the Lords two last witnesses and prophets, that ever shall declare the mind of God the man Jesus, that was crucified without the gates of Jerusalem: the Lord Jesus by us his poor despised messengers hath sent this Writing unto the Christian world so called. Wherefore we declare by virtue of our Commission, given unto us by voice of words from the holy Spirit of the Lord Jesus from the throne of his glory, to make known his prerogative will and pleasure both to the elect world, and reprobate world, a little before his glorious coming to separate between the two worlds, that whosoever despiseth this Writing, whether he be a King, or a Begger, by calling it blasphemy, or heresie, or delusion, or a lye, or speaking evil of it in any kind whatsoever; in so doing they have committed that unpardonable sin against the holy Ghost, or spirit that sent us, Wherefore in obedience to our Commission from the Lord Jesus Christ, whom they have despised, and not us, we pronounce them cursed both soule and body from the presence of the Lord Jesus, elect men, and Angels, to all eternity.

John Reeve *and* Lodowick Muggleton, *the Lords two last true Witnesses and Prophets, spoken of in the eleventh of the Revelation, a little before the coming of him that sent us, who is the Judge of both quick and dead.*

I. *February* the 3, 4 and 5. 1651[2]. three mornings together, much about an houre, the Lord Jesus, the only wise God, whose glorious person is resident above or beyond the stars, I declare from the spirit of truth, that this Jesus from the throne of his glory, by voice of words, spake unto me *John Reeve*, saying; I have given thee understanding of my mind in the Scriptures, above all men in the world. The next words the Lord spake unto me, were these, saying; Look into thy own body, there thou shalt see the Kingdom of Heaven, and the Kingdom of Hell: the Lord spake these words unto me twice together. Again, the Lord spake unto me these words, saying; I have chosen thee my last messenger for a great work, unto this bloudy unbeleeving world. And I have given thee *Lodowick Muggleton* to be thy mouth: at that very moment the holy spirit brought into my mind that Scripture of *Aaron* given unto *Moses*. Again, the Lord spake unto me these words, saying; I have put the two-edged sword of my spirit into thy mouth, that whoever I pronounce blessed, through thy mouth, is blessed to eternity; and whoever I pronounce cursed through thy mouth, is cursed to eternity. When I heard these words, my spirit desired the Lord, that I might not be his dreadfull messenger. For indeed I thought upon the delivering of so sad an unexpected message unto men, I should immediately have been torn to pieces. Again, the Lord spake unto me these words, saying; If thou dost not obey my voyce, and go where ever I send thee to deliver my message, thy body shall be thy hell, and thy spirit shall be the devill that shall torment thee to eternity; then for a moment I saw this hell within me, which caused me to answer the Lord these words, saying; Lord, I will go wherever thou sendest me, only be with me. These were the Lords words spoken unto me the first morning, and my answer unto my God. I being as perfectly awaked when he spake unto me, the Lord is my witnesse, as I was at the writing hereof. Again, the next morning the Lord spake unto me, saying; Go thou unto *Lodowick Muggleton*, and with him go unto *Thomas Turner*, and he shall bring you to one *John Tane*, and do thou deliver my message when thou comest there; and if *Lodowick Muggleton* deny to go with thee, then do thou from me pronounce him cursed to eternity. These words the Lord spake unto me the second morning, and no more. The third and last morning, the Lord spake unto me these words, saying; Goe thou unto *Lodowick Muggleton*, and take such a woman along with thee; and then go thou unto one *John Robins* a Prisoner in new Bridewell, and do thou deliver my message to him when thou comest there. These were the Lords words the third and last morning, and all the words in the Commission of the Lord spoken unto me; only this message of the Lord extends in general to the whole world; because the elect Jewes and Gentiles are mixt in marriages through all parts of this Earth, for whose sakes only we are sent. But as for those natural unbeleeving Jewes, that deny that God is come in flesh, those Jews shall never come to the faith of Jesus, we are not sent unto these. The holy Spirit beareth witnesse in my spirit of the truth of that which I shall write unto you, that the first words that the Lord spake into me, the words speaking came into my spirit and body, with such an exceeding bright burning glory of God like Majesty, that I did not well know whether I was a mortal man, or an immortal God; so glorious are the words of the immortal God that the tongues of Men nor Angels can never expresse it; my body also was changed at that time for a season in a most dreadful manner to behold, of the which there be many can bear witness at this time. Again, for your information that are spirituall, the Lord opened the understanding of my fellow witnesse, and made him obedient with me in the message, of the Lord, as *Aarons* understanding was opened, to make him obedient with *Moses* in the messages of the Lord at that time; and the Lord hath given him as glorious testimonies by Revelation from his holy spirit many a time of the full assurance of this Commission to be from the Lord, as ever the Lord gave to *Aaron* to assure him, that *Moses* Commission was from the Lord; onely *Moses* Commission (he being the Lords first Commissioner unto men) was manifested by natural signes visibly upon the bodies of men and women:

and on the contrary, we being the Lords last Commissioners, our Commission is manifested by spiritual signes, upon the invisible spirits of men and women, because our message is all spiritual, concerning men and womens eternal weal or woe in the life to come.

II. Againe, That you that are elected unto eternall Glory, may understand some thing of *John Robins* aforesaid, I declare from the holy Spirit, that this *John Robins* was that last great Antichrist, or man of sin, or son of perdition, spoken of by *Paul* the Apostle in the *Thessalonians*, who (as it is written) opposeth, and exalteth himselfe above all that is called God; so that he as God, sitteth in the Temple of God, shewing himselfe that he is God: this is he that was to appeare in this last Age, a little before the personall visible coming of the Lord Jesus in the Clouds, with his ten thousands of Saints in power and great glory, to separate between the persons of the true Christians, whose weapons are spiritual Faith, that worke by love and patience, with all other such like heavenly vertues, from the persons of all lying Hypocrites, who call themselves Christians, but they are indeed far worse then Heathens, by killing their Neighbours with the sword of steele; therefore their damnation will be far greater then the Heathens, in the day of the Lords vengeance. Againe, it would be too tedious to write unto you, wherein this *John Robins* did appear to be the man of sin as before said; so that the *Pope* is not the man of sin, as men blindly imagine, for want of the spirit of the Scriptures: but on the contrary, I declare from the spirit of the Lord Jesus, that all men that call themselves Christians, and yet make use of the sword of steel, in any case whatsoever, the Pope and those men are both Christians alike; therefore to be an Antichrist, or a man of sin to oppose God as before said, *I* declare from the holy Spirit, that is, when a man doth exalt himself in the place or person of God, and doth set up a worship seemingly, far more pure then the simple plain worship of God and to manage his design, he doth shew many great lying signs and wonders, as this *John Robins* did, to the amazement of many deceived by him. It was a spiritual opposing of Jesus, which is the only God, by shewing of seeming spiritual lying signes and wonders, as this *John Robins* did, yea, he shewed such signs as the Popes could never shew, nor never shall shew: wherefore that you that are the elect may no longer remain in the dark, concerning the last great spiritual Antichrist, I declare from the Lord Jesus that this *John Robins* did attribute to himself the titles of the only God: first he called himself *Adam, Melchizedeck*: again, he call'd himselfe the God and Father of our Lord Jesus Christ: Also, he held forth a Trinity of Persons; as namely, *Adam, Abel,* and *Cain*: Again, he call'd himself the first *Adam*, saying, after he had been five thousand six hundred and odd years in the dust, he was risen from the dead to deliver his people; then he said, that *Abel* was his son Jesus, the second person of his Trinity: then he called *Cain* the Holy Ghost, and this was his third Person of his Trinity. This *Cain* that was the seed of the Serpent, or son of the Devil, this was his Holy Ghost. I could write very much of his Trinity concerning his Wife *Eve* so called by him, and of a Jesus he said should be born of her of his begetting, and of a

Disciple of his that he called *Cain*, to make up his counterfeit Trinity, but that it wou'd hinder things of more value: again, he declared, that he knew all Angels, their names, and their natures; also he said, he had a power over all voyces; also he said, that he knew what the spirits of men spake that were in the dust: againe, he said, that he was Judge both of quick and dead; again he said, that the Lord Jesus was a weak and an imperfect Saviour, and afraid of death; but he said, that he had no fear of death in him at all; but this *Cain* hath proved himself an old lyar, since his great blasphemy against the Lord Jesus: again, this *John Robins* did declare, that he was to gather the Jews in all Nations, and to lead them into their own Land unto *Jerusalem*; with many more such like things declared by him.

As for his lying spiritual signes and wonders, they were these and such like, unto some that were deceived by him, he did present the form of his person riding, upon the wings of the Wind like unto a flame of fire; also he did present unto some in their beds a great light, like unto a flame of fire over all the Room, that they have been compell'd to hide their faces in their beds, fearing they should be burn'd; but when they hid their faces in their bed, the light did appear more brighter then before: also he would present unto them half Moons and Stars, and sometimes thick darknesse, darker than any natural darknesse whatsoever: also he did present his head only in the day time without a body, to a Gentlewoman that *I* know in her Chamber; also presenting unto her to deceive her, the forms of strange beasts, as namely Dragons, and such like. Again, I declare from the Lord, that this *John Robins* did present the form of his face, looking me in the face in my bed, the most part of a night, insomuch that I cryed in my spirit unto the Lord, and the Lord by his Spirit revealed this great Antichrist unto me, to my exceeding joy, and his everlasting praise. Much more might be spoken of his deceits in this kind; but now I shall declare the manner of his being worshipped as a God, by those deceived by him: they prayd unto him, and they fell flat on their faces and worshipped him, calling him their Lord and their God; also he gave commandment to some of them, that they should not make mention of any other God, but him only: also he gave authority unto some of his Disciples, both unto men, and women to change their wives and their husbands, telling them that they were not united to their own bone. This cursed *Cain* changed his own wife first, for an example, and called her name *Eve*, telling his Disciples, that she should bring forth his Son Jesus, and it should be caught up into Heaven; many of his Disciples following of his cursed example, to their utter ruine, in this life and that to come: also he commanded his Disciples to abstain from meats and drinks, promising them that they should in a short time be fed with Manna from Heaven, until many a poor soul was almost starved under his dyet, yea and some were absolutely starved to death, whose bodies could not bear his diet; for those that believed on him indeed, they brought in their whole estates unto him; so that then he had full power over their souls, and bodies, and estates, and he did plague their spirits and bodies at his pleasure, in a most dreadful manner, if they were not obedient to his commands, of the which I my self was an eye-witnesse. I could speak more of this Prince of Devils, in this last age; but I know I have written enough, for a spiritual Christian to discern something of this great Deceiver in what I have written: when his wickedness was at the full, the Lord Jesus sent me as beforesaid unto this *John Robins* to declare his wickednesse unto him, and immediately to pronounce him cursed in soul and body, from the presence of the Lord Jesus, to all eternity; unto the which I with my fellow witnesse were made obedient; then about two months after this sentence of the Lord Jesus, this *John Robins* wrote a Recantation of all his seeming great matters declared by him, and sent the writing to General *Cromwell*, and so obtained his liberty, when he was out of prison, he gave all his disciples about *London* the slip, and with what silver he had left, that he had cheated from them, *Cain*-like, instead of building of Cities, he went into his own Country, and repurchased his Land, but it was re-bought with the Innocent blood of many poor innocent souls, in the highest nature, that ever any man gained such a sum of silver as he did.

III. Again, I declare from the Lord Jesus, that all those that bear the name of Christians, and yet make use of the sword of steel to slay men, who are the image of God, they are utterly ignorant of the true God, and man Jesus, and enemies to his Gospel, that commands men to love their enemies; therefore their fleshly reasoning causeth them to forsake the Gospel of suffering the Crosse of Christ, and they apply themselves to the Law of *Moses*, to prove it lawful to kill the Gospel of Jesus, instead of yielding obedience unto it. Unto you that are chosen to work righteousnesse, I declare by revelation from the Holy Spirit, that no spiritual Christian hath any thing to do to meddle with any Scripture from the Law, given by the hand of *Moses*, to prove it lawful to warre with the sword of steel, because it was lawful for the Nation of the Jews only, by commission from the Lord, to warre against all the Heathen Gentiles that rose up against the Jews, because they worshipped the God of *Israel*, who was contrary to the Heathen Idol-gods; and this war of the Jews was lawful until God the Father became flesh, to reconcile both Jew and Gentile into that one faith, in the body of his flesh, and no longer: Therefore since God became flesh of our flesh, and bone of our bone, sinne only excepted, I declare from the Lord Jesus, that they that are Christians indeed, they are not under the Law of *Moses*, that is a Sword of steel, but they are under Grace, or the Gospel of Jesus, that is the sword of the Holy Spirit, that makes all true Christians to understand, that in this world their portions is to suffer all kind of wrong from all men, and to return mercy and forgivenesse unto all men, yea and to forgive those that would kill them, because they know all vengeance is the Lords, and he will repay it; therefore they dare not rob God of his glory. Again when the Lord Jesus gave that new Law of love unto all his elect believers, where he saith it was said of old, an Eye for an Eye, and a Tooth for a Tooth; but I say unto you, love your enemies, blesse them that curse you, do good to them that hate you. These be those Christians indeed that may be called perfect; as their heavenly Father was perfect; the Lord Jesus, who did all good, and suffered all wrong, yea, and laid down his life for that whole world of his

Elect, when they were all become his enemies. Again, I declare from the Lord Jesus, that they that are new born by the Holy Spirit, they are so farre from killing, or consenting to the killing of any man, offensively, or defensively, in their own behalfe, or in the behalfe of any other man, that they are afraid of their own evill thoughts, and much more of evil words or deeds, against God or men; because they know nothing but pure righteousnesse, pure love without envy, and pure innocency shall raign in eternall glory with the only eternal Father, the Lord Jesus: And on the contrary, they know all man-slayers, under what pretence soever, and all Covetous, Idolaters, Drunkards, Swearers, Lyers, Sorcerers, Whoremongers, and all those that vindicate unrighteousnesse, through the love of silver, in opposing of that pure Law of love, that commands all Christians not to do as they are done unto, that is the hypocrits righteousnesse: But on the contrary, to do unto all men, as you would they should do unto you; this is the righteousnesse of pure faith, which is the righteousnesse of God, which makes men to fulfil all righteousnesse, for want of this, those unrighteous persons beforesaid must all perish to eternity. Again, I declare from the Lord Jesus, that all those that hate to yield obedience to this pure peaceable Law of love, proceeding from the pure spirit of the Lord Jesus; I say in the great and notable day of the Lord, by his decree, or by a word speaking from his mouth, they shall every one of them rise out of the dust together; not with the same bodies they died, or fell asleep in, because there was somewhat of God in those bodies, whilest they lived, which perisheth with them in death; but the bodies which they shall have, shall be in forme of their former bodies, but they shall be fiery bodies, of spiritual darknesse, yea bodies of all unrighteousnesse, having all their wicked deeds of their former bodies conveyed into these bodies, as fewell to kindle the fire of new sorrows: In these bodies of Hell and utter darknesse, and their spirits in their bodies shall be all fiery Devils; so their bodies shall be their Kingdome of Hell, and their proud spirits, that had pleasure in unrighteousnesse, shall be the Devils, that shall be barr'd in close prisoners within their bodies, from all motioning or thinking of any former comforts, either spiritual, or naturall, to give them any ease at all, because all time is past; then as beforesaid shall their spirits and bodies burn together like a flame of fire, that is all as dark as pitch, they never stirring from the place of their resurrection, nor never seeing one anothers faces more, much lesse shall they see the face of God, just men, or Angels, to all eternity, and the place of their eternall torment shall be upon this earth, where they acted all their bloodshed, and all other unrighteousnesse. Then shall the Sun, Moon, and Stars, and all other natural lights in this lower creation or world, vanish or go out like the snuff of a candle, giving no more light to eternity: then shall this fruitful pleasant earth be like unto dry burning sand, the seas and all rivers or springs of water being dryed up for evermore, as if they never had any being: this whole creation being turned into a chaos of confusion, without forme, and void of all light or sap, either natural or spiritual, to all eternity, as beforesaid.

Again, I declare by Revelation from the Holy Spirit, what was from Eternity, before any creature was formed, that had any sensible life, either in heaven above, or in this earth beneath; there were these two uncreated substances of earth and water, with the uncreated spiritual person of God the Creator, in whose glorious presence these senseless substances of earth and water were eternally resident, that the creator might create or forme by his infinite wisedome out of those dead substances, all variety of sensible living creatures in his own time, for the setting forth of his visible glory to eternity. Again, I declare by Revelation from the holy spirit, that the earth and the water were both dark substances, having no light or sensible life at all in them, but the person of the creator was infinitely full of all glorious light and sensible life to himself, both within and without. Thus it is clear there was death from eternity, only it was not in a sensible forme, as well as there was sensible life, light, and glory, in forme from eternity. Again, eternall life or God, was a substantial forme from eternity, but eternall death or darknesse of earth and water was substance without forme, void of all spirit or life, so that life or spirit only is all substantial forme, and death or darknesse only, is all substance without forme; so that life and death from eternity are not bare words, as blind hypocrites imagine, but the invisible creator of all life or spirits, was a God of a glorious substance, a spiritual body, in the form or likenesse of a man from all eternity. Again, I declare from the Lord Jesus, that the glorious sensible life or light in the person of the Creator, could not possibly be known by Men or Angels, but by his creating or forming of some creatures to live sensibly in death and darknesse, shame and misery, and by creating other creatures in opposition sensibly to live in life and light, joy and glory. Again, the infinite glorious prerogative power of the Creator, could not possibly be known to any of his creatures, to make a distinction between the glory of eternal life, and the misery of eternal death; but by his forming of creatures of the same lump to be vessels of honour and vessels of dishonour to eternity: but of the contrary, if the Creator without distinction had formed his creatures to be all eternally glorious like himself, then the glory of his prerogative power of infinite love or mercy, and infinite justice or wrath, and all his infinite new wisdom increasing or flowing in his glorious person as a fountain of living waters must in a manner have been shut prisoner in his own person, and the creatures must have been all as Gods, instead of creatures, and so the Creator would have had no glory in his Creation at all of the prerogative power of his Godhead. Wherefore I declare by virtue of my Commission from the onely wise God and everlasting Father, the man Jesus in glory, that all those that are made to yield obedience in love to the prerogative power of God, are his Elect ones appointed for blessednesse to all Eternity; but on the contrary, all those that are offended at the prerogative power of the Creator, and love to dispute against it, are all Reprobates, and appointed to be cursed to all Eternity.

IV. Again, for your Information I declare from the holy spirit, that the Creation above or beyond the starrs of the holy Angels, who are spiritual bodies, in their persons formed like men, and all other creatures that God hath made in the heavens above, of that substance of earth and water afore-said, that was from all Eternity, in the presence of his eternal spiritual person, I declare from the Lord Jesus, that God the Creator hath made that creation in the heavens above, as visible to be seen, as this creation is seen in this earth beneath. Again, I declare from the holy Spirit, that the glorious person of the onely wise God and eternal Father the Lord Jesus, is as visibly seen of the creatures, where his person is resident, as a man is visibly seen of the creatures in this earth beneath where his person resides: as for this creation in the heavens above, it is to set forth the glory of his immortal person, that all the creatures in his presence visibly beholding the glorious person of their Creator, both holy Angels, and other creatures according to their wisdom or understanding, might give him the glory of their eternal happinesse of this their creation: and on the contrary, if the Creator were not visibly seen by the eyes of his creatures, then no creatures could possibly know him to return any praise or glory unto him at all, for the happiness of their condition. Therefore it is a cursed lying imagination for any man to think that the glorious person of God is not as visibly seen of his creatures in the heavens above, as the person of man, who is the image of God, is visibly seen of the creatures in this earth beneath. Again, you must not think after a fleshly manner, that the creatures above the starrs are male and female for natural generation, as they are in this creation beneath the starrs: for a woman had never been made but for generation, that the immortal God might have a womans womb in this world, to cloath himself with flesh, and that the Reprobate Angel, which is the Devil, might have the womb of a woman to cloath himself with flesh also, to bring forth Gods glorious design, between the seed of the Woman, and the seed of the Serpent; wherefore, I declare from the holy Spirit, that the holy Angels, and all other Creatures that are in the presence of God in the Creation beyond the stars, are all spiritual male creatures, never encreasing in their numbers, not being fleshly, desiring generation, but their spirits or natures, instead of fleshly pleasures in generation, are full of spiritual and heavenly joyes, of a more transcendent glorious content within themselves, and visible glorious contents in their beholding of the glorious face of God, and the faces of one another, and the glory of that place they enjoy, the which exceeding glory shineth forth through that heavenly Kingdom, from the bright burning glorious person of God the Creator, the Lord Jesus Christ, who alone hath all the glory of his Creation in the Heavens above, wherein dwelleth nothing but righteousnesse in Glory.

Again, I declare from the Lord Jesus, that no man can understand, or know any thing of these things that are invisible unto our natural eyes, but by the Spirit of Revelation; therefore it is written, that faith is the substance of things hoped for, the evidence of things not seen: again, it is written, through faith we understand that the worlds were framed by the word of God, so that things which are seen were not made of things which do appear; so that in the Letter of the Scripture, it is clear to you that see by the eye of Faith, that God hath made or framed two Worlds, or two Creations which is all one; for you know to frame a thing, or to make a thing, is all one. Again, unto you it is clear, there are spiritual visible things, in that world above or beyond the stars, as well as here are natural visible things in this world beneath the stars; because you may understand that this world, and the things that are visible therein, were made or created out of that world which is invisible to us, who are in mortality, but visible to those who are above in glory; so that now, you that are appointed to enter with spiritual bodies into that glorious Creation, or world beyond the stars, may under-stand a little clearer of your inheritance in that Kingdome made without hands, or City eternal in the Heavens, where you shall visibly see with your eyes the face of God, Men, Angels, and all Creatures, in that creation above the stars, as you see the face of man, and all other creatures in this creation beneath the stars, with glorious new Songs of spiritual and heavenly praises unto a glorious God, to all eternity. This proves the truth of these Scriptures, where it is written, *My kingdom is not of this world*:and of this saying, *Lord remember me when thou comest into thy Kingdom*: and of that saying, *In my Fathers House*, or Kingdom, *are many mansions*: and of that saying, *For thine is the Kingdom, the power, and the glory for ever*: and of that saying, *The Kingdoms of this world are become the Kingdoms of our Lord, and of his Christ*: this world was the Heavens above; and of that saying, *neverthe-lesse, we look for a new Heaven and a new Earth, wherein dwelleth righ-teousnesse*, and of that saying, *He hath made us Kings and Priests unto God, and we shall reign with him upon the Earth*. This is that glorious new Heaven, and new Earth in the presence of God, above or beyond the stars; but blind carnal hypocrites imagine, that Gods reigning with his Elect ones, will be upon this bloody Earth, because they have no spiritual Eyes to see or know that new Heaven or new Earth, above or beyond the stars, where nothing but pure righteousness reigneth in glory for everlasting, or world without end, *Amen*.

V. Again, concerning that Serpent before said, so called of the Lord for his subtilty; I declare by Revelation from the holy Spirit, that God created his spiritual person more glorious then the persons of all the holy Angels that are in the presence of God in Heaven, because this mighty Angel, by the wisdom and secret Counsel of God, was to be as a God, to bring forth his seed, or generation of wise, and prudent, subtile Serpent men, and women to oppose the Creator, and his innocent seed, or generation of simple plain-hearted men and women, that are of the spirit of faith and pure love, with all other heavenly vertues; for the nature or Spirit of God, is faith and love, and all other divine vertues, infinitely living in his glorious Person; the which faith is all power of righteous actings, naturally flowing from his pure spirit, as from a pure overflowing fountain of living waters: but on the con-trary, the nature or spirit of this God-like Angel, and all the rest of the holy Angels in their Creation, were pure reason, from whence naturally flows no good at all, but what comes into them continually by Revelation from that pure spirit of Faith, in the person of God their Creator; and this is that spiritual *Manna* that keeps the holy Angels natures or spirits pure in the presence of God; for it is the nature of that pure reason in the holy Angels continually to desire the knowledge of that spirit of wisdom in the Creator that made them, and the overflowings of that new wisdom in the spirit of the Creator by the decree of God, it is that spiritual food that keeps the holy Angels pure in their glory, or else not one of them could stand upright in the presence of God, not one moment, but they would all become serpent Devils, and fall down into this earth, as that great Angel did, presently after the Lord withheld the revelation of his glorious wisdom from him: then this Angel for want of his spiritual food of revelation, that kept his spirit in obedience to his Creator, presently his spirit began proudly to imagine and think high and lofty thoughts concerning his own person, and great wisdom of spirit within him, wherefore secretly he was lifted up in his spirit to disdain the persons and wisdom of all the holy Angels, in comparison of the glory both of his person and wisdom, pride being begun in him, *Lucipher*-like he soared higher in his pride, for he thought both his person and wisdom to be as glorious, if not more glorious then the person and wisdom of the Creator, wherefore he being very proud of his own wisdom, he imagined that if he had been the Creator he would by a word speaking have created the Angels, and all other creatures without Earth, or Water, as God made all things of; for his proud spirit thought he could by a word speaking have created all creatures of nothing at all, therefore he counted his wisdom, rather greater, and of a more higher nature to have formed all things for a greater glory to himself, if he had been the Creator, then the Creators wis-dom in the things or Creatures formed by him; so imagining his wisdom above the Creators, he thought himself more fit to reign over the holy Angels and all other creatures then the Creator; he being wise in his own conceit, became an absolute Fool: for out of nothing comes nothing, and out of nothing comes no form, or nothing can be formed; for to create or make a living form or creature out of senslesse matter or substance, of Earth or Water, by a word speaking, of what nature or form the Creator pleaseth, whether contrary to his own nature and form, of his own nature and form, this is the power and wisdom of my Creator, the Lord Jesus; for he by his infinite glorious wisdom, by a word speaking did create all living creatures in the two Creations or Worlds, of unsensible Earth and Water, that was without his person from all eternity in his presence with him, because his eternal glorious person you know, must have a place of residence, therefore reason it self cannot deny the eternity of Earth and Waters, and the person of the Creator; let it imagine never so much, nor never so long: again, as beforesaid, when the time of this proud and lofty Angels glory was by the decree of the Creator, expired in the Heavens above, to the exceeding joy of all the holy Angels, unto whom the Lord revealed his exceeding pride, the Lord then cast down this Angelical wise Serpent into the Earth; therefore it is written, *wo be to the Inhabiters of the Earth, for the Devil is come down amongst you*, this Angel that was cast into the Earth, is that Devil beforesaid, and his nature or spirit of pride and envy, and all other wick-ednesse being changed, his names or titles are changed according to the uncleannesse of his nature, and now instead of the name of an *Angel of light*, he is called an *Angel of darknesse*, as in *Jude*; yea he is called a *Serpent, a Dragon, a Devil Satan*, or an *unclean spirit*, or *that wicked one*, suitable to his cursed nature; but the Lord changed not the form or person of this Reprobate Angel at all, but his names or titles only as beforesaid, according to his nature.

Again, I declare by Revelation from the Holy Spirit, that that Serpent spoken of in the Scripture that tempted the Virgin Wife *Eve*, he was a spiritual body in the form of his person like unto a man; yea, I say from the Lord, that this Angel-Serpent was more amiable or glorious in the form of his person to the outward appearance of *Eves* eyes, then the Person of the man *Adam* was; wherefore, by the prerogative power, and secret wisdom and Counsel of God, to bring forth his glorious design, it was the outward comlinesse of the Serpents person, and his seeming wise and glorious God-like counsel, by the decree of God, became a snare to deceive and overcome the innocent Virgin Wife *Eve*, as many a poor innocent Virgin in these dayes are deceived and overcome, by the outward comlinesse of mens persons, through their Serpent-counsels and cursed temptations; wherefore it is written, *the woman was deceived, and not the man*.

Again, I declare by Revelation from the holy Spirit, that when this Angel Serpent, by his seeming wise God-like Counsel, had overcome innocent *Eve*, as before said; the very person of this spiritual Serpent Reprobate Angel, entered into the body or womb of innocent *Eve*, and there he dyed, or was changed from his spirituality, and immediately he quickned in her pure undefiled seed, or nature all serpentine lust of all natural uncleannesse, wherefore, she being now naked from her former pure created Virginity, presently she is full of natural lust after her innocent Husband, that had no desire to a woman at all, therefore it is written, *and she gave also unto her husband with her, and he did eat*; then were they both naked from that pure spiritual life of their virgin creation of God-like content within their own spirits, and in the room thereof they are both full of all natural lusts whatsoever; they being both defiled with the spirit of the Serpent-Angel of unclean reason and wicked imagination and this was that cursed effect of their becoming as Gods, knowing both good and evil, until they were both born again by the spirit of Faith, to the full assurance of a more glorious Inheritance then that which was lost through the eternal love of God to his lost Image.

Again, I declare from the Lord Jesus, that, that *Cain* that was the first born of *Eve*, he was the very seed or spirit of that reprobate Serpent angel in the body of *Eve*, and the first born child or son of the Devil and so he became, and none but he alone, that *Belzebub*, the Prince of Devils, and the only father of all those Angels of darknesse spoken of in the Epistle of *Jude*, that are kept or reserved in chains of darknesse, of unbelief, unto the Judgment of the Great Day.

Therefore, where it is written of the warfare between *Michael* and his Angels, and the Dragon and his Angels, that *Michael* is the Spirit of the Lord

Jesus, in his Angelical believers, whose spiritual weapons are faith, and love, and patience, and such like, unto the death, because they see a crown of Life, in yielding obedience to the crosse of Christ. The Dragon, that is the spirit of cursed *Cain* in his persecuting believers, whose carnal weapons are swords and guns, and all kinds of murdering weapons whatsoever, flowing from ignorance, cursed covetousnesse, and vain-glorious envy selling their eternal birthright for a messe of pottage, because the Lord Jesus hath no delight in their persons. Again, it is written, *and the Dragon was cast out, that old Serpent called the Devil and Satan,* he was cast out into the earth, and his Angels were cast out with him; that *Cain* before-said was that Serpent Dragon Angel, and his Angels are that fleshly seed of his, or off spring or generation of serpent, wise, prudent men and women that mind earthly things: These are those Serpent reprobate Angels, that go up on the bellies of their spirits, and lick up the dust of the earth all the dayes of their lives: that is, their spirits lick up the gold and silver, and put it into a bag, for their generations, and this is the food of their souls, and such like all their dayes. This is that spirit of unclean reason and wicked imagination that was in *Cain*, and now is in all his Angels, who are the Lords of this world, whose spirits wholly thirst after things that perish, and they are never in their proper center, but when the thoughts of their spirits are feeding upon riches, or honours, or friends, or fleshly delights, or long life, and such like. This was the food of that Serpent *Cain*, that slew his brother *Abel*, because he was more righteous then he; and this is the food and no other of all those Serpent angelical men and women, both great and small, that are the very sons and daughters of cursed *Cain*, hating all spiritual righteousnesse in all spiritual *Abels* as he did. Therefore as beforesaid, cursed together with that Serpent Reprobate Devil their father *Cain*, from the presence of the Lord, just men and Angels, to all Eternity.

VI. Again, for your Information, in whose persons the Lord by his holy Spirit delights to dwell: I declare by Revelation from the holy Spirit of the Lord Jesus, a little of that wonderful unspeakable mystery of God the Father, cloathing himself, or manifesting himself in flesh: it is written, *she was found with child by the Holy Ghost.* Again, it is written, *for that which is conceived in her, is of the Holy Ghost; and the Word became flesh; and behold a Virgin shall be with child, and shall bring forth a son, and they shall call his name* Emanuel, *which being interpreted, is God with us.* Again, it is written, *For unto us a child is born, unto us a son is given, and the government shall be on his shoulders, and his name shall be called Wonderful, Counsellor, the mighty God, the everlasting Father, the Prince of Peace; of the encrease of his government and peace there shall be no end*: From these Scriptures, it is very clear in the bare Letter, unto you that see God by the eye of Faith, that that holy Child Jesus, that was born of the Virgin-Wife *Mary*, he is the only God and alone eternal Father unto you that have faith in a personal God, or a God of one distinct person, and no more unto you alone, for whom is prepared a Crown of immortal glory. I declare by Revelation from the Holy Spirit of the Lord Jesus, that the Holy Ghost beforesaid, was the Glorious Person of that one only Wise God, and Everlasting Father, and Creator of all things, that entred into the Virgins womb, and dyed, or changed his immortality or spirituality in the body or womb of the Virgin, and immediately quickned or conceived himself of the very nature or seed of the Virgin; a pure natural child or son, in whom, as it is written, *the fulnesse of the God-head lived bodily;* so that as the Serpent-angel beforesaid, entred into the womb of the Virgin-Wife *Eve*, and defiled her pure nature, or seed throughout, and dyed in her womb from his spirituality, and quickned in mortality, and brought forth himself the first born child or son of the Devil, and so he became the father of an innumerable company of Serpent reprobate Devils of men and women; so in opposition of that reprobate Angel, and Prince of Devils beforesaid, the glorious person of the eternal God entred into the womb of the Virgin-Wife *Mary*, and dyed in her womb from his immortality, and purified her nature or seed throughout, that was unclean before, and quickned himself in pure mortality, and brought forth himself the first born son of God, and the only eternal Father of an innumerable company of elect sons and daughters purchased by his own precious blood: Thus immortality dyed and quickned in mortality, and this pure mortality dyed and quickned in immortality and glory again, in that very same flesh or person that dyed, and now reigneth in glory in the highest Heavens, and the lowest hearts, God alone blessed to all eternity. Thus Eternity became Time, and Time is become eternity again; for there is nothing but an eternal immortal God, that is the Creator of all life, that can by his own power, live and dye, and live again: But on the contrary, no creature hath any power at all, neither to live, nor to dye, but by the decree of the Creator alone, the Lord Jesus Christ. Thus you that see by that single eye of Faith, may understand in some measure the difference between the seed of the woman, and the seed of the Serpent; for ever since the Angel-Serpent, by his wise cursed Counsel, took possession of the Garden of God, the bodies of our first parents.

I declare from the Holy Spirit, that there is no Devil at all without the body of man or woman, but what dwells within the bodies of men and women; so that, that Devil so frequently spoken of in the letter of the Scripture, that tempts men and women to all unrighteousnesse, it is mans spirit of unclean reason, and cursed imagination, that unsatiably lusteth after things that perish; until the Holy Spirit of faith enters into the man, and purifies his unclean spirit, and reveals unto his dark understanding spiritual and glorious durable things, and that makes a man trample this perishing world, and all its vain-glory, under the feet of his spirit as dung, as it is, in comparison of the glory that is to come, in that world above the stars that remain to all eternity.

VII. Again, it is written, *a woman shall compasse a man*: that woman was the Virgin *Mary*, and that man was God the Father. Again, it is written, *a woman cloathed with the Sun, and the Moon under her feet, and upon her head a crown of twelve Stars*: this woman was the Virgin *Mary* beforesaid, and the Sun that she was cloathed withal, was the only begotton Son of God, the eternal Father in the Virgins womb; and the Moon under her feet, that was the worship of the law of *Moses;* for she being cloathed with the sun, she was filled with the Revelation of the everlasting Gospel of that Son within her, which was of a more transcendent glory, than that of the Law: and that Crown of twelve Stars upon her head, that was the twelve Apostles that sprang from her head Jesus to preach the everlasting Gospel of Truth and Peace unto his Elect: thus that saying, *that every seed shall have his own body,* is a little more clear unto you that have faith in a personal God, then it was before: you may understand that God the Father was a spiritual man from eternity, and that in time his righteous spiritual body brought forth a righteous natural body, that the Father to shew forth his infinite love and humility, and to bring forth a new transendent glory to himself, might become a son, yea and a servant unto his creatures, in the very condition of a creature for a season, that he might exalt his elect creatures into the same condition of the Creator, in his glory in the highest Heavens to all eternity, when the curtains of this lower Heavens are drawn and vanisht like smoak never more to be, time being past. Again, it is written, *he that hath seen me that's seen the Father, and the Father liveth in me, and I live in him, and I and the Father are one*: the only meaning or mind of the Lord Jesus in those words is this; his Spirit living within his body that was the Father, and his visible body that was the Son, both God and man in one person, and so but one personal God, the man Christ Jesus, he perfectly knowing himself to be the only God, he said unto the Jews, *except ye eat my flesh and drink my blood, you have no life in you*: again he said, *except ye believe that I am he, ye shall dye in your sins*: his very mind in those words was this, except they did believe, that that very person of his, of flesh, blood, and bone that spake unto them, was the only God and eternal Father, and alone Saviour of all that were to be saved, and that there was no salvation to mankind, but thus spiritually eating of his flesh, and drinking of his blood, except they did thus own his person, to be their Lord and only Saviour, they must all die in their sins, and perish to all eternity, because there is nothing but the precious blood of a God, can possibly clense the spirit of man from the power of sin; therefore if the very Godhead had not died; that is, if the very soul of Christ (which is the eternal Father) had not died in the body, or with the body, to quiet or satisfie the cry of the guilt of sin in mens spirits, all men would have perisht to eternity; because the spirit of unclean reason the Devil in man, whose nature is all sin, did reign in the very bodies of the Elect, as their Lord and King, and they were free from the power of righteousnesse, until the precious blood of a God, by the Holy Spirit of Faith, was sprinkled in their consciences, that by the pure life of spiritual love to God and man, they might break the Serpents head of sin, of reigning any longer in them: but on the contrary, they that have no faith given them, in the precious blood of God to clense their spirits from the power of that Devil sin in them; their sins will be their Lord and King, and they must perish together eternally as beforesaid; Again, by this time it is very clear to you that have the faith of Jesus, that the Serpent Angel beforesaid was a spiritual body or person in the form of a man, before he entred into the womb of *Eve*, by that seed or son of his called *Cain*: Thus every seed or spirit by the decree of God, brings forth his own body according to its nature or kind; God the Father being a spiritual man from all eternity, in time begot and brought forth himself a manchild in mortality, of all pure righteousnesse, therefore he was called *the expresse Image of the Father*, because he was indeed the very Father, and that made him say, *he thought it no robbery to be equal with God;* and that was the cause that made him say, *that all power was given unto him both in heaven and in earth*, because he knew perfectly that there was no other God but himself to possesse all power; and this made the Prophet *Isaiah* to attribute the chief titles of the everlasting Father, unto the Son, that was to be made of a Woman, or of a Virgin; because the Prophet knew very well, that the Father and the Son was but one unseparable person in immortal glory from all eternity, and so he knew they were to become in time, one unseparable Person of all purity, in mortality: and I with him know from the same spirit that revealed it to the Prophet long before God became flesh, that that pure mortality, both spirit and body that died together, they did both immediately quicken together, a new life in death, or out of death, and they unseparably, both Father and Son in one person, did ascend together, into that immortal glory that they possesse together from all Eternity, and so they now enjoy it again, in one transcendent glorious person, both God and man to all Eternity.

This proves the truth of these sayings, *Glorifie me with the same glory I had with thee before the world was*; and of that saying, *My glory I will not give to another*; and of that saying, *Before Abraham was, I am*; according to that saying of God to *Moses*, when he bade *Moses* tell *Pharaoh* that *I am* sent him; and of that saying, *He thought it no robbery to be equal with God*; and of that saying, *I am the living bread which came down from heaven: if any man eat of this bread he shall live for ever*; and of that saying, *This is the bread which cometh down from heaven, that a man may eat thereof and not die*; and of that saying, *For the bread of God is he which cometh down from heaven, and giveth life unto the world*; and of that saying, *I am the bread of life*; Again, Not that any man hath seen the Father, save he which is of God, he hath seen the Father; and of that saying, *What and if ye shall see the Son of man ascend up where he was before*; and of that full saying that proves Jesus to be the Father, *He was in the world, and the world was made by him, and the world knew him not*; and of that saying, *In the beginning was the Word, and the Word was with God, and the Word was God, the same was in the beginning with God, all things were made by him, and without him was not any thing made that was made.* Whosoever is not stark blind, by this Scripture must needs understand that there is no Creator nor Father, but the man Jesus only, the Lord of life and glorie; and where it is said, *through faith we understand and that the worlds were framed by the word of God, so that the things that are visible or seen, were not made of things that do appear*; and of that saying, *I am Alpha and*

Omega, I am the first and the last, and behold, I create all things new; anu of that saying, *I am he that was dead, and am alive, and behold I live for evermore.* This was the man Jesus that sate upon the Throne of the Father, with many other Scriptures too tedious to relate, that prove clearly to all that are appointed to eternal glorie, that the Lord Jesus Christ that died without the gates of *Jerusalem*, is the only God, and everlasting Father, and alone Creator of all things that were made, both in heaven and in earth; Therefore I declare from the Holie Spirit of the Lord Jesus that sent us, that whosoever prayes in his spirit or tongue unto any other God or Spirit, but unto my God the man Jesus, that sent me, he prayes unto a Devil of his own imagination, instead of a God; for that man Jesus then to come, was *Davids* only God and Saviour: therefore he said, *The Lord said unto my Lord, sit thou on my right hand until I make thine enemies thy footstool.* And this Jesus was all the true Prophets God in the time of the Law, and this Jesus was the holy Apostles God, and all the Christians God in the time of the Apostles Commission, or Dispensation, or Administration, that lasted about three hundred years; and this glorious man Jesus, is my God alone, and the God of all spiritual Christians in this last age, until he comes in his glorie.

VIII. Again, but some may say, if Jesus Christ be the only God and eternal Father, who was that Father that he spake so much of when he was in mortalitie, where he said, *My God, my God, why hast thou forsaken me; and Father, into thy hands I commend my spirit*, and such like; To this I answer, by Revelation from the Holy Spirit, that *Eliah* spoken of in the Law, that was taken up bodily by a Whirlwind into Heaven, where the likenesse of a Chariot and Horses of fire appeared to *Elisha* at his departure:[1] I say from the Lord, that the body or person of that *Eliah* was taken up and glorified in the Heavens by the Creator for that very purpose that he might represent the person of God the Father for that time or season, whilst God the Father went that journey in flesh as aforesaid: Again, it is written, *he shall give his Angels charge over thee*; those Angels were *Moses* and *Eliah*, who being both glorified, they did both represent the Person of the Father, in the Heavens above the Stars, as they did represent the Person of the Son and of the Father, when they were in earth beneath the Stars; when *Moses* was upon this earth, he represented the Person of God the Son that Lamb Jesus, that was then to come in flesh; in these things, first *Moses* was called the Meekest man upon the face of the earth. Again, he was a great Type of Christ in this, in offering up himself to be blotted out of the Book of Life for the salvation of *Israel*, as the Lord Jesus became a Curse for his elect *Israels;* likewise, *Moses* was a great sufferer at the hands of *Israel* with much patience; as the Lord Jesus suffered with all patience at the hands of his own People or Nation. Again, *Moses* was made an Angel of the Covenant of the Law unto all *Israel*, as the Lord Jesus was made or became an Angel of the Covenant of Grace or the Gospel unto all the elect *Israel;* so, that whosoever despised the Law of *Moses*, was to dye a natural death without mercy; as a Type of the eternal death of all those that despise the Grace or Gospel of

Jesus; and in this he was a great Type of the Lord Jesus when he said, *God should raise up a Prophet unto you like unto me, him shall you hear*; much more might be spoken of *Moses* representing of the Person of God the son, but I suppose it is sufficient for any moderate man. Again, when *Elias* was in this World, he did represent the Person of God the Father, in these things: first in a God-like manner by commanding fire to come down from Heaven to destroy his enemies, and it was so again by his commanding like unto a God all the Priests of *Baal*, that were the National false Priests to be put to death, for drawing the hearts of *Israel* from worshipping of the true God, and that was a Type of the eternal perishing of all the National Priests of *Baal* in the World at this time, who are Ministers of the letter only, but call themselves Ministers of the Spirit, and yet the Lord Jesus sent them not: These are those croaking frogs that keep the people in darknesse, unto whom the people give their silver for nought.

Again, *Elias* by his asking of *Elisha* in a God-like manner, what he should do for him before he was taken up from him, with his granting of *Elisha* a double portion of his Spirit, if *Elisha* saw his departure from him.

Again, *Eliah* spake in the Authority of the Father, when he told King *Ahab* to his face, that it was he, and his Fathers house that were the troublers of *Israel*, by their departing from the living God, with more such like actings of his, after a God-like manner, shewing clearly his representing the person of God the Father when he was upon this earth; which was but a Type of his representing the person of God the Father in the Heavens afterwards; but some may say, it seems very strange, the Lord having so many glorious Angels in his presence, that he should passe them by, and take up a mortal man, or a sinner into that exceeding glory, of the representing of the person of God the Father, as beforesaid: To this I answer from the Holy Spirit; all the Counsels of my God the man Jesus are quite contrary to mans unclean reason; yea, and contrary to the pure reason of the holy Angels also, that God alone may have all the glory, of the revelation of his unsearchable Counsels of wisdom from his Elect men and Angels. Again, I declare by Revelation from the Holy Spirit, that the man *Adam* in his Creation, was of the very nature or spirit of Faith, with all divine vertues of pure love, patience, meeknesse, and such like spiritual vertues in his spirit or person, which were the very same divine vertues that lived in the spirit or person of God his Creator; only in the person of God every spiritual vertue in him, was infinite above all measure, but in the person of the man *Adam*, although they were the very same heavenly vertues, yet in him they were in measure: thus man in his Spirit was created like unto the Creator, of the very same Divine Nature; only they differed in this, for the body or person of God was all spiritual or heavenly, not subject to mortality; but the body or person of the man *Adam* was natural or earthly, subject to mortality at the pleasure of the Creator; for, if the body or person of the man *Adam* had been spiritual in his creation, as his spirit was, then there would have been no difference between the person of the Creator, and the person of the creature: Thus the man *Adam* was made like unto God, a pure natural person, of all righteous-

nesse in mortality, like unto the spiritual person of God, which is all righteousnesse in glory.

Again, it is written, the first *Adam* of the Earth earthly; the second *Adam*,
the Lord from Heaven heavenly: Thus you that see by that single Eye of
Faith, you may know, that *God* became flesh or a man, as well as *Adam*,
who was called *the Image of God*, because God was a spiritual man from
Eternity, as abundantly beforesaid: Now you must understand the reason
why Jesus the only God was called *the second Adam*, was this; because the
body or person of the Lord Jesus was a pure natural body of all righteousnesse in mortality, just like unto the body or person of the first *Adam* before
his fall; only Christ the second *Adam* had the spirit of Faith in him above
measure, and the first *Adam* had the spirit of Faith in him by measure, as
beforesaid: again, the second *Adam* differed from the first *Adam* in this, he
being made a man of sorrows, but the first *Adam* knew no sorrows before
his fall; and why did he become a man of sorrows? it was to redeem the
Elect seed of the Spirit of Faith overcome in his image the first *Adam*, by
the Reprobate Angel-Serpent, as beforesaid. Again, as for the natures or
spirits of the holy Angels in their Creation, they were pure Reason, quite
contrary to the nature or spirit of Faith in God their Creator; only in their
bodies or persons they were spiritual or swift of motion, like unto the spiritual person of God their Creator: but if the nature or spirit of the holy
Angels had been of the spirit of pure Faith, as they were of pure Reason,
then there would have been no difference between the person of God their
Creator, and the persons of the holy Angels in their Creation who are but
creatures as well as men; therefore not the holy Angels, for they are not of
the nature of God, as it is written, *he took not upon him the nature of
Angels, but the seed of Abraham* but *Elias* as beforesaid, by the secret wisdom and counsel, and love of God unto man, above Angels, was exalted
upon the throne of glory for a moment, to represent the person of God the
Father, and he was made the protector of my God, when God became a
child; and it was *Elias* by vertue of his Commission, as a faithful spiritual
Steward upon the throne of glory, that filled the Lord Jesus with those great
Revelations of his former glory, that he possest in the Heavens, when he
was the immortal Father; and it was *Elias* that spake those words from
heaven, saying *this is my beloved Son, in whom I am well pleased*; hear him
again when Christ was transfigured upon the Mount, that his garment glit-
tered with the glory of his transfiguration: it was the visible glorious appearance of the persons of *Moses* and *Elias* talking with him, that were the
instrumental Commissioners of that visible glory of the Lord Jesus unto his
Disciples, who said, *Master, it is good for us to be here*: for that glory was
so great, that they would have been building of Tabernacles for a continuance in it. Again, I declare from the Lord, that *Elias* by vertue of his Commission did fill Elect man and Angels also with Revelation, to keep them in
obedience until the Lord Jesus was upon the Throne of his glory again, so
that when the Lord Jesus (who was an absolute creature, cryed in his agony
unto his Father, & when he prayed unto his Father, that that Cup might

passe from him, if it were possible; it being a dreadful Cup for his innocent flesh and blood to drink, he being as sensible of pain in his body, as we are in our bodies: and when he cryed out, saying, *my God, my God, why hast thou forsaken me?* and *Father, into thy hands I commend my spirit:*[2] I say again from the Lord that *Elias* by Commission from his man Jesus was that Father that he thus cryed unto in his mortality, *Elias* being then in glory; and the chief ground of all those actions, and sufferings, and cryings out of the Lord Jesus in the condition of a creature, unto a Father or a Creator, was to fulfil the Scriptures foretold by his Prophets in the time of the Law: therefore he said, *Heaven and Earth shall pass away, but my word shall not pass away*: again, but you may say unto me, did God the third day rise from the dead by his own power or by the power of his Deputy *Elias*? to which I answer, he by his own decree, and spiritual compact with *Elias*, and by that spirit of Faith in his innocent body, the which Faith died in his pure body, and quickned immediately and brought forth at the appointed time, that natural innocent body out of the grave a pure spiritual body, which naturally (at the time appointed) ascended into glory; for, it was impossible for God by death to be held in the grave; because his person being pure, his pure spirit and death could not remain together, because there was no sympathy or agreement or union between them; yea, they were so contrary, it was impossible for them to be together, except one of them were absolutely extinguished; wherefore death being too weak, the Lord Jesus, who is the only God of all created life, brake through death, and hell, and the grave, and through all the sins of his Elect, by the shedding of his most precious blood, and so entred into his eternal glory, that all those that have Faith in his glorious person may be delivered at the appointed time, from sin, hell, death, and the grave, and enter into eternal glory with him when he comes in the clouds of Heaven.

Again, the reason why mens bodies in death, or after death, do rot or stink in the grave, and come to dust, is, because there was sin in their bodies whilst they lived, the which sin and death had a sympathy, and as it were a sweet communion together, whereby death had full power as Lord and King to keep the spirits and bodies in the dust, until the time appointed of the Lord of life: but on the contrary, if men had no sin in their natures or bodies, they might live, and die, and naturally rise again, by their own power, in their own time, as the Lord of life did, whose body was too pure to see corruption.

Thus unto you that have Faith in the Lord Jesus, it is not strange, that *Elias* should represent the person of God the Father, until the Lord Jesus ascended into the right hand of all power and glory of his Father *Elias* again: then when Jesus was set down in the Throne of the glory of the Father again *Elias* then as a glorified creature, did return all praise and glory unto the Lord Jesus his Creator: so that now it is the Lord Jesus alone, by his holy Spirit, that revealeth all spiritual and heavenly wisdom to elect men and Angels; *Elias* having now with exceeding joy, surrendred up his spiritual and glorious stewardship of representing the person of God the Father, unto the right owner, and sole Heir of Heaven, and Earth, and all therein is, the Lord Jesus Christ, the eternal Father, God alone, blessed to all eternity: I know I have spoken enough to the spiritual Christian of his Truth.

IX. Again, I declare by Revelation from the Holy Spirit, that about this fourteen hundred years there hath not been one true Prophet nor Minister, sent with a Commission from the Lord Jesus, to declare, or write, or preach the everlasting Gospel of truth and peace unto his Elect: Wherefore I declare (by vertue of my Commission received by voyce of words from the Lord Jesus) that all the Ministry in this world, whether Prophetical or Ministerial, with all the worship taught by them, whether invisible or visible to the people, it is all a lye and an abomination unto the Lord; both the Ministry and their worship are as acceptable unto my God the man Jesus that sent me as the cutting off of a dogs neck. Now unto you that discern truth from the Lord, I shall give you light into this truth: first I declare, that all the true Commissionated Prophets of the Lord, in the time of the Law from *Moses* unto *John* the *Baptist*, with all the true commissionated Apostles and Min-isters of the Lord Jesus, in the Gospel, they had every one of them in their Commission a power given them, to set life and death before men, or to declare blessing or cursing unto men, which is all one, according to their administrations received from the Lord. Again, I declare from the Holy Spirit, that the Lord Jesus did purpose within himself, to send his Messengers three times to the world, & but three times to this bloody unbelieving world, and no more, for a witnesse or testimony unto them, and to make known unto his Elect, that he alone is the only God and everlasting Father; wherefore you shall find it written, *there are three bear record in Heaven, the Father, the Word, and the Spirit, and these three are one*: again, it is written, *there are three bear witnesse in Earth, the Water, the Blood, and the Spirit, and these three agree in one*. Again, I declare from the Holy Spirit, that those three in earth are the Lords three dispensations given to his Proph-ets or Messengers beforesaid; the Water was the Commissions of *Moses*, and the Prophets under the Law; the Blood was the Commission of the Apostles, and those Ministers of the Gospel chosen by appointment from the Lord; the Spirit, which is the third and last Witnesse, by Commission from the Lord, are those two Witnesses spoken of in the *Revelation*, prophesied of by *John* the beloved Disciple of Jesus, that were to come in the last age, whose Message, or Ministery, or Prophesie, is all invisible and spiritual, cutting off, or condemning all fleshly formal worshipping of an invisible spiritual personal God, taken up by vain-glorious men from the Letter of the Scripture, which were the Prophets and Apostles Commissions, because they want a Commission from the Lord.

Again, I declare from the Holy Spirit, the Lord spake by voyce of word, unto his three Commissioners that he hath sent unto the World; yea, I know God the Father spake unto *Moses* as a man speaks unto his friend, as it is written; and I know that God spake unto the Apostles in the person of the Son, as it is written, because I know the Lord Jesus spake unto me in the person of the Holy Ghost, or Spirit, as beforesaid; only, the two former

Witnesses saw the person of God in part visibly, but I saw the glory of his person invisibly, or within me, because I am the Messenger of the Holy invisible Spirit.

Again, concerning those three bearing Record in Heaven beforesaid; the meaning of those words are this, God from Heaven, in a three-fold name or title bear witnesse by Signes and Wonders, unto his three Commissioners, according to their several administrations given unto them, unto *Moses* and the Prophets; this personal God bare witnesse in the name or title of the Father; unto the holy Apostles God bare witnesse in the name or title of the Son; and unto us his third last Messengers, God beareth witnesse, in the name or title of the Holy Spirit, because our Commission is all spiritual, we have to do only with the invisible spirits of men, concerning the eternal estates of men and womens persons, in the great and notable eternal Day of the Lords account; therefore instead of natural signes upon the bodies or persons of men and women, as in the two former Commissions of the Prophets and the Apostles; the Lord Jesus beareth witnesse, that he hath sent us, by spiritual Signs or Wonders, upon the spirits of those that are sealed up through our mouthes, unto eternal life and unto eternal death, as many do bear witnesse, whose eyes are opened at this day in *England*, in this great City of *London*.

Again, This is a true testimony unto you that have faith in the Lord Jesus, that he hath sent us by his Holy Spirit, because there is none upon this earth that beareth witnesse unto that man Jesus that was crucified at *Jerusalem*, to be the only God and everlasting Father, but we only; as *Moses*, the Prophets and the Apostles bare witnesse in their times unto this Jesus, to be the only God, and alone eternal Father: but on the contrary, there is hardly a Minister in the world that confesseth an invisible God, but they preach unto the people either a God of two Persons, or a God of three Persons, that is a Monster, instead of one true personal God; or else they teach the People to worship an infinite Spirit, that is every where, without a Body or Person; but he is fain to borrow his creatures bodies to live in; that is a God of words only without any form or substance, or an infinite nothing, that never can be comprehended nor apprehended in the least by any formed creature, a cursed lying imaginary God from mans own unclean blind reason, which occasioneth all kind of blood and cruelty to be committed in this wicked world between man and man; for if men understood indeed, that there is but one only wise God, and that this God is a distinct body or person, then would men understand, that all those that are led of the voyce of the Holy Spirit of God, the man Jesus, to work righteousnesse in their bodies, they lived in, they only shall appear with bodies of all righteousnesse like unto their God the man Jesus, visibly to behold face to face the glorious body of the God of all Righteousnesse for everlasting world without end.

Thus it is clear to the understanding of all those that are appointed to know the true God, the man Jesus unto life Eternal, that there is no true Ministry in the World, because they teach not the true God unto the people, therefore as it is written, *they are blind leaders of the blind*, therefore they must needs both fall into the Ditch; Oh! it is an eternal Ditch: These are those Merchants of the Letter of the Scripture, that make the blind Nations their pray; these are those ravening Wolves that come in sheeps cloathing; these are those dumb dogs in spiritual things, that bark a true Prophecy and heavenly revelation that a man declares by Commission from the Lord Jesus; these are those that the Apostle *Paul* complained on in his time, that bewitched the people to turn from the spiritual Gospel to the legal form, who began by the Apostle in the spirit, but were deluded by false Hypocrites to be made perfect in the flesh; these were of those Hypocrites that were in Christs time, who under pretence of long prayers devour Widows houses; these are those hypocrites that are always teaching of God what he should do for his own glory, when indeed it is their own glory, (in lusting after things that perish) they desire, when they thus pray, or preach, or prate; these are those bloody hypocrites, and workers of iniquity, that the Lord Jesus will never own, because he never sent them.

X. Again, I declare by revelation from the Holy Spirit, that there is no Magistrate in this world, that bears the name of Christian, that hath any Authority or Commission from the Lord Jesus to set up any visible form of Worship whatsoever, to compel the spirits or consciences of men to bow down to his image, that he had set up for his own glory, because ever since the Lord Jesus ascended into his glory, he alone is the Teacher of all his Elect by his Holy Spirit; it is truth, in the time of the Law, before God became flesh, there were many Magistrates and Priests commissionated from the Lord, to set up, and to declare the true Worship of God unto all *Israel*, and it was death by the command of the Lord, if the people despised to yield obedience unto it, because it was the Lord's Worship and not mans worship, set up from his own lying imagination, that would be a God, but he is a devil; for his creating of a Worship to deceive the people without a Commission from the Lord, and by taking the prerogative power and glory of God to himself, who will not give his glory to another, as it is written; therefore in the Revelation, the Dragon there spoken of, is the Imagination of the Beast, and the Beast is the body of the Magistrate, wherein that Dragon imagination liveth; and the false prophet there spoken of, is the Magistrates Priest, and the Image of the Beast, is that false worship set up by the imagination of the Magistrate, and the serpent-counsel of his false prophet or Priest, to deceive themselves and the people with them; therefore it is written, *And all that dwell upon the Earth shall worship him whose names are not written in the Book of Life, of the Lamb slain from the foundation of the World*: that is, all Reprobates, both rich and poor, shall bow down onto that false, idolatrous worship, set up by Heathen Magistrates, and their Heathen false prophets, the National Priests, who call themselves Christian Magistrates, and Christian Ministers, and are blindly called so by the people also; and yet both of these Devils together persecute with the sword of steel all spiritual Christians under the name or title of Blasphemers, Seducers, Heretic, Deceivers of the people, and such like; because the spiritual Christian cannot bow down unto that carnal Antichristian formal worship, set up by those carnal Magistrates, and their carnal Ministers beforesaid, who being both lovers of the glory of this world, loving to be honoured as gods, for that cursed heathenish idol-worship from their own invention set up to deceive themselves and those appointed to damnation with them; wherefore the Dragon Magistrate, and the false Prophet his Serpent-Ministers, that committed spiritual fornication together, and all those of their own spirits, shall every one of them, in the day of the Lords vengeance burn in their spirits and bodies together as a lake of fire: those spirits and bodies that they shall appear with in the Resurrection, shall be that lake of spiritual fire and brimstone, that by the decree of the Lord Jesus shall burn together to all eternity; this is that giving her own blood to drink, who eat up the innocent as bread, and thought they did God good service, in shedding of the blood of the Lambs of Jesus, as their forefathers did; then will these Scriptures be fulfilled, *And those mine enemies that would not that I should reign over them, bring them and slay them before me*: And, *Go ye cursed into everlasting fire*; And the Carcasses of the Rebels shall be cast out, where the worm never dies, and the fire never goes out; *And Tophet is ordained of old for the King*; That *Tophet* is the body of man, and that King is the spirit of unclean reason in man; *for behold the day cometh that shall burn as an Oven, and all the proud, yea, and all that do wickedly shall be stubtle, and the day that cometh shall burn them up, saith the Lord of Hostes, and ye shall tread down the wicked, for they shall be ashes under the soles of your feet, in the day that I shall do this, saith the Lord of Hosts; Fill yee up the measure of your Fathers, ye Serpents, ye generation of Vipers; how can ye escape the damnation of Hell? for he shall have Judgment without mercy that hath showed no mercy; but the fearful, and unbelieving, and the abominable, and Murtherers, Whoremongers, and Sorcerers, or Astrologers, and Idolaters, and all lyars, shall have their part in the lake which burneth with fire and brimstone, which is the second death*.[3] Again, the bloody persecutors beforesaid, instead of feeding and cloathing the hungry Saint, quite contrary, they do not only take away the food and rayment of the Lord Jesus, in his Elect innocent lambs; but they crucifie the Lord of life afresh, in the shedding of the blood of his Believers, because they yield obedience to the spiritual Law of faith and love, or command of the Lord Jesus, either by Prophecying or writing, or speaking the Truth by command from the man Jesus, who is the only spiritual Magistrate and Minister unto all that are appointed unto eternal glory wih him, in that glorious Creation of that new Heaven and new Earth above the stars, when this creation beneath the stars is utterly destroyed, and fitted only for persecuting Dragon-Serpent-Devils to lament, howl, and weep to all eternity, upon this earth, where the Saints by them were put to grief for a moment.

XI. But some may say unto me, do you not allow of the civil Magistrate to govern the rude people? To this I answer, The Magistrate is very needful in every inhabited land, for the government of the People in all civil things, to do equal justice between man and man: if such a Magistrate could be found, it would be a rare thing. Again, I declare from the Holy Spirit, although the Magistrate be but a heathen Ruler, as he is; wherefore Christ said of this Magistrate, unto his Apostles, *the Kings or Princes of the Gentiles exercise Lordship over them, and they that exercise Authority upon them, are called Benefactors, but ye shall not be so, but he is that is greatest among you, let him be as the younger*: yet I say from the Lord, the Magistrate beareth not the Sword in vain, but he is a type of the true spiritual Magistrate, that can do nothing but equal Justice between the just and the unjust the Lord Jesus Christ. Wherefore, all men ought to yield obedience to the civil Laws of the Magistrate, either by executing of his Lawes, or patiently by bearing the curse of the Law upon their own persons, leaving all vengeance unto God, or else they rebel against God, and they are in danger of an eternal curse, because the government of this world and the glory thereof belongs only unto the wise and prudent heathen Magistrates in this Earth, who are the very sons of *Cain*, that old Serpent-Dragon-Devil, that slew his righteous Brother *Abel*, that he and his Seed that are of his own spirit, might be the Lords and Rulers of this world for ever; because *Cain* thought, and his dark Angels thinks that there is no world at all, but this only; they have purchased the Lordship of this perishing world at a dear rate, for it was the price of the innocent blood of righteous *Abel*, it is their only heaven. Therefore let us that have received faith to believe in the glorious person of the Lord Jesus, by his power patiently suffer the cursed spirit of *Cain* in his heathen Magistrates, to shed all our innocent blood, if our God will have it so, that they may fill up the measure of their fathers sins, from the blood of righteous *Abel* and the holy Prophets to the precious blood of the Lord Jesus, and the holy Apostles, that our blood that are the two last Witnesses and Prophets of the Lord Jesus, may make the last persecutors of Christians compleat Devils, with their Father *Cain*, who was the first bloody persecutor of the first suffering Christian; therefore it is written, *that Christ was a Lamb slain from the beginning of the world*, he being slain in believing *Abel*. I say from the Lord, by the power of his Holy Spirit, patiently let us yield up our lives with our God, unto those perishing gods beforesaid; because we that suffer with him are appointed to enter into an eternal Kingdom of glory in another world, hid from the wise and prudent Rulers of this vanishing world, therefore it is written, *which of the Rulers have believed in him*? again, as it is written, *Why do the heathen then so furiously rage together, the Kings of the earth stand up, and the Rulers take Counsel together, against the Lord and against his anointed, or against his Christ.* Again, as it is written by *Paul, howbeit, we speak wisdom among them that are perfect, yet not the wisdom of this world, nor of the Princes of this world, that come to nought.* Again, it is written, *which none of the Princes of this world knew; for had they known it they would not have crucified the Lord of glory.* Again, that world that we are to reign in after we have suffered, it was purchased also by blood, but it was the price of the precious unvaluable undefiled blood of our God the man Jesus, who by his Holy Spirit that sent us only, maketh us willing to taste a little of his Cup that he so deeply drank of: the servant is not greater then the Master, because we are to sit down with him upon his eternal Throne of glory, to behold his face, in the presence of all his holy Angels; then these Scriptures will be fulfilled, *Blessed are they which are persecuted for righteousnesse sake, for theirs is the Kingdom of Heaven. Again, Blessed are ye when men shall revile you, and persecute you, and shall say all manner of evil against you falsely for my sake, rejoyce and be exceeding glad, for great is your reward in Heaven; for so persecuted they the Prophets which were before you. Again, Then shall the righteous shine forth as the Sun in the Kingdom of their Father. Again, For the son of man shall come in the glory of his Father, with his Angels, and then he shall reward every man according to his works. Again, Then shall the King say unto them on his right hand, Come ye blessed of my Father, inherit the Kingdom prepared for you from the foundation of the world: Again, then shall he say unto them on the left hand, Depart from me ye cursed into everlasting fire prepared for the Devil and his Angels.*

XII. Again, I declare by Revelation from the Holy Spirit, that since the fall of our first Parents, that the spirit and body of man are both mortal, and that by the Decree of the Creator, the soul and body of man are both procreated or begot together, and they are both of one nature, and so both but one Creature; for it is the invisible spirit that liveth in the seed and nature of man, that by the Decree of God creates or begets that form of flesh in the person of a man or woman according to their kind: and thus it is with this whole Creation, every seed or spirit naturally, by the wisdom of the Creator brings forth their own bodies or kind, whether Man, Beast, Fish, or Fowl and all things else that grow, naturally brings forth in their season according to their natures: because the Creator by his secret Counsel and Wisdom decreed within his glorious Person, before any thing was created or formed by him, that all things or Creatures that should be created or formed by his infinite Wisdom, should bring forth their own bodies or kind only, and no other for ever: therefore, when men and beasts seeds are un-naturally mixt together, contrary to their kind the Lord discovers them both to their destruction, and his glory. Wherefore, I declare from the Lord Jesus, that it is a cursed Imagination in any man to think when men die, their spirits may go into other forms and bodies, contrary to their own natures or kind; as many a cursed lying Atheist prates, that denyes the Resurrection of mens bodies, through the love of some dark fleshly lust they live in: They are in spiritual darknesse, understanding nothing of the power of God, and so erring, not knowing the Scriptures, as it is written, nor the power of God; therefore, it is a common thing for these blind Atheists in their discourse, to say, when men die, their spirits may, or do go into a Horse, or into a Root, or into a Flower, with many more such like cursed expressions, they being more ignorant, if it be possible, of the Lord Jesus, through the love of fleshly pleasures, then the brute beasts; therefore they reason against their own reason, and say, this Creation or World had never any beginning, nor never shall have any ending, two cursed lyes.

Again, They called perishing nature *God*, or *Creator*, saying, God is all things, and all things is God: Thus these blaspheming Devils, liken the incorruptible Spirit of God the man Jesus, not only unto the unclean spirit and cursed imagination living in the body of corrupt man, but unto the spirits of unclean beasts, and creeping things, as those Atheists in the time of *Paul*: These are those who received the truth to prate of it only, but not in the love of it, having pleasure in unrighteousnesse, therefore given up to strong delusions to believe a lie, that they might all be damned, then these Scriptures will be fulfilled, *He made all things for his own glory, and the wicked for the day of wrath.* Again, *He shall come in flaming fire to render vengeance upon them that know not God, and obey not the Gospel of Jesus Christ*: Again, *But these as natural brute beasts made to be taken and destroyed, speak evil of the things they understand not, and shall utterly perish in their own corruption*: Again, *Having eyes full of adultery, and that cannot cease from sin, beguiling unstable souls, an heart they have exercised with covetous practises, cursed children, which have forsaken the right way and are gone astray, following the way of* Balaam *the son of* Bosor, *who loved the wages of unrighteousnesse*: Again, *Raging waves of the sea, foaming out their own shame, wandring stars, to whom is reserved the blacknesse of darknesse for ever*: Again, And also *Enoch* the seventh from *Adam*, prophesied of these, saying *behold, the Lord cometh with ten Thousands of his Saints, to execute judgment upon all, and to convince all that are ungodly among them of all their ungodly deeds, which they have ungodily committed, and of all their hard speeches which ungodly sinners have spoken against him.*

XIII. Again, Unto you that see by the Eye of Faith, from the Lord, I shall shew you that general Error amongst men, concerning the spirit of man in death; some say the spirit dyeth not at all, but immediately goeth into Heaven or into Hell and the body goes to the dust only; others say, the spirit dyeth not, but goeth into another form either of man, or some other creature as beforesaid; others say, or think all mens spirits go into a Hell or Purgatory when they die for a season; others blasphemously say, that the spirit of man is God, and that the body only dies and turns to dust; these say also, God is an infinite Spirit, and all spirits came from his Spirit, and so return into his spirit again; others say, the spirit and body, or think it turns to dust for ever: indeed, almost all men are in darknesse, because they walk by thinking only about things of eternity; but about things that perish, they think them hardly ever sure enough unto them: wherefore unto you, whose bodies are the Temples of the Holy Ghost; from the Lord Jesus, I shall declare unto you the truth of this secret; you may know, that the spirit is nothing at all without a body, and a body is nothing at all without a spirit; neither of them can live or have a being without the other: you may know it is the spirit only in the body of man, that lives, and speaks, and walks, and works, and eats, and drinks, and dies; for the spirit is a natural fire of Reason, which is that life of light, heat, or motion, that as a fire kindleth life and strength through all the flesh or body of man; only the principal part of the understanding of this natural fire or the spirit of Reason, liveth in the head of man; because that is the glory of the man; so that the spirit or soul is the man, although it cannot possibly be without the form or body: wherefore when man dies, and turns to his dust, it is that natural spirit of the fire of Reason, that was the life or spirit of the body that dyeth, or is quenched, and goeth out within the body as fire goeth out in an Oven that is closed; so doth the spirit of man die within his body from all sensible life, heat, or motion, until the visible coming of the Lord of life in the Clouds of Heaven at the last day: therefore it is written, *Dust thou art, and unto dust thou shalt return*, when the Lord spake those words, he did not speak to the flesh or outward form or body of the man, but he spake to the inward spirit or soul that understands the words of a spirit: again, it is written, *in the day thou eatest thereof thou shalt dye the death*: that is, if thou through diso-bedience to my command, dost forfeit the image of thy Creation, then thou shalt see mortality or death within thy own body both spiritual and natural, and the fear of eternal death also. Thus it is clear to you that believe in the Lord Jesus, that the spirit of man dies and turns to dust within the body; because nothing can possibly die, but it must first live; so likewise, nothing can possibly quicken or live again, but that which is absolutely dead, or dust, or asleep, void of all motion, heat, life, light, or sense, being utterly annihilated to its self, and all other creatures, only being alive in the memory of God, that God alone the man Jesus might have all the Glory in the new creating of Mankind at the last out of dust, as he had in creating of man at the first out of dust, according to that saying in the *Revelation; Behold I create all things new*, in answer to that Creation in *Genesis*: Thus it is with the grain or body of Wheat, except it dies, it never comes to perfection, but abides alone in the dust for ever: But on the contrary, if the spirit of life which is in the body of Wheat doth absolutely die within its body, then by the decree of God, it quickens out of death unto a new life immediately, and brings forth a glorious Resurrection in due season, of many bodies in the same form, like unto that which died, of the very same nature: Thus it is by the decree of the Lord Jesus, with the natural spirits of all the Elect, first they are dead in sins and Trespasses, before they are capable by the spirit or truth to live in righteousness; so likewise, the spirits of men and women must be absolutely dead, when they fall asleep in the dust, or else they were never capable to rise again, neither in glory nor in shame; so that by the decree of God, all life, both spiritual and natural must first enter into death, that through death, or in death, they may quicken a new life of a glorious encrease, both spiritual and natural; so that death in its place is as useful for the Creators raising of glory to himself as life is in its place; this proves the truth of these Scriptures, *He poured out his soul unto death*: again, *The soul that sins shall die*: again, *He cryed with a loud voyce, and gave up the ghost*: again, *In the day thou eatest thereof thou shalt die in death*: again, *His soul was made an offering for sin*: again, *He was put to death in the flesh, and quickned in the spirit.* I know I have written enough to satisfie (in the proof of this truth) all spiritual Christians.

XIV. Again, it is written, *and those that sleep in Jesus shall rise first*; that is, those that fell asleep in the believing of the visible coming of the glorious person of the Lord Jesus in the clouds of Heaven in power and great glory, their bodies shall be raised first out of the sleep of death, because they were united by faith unto the person of their Lord Jesus, who was the first that ever rose from the dead by his own power, who raised life in death or out of death; therefore he was called the first fruits of the resurrection, or of life from death: again, you that see by faith may understand, that not the same bodies that died or fell asleep shall appear any more at all, then the body of wheat doth as beforesaid, which *Paul* fitly compareth together in their resurrection, where it is written, *but God giveth it a body as it pleaseth him, and to every seed his own body*, that is as beforesaid, that grain or body of wheat that died, quickened a new life out of death, and brought forth in a glorious manner in due season, many bodies of the same form of that that dyed, and yet that body that died appeared no more: so likewise it shall be with all that died in the faith of Jesus, not the same bodies or persons they lived in, and died in, shall appear again any more, but that spirit of faith mixt with pure love, and all other spiritual vertues, that were in their former bodies, by the which they died unto the power of sin, and lived unto the power of righteousnesse, that divine seed of faith sowed in the former body died with the first body, & immediately quickned a new life out of death by the decree of the Lord Jesus; for you know there is no time now unto God, nor unto them that are dead, and so brought forth a spiritual body in its form like unto that in the dust; yea of a body of pure righteousnesse, the same nature of that holy spiritual faith, that raised it out of death; yea, a glorious body, brighter then the Sun in its strength, and as swift as thought, yea, bodies of such a bright burning glory, that no persecuting Canaanites can behold and live, because our spirits and bodies according to our faith, and shall be made like unto the glorious body of God the man Jesus, the which no man in mortality with his natural eye, can behold and live: then shall all the Elect in the twinkling of an eye, both those that slept in the dust, and those that are alive at that time, whose bodies also shall be changed like unto those that slept; then I say, they shall all ascend together as one body, to meet their Head, the Lord Jesus in the Aire; and with their King they shall enter into his Kingdom of eternal glory, where that new Heaven and new Earth are beforesaid, there with holy Angels to behold the glorious face of the only wise God, and everlasting Father, the Lord Jesus Christ, with new glorious songs and praises unto their Redeemer, that was dead, as it is written, to redeem us by his precious blood from eternal death; and now behold he liveth for evermore, therefore we eternally live with him.

XV. Again, I declare by revelation from the Holy Spirit, that when the Elect are thus glorified, they are absolutely of the very same glorious nature both in spirit and body as God is; as God and they were both of one nature in mortality, sin only excepted: wherefore as the spirit of faith and love, infinitely in the glorious person of God, overfloweth as a fountain, continually with revelation of new Heavenly wisdom, from whence flows new joys and glory to himself, and the holy Angels; so shall every Believer according to his degree in glory, be as a Well springing up unto everlasting life, of revelation of new wisedom, from whence flows new joys and glory within his own person, like unto his God; only they shall naturally returne the glory and praise unto their fountain the Lord Jesus, for this their exaltation upon the glorious Throne of his own likenesse; for it is the righteous actings and sufferings that was in the innocent body of the Lord Jesus when he was in mortality, that by his infinite wisedom is made naturally that glorious fire to kindle new Revelation of Heavenly wisdom within his body, for the increase of his glory to all eternity as beforesaid; so likewise all those righteous actings and sufferings for truth sake, that were acted and suffered in our former bodies, by the appointment of our God, shall be conveyed into our new spiritual bodies, that are like unto our God, and shall be that glorious fire naturally to kindle revelation of new wisedom, from whence flows glorious new songs and praises unto our Redeemer the fountain of all our glory, for everlasting world without end, as abundantly beforesaid; then shall these Scriptures be fulfilled, *to him that overcometh will I grant to sit with me in my throne, even as I also overcame, and am set down with my Father in his throne*: Again, *and he that overcometh and keepeth my words unto the end, to him will I give power over the Nations, and he shall rule them with a Rod of iron, as the vessels of a Potter shall they be broken to shivers, even as I received of my Father; and I will give him the morning star*: Again, *him that overcometh will I make a Pillar in the Temple of my God, and he shall go no more out, and I will write upon him the name of my God, and the name of the City of my God, which is New Jerusalem, which cometh down out of Heaven from my God, and I will write up on him my new name*: Again, *he that overcometh shall inherit all things, and I will be his God, and he shall be my son*: Again, *henceforth I will not drink of this fruit of the Vine, until that day I drink it new with you in my Fathers Kingdom*: Again, *and from Jesus Christ, who is the faithful witnesse, and the first begotten of the dead, and the Prince of the Kings of the Earth*: Unto him that hath loved us, and washed us from our sins in his own blood, and hath made us Kings and Priests unto God and his Father, to him be glory and dominion for ever and ever. *Amen*.

XVI. Again, from the holy Spirit, I shall shew you the difference between elect men and Angels in glory: the Angels natures or spirits being pure Reason, they must always be supplyed by Revelation from the spirit of faith in the person of God, to keep their spirits in pure obedience unto their Creator: but on the contrary, the Believers Spirits being of the very same divine nature of God, they are but one voice or spirit, speaking all pure obedience within themselves unto their Redeemer, to whom alone be all Glory and praise from my Spirit, with his Elect men and Angels to all eternity.

FINIS.

FOUR

JOHN SADDINGTON

The Articles of True Faith

The Articles of True Faith

The Articles of True Faith Depending upon the Commission of the Spirit Drawne up into XLVIII heads by John Saddington an Ancient Beleiver for the benefit of other Beleivers, that now are, or hereafter shall come to beleive And to confound and disprove All Despisers that say wee know not what wee Believe. Anno M.DC.LXXV.

Here I have Written the Articles of my Faith which will witnesse to be true, with the death of my soule if it be required of me. Therefore, let not the words of any Canaanitish Devill Prophane Esau Scoffeing Ishmael or Railing Rabshoceh be credited. When they Vilifie & Belye the Beleivers of the Witnesses of the Spirit in saying they do owne neither God nor Devill or when they cast any other Scandalous Reproaches contrary to Truth upon us that truly know God.

The Articles

I. I do firmly beleive That there is a God full of all glory above or beyond the stars.

II. I do beleive That God is a God of substance, and that that most glorious, most wise and, All-mighty God, that is so often spoken of in Holy

Scripture, was a spirituall glorious body in forme like a man from all Eternitie.

III. I do beleive That the most wise God did create the Holy Angels of that dust above the stars, with glorious spirituall bodies in forme like himselfe.

IV. I do beleive That God did withhold the spirituall food of inspiration from one of those glorious Angels which he had created. And then for want of that spiritual food which kept his nature in obedience to his Creator, he immediately began to imagine within himselfe high and loftly thoughts against God his Creator.

V. I do beleive That that Angel did thinke himselfe more fitt to rule over his Fellow-creatures than God his Creator, for which Pride & Presumption that Angel became accursed in himselfe & for his Rebellion did God afterward fling him downe into this world & call him a Devill, a Serpent, &c.

VI. I do beleive That Earth & Water were from Eternity but without forme, untill such time as the most wise God did create them in to formable bodies.

VII. I do beleive That God created the man Adam of the dust of this earth and then breathed into him the breath of life, which became a liveing soule in Adam & then was Adam in the forme of God his Creator, though not so glorious.

VIII. I do beleive That Adam was created so pure that Death could not have seized him had he continued in his created Purity.

IX. I do beleive That as soone as Adam had sinned then did Death enter into the world and arrest Adam with such a great action of Debt, that in neither Soule nor Body could escape out of his hands for as both had sinned so both were carried to ye prison of ye grave.

X. I do beleive That when God said to Adam, Increase and Multiply, and when he said let evr'y seed bring forth its owne body, then did the wise Creator give power to all seed both in man & beast in herbs & trees to bring forth theire owne bodies without any more additionall help from him.

XI. I do beleive That God created the Sun, Moone and Stars, and placed them in the Firmament of Heaven for Signs and for seasons, and appointed every one of them his office, and as God commanded them at first, so still do they supply this world with all manner of weather, as heate, cold, Raine, Snow &c. without troubleing the Creator in the least.

XII. I do beleive That the soules of all men since Adam were generated and came forth of the loins of theire Fathers with theire bodies and must dye with them, and lye in the Earth with theire bodies untill the Resurrection day.

XIII. I do beleive That the Tree of Life and the Tree of Knowledge of Good and Evill which Moses spake and wrote of were no wooden trees growing out of ye ground.

XIIII. I do beleive That the Tree of Life which Moses wrote of was the same God that created the world.

XV. I do beleive That the Tree of Knowledge of Good and Evill was that Serpent Angel which God cast out of Heaven downe to the earth for his Rebellion.

XVI. I do beleive That that Outcast Angel was yt Serpent which tempted Eve, and that he was at that same time a spirituall body in the forme of Adam.

XVII. I do beleive That that Outcast Angel or Serpent—tree of Knowledge of Good and Evill did enter into the wombe of Eve and dissolve his spirituall body into seed, which seed dyed and quickened againe in the wombe of Eve.

XVIII. I do beleive That Eve brought forth her first borned the son of the Devil & very Devil himselfe.

XIX. I do beleive That there is no other Devill but man and woman since ye first Devill, that Serpent Angel Devill became seed in ye wormbe of Eve & cloathed himselfe with flesh and bone.

XX. I do beleive That Caine was not the Son of Adam though he was the Sone of Eve.

XXI. I do beleive That the seed of the Woman and the seed of the Serpent are two distinct generations of men and women in this world.

XXII. I do beleive That the seed of the Woman is the generation of faithfull people which proceed from the loins of blessed Seth, who was the Son of Adam, who was the Son of God.

XXIII. I do beleive The Seed of the Serpent is the generation of Unbeleivers, or reprobate men and women which proceed from ye Loins of cursed Caine ye sone of ye Devill, & ye first lying & murdering Devill yt ever was.

XXIIII. I do beleive That those men & women that blaspheme against God & despise his Messengers are those Angels which are said to be cast out of Heaven with the Devill their Father.

XXV. I do beleive That that difference & Opposition which ariseth between Beleivers and Unbeleivers concerning their Faith in God, is that enmity which God said he would putt between the Serpent and the Woman, and between his seed and her seed.

XXVI. I do beleive That Moses, David, Isaiah, Jeremiah and severall others were true Prophets and Pen men of Holy Writt.

XXVII. I do beleive That God tooke up Moses & Elias bodily into heaven, & there glorified ym to represent his glorious person while he went yt fore Journey in ye flesh.

XXVIII. I do beleive That God gave Moses and Elias full power to governe Heaven and Earth for [the] time he was in this world.

XXIX. I do beleive That Moses and Elias were those two Angels that were to watch over Christ when he was in mortality lest at any time he should dash his foot against a stone.

XXX. I do beleive That the most glorious and wise Creator left his Throne of Glory for a time, and came downe in to this world, and entered into the Virgins wombe, and there died or layed downe his Immortalitie by dissolving into seed and immediately quickened againe into Pure Mortalitie.

XXXI. I do beleive That that Child Jesus which was borne of the Virgin-wife Mary was both the Son of God Everlasting Father and Creator of all things that were created.

XXXII. I do beleive That the Flesh of Christ was the Flesh of God and the Blood of Christ was the Blood of God.

XXXIII. I do beleive That Christ lay'd downe his Godhead life for a moment when the graves gave up their dead and the Vaile of the Temple was rent in Twaine.

XXXIIII. I do beleive That no other Blood but the Blood of the Eternall God could wash away the sinnes of the Elect.

XXXV. I do beleive That Christ's death was so effectuall that all those for whome he died will be raised againe for Eternall Life and Glory.

XXXVI. I do beleive That Christ was a quickening spirit; And that he did quicken out of Death to Life by his owne Power.

XXXVII. I do beleive That that ever blessed Soule or Spirit which in Holy-Writ is called the God-head did quicken in that body of flesh and bone of Christ which was laid in the Sepulchre and raised it againe from death to everlasting life.

XXXVIII. I do beleive That blessed body of flesh and bone of Christ neither did nor could see corruption or be left in the grave because it was a pure Mortall body without Sinne, Spott, or Blemish before his death.

XXXIX. I do beleive That Christ was visibly seen by ye Apostles and by Private Beleivers after his Resurrection.

XL. I do beleive That Christ did and was visibly seen to ascend into Heaven with that same body in which he suffered death and arose againe.

XLI. I do beleive That the Apostles Doctrine and Declaration of Christ is true.

XLII. I do beleive That that Spirituall God-head or God-head Spirit which was before any thing was created and which created all things that were created is now in Heaven, cloathed with that blessed body of Christ Jesus glorified.

XLIII. I do beleive That God will raise the Soules and bodies of all men out of their graves: Some to an everlasting glorious life and other some to an everdying painfull death which will never end.

XLIIII. I do beleive That God spake to John Reeve to the hearing of the eare, And that God chose John Reeve to be his last Messenger to this Un-beleiving world, And that God gave him Lodowicke Muggleton to be his Mouth to declare the Mind of God to Us in this our Age.

XLV. I do beleive The Doctrine and Declaration of John Reeve and Lo-dowicke Muggleton to be as true as the Doctrine declared by Moses, the Prophets and Apostles of old.

XLVI. I do beleive There will be no Salvation at the day of the Lord for those (that were in the time of Moses and the other Prophets) who did not lay hold on Gods promises made unto them by his Prophets when they prophesied That God would send a Son a Saviour or become a Child him-selfe to Redeeme his People.

XLVII. I do beleive There will be no Salvation for those that were in Christs time who heard of him, but could not beleive him to be the Son of God and Saviour of the world.

XLVIII. I do beleive There will be no Salvation for those that are in these our dayes who have heard of the Witnesses of the Spirit and have seen or heard their Declaration; And yet cannot beleive that Jesus Christ is the Onely Wise God; Father, Son, and Holy Spirit in One single Person Glorified. And that it is Life Eternall, truly to Know Him So to be.

48

FIVE

THOMAS TOMKINSON

The White Divell Uncased

The White Divell Uncased   November ye 6th 1704.

Mr James Steward or Scott, for so you call your selfe, and I shall call you so too. I have lately seene a pamphlet of yours being wrote against us and acted forth from a most malesious hearte and a poysoned tounge not for any evell wee have dun you but because our prinsepals runs counter to yours, all this you pretend you catched by it and beleived it for some time but I see very well by your languidy that you never beleived it att all but Jesuiticaly came creeping in to spi out our libertye and to get knowledg of all thinges on purpose to write against us.[1]

And you begin to show your selfe in your Titlepage, beeing called *Muggleton Unmasked* or *his Atheisticall principols discovered* and under this title you have sett down two Scripture verses, as the subject of your Masterpeece and added two more to them page 5 and these 4 Scripture verses must make good prose to your Bookes title and to bee prose sufesiant for the unmasking of Muggleton and must prove him not onely a false prophet but an Athesticall one.

But Mr Scott I must in the first place tell you that I my selfe am a Muggletonian and have lived in the knowledg and faith of that doctrin above this 40 years. Give me leave then to argue this mater with you, because I shall later prove these prinsepals and disprove yours, then your English man you bring and make the Representer of our prinseples, but sure must speake noe otherwayes then you would have him: but this Answer of mine shall bee the white divell uncased.

And now I come to Answer your 4 Texts of Scripture in order the first is

[1.] Beleive not every Spirit (saith John) but trye the spirits whether they are of God because many false prophets are gone out in to the world 1 John 4. 1. [Margin: 1 John v 7.]

[1.] Answer. This Scripture will not prove Reeve and Muggleton false, for the Apostle haveing established the church in the doctrine of Christ exhorts them to hauld to it and to keepe it in mind, for if that light and life or unction did abide in them, it would inable them to distinguish betwixt truth and erer and soe might by it try the spirits and actions of men.

But John did not bid you or any man else to try [the] spirit, for a spirit of erer can not trye a spirit of truth that hath his comesion from heaven nor to any that is a beleiver under ye comesion. [Margin: 1 John 2. 22.]

Againe these false prophets the Apostles speake of where at that time and in his dayes were gon out in to the world and further saith that there was many gone out. Therefore they could not bee Reeve and Muggleton.

But what was the doctrin these false prophets preached for by there Doctrin there spirit is known but Scott will not tell us what it was yet the very next vers declares it in denying that God was come in the flesh. [Margin: 1 John 4. 2.] Now you blind Scott, doth Muggleton deny this, nay doth not Reeve and Muggleton positively afferme it in opposition [to] all spirits and doctrins of men to all that are chosen by men and have not their call from God[?] Therefore, Scott hath brought a whip to his own back for John justefies this doctrin and those prophets justefies Johns doctrin soe that that Scripture that Scott bringes to unmask Muggleton justefies and serves to unmask all nationall preists in the world and proves them false. Soe Scott lyes in waite to catch us and is catched in his own snare. See Esa. [1] vs. 14–15. chap 13 vs. 13.

[2.] Scots second evidence to prove Reeve and Muggleton fasle is 1 Tim chap 4 verses 1, 2, 3. The words are as follows[:] Now the spirit speakes expresely that in the latter times some shall depart from the faith giveing heede to seduceing spirits and doctrines of divils speaking lyes in hyporisie having those consciences seared as with a hott iron forbiding to marye and commanding to abstaine from meates &c.

2. Answer. This Scripture will not doe Scotts busines but will give Scott another last and bange with noe les then an iron rod. First this scripture tells us of two spirits and that the one in oposition to each other. This proves the truth of our principle of two seeds which Scot rejects p. 23.

The other seduceing spirit from which flowes lyeing doctrin is the spirit of corupt Reason and there is noe Reason in this world but what is corupt. That Reason that is in the Angels (it beeing their own nature) is pure because the spirit of faith in the person of good suplyes their desireing natures (for Reason is strong desire) with Revelation of divine wisedom which keepes them in obedyance, otherwayes they would Rebell as that

Angell did as was flung down from heaven which Angell by trancemuting
him selfe into flesh soe became the god of this world, and when that seede
acts itselfe forth in . . . [page torn; one or two words lost] way there hee
tranesformes into an Angell of Light and will bee soreing up to the place
from whence hee came to have salvation which god will or noe. And in
this his kingdom will bee over all, and Judg of all Inferioretye or Equality
is an Abomination to that spirit, and from hence it is that their preaching
and teachinges are called doctrins of divels, which could not have beene
had they not preached from the divell, and there Devillish doctrin was in
forbiding marige. [Margin: 1 Pet. 1. 12, Revel. 12. 9, 12, 2 Cor. 11. 13,
14.]

   Now I would have this Scott soe far convinced that those false prophets
could not be Reeve and Muggleton for they never forebade mariage or
meates and tho it bee said they should bee in the latter dayes, those latter
dayes to have at the End of the Apostles commission and where to act by a
ministry sett up by Emperyall power. And John propheside of this as well
as Paule how that the courte without the temple (which was the letter of
the Scripture) was to be given to the Roman gentiles who should tread the
holy city under foote and these are those aweful seducing spirits that taught
lyes in hipocresie, for severall hundreds of years, and there hipocrasie was
in saying first that god had chosen them his ministers, whereas they were
but chosen by men, second by that god had espoused and maryed them to
him selfe, and soe were not to touch any man. And herein lay there hipocrasie in there pretense of holyness, but notwithstanding that pretense, they
beeing consious of there own faultes (wanting the purefing spirit of there
chefe priests and Lord Bishops allowed them selves & the rest of the clergie
libertye to keepe concubines which in plane termes are whores, and in this
was there consciances seared as with a hott iron and in this they sined untill
they were not made sensable of sin. And now Scot, these things consederd,
doth it not give a dedly blow against the purite of your church [what] the
Romish church did, and doe they not still forbid maridg to those priests and
alowe them concubines, and doth not the pope maintaine open Brothell
houses and several of those seducing spirits doe teach that those priests that
keepe concubines do live more chast and holy than those that have wives in
matremoney[?] And it is further said that there is Therty Thousand brothell
houses in Roome—whereof ye pope receaves Therty Thousand Duckits or
Crownes a year as an Aniall pension for those harlots Libertye, and there
Saint Agustene[2] who lived in the 4th centurye and was Bishop of Hipou
writes in the behalf of them saying take harlots away and you fill the countrye with [one or two words indecipherable]. It is said this Bishop kept a
concubine him selfe (as which did not) and its writen of Pope Clement the
5th[3] that hee was an open whoremaster—its this curupt church that pleases
curupt Scott.

   3. Scots third scripture evedence against us is 2 John vers 10. The words
are these, If there came any of you and bring not this doctrin receave him
not into your houses neather bid him gods speed.

3. Answer. Doth this prove Muggleton false any more than the other before treated on, for this doctrine was the same as John had preached before as in the 7th vers that hee that denyed that Christ was come in the flesh was Antechrist.

But perhaps Scot will say that Christ did become flesh but god the father did not, now if Scot will have Christ to be god then Scot must have two gods, one god became flesh but the other did not. What confusion is this, but to us there is but one onely god and that this god became flesh and that god which became flesh created the worlds as Paul saith and John saith and that whoever hath not this Christ for his onely Lord and Saveour hath denyed the father because the father was in the person of Christ and not without him and therefore Christ is called the very god the true god & eternal life. See 1 John 1. 3, Ephe. 3. 9, Col. 1. 16, 1 Tim. 3. 16, 2 Cor. 5. 19, 1 John 5. 20. By this last scripture all gods besids or distinct from Jesus Christ are false gods and idols.

Soe that whosoever brings a doctrin denying this god comen in the flesh is an Antechrist. And none that knows the truth as the truth is in him who is the Alpha and Omega can bid him god speede or joyne with him in his devosion because his spirit or doctrin is from Abell and so from Seath who were from Christ his coming in to ye world when Abell was bound as Antechrist came in to ye world when Kaine was bound and Scots spirit and doctrin is from thence.

4. The 4th evedence Scot pretends to bring against us is Gal 1 vers 8, 9. Ye words are these, If any man preach any other gospell then what you have receavd let him bee acursed. Scot saith that this is a dredfull curse upon us and that if wee depend upon our prophets we depart from the gospell they beeing, saith Scott, diametrecall oposite.

4. Answer. This scripture doth not prove our prophets false nor wee in danger. Nether will there Gospell prove contrary to Pauls Gospell but unanimous and agreeing, for the Gospell that John & Paule preached Reeve and Muggleton preach the same as, justefication by faith in Christ Jessus as there onely god and saveour, and that hee descended from heaven and became flesh of the vergin wife Marye and borne of her as other children are, and sufered death under Pontius Pilate, was dead and buried and rose againe the third day by his own power, and assended in to heaven and there sits on the right hand of all magestye power and glorye from thence hee shall come to put an end to this world and to raise all man kinde and to be the Judg of all both quick and dead and to give rewards to all both small and greate. [Margin: Gal. 2. 16, John 6. 62, Ephe. 4. 9, Rom. 7. 5, 1 Cor. 15. 3, 1 Thes. 4. 16, Heb. 8. 1, John 10. 18.]

This is the Gospell that Paul preached and this is the Gospell that Mugleton preached and cursed will all bee that dispise it. And Scott will find the curse of these prophets to bee as dredfull as Pauls curse was against those Apostate Galathians, as had began in the spirit and were deluded by false hipocrits to bee made perphect by the flesh or naturall reason, for this is evedent that those two prophets have there comession from the same god as Paule had and by voice of words from Christ as Pauls had, and Pauls had noe other god but Christ Jesus onely as may bee seene by those scrip- tures 1 Cor. 3. 11, Rom. 14. 9 & 9. 5, Ephes. chap 4 vers 4, 5, 6, Heb. 1. 3, chap 1 vers 9, 10, 11, Col. 1 14, 15, 1 Tim. chap 1 vers 11, 12, 16, Col. 1. 9 & 3. 14, 1 Tim. 4. 7, 1 Tim. 6. 14. Woe unto all such as will not have this god to reigne over them, Luke 19. 27 and 1st. 33. [Margin: Gal. 3. 3 & 1. 1, Acts 9. 5.]

Soe much now in answer to Scot as from those 4 places of Scripture brought by him against us, but I am minded to folow Scot a letle further and take him as hee goes in his pamphlet and unmaske him there as I have dun heare.

[5.] Scot in his preface craves gods parden and all mankinds that hee hath offended in it.

5. Answer. That God the Scot begs pardon of is noe other but the divell, and all mankind that are offended with Scot for beleiveing our prinseples are the seede of the serpent, so Scot you beg pardon of that god and that seede that fight against truth and god in those your prayers you offer Sac- refise to the Divell. [Margin: Deut. 32. 17, 18, 1 Cor. 10. 20.]

6. Againe Scot in page 2ed saith that hee was so catched in maintaining our arguments and haveing noe hole to creepe out at, hee cursed the oposers therof for those paines but said his soule was trobled for it afterwards.

6. Answer. Here Scott hath condemned himselfe for a damned hipocret for hee never beleived it but onely pretended & beleived as doth planly apear in his pamphlet.

[7.] Againe Scot judges it a wicked thing in Mugleton for saying that god doth not take notis of every pertickelar man and man is not to mind god but his prophets onelye.

7. Answer. I must here declare the prophets doctrin for Scot will doe him noe justis but speake those things that are for his purpose and leaves those out yt should explaine it, for the prophet said that if god did take notis of all actions there would bee a present ephect of blesing and curseing as in times past yet saith hee I doe acknowledg that god doth take notis and mind every pertickuler saint & every pertickuler devill as thus: god hath written the law in every mans heart & this law is gods watchman and stands in gods stead to condemn the conscience of every man that hath not true faith in his heart whilst in this life, to free him from ye law of sin and death so that gods person minds it not but leaves the whole power to the law that is written in the heart. But Gods power is to be seene when he shall raise the man again and that Law in his heart shall Quicken again by Gods power and stand as God and Judge to condemn the conscience of every man that hath not faith in his heart whilst on Earth to free him from that Law of sin and death.

Now Scott speaks not one worde of this Law as if man was not con- cern'd with any Law att all but all together with God in his own person and soe the Law must be as uselesse. Yet Scott might have seene this cleare enough in scripture had not the god of this world blinded his eyes, how that it was ever Gods ordinary way of teaching the heathen for they had no written Law given them nor noe prophets sent amongst them. God did not minde them any otherwayes then by his Law written in there hearts, nor punish them for there Idolatry, for they were not in covenant with God as Eserall [Israel] was and therefore it was said by the Apostle that God winked at them and left them to there following after him by that Law that was naturally written in there hearts, and that Law witnessed in there consciences eather for them or against them, according to there actions, as Paule saith eather accusing them or excusing them for saith Paule they doe by nature the thinges contained in the Law for the Law speakes in the hearte eather life or death and the heathen heares it as if God spoke it himselfe. [Margin: Psal. 10, 43, Acts 16. 30, Rom. 2. 14, 15, Rom. 1. 19, 20, Gen. 4. 7, 13.]

But Scott imagening God to bee a spirit without any bodye or person and that hee is every where att one and the same time, it is easye for such a God to take notis of every thinge, hee being every thinge himselfe, for this is the doctrin of Scotts church and therefore said there greate Saint Augustin,[4] God is every where present att one and the same time, and that noe place includes him, and that hee can bee present unperceived, and depart away againe unremoved and soe with the heathen philosohers hee views God to be a power defewsed through the whole universe as Plyney, Thalye, Plato[5] and severall others.

Soe that I doe looke upon most prophesers of Relegen, to bee the very same with the Quakers in this prinseple, and the Quaker talks the very same with the heathens for the Quaker takes this morall Law written in the hearte to bee God and Christ, soe that there Light of Christ they soe much talke of that is within them, it is but this Legall Light, and not the Evangelicall, and where they tell us that Christ inlighteneth Every man that comes in to the world, that Light of Christ which is generall to the whole world is that Legall Light. But this Evangelicall Light is for the seede of his owne bodye, and this morall Law was written in the Angels nature of Reason which motioned forth in them that all obedyance was due to God. Now if it bee required of us how this Law came to be written in the heart of men, they may knowe if ye bee worthye that God by his secret determenation did sufer of these Angels to become very man, and soe the Angels seede and nature, haveing conjunction with the nature and seede of Eve which was of Adams seede and nature and soe by generation the Law came to bee written in every mans hearte and man finds it there but knows not how it came there. [Margin: John 9. 16, Acts 7. 53, Gal. 3. 19, Gen. 6. 2, 4.]

And this Law in the heart is in the place and stead of God, to take notis of all in one Action and will condemn men that hath not faith, in his hearte to justifie him in the Light of God and in his owne conscience by that Law of faith written in his hearte, as it is said by John, if thy heart condemn thee not then hast thou bauldness to ye throne of grace. [Margin: Titus 3. 11, Rom. 2. 1, 1 John 3. 21.]

Again is it any disadvantage to a sainte that God doth not take pertechular notis of him when as hee hath written the Law of faith in his hearte which Law Justifies him in his faith as if God spake to him in his own person, for by this Law there is an Increase betwext God and its own soule and hath comunion and as I may say private talke with God, for faith is the substance of things Invisible as Reason is the Evedence of thinges seene, felt or hearde. And how comes this faith but in the believing the Reports of a true prophet[?] [Margin: John 1. 19, Jer. 31. 33, Rom. 5. 12, 2 Cor. 13. 5, Heb. 10. 16 and 11. 1, Rom. 10. 14.]

And this brings mee to answer to Scotts next charge against us which is, That wee are not to mind God but his prophets onely.

I neede not say much in this, for who is it that men are to minde but Gods prophets since because they are Gods Ambasidors and sent with Condessions of peace, soe that noe man can come to God but by his prophets and therefore saith Christ hee that receeveth you receeveth mee and hee that receeveth not you my mesengers shake off the dust of your feete as a witness against them. A prophet stands in the place of God, doth not God himselfe say soe by Moses and the prophets of Esserall [Israel] being soe Asstonished at God's presence cryed out to Moses saying, Doe thou speake unto God for us, but lett not us speake unto God lest wee dye, soe Moses was to bee a mediator betwext God and the people and every prophet is a blessing to those people that receeves him for such a one standes in the gap to make up the hedge and secure the Righteous even to such as receave him. [Margin: Mark 6. 11, Mat. 10. 40, Exod. 7. 1, Ezek. 22. 30.]

A prophet is in mighty power and his comission is large. Therefore saith God to Jaramiatt I have sett thee this day over nations and kingdomes to roote out and to pull downe to bend and to plante, so that who dare contend with a prophet[?] None but reprobates. And whosoever they bless are blessed and whoever ye curse are cursed. [Margin: Jer. 1. 10; Jer. 27, 29, 33, 40.]

[8.] Scott in page ye 4th bringes his Engllish man to pleate our prenseples with Lyes in his booke saying Muggleton hath made saints of the groasest of sinners on earth in cheateing, robing, stealing, and in page 14 Scott adds murder to it.

[8.] I answer, there can bee noe defense against slander and a lying tounge, yet this I can say, that prophets, Apostles, and Christ him selfe when on Earth hath made Saints of groasest sinners and beeing soe made they sinned no more and it is wonderful to conseder the prerogitive power and will and pleasure over his creatures, as that hee should transmute one of the most gloryeste Angeles in heaven to become the chefest Divell in hell or flesh and to convert one of the greatest divels by nature on Earth to become one of the most gloryouse saints in heaven: Kaine and Mary Magdelen will evedence the truth of this in due time. [Margin: Mat. 2. 13, 1 Tim. 1. 15, Mark 16. 9, Ezek. 1. 13, 14, Luke 7. 44, John 20. 16.]

[9.] Scott in page the 6th tels us that Christ said a spirit had noe bodye and Muggleton saith there is noe spirit without a bodye, doth not this saith hee make Christ a lyar[?]

[9.] I answer, The prophet doth justifie Christs words if rightly understoode and makes Scott and all other men lyers that say a spirit may subsist without a bodye, for Christ did not say a spirit could live without its bodye, but saith a spirit as they imagined could not possibly bee seene with visible eyes because the nature of it is all wayes invisable and can Scott ever thinke that hee with fleshly eyes can see and behold a spirit that hath noe bodye or substance[?] The true God makes bodye and spirit togeather but Scotts God makes spirits without bodyes to frite such as Scott withall in there haunting of houses soe that Scotts God divell and soules are all spirits and can live without bodyes and that imortall soules can live in mortal bodyes, this is heathenish darkness. [Margin: Luke 24. 37, 39, 40.]

[10.] Scott page 8 to page 14 is all abought Merackles without which hee can . . . [damaged page; one word lost] nothing.

10. Answer. If Merackels were besaught now it would availe Scott nothing. Neather would it if hee had lived in the dayes of Christ for the Lord not revealing to the Reprobates inwardly by his blessed spirit therefore hee allwayes tempts his God divell like as hee is for an outward visible signe to make him believe in an invisible God. But the elect are kept from tempting there God, being made to wait for an invisible signe or Testemony whether the comession or prophet bee from the Lord or noe, hee that believes makes not haste. Hee can waite for Revelation whilst the Reprobate lookes after Merackles and regards not prophesie. [Margin: Exod. 7. 2, 3, Psa. 70. 1, Mat. 12. 30, Esa. 25. 9, 20, 17.]

[11.] Scott in his page 14, 15, 16 is all railing and not worth the answering being nothing but rakeing upon the dust hee came to fling in our face and in the comession, scafingly askes us Whether there was not a great many of howling divels abought the stage when Muggleton stood there.

11. Answer. Wee grant it that there was a greate many of sinning divels there at that time and if you Scott were there you made one of them, and looke how many men and women flang any thing at him or reproached him or Rejoyced in his suferinges, so many howling divels were there which might be Legions.

[12.] Scott in the same page saith he scoffs at all prayer.

12. Answer. Here is another fals charge, for none of us that are true in faith, can Scott at any mans worship say if they bee satisfide in there formal way of prayer. It doth not offend us and wee doe not condemn them for it. Neather would we have a glidening[6] tounge hipocrett to condemn us for worsheping our God in spirit and truth for wee are satisfide that the inward speakinges of the spirit of faith in all stilnes of soule is the onely prayer that God acccepts. And the true Christian sounds a Trumpet noe more in his prayers then his Almes. And the prayers now of the true church are turned in to spirituall praise, haveing attained that gift of the Assurance of Everlasting life by faith in the true God the Lord Jesus Christ blesed for ever. Amen. [Margin: Psal. 4. 4, John 4. 23, 1 Cor. 14. 10, Jude 20, Mat. 6. 5, 6, Revel. 14. 3.]

[13.] Scott in pages 16, 17 cales back some of his Ralinge from condemning us all of imoralitye but saith there is some Morall men amongst them and names them as Tomkinson, Ruby, Chapman, Cooke, Ralph and

Attkinson, and first hee saith that these men have ever appeared willing to doe justis, but I know of many more of unjust practices who tho they dare not toy with Gods vaice regents who uphold the Law yet will they speake evell of the Law &c. and some of them have been soe Malishously wicked as to write unto there Brother, against the Law of God. And because hee opposed there unjust impietye they reported him a Jew, and soe continue to vilyfie him although hee bee a man that hath vendecated there prinseples more than all of them could or can doe att this daye.

13. Answer. I am glad Scott hath founde some morall men amongest us tho its but a few as hee names amongsest a greate many, but tho Moralety is a great vertue and hath a blesing in itself in thinges of this life. Yet to such as have receaved the Arackles of God thye Law and the prophets as under the first Testaments of Comesions, if they did not believe the prophets spirituall declareations they could not posibly bee saved. Yet like wayes under the second comesion if they then did not receive and beleave the doctrin and declaration of Christ and his Apostles they could not posibly bee saved lest there Moralety be never soe great and soe it is now whosoever dispises the truth or is shut up from the beleif of the truth when they heare it declarted will certainly perish bee they never so moraly just. Therefore we rest not or stay ourselves upon moraletye for justification before God, but upon faith in Christ Jesus, and this faith in Christ Jesus gives the saintes power to worke righteousnes and doe justise and love mercye and to walke humbly with God in whose soule it is rooted and grounded. Soe this Law of faith is a law to itselfe and lives above all law, and yet is obedyant to all Laws both of God and man (lawes against consciance exepted), for the Law was not made for this nature of faith, for faith can not offend, but it was made for the wicked to ceepe them in awe or condemn them for the breach thereof. [Margin: 1 Tim. 4, Acts 13. 4.]

Wherefore then if any man pretend to be a beleiver of this comesion of the spirit and shall live in sedession and evell practises or doe not beleive in both the prophets joyntly or speake evell of the Law eather morall or sociall, they are not owned by us to bee true beleivers or members of our church, for it alowes noe such thinges, for noe true beleiver can not speake evell of the Law morall because faith hath freed him from the condemnation thereof, but that person that Quarels with the Law is because hee is giltye of the breach of the Law and soe the Law persues him as his Enemye. Thus a malifacter railes att the Judge as condemned him, when as the jury is in noe falt for gieving sentance of death it being just received for evell cometed.

But suppose such should be crept in amongst us as you crept in amongst them. It can not be helped for soe it was in ye Apostles dayes as Jude 4, Phil. 1.15, 3. 19 but are to such as cause the truth to be evell spoken of through the evell lives and practesses.

[14.] Scott in his 10th page gives an Account of his belief in the Trenety and makes Athanasius author of his faith by which hee condemns our faith of one personall God Christ Jesus.

14. This Athanasius is Scotts great Apostle and hee cales him Saint Athanasius because hee had beene sainted by the pope, seeing hee had laid a
foundation for that church to build upon and from hence they called him
the Eye of the World[7] and the foundation of faith and soe was made greater
then the Apostles. And this faith takes begining from a bishop sett up and
established by the Emperor who caled counsell [margin: called the counsel
of Neece[8]] of learned men who did consult and make lawes from the Letter
of Scripture and there own Reason. Touching the Trenetye, Touching the
Scriptures, Touching publick prayers, Touching Baptism, Touching the Comunion, Touching keeping holy dayes, Touching churches and chapels, and
Touching concecration of Bishops, and had it not beene for one man with-
standing them, they had then made a law against priests mariages.

But Athanasius being ordered to draw up the forme of there creede con-
cerneing the Trenetye, which hee did, and the major part argreed to it, and
it was establised by law and concluded with all that the sonne of God was
hummantion, that is to say consubstansiall to the father. And from these
two darke words, that darke church tooke begining, of which Scott is a
member, and that that church and that worship being established by law by
allmost all the princes in Europe in soe much as the most wickedst of men
can stande themselves under it. [Margin: Revel. 1. 2.]

[15.] Scott in page 21 bostes himself a member of a gloryous visable
church and ministrye which hee saith hath beene handed downe sucessively
from the Apostles all lawfully caled through all the centures to this day and
so is like a city on a hill which can not be hid.

15. Answer. This is a Romish brag and it would bee a hard taske for
Scott to prove it unles it were from Constantine's time and soe begin with
Pope Silvester[9] and let Peter alone, for Tertullian[10] who lived in the 5th
persecution did not finde ordenation then, for hee said it was a comon thing
for false Apostles to ordaine. And I much question the truth of there history
in there catalog of bishops, through the 3 first centures, for ye nerer they
came to ye Apostles the more uncertaine they are, for some of there histo-
ryans say that Peeter was the first bishop of Rome sate 24 yeares, others say
hee was never there, some say Clemand sucseeded him, others say Linus,
others say Linus was before Clemand,[11] soe there is no certainty. . . . [dam-
aged page; two words lost] ordination or sucesions, as for instance in there
catalog of Bishops, Mcecelian[12] is said to be bishop in ye yeare 296, and
this bishop denyed Christ, and offerd insence to the divell to save himselfe.
Where was the visabelety of your church then? Now had hee beene truly
ordained & had receved ye holy ghost thereby, then hee could not have
faled. But I reade of Sixtus the Second[13] who was Bishop some 20 years
before Meclesion, and your history saith hee persecuted Salinlus, and hee it
is said was a bishop too, and held the doctrin of our personall God Father,
Son, and Spirit. Now if Sixtus had beene a true ordained Bishop hee could
not have persecuted Salinlus nor any other man of what perswasion soever,
for Gods ministers never persecuted but were persecuted.

And where Scott saith there church is like a Citye itselfe, even Spirituall babylon, and tho it is the mother of harlots, yett hath it raigned over all the Kinges of the earth, for the Gospell, as one said, was a foriner before Constantine the Emperor but then it became a Citysen and was noe more hid in woods and caves of the earth, for then the ministry sett up by Emperyall power, had provided for them plentyfull maintanance some hundreds, some thousands a yeare with brave houses to live in and prisons here for them to punish such as bowed not to them, and allsoe great churches with stone walls and high steeples babill like, to worship there God in, in stead of a Jerusalem temple and soe lived like prinses and were prinses companions, but his holynes the Pope surmounts all in riches haveing more church lands then 3 or 4 of our Countes. And history tels us that the value of the pope's first fruites from bishops under him amounted to above five hundred thousand thousand pounds besides elections, dispensations, Tolerations for his bulls and his Peeter pence which all together was infinite.

This is Scotts sucesser to Peeter but as Thomas Aqueenus[14] said to ye pope your holynes can not say as Peeter, Rise and Walk, but you can say Silver and Gold we find enough. But now Scott's church comes handed down in this pompe and grandure. Scott scornes to have it said hee will goe to heaven with such poore prophets as Reeve & Muggleton. Noe, noe, hee will goe alonge with this great Citye Babylon so gloryously decked, and perhaps hee may borow the popes chartt to Carye him thither and to free him for goeing by purgetory seeing hee hath dun him such servis as to damn Reeve and Muggleton with his bell, Booke, and Kandle[15] and all his folowers.

[16.] Scott goes on saying that our prophets aimed the time well to come forth att such a time as all Brittaine was in an uprore, the Cromwelian partye minding nother but there conquests and the murdering of there Kinge and his best subjects.

16. Answer. It was . . . [damaged page; one word lost] providence of God to chuse them att such a time. Other wayes they could not have had so much time as to finish there Testemonys for there was such a ministrey and church governmente before that was broke forth as would have taken away there lives, for there Commession Courte and Star chamber equalled the popeish Tyrenye, and were such as these the Kinges best friends. Naye certainly had not the Kinge adheared to them, he had cet his throne, but it was they that stured up the King against Tender Consciances, for att that time the bishops doctrin, litergie, and worship difered little from poperye, for the Convocation owth of the clargie the yeare 1640 was that they did aprove of the doctrin and disipline of the Church of England as containing all thinges necessary to Salvation, and that they will not Consent to alter the governmente of this church by Archbishops, Bishops, Deacons, Archdeacons, &c.

Now in this convocation owth the Scripture was as good as sett asside and made useless for there littergie stoode in the round of the Scripture was as good as sett asside and made useless for there littergie stoode in the round of the Scripture and soe noe man needed to seeke further for Salvation, if hee would give consente to there littergie and church dissipline, and those people more consciensious then the rest could not doe soe, and that was one occasion of the war.

And now pray Mr Scott was not this apining of there faith on those Lord Bishops sleeves. And this you like well enough, because such as those are chosen by Kingly authorety and Earthy authoretye, but you hate such men as are chosen by heavenly authoretye. Such as aforsaid you like well enough, and all these preseding, which is manifest was very crewell, for in Arch Bishop Laudes[16] araignment hee was charged for cutting off mens eares, searing there cheekes, slitting there nosses, whiping them openly in the stockes, and att carts tayles, banishing them there countrye, and shutting them prissoners, and all soe accationed that bloodye war betweene Englsnd and Scottland. There was 14 Articles of Impeachment against him put up in the house, and Mr Pim in his speech cales the bishops Trumpeters of Sedession. And Gremstan in his speech to the house cales them woofles that devoured the sheepe and wasps that sting in the tayle &c.

Bishop Wren[17] was like wayes araigned before that Parlement 1640 and 25 Articles of Impeachment against him, one was of his booke of Articles that every church warden must sware, containing in it 139 Artickles and 897 Questions, which noe one judges many of them redeckulus, and imposible to bee perpharmed, and he persecuted them that would not sware to them. These are the men that Scott calles the Kings best friends, soe wee may see what a man this Scott would bee if hee were in Authoretye. Would hee bee anything les then a persecuting divell in hose and habbitt as by his next charge doth apeare.

[17.] Scott in page 16 railes at that saying of the prohets concerning Elias beeing putt in Authoretye of a father whilst Christ was here on earth . . . [damaged page; one word lost] redemption for all his elect calling it a monstrous Blasphemy and cursed Impietye, crying out saying, O thou Tratorye to the Divell to sett over him his creature.

17. Answer. Scott beeing soe hardened exalted in pride that hee can know nothing how redempsion was wrought or by whome, and it is impossible for proude flesh ever to beleive that God should become flesh, and the creator to become a creature, yea and a servant to his creature, and to humble him selfe unto him selfe sufering to cause his humanity to speake, praye, or crye unto his divinitye within him or unto his own spirituall charge comitted unto his Angels without him for a manifestation of his unserchable wisdome, power, and glory in shame and weakening as well as in power and glory. But this is not to be comprehended where pride raigns, neather are such perles fitt to bee given to swine. But I shall present to the humble soul all Scriptures for a confermation of what is heare written by which may bee seene . . . [damaged page; one word lost] Angels they whom that watched over Jesus both at his baptism . . . [damaged page; two words lost] and figuration at his pasion, at his resurection, and at his assension . . . [page damaged; two words lost] that gave John Baptiste his comesion, and let Scott

frett himselfe and barke att these thinges as noveltes as the dog barked at the moone. [Margin: damaged page margins; some references lost; Esa. 63. 10, 11, Luke 10. 21, John 17. 5, 24 compared with John 14. 9, 10, Luke 22. 42, 43, Psa. 21. 11, Mat. 27. 46 and 28. 2, Luke 24. 4, Luke 1. 12, Mat. 17. 13, Mark 9. 5, 12, Acts 1. 10.]

[18.] Scott in page 24, 25 saith he hath heard tell of the divels entring in to the serpent and soe tempted the woman but, saith hee, how the divell should come in to the woman is a novell move fitt to be tould amongst the Athenians, then amongst Christians, and to talke of the divell entring in to her womb & makeing it eateing is a languidy fit for a mounte bank & tupany stage.[18]

18. Answere. If Scott do beleive that Christ is God then I would aske Scott whether hee can tell how God came in to the Vergin Marys womb if acording to the holy Scriptures, the holy ghost or holy God over shadowed the Vergin Marye. Why might not ye serpent over shadow Eve? It is the same thinge [small five-word insertion, unreadable]. And the prophet Reeve saith it is called Eateing for two respects: first, that neather man nor Angell should know his secrets untill itt was his divine pleasure that hee might receave praise and glorye allone from all those hee should reveale theme to [margin: If ye holy ghost over shadowed ye Vergin Marye, why might not the serpent Angell over shadowe Eve, they beeing both spirituall substance.]; secondly, the spirit of God called it Eateing because of the scaursitye of that speech, for the Scripture languidg is much like unto a modest vergin who is loath to have her secret parts mentioned in the least tho they are as usefull in there kind, and as honourable, because the onely Lord of all Life and Glorye hath honered theme him selfe by his blessed bearth. [Margin: Soe Scott may scoff at over shadowing as . . . (damaged margin; one word lost) at Eatinge.]

Againe, I demand of Scott where hee hath read or heard of the divell entring into a natural serpent. Was it amongst those Athenians spake of, for I am sure you never heard it from the Scriptures. But Scott doe you not comett blasphamy against God and charge him with injustis in this thinge, for wee reade that God gave Sentance upon Adam and upon Eve and upon this serpent act for natural lust and so creape Scott free and made free by Scott and thus this blind Scott hath heare charged God with injustis but Scott will finde and say that serpent to be the divell that was cursed and hee of his seede and soe cursed in him and the seed of the woman will bruse this serpents head.

[19.] Scott page 29, 30 barkes at that prenseple of saying that the substance of earth and water were from eternetye and then askes the question, saying, Doth not all the knowing world experimentaly understand that from aire are all other elementys produced?

19. Answer. It is not all the knowing world that understands as Scott doth, but the unknowing world is in Scots spirit of erer as doctor More[19] for one, for treating on the Scripture of the Spiirit of God moveing upon the waters, saith that that Spirit of God was winde, and will have everything

made of aire, and saith that the divels have bodyes of aire, and that the soules of the wicked after death doth inhabite in the aire with divels and that the Angles are of aire and all thinges of aire. [Margin: Gen. 1. 2.]

[20.] This is Scotts knowing world that will have all thinges made out of noethinge; that which is materyall to be made out of that which is imateryal, matter out of noe matter, a plaine contradection and nonsence.

[20.] Scott, if he must have anythinge to make every thinge of, it must be aire which is noe substance a God of aire, a divell of aire, Angels of aire, heaven and earth and the soules of all men of aire, and at last all thinges must turne to aire again, and here is discovred the prince of the aire in all these airey disputes and rules in all Scotts knowing world which are the children of disobedyance and unbeleife.

[21.] Scott in page 33 roars against the mortalety of the soule by the parable of Dives and Lasarus and two or three places more and from these places condemes us as a vile people, haveing our consciances seared as with a hott iron and given up to beleive lyes and are bewitched with such prinseples with abundance more of divellish ralery.

21. Answer. That the soule is mortall and doth dye with the bodye till the Reserection day is one of the clearest thinges to prove as anything in Scripture, and those places of Scripture that Scott speakes of have beene clearly opened by the prophets and it is needles to speake of them againe, onely this I must tell Scott that the heathen philosohers and not the prophets were the first brothers of it, as Thales, Democrates, the Stoicks and Plato. This Plato lived in the time of the prophet Jeramyath, and Scotts famous church preaches up Plato more than they does the prophet Jeramiath. [One line crossed out.]

[1.] Yet I have read the Pope John 22[20] openly asserted that soules are mortall and that they dye together with there bodyes till the reserection day and . . . [torn page; one or two words lost] of the cardenals withstode him (said Calvin)[21] but the scooles of Paris moved the Kinge of France to compass him to recante it, the Kinge forbiding his subjects to comunocate with him, unles hee did out of hand repente and the Kinge proclamed it by an Herald, the pope compelled by that nessesetye adjured his erer, but tho the uneversetye of Paris condemned it of heresie and hee abjured his erer, yet hee cept it secretly to him selfe. And him that was called Saint Irinius[22] was of the same opinion, and soe was there Saint Bernard[23] the monke with many others, being convenced by these Scriptures folowing both of the souls production and death. Gen. 1. 28 and 5. 5 and 46. 26 and 49. 33, Esa. 38. 17, 1 Cor. chap. 15 vers 19, 32, Acts 2 vers 29, 31, 34.

2. It is clear by these Scriptures folowing that the pure soule of Christ did dye then well may arise. Esa. 53. 10, 12, Mat. 26. 38, John 10. 18, Acts 2 vers 29, 31, 34.

3ly. That there can bee noe Eternall Life attained too till Christ comes and the saints doe . . . [damaged page; one word lost] for that day. 1 Thes. 1. 10, Phelep. 3. 20, Heb. 10. 36 and 9. 28, Revel. 22. 19.

4. Noe rewards given till the reserection day. Revel. 22. 12. Mat. 28. 19, Revel. 2. 10, 1 Pet. 5. 4, 2 Tim. 4. 8, Col. 3. 1, Revel. 6. 11, John 3. 28 . . . [damaged page; one reference obscured].

And thus Scott I have answered all the choise and materiall maters, you have bosted against us in your raileing pamphlett, and have folowed you to the 35 page which is the last page where I leave you vometting out the remeander of your poyson upon the prophet Muggleton, who was an inocent person and never broke the law in his life, but was faithfull in his comession. And yet you have murdered him with your heart and tongue as Kaine your father did, and his brother with heart and hande, and vengance . . . [damaged page; two or three words lost] you as it did Kaine, for it is not soe much the Muggletonians . . . [damaged page; two or three words lost] doth and will persue you, for God him selfe did say that hee . . . [damaged page; two or three words lost] two edged sword of his spirit in to there mouthes and that whoever pronounced cursed through there mouthes were cursed to eternety and in there first declaration, they gave this curse upon all both high and loe bee hee Kingte or begger that should call it heresie, delusion, a lye, or of the divell, or speaks evell of it in the least, and that curse being then given in there first declaration, took ephect from that time, and will doe to the end of the world. Therefore, whoever have read these writinges or have heard of there messige and doctrine or shall hereafter, and have or shall dispise it, are concearned in this curse, and have brought it upon there own heads, and must sufer for it to all eternetye. And soe, Scott, deliver your selfe from it by proving God and these prophets lyers if you can as you have proved your self one, for the prophet Muggleton tho his memory much failed him, yet nothing hapened to him but what was common to all men and he was sencable to the last, for the weeck before hee dyed hee was sencable of his death at that time and justifide the comesion. And before severall witnesses hee delivered in to my hand, that manuscrept of his intitled the Acts of the Wittneses of the Spirit, being wrote with his owne hande, for to be printed by mee after his dissease, which was perphormed. And if Scott can stur up the powers of the nation to persecute us, or to persecute mee for this my answer to his wicked pamphlet, hee may use his power and I shall use my faith to justyfye this comesion of the spirit and the doctrin there of to be true and if there law can doe it, to seale it with my blod.

Thomas Tomkinson

SIX

Letters

1. Copy, John Reeve to Christopher Hill of Maidstone, Kent,
11 June 1656. Add. MSS 6071/10.

Dear Friend in the Eternall Truth My Love to you and the rest of our
Spiritual Friends remembered.

Brother Hill,

It seems very strange to me That you with the rest of former Friends,
make no Enquiry atte me whether I am dead or alive. What, Have the
unnecessary things and Cares of this World Swallowed up your former Love
to the Truth? Though I am moved in this manner to write unto you, I trust
you have not so learned Christ.

Friend, The Reason of my not sending unto you this Long Season, is this,
because my Wife and I were both very Sicke and Weake, of which Sicknesse
the 29th of March last my Wife died.

Immediately after I had buried my Wife, the Lord our God called me to
visit some of his people living neare the Citty of Cambridge as he once called
me to visitt you. Yea it was in the very same manner for one of the Chiefe
Speakers of the Ranters being convinced by this Truth who formerly had
deceived them, took a parcell of my bookes and presented them to them,
upon which they greatly desired me as you formerly did. I hope there is
about half a score of them that have received the Truth in Sincerity of heart,

193

they are Husbandmen and tradesmen that labour for their bread as you do. They rejoice in those that really possesse this Truth though by Face unknown.

Christopher Hill,

You seem to forfeit your Engagement to your Father-in-Law. You know the Time is expired concerning your payment of the Money which was lent to you, and not to him. Wherefore as you love the Truth I desire you to send me the Fifteen Shillings remaining behind speedily, that I may restore it to the right Owner.

Now concerning my owne Condition, it is thus: On May Day last I was Senseless two or three times Insomuch, that if a Faithful Friend had not been by me with a little Cordiall I had immediately died. I still continue very sicke and weake so that of necessity I must either mend or end in a little Space. As for reliefe now I have most need of it, it hath been very small of late. I wish it may not be a burthen to the Conscience of some when I am gone; The widdowes mite will be a witnesse against all Carnall Excuses in these that own this Truth. It may be you may thinke I have no need of your Charity now because the merchant for a little Season allowed me Five Shillings a Weeke, but if you thinke so you are much mistaken, for I have had none from him a pretty while neither doe I know whether I shall have any more from him at all, for when he tooke Ship for Barbadoes he had not where withall to leave for his Wife and Children, through the unjust dealings of unreasonable men. Brother Hill You may remember you sent me word That if the London Christians would contribute Weekly or Monthly to my Necessity you would do the like. You will do well to keep your covenant.

And so I committ you to the most High and remain Yours in all Righteousnesse

John Reeve

My dwelling is in Bishopsgate Street, near Hog Lane end, with three sisters that keep a Sempsters shop.

Direct your Letters to our brother Muggleton, to be conveyed to me and the 15s to him for me, You know where he dwells. It is in Trinity lane, over against a Browne bakers.

2. Copy, John Reeve to Christopher Hill, 1656.
Add. MSS 60171/11.

For his Loving Friend Christopher Hill, Heelmaker in Stone Street, in Maidstone in Kent. These.

Brother Hill,

I have received your Letter and your kind token for which I acknowledge your kindness to Truth.

As for my neglect in Writing to you, my great Troubles of Sickness and Mortality hath Hindered it, I hope whilst I am able to write for Time to come you shall not charge me with any such neglect. In the mean Season I do not desire your Charity unlesse you can spare it. Remember my kind Love to your Mother Wyles, to Thomas Martin and Goodman Young. And I rejoice in the Lord for you that the Truth abides in you. As for the fifteen Shillings, I am glad of your Care for the Truths sake because it was lent to me upon that Account.

No more at present but desiring my God abundantly to establish you in all Spiritual Excellencies, unto whose Infinite Grace I commend you all and remaine yours in all righteousnesse.

London the last 1656   John Reeve

3. Copy, John Reeve to Christopher Hill, no date.
Add. MSS 60171/12.

Brother Hill, in the Eternall Truth.

My Love to you and Rest of your Friends. This is a Spiritual Love Letter that I am moved to write unto you. Wherefore by Virtue of my Commission I pronounce thee, Thomas Martin, William Young and Elizabeth Wyles the Blessed of the Lord to Eternity. The Remembrance of this the Lords Blessing will do you no harm when I am in my Grave. In the meane Season our good God cause you to love one another more than your Temporal Enjoyments and that will become a Heaven upon Earth in your Innocent Soules; Faith fetcheth Spirituall Comfort from the Fountaine to each particular Soule but Love fulfilleth all Righteousnesse both to God and Man. Oh the Transcendent Excellency of the Love of Christ in his new Borne People. It is not to be exprest by the Tongue of men or Angells.

John Reeve

4. Copy, John Reeve to Mrs. Alice Webb,
15 August 1656. Add. MSS 60171/13.

Loving Friend

Desiring your Eternnall Happinesse in that Place of Glory above the Starrs I am moved from the Spirit of the Lord to write these Lines unto your serious Consideration.

This I know assuredly as God knows himself That Jesus Christ from his Throne of Glory spake to me by Voice of Words three mornings together, which Speaking of his hath opened my dark Understanding to declare such

Spirituall Light to the chosen of God, as never was so clearly manifested before; Especially in these six Foundations

First, What the person of the true God is, and his Divine nature.

Secondly, What the persons of the holy Angells are, and their Nature.

Thirdly, What the Persons of the Devills are and their natures, and what the person of the Devill was before he became a Devill and begot Millions of darke Angells or Devills, it being all one.

Fourthly, In what Condition the Man Adam was created in, and by what meanes he lost his first Estate and the effects of it.[1]

Fifthly, What Heaven and Glory is, and the eternall residence of it.

Sixthly, What Hell and Eternall Death is, and the Place where it shall be to Eternity.

This I know certainly That before the Lord sent me to declare his pleasure unto his people No man upon this Earth did clearly understand any one of these Six Fundamental Truths, Which to understand is Life Eternal, and the Ignorance of them is Death Eternall, now the Lord hath sent his two Messengers to declare them. I meane all those that may be informed in these Spiritual things, and doe reject us (that are the Lord's Messengers of these things of Salvation) through the Love of Carnall things, they must all perish to Eternity.

Againe, Wee know from the Lord by that Infallible Spirit that he hath given us, of divers persons that shall be eternally blessed with us: and all that wee pronounce Cursed to Eternity are eternally Cursed, as sure as Jesus Christ the Lord of Life is blessed, because it is his Curse and not ours.

Again, if the Lord Jesus doe not beare Witnesse unto our Testimony and make it evident That he hath sent us in a few Months then you may conclude that there was never any true prophets nor Christ, nor Apostles nor Scripture spoken from the Mouth of God to Men. But there is nothing but the Wisdome of men and Nature their God. But this we know That those that are joined with us are Partakers of those Truths and shall be blessed for evermore and shall in the meane time patiently wait for the fullfilling of our prophecie and shall have Power over their Thoughts, Words and Deeds purifying their hearts by Faith in the person of God even as he is pure; trampling all the Riches and Honour of this World under the Feet of their Soules as Dung because they have tasted of that Glory to come that no Tongue of men or Angell can expresse. And this makes them not only love one another in Carnall Things but for the Truths sake they are ready if need require to forsake all relations and Life itselfe for one another, and is that power of that one only Faith and Truth declared from the Spirit of God the man Jesus by us which none enjoyes but those of this Faith.

Much more might I write, but speaking Face to Face, if it may be, is farre more profitable: Farewell.

John Reeve, The true Prophet of the only true Personal God the Lord Jesus Christ upon the Throne of Immortall Glory in the highest Heavens.

5. Copy, Lodowick Muggleton to Mrs. Elizabeth
Dickinson of Cambridge, 20 August 1658. Add.
MSS 60171/21.

Dear Friend in the Eternal Truth, Elizabeth Dickinson My Love remem-
bred unto you and your Husband as being in the same Faith also.

I am very well persuaded of your Eternal Happinesse and I would willingly say unto you, as our Lord did in another Case to the worman that
was troubled with the bloody Issue who said within herselfe That if she
could but touch his Garment shee should be made whole and according
to her Faith it was unto her for shee felt in herself That she was healed
of her plague and not only so but shee had assurance of Everlasting
Life which was farre beyond the Health of her body Which Faith of hers
did drawe virtue out of our Lord Which made him to say That virtue
was gone out of him and he looked round about to see her that had done
this thing And he said unto her, Daughter thy Faith hath made thee whole
Goe in peace and be whole of thy plague As if our Lord should say it was
her owne Faith that did fetch Virtue out of him and it was her owne Faith
that did heal herselfe, as if he had no hand in the thing he was but the
Object of her Faith, it was her Faith that did drawe that from the
Object.

And so it is with you, John Reeve and myself, the chosen Witnesses of
the Spirit, wee having the Commission and Burthen of the Lord upon us.
Wee are made the Object of your Faith And as your faith is strong in this
Commission of the Spirit so shall the Virtue flow from it to your Eternal
Rest and Peace so that you shall be perfectly whole as to the Relation to the
Feares of Eternal Death, as that woman was in her body of the bloody issue
And our Faith being in me as the Object in relation to the Commission of
the Spirit it is your Faith will make you whole, For my Faith is in you
concerning your Eternal Happiness. Let yours be in me and you shall fare
no worse than I doe, for you shall have the end of your Faith even the
Salvation of your Soul as well as I, And that thou may be sure I doe declare
you one of the blessed of the Lord to all Eternity.

But as for those Feares that do arise in you from the Weaknesse of your
nature, or from a Distemper in nature I cannot promise you Deliverance
from it, But it is very probable That the Assurance of Eternal Life will mit-
igate and Weaken the other.

I thought good to write these few lines unto you for your further Con-
firmation of your Eternall Happiness after Death.

No more at present, but rest your Faithful Friend and true prophet of the
Lord,

Lodowick Muggleton.

6. Copy, Lodowick Muggleton to Larennce
Claxton [Laurence Clarkson], 25 December 1660.
Add. MSS 60168/6-7.

Lawrence Claxton,

I haveing seriously considered your many foule & proud covetous actions
Since you came to the beliefe of your Commission, but more especially of
late since you have been allowed some means from the Believers of your
Commission which hath made you so Lord-like that you are growne so
spiritually proud so that you are Now gotten in your owne conceit to be
the chiefe man in the spiritual commission so that your pride hath gone by
degrees so high untill you have gotten in John Reeves chaire or place so that
you are up as high as you can therefore it is high time for you to fall,
therefore seeing that occasions & offences will come that the secrets of the
heart may be made manifest therefore I do see a great provedence in that
buisness of masons wife, for that hath been an occasion to bring forth those
differences which have been amongst the Believers of this Commission, likewise it hath been a meanes to ensearch the bottome of your hart For ever
since the beginning of this defference, after you did understand that your
Commission was like to be taken away from you, you have stroven with all
you might boath with Saint & Devil, to uphold your authority without me,
Therefore you have made use of your beloved Frances & Ananias. And
Saphira[2] like you have consulted with the venemous serpent your wife in
that shee did shew Mr. Hatter & Mr. Hudson that place of Scripture concerning Aron & Miriam which I know that she could not do of herself
except she had heard your judgment of it, which concent of yours on that
place would do you little good only this your judgment on that Scripture
with your continually consultation with the Devill your wife, that Enraged
your wife so far as to Vaunte herself against Believers of this Commission
& against me, for which I do pronounce your wife cursed and damned to
Eternity, though she hath been damned by John Reeve allready therefore I
have sett to my seale that John Reeves Damnation shall be true upon her.

   As for your selfe because you have stroven to maintaine your Authority
without me, & for that purpose you have written this booke wherein you
have quite excluded me & have made the commission only John Reeves &
yours, For your writing do shew forth the very pride of your heart therefore
I do declare against that book & against you that I do renounce & disowne
you upon any such accompt as to be a Messenger, Bishop Or servant any
more to this Commission, neither shall you write any more nor speak in the
behalf of this Commission for I shall Utterly Disown what ever you do or
say of that nature neither shall the Believers of this Commission allow you
any maintenance neither Cambridge nor Kent upon any such account as
Looking upon you to be a messenger for you shall become as one of the
Least Believers of this Commission and shall become a Shame and Reproach
to saints and devil, which shame and reproach shall strike as a loathsome

Leprosie unto you during your Life, for you shall never come to any honnour of this Commission any more [for] you have had your last that Ever you shall have in this world, because you shall know that you have kicked your heel against your master and that there is a Prophet yet in Israel that hath power over you notwithstanding you have made yourself equal with John Reeve you shall know that John Reeve was as Elijah and that I am in the place of Elisha and that you are in the place of Gehazi.[3] This is my Resolution.

Written by Lodowick Muggleton the last true prophet and witness unto the true God the man Christ Jesus in Glory.

December 15 1660   Lodowicke Muggleton

7. Copy, Lodowick Muggleton to William Cleve, near Cambridge, 1665. Add. MSS 60171/73.

William Cleve, I received your Letter by your brother, dated March the 3d, 1665[6], which Lines I am very sorry to heare or read, though I have heard much more than you relate, But I never did love to heare of other Folks Sinnes but alwayes loved to heare of their righteousnesse, But Messengers of God are alwayes troubled with other peoples Sinnes more than with their owne. Neither have the Sinnes of others been a small Disgrace and Disparagement to me because they owne me upon a Spirituall Account.

So that I could even wish I had never been a Messenger of God, yet I knowing it was the portion of my Lord himselfe and others of his messengers to bear the Shame and Reproach of the Sinnes of others, I am made the better able to doe the same, For though the Shame and reproach of other's Sinnes doth reflect upon me and all in my Condition, yet the punishment of Sinne will be to those that act it.

And whereas you say you was drunk with Wine and Beer and upon that you committed Adultery.

To that I say, If it had been but an act of Drunkennesse or a bare act of Adultery though they are both wicked Acts yet they would have been more tolerable of Forgiveness than this Act of yours was for you acted with one that was neither Maid, Widow or Wife but a Common Whore, and not only so but a defiled Whore, defiled with the Pox for shee is now in the hospitall for cure, and you having to doe with her you have received of the same Disease with her, For Doctor Powell doth affirme you have it but not quite cured. Also he doth upbraid Mr. Tort me and all the Believers that own me, Saying This is your Faith, They can gett the pox and then come to me to be cured, He Speaking this by Mr. Nusome and you, So that we are all ashamed to owne such Believers So that this Commission is mightily shamed by those things lying heavy upon us all, But I have no desire to aggravate your Sins but would rather have smothered it, neither would I have discovered it to any though the Crye of it hath sounded in my Eares by others, yet I stoped mine Eares against it as one not willing to heare And the Reason why, because you owne Truth but had not the power of Truth in you, Which power I could nor cannot give if it be not planted in your Nature. I cannot help that.

And as for my speaking peace to your troubled soule, I would to God I could doe soe and be Justified in my owne Conscience, but I cannot speak peace to Sinnes of that nature though your sinne is not that unpardonable Sinne which can never be forgiven in the world to come, But your sinne is more hard to be forgiven in this World than the other For the sinnes you have acted, it carryes the Curse immediately along with it all the dayes of a Mans Life, but the other aforesaid may doe well enough in this Life but the Curse will follow hereafter.

So that this is all that I can say unto you That for my part I shall neither Justifie you nor condemn you, Neither will God himselfe condemne you for it; but if you can by your Faith Repentance and Newnesse of Life, encounter with your Sinne and recover the peace of your Conscience, and the health of your body I shall be very glad you may For Sinne is a strong enemy.

So I must leave your faith and the Guilt of your Sin to strive together and which getteth the Victory will be Lord. And so I Rest in Sorrow for you.

Lodowick Muggleton

8. Original,[4] Lodowick Muggleton to Mr. [John?] Martain, minister of Orwell in Cambridgeshire, 19 January 1666/7. Add. MSS 60168/10.

Mr. Martyn,[5]
Minister of Orwell in Cambregesheire
London 19 January 1666[7]

I understand that you had a desire to see mee & to have som discourse with mee & that you were at a place in Orwell to enquire for mee & not only so but you brought allso with you the high Constable & petty Constable, & another man with you to discourse with mee. Doe you thinke that any man that hath any wisdom that can give any reason of his ways would thinke that you was good to bringe your armies with you to discourse with an naked man & not only an army of men but great officers of the temporall sword that they might not only beare wittnes of what words should pass betweene you and mee or catch me in what Questions you should aske me, But if they could have got nothing out of mee worthy of persecution then by virtue of the power of those two Constables you would have laid hold of mee as a deceiver of the people. These things have been acted by such serpints as you in former times to prophets, apostles & to Christ him selfe. How oft did the priests & Levites such as you are tempt the Lord Jesus by askinge him questions thinking to catch him in his words that they might have therewithal to accuse him before the temporall power.

It is not longe since that I was served so by a priest or minister so called & so caused the temporal magistrate to commit me to prison but what this minister got by it, it was no less than eternal damnation which will assuredly be upon him as it is upon mourdringe Caine who kiled his brother & Judas who betraid his master; for how is it possible that any persecuting spirit who persecute men for consence sake, not breaking any temporall law, should escape the damnation of hell? For this I must tell you that persecution merely for consence sake is the sin against the holy ghost but more especially for men to persecute true prophets upon the account of deceivers there is no pardon for this sin; but I have found by experience what the power of a prophet is & I have found by experience allso that none are so great enimies to true prophers as those called the ministers of the nation are. I find the prophets in the law were persecuted more by those sort of men than any in persecution than any others so that the seed of the old Serpent the Divell is doth run in the line of those sort of men. It is as natural for those sort of men to persecute for consence sake & persecute prophets & so sin against the holy ghost as it is for fish to swimm in the water so that I do noe ways admire the thinge but doe see it must be so and it can be no otherwise. Yet this I would have you to know that if your intent had been real then would you have come alone & have discoursed with mee privately & not to bringe great officers of the parish with you to hear us discourse so that your intentiones were not good towards me but by consequence very evill; & it was the ready way to have procured the sentence of eternall damnation. But in regard I do not heare that you did any ways revile & speake evill of mee or of the doctrin declared by mee by callinge it blasphemy or mee a deceiver or such like terms, whatsoever your intent was in bringing [those men] with you. These things considered, I shall wave the sentence [of Damnation] upon you for the present for this your wicked intent [towards me], only this yoke I shall put upon your necke by [Virtue of my] commission from God. The thing is this: I understand that [you being a] pretended minister of the gospel of Jesus Christ [I suppose you will] own yourself a true minister of the gospel of Jesus Christ else what doe you get up into a pulpit to preach to the people, for yet you professing yourself a minister of Christ, I heare you present or cause to be presented divers of your parishioners for not cominge to church. Is this the practice of a true minister of Christ? Surely no. Did you ever read in Scriptures that any minister of Christ did so? Do you follow the example of the good shepherd? The Lord christ speaketh of the good shepherd havinge an hundred sheep & one of those sheep went astray, the good shephard left the ninty & nine to seeke that which was lost or gone astray & when he had found it what did he doe to it? Hee brought it home in his arms & did nourish & cherish it and took more care of that which was lost or gone astray than he did of all the rest that never went astray. This is the property of a good shepherd.

The moral is this: every true minister of Christ is a shephard & the people of his parish are his sheep & the shephard doth feed his sheep with such heavenly pasture, that is with such savinge doctrin which giveth the sheep assurance of everlastinge life so that their souls are fatted with the joys of heaven in the full assurance of everlasting life and this heavenly pasture, it casteth out all fear of eternal death. This ought to be your practis & your power if you were a chosen minister of Christ but how contrary to a true minister doe you act for if any of your sheep be gone astray, that is to error as you call it, & dissent from your worship, then instead of bringing them home in your arms & giving them bread to eat & watter to drink to nourish their bodies & good admonition, exhortation & the true interpretation of the Scriptures to feed their souls, in stead of this you present them & labour to excommunicate them & send forth the constables, church wardens & officers to apprehend them to bringe them before the temporall magistratres & so cast them into prison or else get the wooll off their backes & leave them bare. Is this the practice of a true minister of Christ? I suppose any conscientious man would be ashamed to own himself a minister of Christ & yet doe these things but it is the custom of most nationall ministers to do soe, therefore I doe not marvel at it because I know there is none of you chosen ministers of God but beinge chosen by men ye act as men, yea as wicked men. And seeing you are made a minister by men & from men & not from Christ, why are you not contented with that waiges that men have appointed for you & let mens conscences alone? Therefore I shall say unto you as John Baptist said to those soldiers that asked him saying, *And what shall wee doe?* You know his answer was *They should be content with their waiges and doe villence to noe man*—So I say unto you be you contented with that waiges the parish hath alotted for you & present and persecute no man for his conscience.

So as I am a minister, messenger & ambassador chosen of God, by virtue of my commission from him I shall lay this burthen upon you: That if you shall present or cause the constables, church wardens or other officers to present any man or woman under your ministry for matters of conscence or for not commung [to Church, Let the people] be of what opinion soever allways provided they pay you [what is allotted] for you & the parish & state-assessments, but if you shall present [or cause to] be presented any for the causes aforesaid after the receipt of [these lines; Then] from the Lord Jesus Christ the only wise God I doe [pronounce you Cursed] & damned both in soul & body from the presence of [God, Elect Men, and Angels] to eternity.

[Lodowick Muggleton]

9. Copy, Lodowick Muggleton to Walter Bohanan, 23 January 1671/2. Add. MSS 60181A/21-26.

Walter Bohenan [Bohanan],

This is to let you know that I have seene three of your rebellious Letters for which cause I was not willing you should see the Answere to those Nine Assertions layd down by William Meadgate that grand Rebbell.[6] Your Letters are full of Nonsense and not good English—And you have layd downe the Assertions false Lies and not true—Those Nine Assertions written by Meadgate were well layd down and I owene them all to bee true as they are layd downe and l have given an Answer unto them all—and no Rebbell shall see them if I can helpe it—But it seemes that you have undertaken not onely to answere the Assertions but to give Judgement upon them—And not onely soe but you vapour and threaten mee—That you will force mee to give Answere to them as if so you were a commissioner to Judge mee—I shall not speake of many of your wicked Nonsensicall Rebellious Words, it would bee too tedious—Onely these few.

First you say you doe believe that I and all the Devills in the World cannot hurt you—For my power you say you are not afraid of it noe more than of a Child of one Day old.

Secondly you say If I doe give sentence upon you before I have Answered the Assertions—you say you will force me to it if you and I doe live in England and that you will bring mee on the Stage—This is Judas like.

Thirdly you say that you have more Ground to bee offended att mee then I have to be offended att you—For you say you do affirme that I have fallen from the Truth and that I have gone about to overthrow John Reeve and have contradicted myselfe—This is Devil like to Judge his Lord and Master.

Fourthly You say you will make mee believe a lye and more then one but many lyes—contrary to all the prophetts and John Reeve's Writeings—Here is the marke of a Reprobate to charge his Teacher with lyes from dead mens Writeings—These are but a few of the Fruits of your Rebellion—And here is enough to condemne any Rebbell to Eternity if there were not more—But this I shall say unto you You have shewed your selfe a Right Scotchman— A dissembling false hearted man of the Scotch nature—And it will bee a rare thing to finde a Scotch man or woman true hearted either to God or man—For I have been in this Commission almost twenty yeares and I never knew but two Scotch, one a woman and one man, that made a profession of this faith—And they proved both false hearted to God and man—The Woman fell off from John Reeve in his time—for which hee Branded her with a Title of false hearted Scott and now you the man hath fallen from that Faith you once had in mee to Rebellion—for which I shall Brand you with the Mark of Reprobation—For have not you shewed your selfe a Reprobate, a Cast away, a false heartles man—Did not you aske a Blessing of Eternall happinesse of mee—Whereupon I asked you if you did believe that I had such power you said you did believe I had such power else said you why should you ask it of mee—And upon your request I gave you a Blessing of Eternall happinesse—And you continued in my Favour and in the Favour of many Believers for a while—But now you have despised the Blessing as Esau did his Birth right—For the Blessing of a Prophett is a good Birth right if it bee not despised—But you hath despised it and disowned it and For-saken the Blessing of a live Prophett and doth cleave unto dead mens words—And to the Doctrine of those that are dead—But hee that God hath presented alive to be the Judge of John Reeves Writeings—And Judge of the Writeings of the Prophetts and Apostles which you never knew—Neither did you ever know any light or knowledge from them but what you received from mee—Yes you have lift your selfe upp in rebellion against mee and have despised the Blessing therefore you shall have the Curse of a Prophett in the roome of it—And see if that will stick more Close unto you then the Blessing did—For this I say you shall never cast the curse off as you have done the Blessing but it shall remaine upon your Spirit for Eternity—For your condition is much like unto King Sauls—The good Spirit of the Lord departed from him and another Spirit was sent from the Lord unto him—That is while he kept in obedience to the Prophett Samuell—The good Spirit of peace from the Lord in his Seed gave him peace of conscience—But his Rebellion and disobedience to the Prophett Samuell caused that peace of conscience to depart from him—And the evil Spirit in the Seed of reason of Rebellion and Disobedience was sent unto him—And that became a wound in his conscience that never dyes—And a fire in his conscience that will never bee Quenched[7]—This will be your condition for your rebellion and Diso- bedience to mee—For while you kept in obedience to mee the prophett of the Lord—The good Spirit of the Lord in your Seed that believed in his Prophett it preserved you in peace of conscience in that I gave you the Blessing—And now through your disobedience to the Prophett of the Lord and Rebellion against God—For it is all one of God himselfe were in my place you would say as much to him as you do to mee—And the good Spirit of the Lord is departed from you—And an Evil Spirit from the Lord is sent unto you—Even the fruit of your disobedience and Rebellion—Which is the curse of God—You being rejected of God and of the Prophett and pass out from the society of the faithfull for ever—Soe that the wound of Rebellion will never dye in your conscience—Now the fire of Hell will never be Quenched—Soe that you shall know that this Torment is for nothing else but for your disobedience and Rebellion against the Prophett and as for your vapouring saying that I nor all the Devills the words cannot hurt you—And that my power is noe more feared by you then a child of a day old—These words you have learned of Meadgate that Dragon Devill who hath roared out of his Rebellion like a Madd Bull and you have learned of him to call the Prophett of the Lord Devill who was his Lord and Master and yours alsoe—And for all your vapour you shall finde that my power shall reach you where ever you goe—If you ascend upp to Heaven in your Imagina- tion—My Faith and Authority shall pull you downe from there—And if you goe downe into Hell I shall finde you out there—And your Act of rebellion and my Judgement shall bee Executed upon you there—And if you goe to the utmost parts of the Earth you shall not fly from that curse that shall follow you—See that you shall know that the most high hath chosen mee and rejected you—And as for your Threatning mee that you will force mee to Answer the Assertions if you and I live in England—And that you will bring mee upon the stage—Doe not you show your selfe a Cain and Judas Devill—You would betray your Lord and Master as Judas did his if it lay in your power—And kill as Cain did his Brother because hee was accepted and Cain rejected—Soe because God hath accepted mee and sett me in his place and hath rejected you—Therefore you would betray me and bring mee upon the stage—Your evill Spirit is willing I perceive but your power is weake—And will you dare to talke of bringing a man upon the stage that is free born and free by service—You that is a Forreigner an Alien One that is by Act of Parliament counted a Vagabond, a Runagade, a Fugitive in a Nation which is not your owne who is not free borne nor free by redemption—Yett you will dare to bring mee upon the Stage because I condemne you for your Rebellion—And this I say if I were as treacherous in heart as you are—I could quickly cause you to bee removed from Ware If not out of England[8]—And I shall lett that passe—And I would faine know how you can force me to tell you soe the Answere to the Assertions or to bring mee upon the stage—You may doe what you can now I shall provoake you to it—And here you may see the Pride and Presumption against your owne soule in that you have lifted your selfe upp against your Lord and master— And whereas you say and affirme that I am fallen from the Truth—Is not this the words of a Rebbell—That learned and was taught this way of Truth and what Truth is by mee—Neither had you any light or Truth att all but what you received from mee your Lord and Master—And yett the Spirit of Rebellion in you is growne soe wise to Judge your master that taught you to bee fallen from Truth—Soe that you know how to teach your Master better than hee can teach you—But how can I expect any better from the Spirit of rebellion—After you say I would make you believe lyes—Who made you a Judge what is lyes and what is Truth—You say that I goe about to overthrow John Reeve—And that I would make you believe many lyes contrary to all the prophetts and John Reeves Writeings—As to this I say what have you to doe with John Reeves Writeings now hee is dead—Neither have you to doe with the Prophetts nor the Apostles Writeings they are all given into my hands that is alive—And you ought all to bee taught of mee that is alive else you cannot bee taught of God—And whereas you say I contradict John Reeve—To this I say I have power to soe to doe—And I hath power to doe soe in some things when hee was alive—And I did contradict him in some things when hee was alive—And John Reeve did write some things that was error to mee and Error in it selfe which I did oppose him to his face and hee would not deny it—Yett notwithstanding John Reeve was Infallable and did write by an unerring spirit—This will seeme a Riddle except it be unfolded as thus—As to the Doctrinall part conteyned in our writeings the Six principles they were written by an unerring and Infallable spirit in John Reeve—And the Interpretation of Scripture written by him was Infallable—But John Reeves experienced Judgement and Apprehension of Gods taking Imediate notice of every man was Error—And that God did supply every perticuler man and woman Imediately from his owne person this was error in John Reeves Judgement and experience as I did prove to his face—And the things being written before and discourse and considering they were of noe great consequence as to Eternall happinesse they were lett passe—Besides none can Judge of a prophetts writeing—But hee that is equall in power with him—Being chosen of God I have power to contradict

him in his Judgement—But noe man else in the world hath power to contradict him in his Judgement though it was Error—It would have beene
rebellion in any Believer to doe as I did—And now I being the last liver—
Itt is rebellion in you to call any thing lyes or Error that I doe Justifie to bee
true—For noe man is to call mee to an Account or to resist my Judgement
in Spirituall matters but God onely and I am sure hee hath and will Justifie
mee in what I have done and in what I doe of this nature—Besides whome
ever are chosen equall in power they may contradict one the other in some
things and yett both Infallable men in Doctrine but not in Judgment and
practice—As for Example Peter was an Infallable man and did write by an
Infallable and unerring Spirit as to the Doctrine of Christ—Yett he owned
in his Judgement and practice—Yett hee gave way to circumcise Titus who
was a Greeke contrary to his commission from Christ and it was unlawfull
and a great Error in Peter—For which cause Paul an Apostle being equall
in power withstood Peter to his face and reproved him sharpelly of Error
and dissimulation to his face—Now should any Believer of Peters Doctrine
have said soe to Peter thou art a Lyer and noe true Apostle now hath not
an Infallable spirit but art in an Error—If this should have beene spoaken
by any private believer as it was by Paul who was equall in power—I would
not have beene in that Believers condition for all the World—Againe did
not Paul write by an Infallable Spirit as to the Doctrine of Christs death
resurrection and Ascension Peter and hee did agree in that—But Paul comitted an Error in his Judgment and practice as Peter did—When hee pretended a vow and shaved the heads of some Greekes which was unlawfull
for him to do, it was an Error and dissimulation in him yet no private
Believer durst reprove him for it—Yett this was a great Error in his Judgement and practice, it had like to have cost him his life—And should any
dare say that hee writt his Epistles by an Erring lyeing Spirit—So like wise
Paul and James two Apostles equall in power—Did contradict on the other
in their Judgements—For Paul saith Rom: 3d and 28th Saith hee therefore
wee conclude that a man is Justifyed by Faith not the Deeds of the Law—
And James the 2d and 24th saith you see then by workes a man is Justifyed
and not by Faith onely—Here is a quite contradiction to Pauls Judgment—
And should any Believer in their tyme dare to say that either of those did
write Error and lyes And that they were not Infallable men in their Doctrine
of Christ because they differed in Judgement in point of Faith and workes—
This is much like John Reeves believing God did take notice of every per-
ticular man and my Judgement that God did not take notice of every man—
Nor shall any dare to say that either of us are lyers because we differ in
Judgement in some things—Besides this is a common thing in the Scripture
for prophetts and Apostles to differ in Judgement and practice but not in
Doctrine—As the four Evangelists they contradict one the other very oft—
And the words of Christ himselfe contradict one the other in a many places
which would be too tedious to name—Now because Christs words doe contradict one the other in some places, Shall any dare to say that hee spake
lyes and taught Error and that which he spake was contrary to all Truth—Or

that hee was not a true Christ—None but Devills did say soe when hee was upon Earth—And should any in the Apostles Matthew Marke Luke and Johns tyme dare to say that any of them Writt lyes and error because they contradicted one the other in poynt of Judgement and experience—None but Devills did finde fault and cavell with them when they were alive—And soe it is now with John Reeve and mee—None but Devills would have made a fraction and disturbance amongst the Believers about John Reeves Writeing of Error—For this I must tell you—That noe man upon Earth is to Judge what is Infallable and what is not but the Prophett onely that is alive— And if men will not take things upon his worde and Judgement—Whoever refuseth it upon his bare words will perrish to Eternity—Therefore thy Spiritt of Rebellion hath deceived you and made you forsake the Prophett that is alive—And to cleave unto John Reeve that is dead—And to trust to the Scriptures which were never spoaken to you nor given unto you—But those people they were spoaken unto did receive benefit by them if they did believe in that tyme when that Faith was in being—But John Reeves Writeings nor the Scriptures will do you noe good now you have rebelled against the Prophett that is alive—Neither will that Faith in them deliver you att all from those Eternall Torments—Neither will those dead Prophetts deliver you from your Rebellion—Nor helpe you to the knowledge of truth now they are all dead—But this live Prophett shall Torment you and those dead ones shall not deliver you from my power—And as you have walked in the stepps of Corah, Dathan, and Abiram those notable Rebbells—Who rebelles against Moses and Aron[9]—And what was the fruits of their Rebellion—Did not Moses the Prophett of the Lord cause the Ground to open and swallow them upp alive for their Rebellion—And this you shall know though I cannot cause the Earth to open its mouth as Moses did—Yett this I can doe by my commission of the Spirit—I can open Hells mouth and that shall swallow you upp alive and keep you there eternally for your Rebellion where your worme of conscience shall never dye and the Fire of Hell shall never be quenched—That you may know to your endlesse paine and shame that you Rebelled and forsooke the blessing of a true Prophett alive on Earth att this day—And cleave unto John Reeve and those prophetts that are dead which you never knew—And for all your pride, presumption, and boasting lifting your selfe upp against the Lords Anointed and Chosen Prophett—And it will be a wonder if Gods vengance doth not make you exemplary in this world to bee a Fugitive and Vagabond upon the Face of the Earth before you dye besides your damnation here after—For sins of this nature are punished with greater punishment then any other sin whatsoever but murder— And it would have beene good for you and Meadgate that you hath never beene Borne—Therefore in obedience to my commission for this your wickednesse in falling from the Faith you once had in the Prophett now alive to Rebellion against him and against God—And for many base proud presumptuous speeches in your letters—I doe pronounce you Cursed and Damned in Soule and Body from the presence of Gods Elect men and Angells to Eternity—And now doe you see whether God will take notice of you to

deliver you—Or whether hee will owne you or mee—Or whether your Faith
be stronger then mine—Or whether you have declared Truth or I—Neither
shall any of this Faith Eate or Drinke with you—Or Trade any more with
you if I can helpe it—For you are cast out of Gods sight for ever—And cast
out of the Prophetts sight—And cast out of the Assembly or Society of the
Believers for ever—And now you may seeke new acquaintances in the World
and see if you can finde a better sort of people then those you find a fault
with—And you need not feare as Cain did—That every one that meets with
you will kill you—But your owne evill deceitfull heart to your Principle and
rejected Spirit may meet your Conscience and kill the peace of it.

> Written by Lodowicke Muggleton
> January the 23 1671[2]

10. Copy, Lodowick Muggleton to William Penn, 23 January 1673/4 Add. MSS 60171/182

William Penn Quaker that blaspheming reprobate Divel.

I thought good to send thee an Answer of thy wicked Antichristian pamphlett where thee maiest be convinced though not converted but the more
hardoned in thy blasphemy against the true God in the forme of a Man;
and that Sentence and Judgement that I passed upon you, in the discourse
between us, maybe more surely established upon your heart, even so
strongly, that your God, that is an Infinite Formless Spirit without a Body,
cannot Revoke it, nor take it off you to Eternitie; and you shall find these
heavenly secrets, which you call foolish Dreams and Impostures to be too
strong for your Antichristian Spirit of Reason the divel in you, which you
call God; neither can I wish for your Soules sake; that you may thinke in
time, and have a deepe repentance, and come to find forgiveness with the
true God, because I know he did reprobate you in the seede of the Serpent;
And that you are Predestinated in the seed to Blaspheme against the true
God, as made man in his own Image and Likeness; that you might Justly be
Damned to Eternitie; so that if it were possible that you should be convinced
now, I have given sentence upon you for your blasphemy, I then must of
necessity be damned if you believe; but I know in whome I have believed,
in that God that hath given me power to give sentence upon such Antichristian divells, that deny the body and person of God; and I am Justified of
God, and Justified in my own conscience; neither will it stand with Gods
glory to Save us both; and if those Revelations of Reeve and Muggletons
hath declared be filthy, Divellish and sottish Imaginations as you call them,
then certainly our End will be Endless pain indeed, but if wee be true, as I
know wee are, Then you have given just Sentence upon yourselfe, that your
End will be endless pain from the never dieing Worme in your conscience
in the Resurrection, when Eternitie doth begin to Rise and time doth end.

> Lodowick Muggleton

11. Copy, Lodowick Muggleton to Elizabeth
Dickinson, Jun.[ior], 6 March 1674/5. Add. MSS
60171/134.

I understand, by Goodwife Love that you are not well, but rather drawing
neare the Grave, And that you would gladly have seen me before you dye,
yet being comforted in your selfe that you shall see me hereafter in Heaven,
I was desired to write a few Lines unto you to add to your Comfort before
you goe hence and shall be seen no more. I have considered your tender Age
and weak distempered body ever since you were borne Yet with tender
Looking to, your weak distempered nature hath been preserved and upheld
to this Day Yet the roote of your disease doth still remaine and cannot be
cast out but by Death, it being born with you, but in the Resurrection this
Vile Distempered body of yours, which is now mortall shall rise an Immortall Spiritual body Capable of Eternal Joy and Glory, where no Diseases
Pain nor Sorrow can come where body and Soul shall live in Joy and pleasure for Evermore. And though I know there can be no feares of Death to
arise in your heart because of the Tenderness of your Age, You being un-
capable of Actual Sin, the Sting of Death is taken away from you, for the
Sting of death is Sin, and the Strength of sin is the Law, but that being not
Capable of the breach of any Law So no Sting of Death can lay hold of
you; I knowing this, would add a Word of Comfort to Strengthen your Spirit
here, and to your happinesse hereafter in the Kingdome of Eternall Glory
where is joy and pleasure at the right hand of our God and King and our
Redeemer for Evermore. And that you may be the more Satisfied and Comforted in the assurance of Everlasting Happinesse in the Life to come I doe
declare you Elizabeth the Younger one of the blessed of the Lord both in
Soul and body, to all eternity. And if you doe live till Whitsuntide, I doe
intend to see you if possible.
    So resteth your friend,

                    Lodowick Muggleton.

The Postern
March 6, 1674[5]

12. Copy, Lodowick Muggleton to Mrs. Hampson
of Cambridge, 11 June 1674. Add. MSS 60171/173.

Dear Friend Mrs. Hampson,

I understand you have some trouble upon your mind about the death of
your Child as if it were bewictht. I thought your faith in what I had declared
concerning Wicthes had been stronger than so to thinke that Wicthes should
have power over Infants, wich are not capable of feare; for feare and beliefe
is the Inlet to all Witchcraft, feare Entred first into the mind, and beliefe

enters into the flood and so men, Women, and Children, comes to be be-wictht; but I suppose your Child was not capable of any of these two; like-wise frights to children may cause fits, like to Wicthcraft fits, yet not be-wictht in the least, besides children in the conception, when they are conceived in the wombe, may partake of that melancholy blood, in the na-ture of the parents or of any other distemper or desease in the parents as I by experience, doe know by my own children; two sonns by my second Wife, as sweete Children as eye could look on, yet partakers of their mother's nature, who was a Comely woman to see to, yet of a Malancholly Dropsicall nature and Humour, if thinges did not goe well in this World, as no man can Assure his Wife all thinges shall prosper alwayes; because trou-bles are as sparks of fier that flie upwards; and fall downe to its center again; especially where children are; The first borne sonn was stricken with a con-vulsive fit, when it was a year old, as it satt upon my knee, when it was merry and it lived till it was three yeares old; afterwards the second sonn I had by her did grow up and prosper till he was three yeares old, after that the Evill did breake out, and it encreased to the Running evill from place to place, and he lived thus till he was nine yeares old, though I used meanes to help him; but all in Vaine; and when the Child died I was glad, knowing all Children I had by her did partake of her Malancholly and dropsical nature, and not any Wicthcraft powers in the least and I know your nature is given much to Malancholly and discontent of mind produced out of your owne surmisings, which are as false as God is true so that you have created to yourselfe feares where no fear is and sorrow where you might have had Joy, and griefe where you might have had comfort and though you are not sensible of the hurt it doth your person, it being grown strong, yett your mind being troubled it corrupts your nature, in that it enters into your blood; and the griefe your husband hath to see you in this condition, that nothing will comfort you, it hurteth his nature also which never was very healthfull since I knew him so that what evill is produced in your bodie by feares and Malancholly you must expect your children must partake, at one time or another, and you have no remedie but patience, therefore I shall say this unto you, I remember when you were first marryed your Malancholly mind wanted rest not only in this Life, but you wanted peace and assurance of happinese in the Life to come, and for that purpose you desired a Blessing of me, which upon your request I gave you, and you seemed to be satisfyed in it ever since; And my faith is stedfast in what I said unto you, therefore let yours be stedfast in me without doubting and you shall never perish, but have everlasting Life; And lett not these Malancholly thoughts of wicthcraft or evill surmises enter into your mind, but lett your faith in God, And in the commission of the Spirit, and patience in temporall troubles refresh your Soule, then will you receive an hundred fold, of peace and satisfaction in this Life, and in the Life to come Life everlasting. This is the true way to have peace in this life, and in the Life to come; And what can I doe more for you than I have done, to sett your mind in peace, yet if you have con-ceived any prejudice in your hart against any of the believers, though it be causeless, yet I shall part you asunder, so that you nor your husband shall have no societie with them, nor they with you, so your peace can be preserved, all shall be well. This is as much as can be said in this Matter, and all I shall say at present, Hoping you will take my advice in what I have said in this paper, that my words may take place in you to your peace of mind here, and eternal happiness hereafter, as it hath done in several others.

This with my true love remembered to yourself and husband, I rest your friend in the Eternal Truth,

Lodowick Muggleton

Postern June 11th 1674

13. Copy, Mrs. Ellen Sudbury to Mr. Thomas
Tomkinson, 10 August 1664. Add. MSS 60182/14.

Dear Friend & Brother in the Eternal Truth,

I Receiv'd your Letter & the Prophet's, and do greatly rejoice to hear of your faith and understanding which I see you have in this Commission, and now there is no need that any man teach you but as the annointing teacheth you, which is the seed of faith in you, it being awaken'd by the messenger of the true God, for these messengers have power to smite the stoney hearts, & when the heart is smitten or awaken'd by the voice of a true prophet, then there comes water of life which is allways springing up in the soul. Oh hear is the staisfying bread and the living water to be had, & happy shall all those be that believe it, there are many believers in these days, but blessed only are they that believe to life Eternal.

I am glad and do exceedingly rejoice to hear your wife begins to have a love & affection to this Commission of the spirit truly, for my part I have drank of many waters, but never drank of the water of life till I met with the witnesses of the spirit, but now I have found that which doth satisfy my desires, and my thirst is allay'd for ever,—

No more at present but mine & my husbands Love to You & Your Wife,

Your ever Loving friend & Sister in the faith of the true God the Man Christ Jesus in Glory,

Ellen Sudbury

14. Original, Thomas Dudson to Lodowick
Muggleton, 2 March 1668/9. Add. MSS 60168/9.

Loving Friend Mr Muggleton

The gentleman from whome ye did desire the booke is steward to the Earle of Lessester[10] for by my working there wee became Acquainted. He also hath writen to you him selfe and hath put the bookes together for they ware at his Chamber and sent them to you among which you shall find 11s 6d to pay for the new booke and the binding the other I received two bookes by Mr Leader of those were last printed and have sent one of them but of the interpretation of the whole booke of the revelation of S John I never had but one of them. If I had any of the mortality of the soule I would have sent it for Mr France loks on that booke to bee very meterial and doth thinke to geet mine if that bee not in the new one when they are bound together. You may send them both to Penshurst by William Lorker Carrier. He will come to his Inne every Tuesday night and it will be very well taken of

Your Friend Tho: Dudson

Penshurst March
the 2nd day 1668[9]

15. Copy, Alexander Delamain[e] to Mr. George
Gamble, merchant in Cork, 14 August 1677.
Add. MSS 60180/6-18.

Truely Loveing Brother

Because Spiritually United in all those divine Qualifications that tends to the perfection of the Saints, & Leads to Life Eternal, the fruition of our faith, which is the most pure & holy Seed of our Blessed God the Man Christ Jesus in Glory, from & by which we Enjoy while in Mortallity, more than the Tongue can Express, In Consolations, Assurances, & revelations, Arising from our Seed Spring Continually. This is that pearle & Hidden Treasure that we cannot Loose, Neither can it be taken from us, Neither doth the world know of, in what a Wonderfull Manner & Measure is our Understanding Inlightned, so that if we Look back into the days & Slavery of our former States, & the Condition, of all out of Truth, we must of Necessity be filled with divine Rejoicings. Because true Knowledge Supposeth Ignorance as Light—Darkness, Redemption, Creation, there is No publick worship this day in the world, that Enjoy perfect Unity in their Assertions, Ceremonies & Persuasions, what discords jarrinnge disputations Several forms & Branches in one profession And most of them full of Vain Janglings, & Dark deep, foolish Controversies, till they Loose themselves, because out of Truth, Nothing but Truth Creates Union, it reveals the true god, & causeth all those that Enjoy her to be of one Mind, to speak one language in Spirituals even the language of faith. We haveing all one god, one faith, all our Assurance is Revelations, Joys, Love, and Spiritual Consolations, are all one & the Same in every one, in Measure, how happy are we that it hath so hapned, that is the Land of our Nativity & in our Life Time we had the knowledge of our Eternal State made Manufest to us, by the Lords true Messenger, that hath brought the glad tideings of Salvation to our Souls at whom & us the World Rageth, & would devour us, & we Must expect it. I am desirous to Augment Your Joys, by being the Messenger of glad Tideings unto you & the rest of the faithfull in Your part, of Acquainting you of the Prophet's Deliverence from Imprisonment on the 19th of July Last, who hath desired me to write to you all, & send these Inclosed, that you may all understand truely from him, all his Sufferings And the Manner of his Inlargement, & what his Desires are, desireing you & me, that you would Communicate your writeings to all the believers of this Commission, we have made our gathering Among our friends in London, & it falls short so that he is forst to have recourse to Country Friends, we have a great many believers in London, but few are able to give, he hath Order'd me to write to all the Believers in England & Ireland, I hope this to you will be Sufficient for your Land, hopeing you will return an Answer as soon as may be so no more at present but Mine & my Wife's love presented to you & your good wife & all our dear friends in truth I rest your Loveing Brother.

In the true faith of a personal God,

Alexander Delamain

16. Original, William Wood, painter, to Lodowick Muggleton, 9 February 1691/2. Add. MSS 60168/41.

Much honoured and Esteemed Sir

I being moved in the spirit of faith to Congratulate you for the great benifits which we have receiv'd from John Reeve and you God's last prophets and Witnesses of the Spirit; by whose heavenly declamations we are sanctifyed and sealed up to everlasting redemption according to the election of grace and our faith which bears witness to the same, and whereas the prophet Reeve now being asleep in the Dust, he hath left you his faithfull fellow Messenger alone to plant and nourish the good food of truth in our hearts which you in obedience to the Lord God our Redemer who sent you have carefully done according to the tenet of your comition to his eternall praise and our ever lasting comfort. You have allso watered each plant with your heavenly revelations: as with ye water of life, which flowes from the eternall fountaine through your Spirit as through a conduit in most graduall streames nourish each plant according as it requires.

You have allso defended the good seed of truth and maintained it against all spirituall vermin that would have destroyed it and have cut them down and seald them up to everlasting damnation, moreover you have under the devine and most indulgent providence of our God livd amonst us in your comition this forty year and seen the seed of truth which you have sowen to grow and flourish according to the determinate will of God and to our exceeding satisfaction and Joy this unvaluable happinesse have we injuoyed by the power of your comition; our Fathers that are now sleeping in the dust hungerd after the same but could not attaine it truth being extinct throughout the earth.

And now sir you have finisht your great work and done like a faithfull steward. You have nothing to do but sit down and rest your old age & to praise your God and our God your redeemer and our redeemer the man Jesus now resident in heaven above the stars till death frees you from a persecuting and bloody world that you may sleep with your fathers for a moment. Then the Lord of the harvest will come with his inumerable host of angels & will call you forth and say according to his divine parable well done good and faithfull servant enter into your masters Joy. Then shall all we that are sanctified by faith in your declaration be raisd from death to eternall life with light spirituall bodyes capable to assend up in ye clouds of heaven with you our Shepherd to meet our God & our Redeemer with his mighty host of angells & then will all tears be wipt from our eyes & we shall praise our God & redeemer for ever & ever. Then shall our persecuting enemies be confined in utter darknesse where their torment shall never have end and we shall rejoice over them and then shall they know that our God that they have dispised is the God of mercy & the God of justice.

Thus greeting you Sir and wishing you all health & happinesse with my kinde and faithfull love remember'd to you and all the rest of our friends I remain

Your friend in truth faith
William Wood

February ye 9th 1691[2]
Braintree

SEVEN

Songs and Miscellaneous

1. Song by Nathaniel Powell. Add. MSS 60208/23–26.

> Hark hark I hear the Almighty's voice
> Saying John Reeve I have made choice
> Of thee my Messenger to be
> To publish Secrets hid from thee.
>
> And to assure what I have said
> The chiefest Judge I have thee made
> My minde in Scripture for to know
> To Publish it to saints below.
>
> O Lord, said I, I thee desire
> Some other person thou 'dst Inspire
> For my great Inabilitie
> To mean's thy Messenger to be.
>
> If thou refuse for to obey
> My Great Commands to thee I say
> Both in thy Body thou shalt see
> Curst hell and Blest Eternity.
>
> Then Lord said I: I thee obey,
> With thy great Spirit, I thee pray,

Thoud'st me Inspire that I may be
A Faithful Witness unto thee.

Then said the Lord it shall be done
Go take thy cousen Muggleton
Him I declare thy mouth to be
And a High Priest to wait on thee.

If he refuseth to obey
My Sacred message to him say
That he for ever be accurst
That God's Commands refuseth.

Then said the Lord and spake it soon
Go take thy Choice Companion
And to John Tane strait repair
And Seal him when he comest there.

Now I Command thee Swift as tide
Take Muggleton thy faithful guide
Go to new Bridewell where thou'lt see
The Antichrist opposeth me.

And when thou dost his face behold
Tell him from I heard him bold
Against me preach his Blasphemy
For which Curse him Eternally.

Next motion said go Summons all
Those cursed lying Priests of Baall
And know by what authoritie
False Incense offer'd up to me.

Bid them desist or else do thou
Show them my fierce and angry Brow
But my true phophets whom I send
My favor's with them to the end.

But say who sent you to Proclaime
Under such falsehood my Great Name
Therefore desist me Streight obey
Or with my Sword I will thee Slay.

Then motion said declare to all
Whose Ignorance misguided call
Me their True God to them declare
Salvation doth to them appear.

Then first declare to them my form
And Nature which is yet unknown

My Form's a Spiritual Man all o're
My Nature's Faith which is all power.

In me their God but where I give
It teacheth duty to believe
Make them to know my dreadful stroke
Unless they come and take my yoake.

Next go describe the Devil plain
Whose first appearance here was Cain
He was once Lucipher on High
But fell & became mortality.

Then Show the Nature of my Throne
It's Spiritual I have thee Shewn
Likewise the angells Nature tell
It's rational thou know'st full well.

Their Body's Spiritual declare
My Secret Message swift to bear
For I that am thy God can do
Wonders as yet unknown to you.

Then tell my flock their souls must dye
That compounds all mortality
They Silent Sleep untill the day
I raise them to Immortall Ray.

Last, tell the place where hell shall be
Its Nature Torments fuelty
This Earth where they their Sins commit
The place they suffer must for it.

Then shall their Bodys be their hell
Their cursed Spirits the Devill
Which burneth with such horrid flame
They'll curse for to provoke their pain.

But you my flock say to the blest
The Lord by me proclaim your rest
With him for ever to possess
A Glorious Seat of Happiness

Then praise the Lord all you that own
His Prophets Reeve & Muggleton
For his most gracious free decree
Peculiar you his Saints to bee.

2. Song by William Wood, painter at Braintree.
Add. MSS 60208/10–12 (partial: stanzas 7–11
only).

In God's decreed time in fifty and one
In the month February from his heavenly throne
He made himself known unto all elect men
The third and last time he shall ever come again
He sent forth two champions of truth to maintain
And to shut up all mouths that prattled in vain
Then let all that are elected his praises forth shew
That had bowels of love to poor mortals below.

And out of their mouths proceeds Spiritual fire
To Burn up all those that to hurt them conspire
With the Sword of the Spirit divine truth to defend
And to cut them all down that with truth do contend
They have also the keys of heaven and helle
No Champions like these in this region doth dwelle.

These Champions have with them rare balm
Which in a great earthquake will make a great calm
It cures all wounds that are made by deaths Sting
It makes the dumb speak and sing praise to their king
It makes the blind see these glorious days
It makes the lame walk and give God the praise.

It makes the deaf hear their divine revelation
Which expels all the fears of eternal damnation
The knowledge of God in them is inspired
Which all the elect so long time have desir'd
The natures and forms of angels they know
What heaven is above and what hell is below.

And of the right Devil and rise of his seede
They have satisfied all true men indeed
The soul it is mortal they truly do say
Though Devils and monsters of men do say nay
With many more secrets they are fully replenisht
Their worke it is done & God's mistery is finisht.

3. Song by Thomas Tomkinson.
Add. MSS 60219/31–32.

Great Jesus our Saviour and God of all Might
To sound forth thy praise is our duty and right

For sending his prophets our Souls to set free
We'll sing and rejoice all for this Liberty.

They have brought us from bondage Shadow and ties
From these formalities that blinded our Eyes
Then this is a day that we merry will be
And sing new songs of praise for this Liberty.

Rome thou art in fetters and we are at ease
Religion hath freedom but yet cannot please
Because it is empty but filled are we
With Joy & rejoicing for this Liberty.

A freedom Subservient to this we mind
Being healthfull and good and by the law enjoin'd
That no one for his faith now troubled shall be
Then we'll rejoice for this Liberty.

Our Joys doth not come from the Mighty redound
Of Preaching and teaching which makes a great sound
Our Joys springs from that from Sin is set free
We'll rejoice and be glad for this Liberty.

4. Song by Thomas Turner. Add. MSS 60208/27–28
(attributed by 60215/28 to Lodowick
Muggleton).

A Song made by a believer when the Commission came first forth
   & Sung by the prophet Lodowick Muggleton, at Braintree.
When men of Learning leave discerning
Perfect truth then flourish shall
The Leighety shall be esteem'd
Now mark what then here will befall
No false speaking no false seeking
Will be heard any more at all
But upright dealing without stealing
Evermore then flourish shall.

The Lion with the Lamb may live then
Peace will reign perpetually
All strife and envy will be vanquisht
And things will go more equally
No more Error to breed Terror
Will be heard any more again
For true bleivers are perceivers
Neither will their faith prove vain.

Not many wise nor many noble
Have imbrac'd Christianity
They gave the world the Shaddow of it
But ever practist Cruelty
The Conscientious not Contentious
Evermore were punished
No compassion but proud passion
Ever great men fancied.

5. Song by John Ladd. Add. MSS 60220/17–18.

A Glorious throne in the Heavens methinks I see
A noble court bedeckt with majesty
A canopy of state what tongue can tell
The untold Gloryes where our God doth dwell.

But to unfold what we don't understand
Gods holy Prophett we have in our land
Who hath a soul adorn'd with matchless faith
Which is Gods nature as the scripture saith.

But to his court where God proclaimes a call
To the Select Angells for to see his fall
The Almighty seats him on a matchless throne
The Elect admire the serpent all along.

A prisoner stands at the celestiall Barr
Where Guilt transports him from that Kingdome farr
The Judge unto the prisoner speaketh now
Where direfull Anger seiz'd the Almightyes brow.

Which to behold the Angells trembling lay
The heavens seemed vail'd then did the Almighty say
Pernitious Actor of a Deed so base
The effect reape nothing to thee but disgrace.

Dost thinke that I who gave a life to thee
Will suffer this rebellion against mee
No thou shalt know my power shall extend
To force thee hence and downward thee to send.

The Almighty God who then with powers calls
Which made heaven crack and down the Angell falls
Into a new found world hee did not know
That ere God's power had extended soe.

Nor hath God done his crimes for to pursue
But woe to the Earth the devil's come to you

With whome hee doth a new Invention try
In hopes to unthrone Eternall Majesty.

Which to prevent great god with anger deare
Decrees new wayes nor will hee leave him here
Then hee into our parent Eve did come
God nooz'd him there and Decreed his doome.

Thus we hee cast by our great God's command
Which to behold the angells trembling stand
But straight new gloryes from their God appeares
Into their hearts and free them from their feares
   For which all praise and glory be ascrib'd
   Unto Heavens King for ever to abide.

6. Song by Alexander Delamain[e]. Add. MSS 60220/16.

On the 17th of January 1676[7], being the day the prophett Muggleton was
tryed at the Old Baily for Blasphemy fined £500: Imprisoned till pay'd and
to stand 3 days on the Pillory.
   One thousand, six hundred and seventysix
   Was a black dismall day which the Devils prefixt
   To bring a great Prophett to their unjust Barr
   Where Reason was clouded and mallise shown farr
   An Indictment of Blasphemy then was brought out
   And the Question was ask'd whether Guilty or not.

   To reap upp the Venome that sensate did spitt
   Too tedious it would be in Verse to relate
   They belcht out their poyson thinking to devour
   The Prophett of God whose strong faith was a Tower
   Of impregnable strength against Mallise and hate
   In attempting to assault which rebounds on their pate.

   When the Jury that for the same purpose was made
   Had brought in their Verdict the Judges thanks pay'd
   And Balaam Jefferyes was left the courts sentence to pass
   Which hee did with a voice that did bray like an ass
   And said thou must stand in the pillory thrice
   And pay a small fine but five hundred pound prise

   Now, now the fight's for the Prophett of God
   Hath conquer'd his foes with the two edg'd sword
   Hell foam'd at his rest while the nine dayes did last
   Which being expir'd the wonderment's past
   Hee rides the white horse and with joy hee is crown'd
   With the love of those saints that encompass him round.

This, this was the day fate sparkled disdaine
That a Dungeon should longer Gods prophett detaine
Hee hath now lost your Hell and that Devilish place
For a palace of Joy that is free from disgrace
Then let us all rejoyce and for his blest sake
And for his day of redemption a Jubile make.

Love, Love be our bliss Love and triumph our Joy
While mallise and hatred damn'd envy destroye
Let the Devils below when wee sing forth a Quire
Of praises to God for they can soare no higher
Than this dismall black Orb where our Joys were supprest
By those who were stampt with the mark of the Beast.

7. Song by William Wood, painter at Braintree.
Add. MSS 60215/19–20.

A song to wellcom the Prophet into Braintree.
Now no more may monsters Bo[a]st
Now Reasons Gods Elect Deceive
Despised ones throw Down mountains
Whilst in truth we Do believe
Grace and truth hath long abounded
And all Monsters are Confounded.

Then let Each Soul that's here be glad
Rejoice now with faithful Zeal
See the Conduit of Salvation
Whear we all have set our Seal
Whilst the Mountains Catch at Small things
Still our Conduit floweth forth all things.

You Great Sire we Greet in Love
The Object Vipers would Destroy
Since your compainy in Braintree
Now once more the Saints enjoy
By a power that divine is
Make our Watter Sweet as Wine is.

Perils great have you Endured
Because you Charge the world with Sin
You're the marke of all their mallis
Shot against by every Sin
But your armor is your Defence Sir
Until Death Release you hence Sir.

Then all Saints in Raptures Sing
With Joyfull souls to make a Quire

To praise the God of our Salvation
Which Did first our Souls inspire
And protected you so Long to
And with armour made you Strong to.

Then in Dust a silent Sleep
You take and bid the Saints a Due [adieu]
Till all time be gone and Ended
Then our God makes all things New
Mountains then Will Shake and Shiver
Then We Saints are blest for ever.

See the Saints in Clouds asending
With acclamation fil's with Joy
Persecuters then behoulding
Which did oft the Saints anoy
We all Ending you atending
Into Glorye Never Ending.

Sad and dismall will they bee
To Reason and his Blind Desier
Seeing the wekist are the Strongist
Adds more fuell to their fier
Fears and horrors whelm them under
Whilst they perish all with wonder.

8. Song by John Ladd. Add. MSS 60223/128–29.

[The following explanation appears at the end of the song: These Verses
were made By John Ladd, and Sung Before the Prophet Muggleton, on the
Nineteenth of July 1681 being kept as a Day of Jubele for his happy Deliverance out of Prison, &c.]

O God how wondrous are thy works
Who can thy Power know
That with one touch so Elevates
Poor mortals here Below
The works of thy Creation Doth
Great Wonders Plainly tell
But our Redemption truely doth
Those Wonders far Excell.

Such are thy Sacred Misterys
When thou doth them Unfold
It Operates by Miracles
As in the Days of Old
It takes ye Scales from off our Eyes
That we Can Plainly See

It opens all the prison Doors
And Sets the Prisoners free.

Its A Strong tower of Defence
Against our Enemy
And doth our warfare Recompense
With victim Victory
Its Pools are also Virtuous
That Being washt we can
With great delight Both lipe [leap] and skip
That neare Before Could Stand.

Its language is a Parable
Both Life & Death sets free
It bindeth some in Chains & sets
The Rest at Libertie
A Jubilee lets ever keep
And make our Souls right glad
We were in Bonds but now By faith
A Liberty is had.

And you Great Sir who Bonds
So lately did Retain
Rejoyce with us at Being Set
At liberty again
With Dangers and Such Perils we
Poor Mortals are opprest
But Death at last will Set us free
With an Eternal Rest.

9. Song by William Wood, painter at Braintree.
Add. MSS 60227/52.

Let's lift up our Souls and rejoice
This is the Thanksgiving Day
When Gods beloved prophet was Releas'd
From Monsters and Beasts of prey
Which for truth no long time was confin'd
In a Dungeon with vipers to dwell
But the Dragon alas was quite blind
To think to keep truth in a Cell.

For now he hath shaked of[f] the Chains
And Ministers Truth to each Brother
Like the Sun in the Firmament shines
From one end of the Earth to the other
What power can extinguish such light

Which Gods Divine person Inspires
It is all the Saints delight
And all our Forefathers desires.

Some Serpents still fill'd with disdain
Think long to be shedding our blood
Till this time they cannot refrain
To Blaspheme against all that good
It is not the prophets alone
But each beloved saint the same
They trample under dirt the Just one
And all that profess his name.

In darkness they hover about
Expecting to find some rest
With nothing but fear and doubt
Their Reasonable Souls are possess'd
With their three person God they cann't help
Disdaining our Union and Love
In the midst of plenty they want
When the Sun it shines bright from above.

Since Serpents in darkness rejoice
Let us praise the true God for light
And obey the true Shepherds voice
That guides all our Souls aright
For tho we as Pilgrims live here
As Sojourners in a Strang Land
We brisk and lively appear
When Serpents they cannot stand.

10. Song by Thomas Tomkinson. Add. MSS 60208/
112–13.

Love what art thou that art divinely bent
Or whence comes thou in to this continent
What is thy birth and where can divines tell
Yea but not such as in Cambridg dwell.

Yet Cambridg school know thy bare name of love
But not the nature as come from above
For tho love there was born and born again
Yet divine breath's not known by learned men.

But love I know thee in thy paths divine
Being of the linnage and thy linnage mine

Therefore I will describe thy pedegree
And speak the praise that doth belong to three.

Love is the daughter of dame faith divine
Love is the queen of virtue in faiths line
Love is the princelyest grace of faith that's given
Love is faiths life and faiths love lives from heaven.

Love is a star of the first magnitude
Love shines so bright as blinds the owlish breed
Love is the pearl of paradise therefore
Love is our glory but the worlds no more.

Love is the balsam which heals our wounds
Love is the circuit of the churches bounds
Love is the loadstone that doth draw to life
Love is the empress to defend from strife.

Love is the fiery chariot sent from on high
Love mounts the saints into eternal joy
Love being such as I've describ'd to be
Love I will love and love do thou love mee.

11. An Acrostic by Tobit [Tobiah] Terry. Add. MSS 60210/2–3.

An Acrostic on the name of John Reeve and Lodowick Muggleton. Amiable and delightful are the ways of truth.

In Vain do Antichristian Spirits strive
*O*r think fallacious principles shall thrive
*H*eaven disallow their Tenants & they fall
*N*o less than Damn'd pharisaica.

*R*eeve rests in dust who had Commission given
*E*ven from the Personal God of Heaven
*E*ternal is his Power his prophets can
*V*anquish whatever's Antichristian
*E*ven all the devilish fallacies of Man.
*A*nd tho' Reeve rests yet this Commission shall
*N*ever be Vanquish'd or be forc'd to fall
*D*evils do your worst & for assistance call.

*L*o here's a Prophet still survives to be
*O*ur Certain guide to true Felicity
*D*ivine expressions as e're was taught
O'rerflows in him his mind's so richly wrought
*W*ith heavenly Wisdom you who e'er believes him
*I*t surely from Eternal death Reprieves him

Come then, ye Faithful ones, here's life's true spring
Kept for your good Salvation to bring
Ever blest Message from heaven's great king.

Multitudes flock to hear Men's false Traditions
Vain is their hopes and desparate their Conditions
God's Messengers are come to blast false Teachers
Great power from heaven Confounds all Earthly Preachers
Let Worldlings then Admire their false Devotion
Ending their Wretched lives in Earthly Notions
Truth in its Center drives & Mounts on high
O'retopping all this world's Impiety
Nothing but faith will reach heavens Majesty.

12. Expense Record, Dinner, 19 July 1682.
Add. MSS 60232/1

At our meeting at Holloway on the 19th of July 1682. At Mr. Hoolbrookes
at the Greene Man, Present there
The Prophitt of God
  Mis. Muggleton

Mis. Delanall _____	00:05:00
Mis. Smith _____	00:05:00
Mis. Webb _____	00:05:00
Mis. Evans _____	00:05:00
Mr. Cooper _____	00:05:00
Mis. Cooper _____	00:05:00
Mr. Atkinson _____	00:05:00
Mis. Atkinson _____	00:05:00
Mr. Gouldique _____	00:05:00
Mr. Rich: Smith _____	00:05:00
Mr. Whitehead _____	00:05:00
Mr. Brocke _____	00:05:00
Mr. Symonds _____	00:05:00
Delamain Senr. _____	00:05:00
Mis. Delamain _____	00:05:00
Delamain Junr. _____	00:05:00
Mr. Burrell _____	00:05:00
Mis. Henn _____	00:05:00
Mis. Roe _____	00:05:00
Received _____	04:15:00

Monyes Paid away the 19th July 1682, at Mr. Hollbrookes at the Greene
Man in Holloway

pd for 18 Pulletts at 14d per Pullett is _____   01:01:00
pd for 18 Sivell Oringes at _____   00:01:08
pd for 6 penny post Letters of advise _____   00:00:07
pd for the prophitt's Coach _____   00:03:06
pd a porter from London wth the fowles _____   00:01:06
pd for 5 δ & ½ of Bacon at 7^d½ per δ is _____   00:03:04
pd for 5 large Collyflowers _____   00:01:00
pd for Bread and Beere _____   00:09:04
pd for Wine _____   01:06:00
pd for Dressing Meate and fowleing Linning _____   00:14:00
pd for 5 Tarts at 16^d per Tart _____   00:06:08
pd for Butter and Cheese _____   00:01:06
pd for the Servants of the House _____   00:02:00
pd to y^e man of the Bowleing Greene _____   00:01:00
for 1 Quartern of Tobacco _____   00:00:06
                                                           ───────
                                                            04:13:07

Appendix A

This alternate version of the Epistle Dedicatory is found in copies of *The Acts of the Witnesses* in the Bodleian and Library of the Religious Society of Friends collections. Among other things, it eliminates the impression that the two prophets were buried side by side by making "Fellow-Witness" plural and omiting "both" from "there they are both to remain" in the final paragraph.

THE

EPISTLE

DEDICATORY

To all True Christian People that do or shall hereafter come to believe in this Third and Last Spiritual Commission, is this ensuing Treatise *directed, with love and peace to you be multiplied: It being a Legacy left you by the Lords last True Prophet, for your further establishment in Truth: As also it is left for a Convincement of the Seed of Reason, when he is in the dust; that by these* Acts *they may see how he hath been slandered, reproached, and belied, persecuted and imprisoned without a Cause.*

For how many Lying Reports hath been not only flung upon them, but also upon the True Believers of them; saying, That we own neither God nor Devil, Heaven or Hell; *and all because they see us use no outward glittering shew in fruitless Forms of Worship; whilst we worship an invisible Spiritual, yet personal God, in Spirit and Truth, which the World knows nothing of.*

For this we know and affirm, that the Doctrine of this Commission of the Spirit is of as great purity and power, as to Godliness, as ever any was, and as they were themselves, ever kept innocent from the breach of the Morrall Law, as to Act; Even so the Fruits of their Doctrine is of the like efficacy in the knowing seed of Faith, by which they have dominion over Sin, as in respect of Act.

And altho' this last Prophet in his Answer to the Nine Assertions, hath shewed his great mercy and clemency to some corrupt Natures, yet it is but to such who act not so; for as the breach of the Morral Law; *as to borrow Money, and not to pay it again; or to be passionate and hasty natur'd, overcome with Strong Drink, or the like, and tho' these are evil, yet reach but to the Borders of the Law, being Frailties in Nature, which disturb the peace of the Mind, for in such things, as the Apostle* James *saith,* We offend all: *But where there is true Faith, it prevents the Act; as this Prophet saith in one place, among many his Words are these,* Faith, *saith he,* overcomes all Sin, Death and Hell, within a man's self, and that none but such shall be admitted into the Kingdom of Heaven. *And the Prophet* Reeve's *Doctrine is thus, saying,* All those that are led by the Voice of the holy Spirit of *Jesus,* do work Righteousness in their bodies whereby they die unto Sin. *Again, saith he, in another place,* The Light of Christ in man doth convert from the Ruling Power of Sin. *And in a Third Place, which is not yet printed saith,* That they that are led by the Spirit of Faith, are kept from the commiting of sin: I do not say, *saith he,* that they have no Motion to sin, but the Spirit of Faith purifies their hearts, giving them power against those Motions, that they commit not the Act; and from hence it is, that all that are born of God, know the Voice of God, and hath this Power over Sin, as I have declar'd, *said he.*

These Doctrines of the Prophets are absolute and possitive, and do give great light into several Scriptures, *as* Matt. Chap. 5. ver. 28. I John chap. 3. ver. 9 *and ver.* 15. *in these places we are to distinguish between the Motion and the Action of Sin: This may also give light into* Rom. chap. 7. *how that* Paul *spake there as to his state by Nature, as also of the strife and struggle between the two Seeds of* Faith *and* Reason, *until the Law of* Faith *was quickened, and power by it attain'd, and then had he dominion over Sin, as* Chap. 8. *and so came to have peace with God, and with his own Conscience.*

And from hence comes the Grounds of true Worship, and flows forth all spiritual Praise, as David *said,* O how sweet is thy Law: *This sweet Law is the Law of Faith; and he or she that is truly possessed hereof, can seal to those words of the Prophet* Reeve, *which saith,* That he that is born of God, his Language and Practice is such as speaks forth the Power of Godliness, to the confounding of all glittering Tongue Hipocrites, and Faithless Formalists.

Now let all True Believers know, that under every Commission this is made the ordinary way of life and salvation; yet to prevent an objection, this is confessed by us: That tho' there is this power in Faith, as aforesaid, yet the Lord for the Tryal of His Creature, may suffer some of his Chosen Ones to fall in the time of a Commission; and for the praise of his Free Grace may grant them one Repentance, or second Free pardon; for thus writes the Prophet Reeve *in a Writing not yet printed.*

The Lord, saith he, leaves some to their own strength, through which he rebels against the Light that is in him, to the wounding of his own Soul; to the end that he may learn, that the power, by which he is preserved from the Act of Sin, and so from eternal ruin, is not in himself, but in the Living God that made him. Therefore the Scripture here and there pointeth forth one that the Lord hath left for a season to manifest his Prerogative Power over his Creatures, and afterwards doth his God-head Spirit move him to a second Free Pardon, wherein he raiseth that Soul to a higher and greater measure of Grace, Wisdom and Humility than it had before; which fulfils that Saying of Paul, Where Sin abounded, there Grace did superabound. *And this was fulfilled both by* David *and* Paul.

Here we see that if an Elect Vessel should once fall after his knowledge and belief in Truth, that his second Pardon doth raise him to a higher degree of Grace, Wisdom and Humility then he had before: This by the Prophet is made a true tryal to know whether a repentance or conversion from the Act of Sin committed be real or fained; as also that a second fall or relapse will prove dangerous; because it is rare to find a Third Pardon, and a Third increase of Grace to that Pardon.

Thus it is made clear that the Doctrine of this Commission of the Spirit hath power of Purity in it, and none that is truly born of God can dispute against it, but rather fear to offend, as the Prophet Reeve *saith,* That a true born Saint is afraid of his own evil thoughts, much more of evil words or deeds against God or man.

Again we see by this Book of the Acts, that these two Prophets were jointly chosen by God, and made equal in Power and Authority; for the Prophet Reeve *saith,* That his Fellow Witness had as great power as he had himself. *And further said,* That he was the Lords last High-Priest: *If this be granted, then it must follow, that there can be no Salvation to such as shall reject him, or his Writings, altho' they pretend to own* John Reeve.

Moreover the mighty sufferings that these Prophets *have undergone for their Testimony sake are admirable; yet notwithstanding all opposition, providence preserv'd them so, as that they both died in their Beds in peace; and not only so, but this last Prophet liv'd to see the downfall of many of his great Enemies, and of his Persecutors.* [The remainder of this line and the following ten lines to the end of the paragraph are marked out with pen and ink, but a sufficient number of words are readable enough to provide the following reconstructed summary: Judge Jefferies was so wicked that Muggleton hoped he lived long enough to see Jefferies fall from his glory in this world, and in fact Muggleton did live to see his desires in this matter granted.]

Now to come to a conclusion of this Epistle: *When the Prophet had wrote this* Book *of the Acts, he kept it by him, not letting any to see it; but about two Weeks before he died, it was put into the hands of one of us, that was his true Friend, and ancient Acquaintance; being seal'd up with his own Seal, in order to be printed after his death: Which now with the assistance of several Friends, through providence it is perfected, and is recommended to the whole* household of Faith, *both by the* Author, *and by us who are made instruments thereof.*

After this upon the First of March, 1697[8], *the* Prophet *was taken with an Illness and Weakness, upon which he said these Words,* Now hath God sent Death unto me: *And presently after was helped to bed, and tho' he kept his Bed, yet we could not perceive that he was sick, only weak and he lay as if he slept, but in such quietness, as if he was nothing concerned with either Pain or Sickness.*

So that it was mear Age that took him away, which was the 14th day of March, *in the latter end of the Year* 1697[8], *he then departed this Life with as much peace and quietness as ever any man did, being about 88 Years of Age, so that he had that Blessing, to come to the Grave in a full Age, like as a Shock of Corn cometh in at its Season. Upon the 16th day his Corps was remov'd to* Larsimus Hall, *and on the 17th day was from thence honourably Attended with two hundred forty eight Friends accompanying him to the Grave, where we went in order* [the remainder of this line and most of the next line are marked out as before] *according to the Custom of Burials, and so to* Bethlehem Church-Yard, *where he was Buried by his Fellow-Witnesses, which was according to his own appointment.*

And thus was the Lord's Last Prophet brought to his Grave in peace, without noise, or without tumult, though thousands of Spectators beheld it, and there they are to remain until the coming of their Lord, their King, and their Redeemer the Lord Jesus Christ, the High and Mighty God, and our God, and blessed are they that know their Voice, and wait for that day, and are offended with these things. Farewel.

FINIS.

Appendix B

The following materials were omitted from Muggleton's 1661 revised second edition of *A Divine Looking-Glass* but appeared in the third edition in 1719, which claimed to be a reprint of the original first edition of 1656. The 1760 fourth edition also claimed to be a reprint of the first; however, the 1719 and 1760 editions differ from each other primarily in the placement of material; capitalization, punctuation, and fonts; and in the fact that the 1760 edition follows a versification format and includes a summary of subtopics at the beginning of each chapter, both of which features it shares with the 1661 edition. However, the 1719 edition does include a summary of subtopics as a separate "Table of the most Principal Heads contained in this Book." These omitted materials reproduced below provide something of the Muggletonian view of temporal government.

[1719 A2^r–A2^v between the title page and the "To the Spiritual Discerning Reader" section omitted in 1661.]

A Divine LOOKING-GLASS: OR Heavenly Touchstone; | Proceeding from the unerring Spirit of an Infinite Majesty, whose | Personal Residence is seated on his Throne of bright burning | Crowns of Eternal Glory in another World. Purchased in this | World from his Divine Self only, by Vertue of powring forth | his unvaluable life Blood unto Death, through the Transmu- | tating of his incomprehensible Glory into a Body of Flesh, sent | forth for a Tryal of all sorts of supposed Spiritual Lights in this | Nation, or World, until the Ever-living True Jesus, that most | High, and Mighty God, Person-

233

ally appeareth in the Air with his Saints and Angels, to judge between the Truth of this Epis- | tle, and all Spirits that shall contest with it under Heaven. Even | so come Lord Jesus, come quickly, and fulfil thine own Promise | in thy Records of Truth, that thy Redeemed Ones may really | know, thou art that unchangeable God which cannot possibly | Lie, though Millions of Unredeemed Mankind thereby should everlastingly Perish. | Or, An Epistle Written by Inspiration from the fiery glorious Spirit | of Jesus Christ, that Immortal *Jew*, and Spiritual Lion of the | Tribe of *Judah*, who alone is the Lord protector of Heavens, | Earth, Angels, and Men. Unto *Oliver Cromwell*, that Mortal *Jew*, | and Natural Lion of the same Tribe according to the Flesh. Who | is stiled Lord protector of *England, Scotland*, and *Ireland*, through | the secret Decree of this most High and Mighty God. And to his | and the Common-wealth's most eminent Council, and Head Offi- | cers in Martial Affairs within his Dominions, as the fore-runner | of the sudden, dreadful Appearing of this impartial Judge of Quick | and Dead, with his elect Angels, to make an Everlasting Separa- | tion between the Persons of Tender-hearted *Israelites*, and Bow- | elless *Cananites*. Even so come Lord Jesus, come quickly. *Amen.* | [rule] | Printed in the Year of our Lord, 1656. And Re-Printed by Subscription in the Year, 1719.

Most Heroic *Cromwell*, who art exalted unto Temporal Dignity beyond the Foreknowledge of Men or Angels. In the most Holy Name and nature of our Lord Jesus Christ, upon the bended Knees of our Souls, we most humbly beseech thee to peruse this Epistle with thy own Eyes, not trusting any Man about thee to view it before thee, why, because there is something Written in the Book which more principally concerns Thee more then all other Men within thy Territories. And in so doing, with Spiritual Delight, by the glorious Power of the Everlasting God. Thou may'st in due season become the only Counsellor to thy Council above all Earthly Princes under Heaven, and not only so, but also a faithful Defender and Deliverer of all Suffering people upon a Spiritual Account within thy Dominions, and if so, what Mortal Persecuting Powers can stand before thee, or Serpentine cursed Plots come near Thee or Thine for ever. [decorative band] *John Reeve* and *Lodowick Muggleton*, Penmen of this Epistle, and chosen Witnesses unto that ever Blessed Body of Christ Jesus Glorified, to be the only Wise, very True God alone, Everlasting Father, and Creator of both Worlds, and all that were made in them in a sober Opposition of Men or Angels. [decorative band]

[1719 titled this section on pages 45–46 "7. How Prayers are heard"; 1661 used the same title but omitted the section itself p. 47.] Again, If it should seem strange unto any Man, that the Creator should cause such Variety of Expressions in Scriptures, in reference to one Divine Person only, if that man be an earthly Prince sitting on his Throne; I would faine know of that Princely Father, if he knew sufficient Power in himself for advancing of his Glory in the Spirits of his Subjects; whether he would not for a Season disrobe himself of all his Princely Greatness, and abase himself in the lowest Appearance of a Subject, and serve his Subjects, yea, and suffer himself to

be exceedingly abused of the Basest of them for his Glory's Sake, and Prerogative Pleasure over those Vassals when he is set on his Throne. Again,
moreover, for the Improving of thy Kingly Power, And advancing thy
princely Glory, wouldst thou not stoop to the lowest Way that could be
imagined, for so mighty a Prince to bow unto, as namely, wouldst thou not
commit the Government of thy Throne unto some of thy Princely Favourites:
and furnish them with Gifts that should make them as fit in Measure for
that Throne, as Faithful as thou art to thy ownself? After that, wouldst thou
not enter into one of thy Virgin's Womb, and transmute thy Fatherly Glory
into a Condition of Sonship; and so have a Beginning from thine own self;
in a New and wonderful Way of seeming Weakness unto thy Luciferian
Subjects, that were ignorant of thy Princely Wisdom and Transcendent Humility? Furthermore, thou being now in the appearance of a Subject thy self,
wouldst thou not yield all Childlike Obedience unto thine own representative
Power in thy Favourites Persons, as a perfect Pattern of all Righteousness
to thy beloved obedient Subjects whom thou delightest to Honour? and for
an everlasting Terror unto those non-favourable Subjects, whose Pride and
Envy caused them utterly to abhor that Prince and his Laws that should so
Abase himself to his own Subjects: Again, Suppose thou wast the sole Emperor of this whole World, and didst possess of thy Body only one Son and
Heir, and being both alive at once, thou shouldst set thy Son on thy Throne
and bequeath all thy Princely Titles unto him; and command all thy Subjects
to honour him as their only Lord and King for ever: What art thou then,
when thy Throne, Titles, and Honour, is invested upon the Person of another? Are thou any more unto that Prince, and his People, than a Round
o, or an absolute Nothing?

   [1719 pp. 50–52, omitted from 1661 p. 52.] Again, my Beloved Brethren,
these last Sort of Literal Comforters are those Speakers and People, which
for the most Part combine together as one Man, and in their solemn Meetings of imaginary Worship, under pretence of their Duty towards God, and
tender Compassion unto the Souls of Men instead of counselling one another
to desire the Holy Spirit's Assistance, of following Peace with all Men to the
utmost, and Forgiveness unto their supposed Enemies, as our Lord Jesus
Christ and his Saints did unto their blood Persecutors for Righteousness
Sake; they spend a great Part of their precious Time, in the discovering of
the Unfaithfullness of Civil Magistrates, but especially of the chief Magistrate of these three Nations in present Power: So that their Holy Meetings
(so called) tend principally to the involving of the three Nations into Blood,
Fire, Famine, Pestilence, and what not? when all Sorts of Men have a Sword
of Steel in their Hand again: Again, suppose the Head Magistrate, called the
Lord *Protector*, be guilty of many unjust Acts of Breach of Covenants in
general or in particular; of the which his own Light of Conscience often puts
him in Remembrance: My Spiritual Brethren, can you possibly imagine or
think that those Speakers or People have any Spiritual Light ruling in them;
which are not only full of scurrilous and bitter Language against the Head
Magistrate, in reference to his former Evils; but are also ready, if they had

Opportunity to unthrone him, and kill him, to cure him of his Maladies; or rather satisfie their own bloody Madness, with which they think God would be well pleased: But some Men may be offended with what I have here written, and say unto me, that they are very willing to yield Obedience unto the just Commands of a Head Magistrate, lawfully chosen by a free Parliament; but that Man which with us engaged against Monarchical Government, ruleth more rigorously in the same Way, therefore he appeareth unto us as a Tyrannical Usurper, over a free-born People, rather than a lawful Magistrate. Whoever thou art that thus reasoneth, To thee I answer by Way of Query, Didst not thou account Old *Charles Stuart* thy lawful Head Governour? And didst thou not swear to be obedient to him and his Heirs in all their just Commands? And yet for all this, didst thou not war against him and his Council, as Tyrants over the People, thro' monopolizing, and the like? And when they were overcome, didst thou not consent to their cutting off as Tyrants and Traytors, or justify it when it was put in Execution? Deny it if thou canst: And now is thy Friend *Cromwell*, with whom thou didst engage thy self, and all that was near and dear unto thee against Tyranny, become the greatest Tyrant of all, because he possesseth the highest Place of Government without thy Consent? Was *Charles* a Tyrant? And is *Oliver* a Tyrant? And art thou a good Christian, because thou wouldst cut both their Throats?

Again, you that have sided with the *Protector*, and his Head Officers against the common Enemy, (so termed), if this present Power by Consent of any Parliament had established your Opinions as the purest Christian Religion in *Europe*, thro' the three Nations, that from your *Roman* See you might subject Mens Persons and Estates, whose Consciences could not bow down to your Idol; Is it not to be suspected, that your Zeal would have been as fiery hot as any Men in this World, for the *Protector's* Government as the most fittest man alive? Again, are not all Civil Powers whatsoever established by the secret Decree of the most High God? And is it not he that setteth Kings upon their Thrones, and pulleth them down again, and setteth up their Subjects in their Stead, to bring about his unsearchable Wisdom of Mercy, or Judgment, towards a Nation? Again, is there any Rule in the Letter of the New Testament to warrant any Spiritual Christian to resist the Civil Magistrate, with the Sword of Steel? Nay, doth it not altogether command the contrary? Likewise, notwithstanding these Sleepers also defile the Flesh, and despise Government which are bold, and stand in their own Conceit, and *fear not to speak evil of them that are in Dignity*, 2 Pet. 1.10. If it should be objected, these were filthy *Sodomites* that resisted both Spiritual and Temporal Dignities: To that I answer, If thou countest thy self a Spiritual Christian, and yet resists the Temporal Power, art thou not liable to the greater Condemnation, because thou rebellist against greater Light? *Then said Jesus unto him, Put up thy Sword in his Place, for all that take the Sword, shall perish with the Sword*, Mat. 26.52. Ye stiff-necked bloody minded Rebels against your own Native Magistrates, behold the Example and Words of the Lord of Lords, and King of Kings himself: And if there be any Light left in you, you may see, that he was so far from allowing any Resistance against the Temporal Magistrate under what Pretence soever, that he layeth it down as an absolute Rule unto all Spiritual Christians, that *he that killeth with the Sword, shall perish with the Sword*: Wherefore, by an immediate Commission from the God of all Truth, I pronounce Woe, Woe, Woe, yea everlasting Woe unto all the Speakers, or people, which pretend Love unto our Lord Jesus Christ, and yet provoke the People to kill their Magistrates, and butcher one another with a Sword of Steel.

[1719 p. 55, omitted from 1661 p. 55; 1760 omits "before I write . . . despairing Reprobate."] In the next Place, before I write of the Language of a despairing Reprobate, give me Leave to reason a little in a Divine Balance between the present Civil Magistrates, and all Men whatsoever which have engaged with them, or against them in the late unnatural Wars.

[1719 p. 57, omitted from 1661 p. 57.] Again, if it be objected, if those in present Power did that Good I speak of, there was something in it, but we find quite the contrary, therefore suppose Things which are not: To this I answer, Be thou a Cavalier, or otherwise, I dare boldly affirm, that the Occasion of your present Sorrows of Death, or such like, ariseth from your Endeavours to cut off the Civil Powers now in Being. Again, would you not do all that lay in your Power, if you were in their Stead, for your own Preservation? Would you gently yield up the Throne unto any one when you are settled in it by Love, or by Force, because he shall pretend Birthright unto it? Is it Birthright or excellent Endowments preserves any prince upon his Throne, or enlargeth his Dominions without carnal Weapons? Again, if Kings preserve their Crowns, or purchase Kingdoms by Policy, Silver, and Swords of Steel, are not those Men as worthy of Thrones that win them with the same Weapons?

[1719 pp. 59–60, omitted from 1661 p. 58.] Again, Thou that art offended with *Oliver Cromwell*, for his accepting the Title of a Lord *Protector*, and governing the People in a Kingly Manner in a more imperious Way in thy Judgment than the former Powers did, if thou hadst had his Opportunity is it not very probable, if thou hadst been an Atheist before, that for the attaining so honourable a Place thou wouldst have become such a Christian, that notwithstanding thy former Covenants thou wouldst have concluded, that the God of Heaven saw this Way of Government most fit for the General Good of the People: Furthermore, and having obtained the Throne, is it not to be suspected, that instead of the intended Good unto the Nations, that thy imperious Hand would have been more heavy than his whole Body that now ruleth? Again, but it may be objected by some, that contrary to *Magna Charta, John Lilbourn* is under Restraint; notwithstanding he was freed in open Court, by an honest Jury of Twelve Men of *England*:[1] To this I answer, Might he not have his Liberty if he could but acknowledge the present Government, or would engage himself not to war against it nor to provoke the People by Writing, or otherways to rebel against it? Thou that lookest upon such Things as these as unreasonable and intolerable to be born, wouldst thou not do the very same Things, if thou wast the Lord

Protector, for thy own Preservation? And not only so but also for preventing
of a new unnatural bloody War, which irrational seeming wise Men would
provoke the People unto, upon the Account of Breach of Vows and Covenants, notwithstanding generally they are guilty of the same, and know not
what they shall do, if they were tried to the Purpose. Again, seeing *Oliver
Cromwell* is become the Head Magistrate of these three Nations in such a
Way which was contrary to his own Thoughts in my Judgment, at that Time
when he solemnly engaged the contrary, wouldst thou be counted a sober
rational Man to set the Nations together by the Ears? Again, to make the
Remedy worse than the Disease, that thou mightest under Pretence of Justice
and Good unto the People, execute thy Wrath upon the Head-Magistrate
for that which he could not possibly avoid, thro' the secret Decree of the
most High God, whatsoever men shall imagine to the contrary, thy Reason
tells thee, thou wouldst not be so dealt withall, if his Case were thine:
Therefore art thou not unreasonable, if weighed in the equal Ballance of
sober Reason it self? Again, if thou really believest there is a Creator, what
needest thou trouble thy self about *Oliver Cromwell*, his Council, or Head-
Officers, in reference to Things that perish? Who can tell for what End the
protector of Heaven and Earth hath so highly exalted him? Again, if thou
hast but a little Patience, and shalt see the Lord Jehovah make Use of *Oliver
Cromwell* to be an Instrument of Acts of General Good beyond thy Expectation, tho' in a Kingly Way, wilt thou not then be asham'd of all thy Reasoning, in Reference to his Ruin? Again, if on the contrary, he should be an
Instrument of Cruelty above others before him, and so in a short Time be
removed by the Creator himself, will it grieve thee then, that thou wast not
guilty of his Blood? Again, doth any Men in the World possess such a kind
of continual Peace, as those men which are tender of the Lives of the worst
of Men? Who are thou then that wouldst be counted a sober Rational Man,
and yet wouldst do that to another which by no Means wouldst have done
to thy self?

[1719 pp. 62–63, omitted in 1661 p. 60.] Again, this sort of Spiritual
bloody Persecution of long continuance, being come to the height, whoever
thou art, that are offended with the present Power because they have not
establish'd such a Government as was by many imagined; it is because of
thy rational Atheism, or spiritual Weakness in the wonderful Transactions
of the most high God in this present Age: Again, whatsoever *Oliver Cromwell*, his Council and Adherents are Guilty of, it is best known to God, and
the Light of their own Conscience. But this I positively affirm, by an immediate Commission from the Holy Spirit, that the God of Glory, that Spiritual Lion of the Tribe of *Judah*, hath exalted *Oliver Cromwell* a Lion of
the same Tribe according to the Flesh, into the Throne of *Charles Stuart;*
that the Yoke of Jesuitical Persecution, for Conscience sake, may be utterly
taken off the Necks of his People in these three Nations. And that all those
Powers which endeavour to exalt the *Roman* See of *Charles's* Seed upon his
Throne again, may be cut off as Spiritual Rebels against the Everlasting God,
and his glorious Apearances in the Spirits of his Redeemed Ones out of

Darkness into his marvellous Light, I say again, by full Assurance from the Everlasting *Emanuel*, that whatever *Oliver Cromwell* hath been suffered to act for attaining the Lordship of Three Crowns or Kingdoms, or whatever Depths of Counsel shall proceed from him and his fellow Counsellors, for enlarging their princely Territories; yet because he denies Throning himself as a Spiritual God in the Consciences of his fellow Mortals upon what account soever; though all the princes of the Earth Band together against him, which are guilty of Spiritual Tyranny, they shall Prosper as those that fought aginst *Joshuah* or *Judah*.

Again, If thou shalt peruse this Epistle, and in thy Heart shall say, these are but Words only, and many in these Days of Liberty of Conscience have declared strong Expressions, with pretended Commissions from the Lord Jehovah, and have appeared with lying Signs and Wonders to confirm them, thro' which many have been deceived and utterly ruined both in Body, Mind and Estate, and whether thou art one of this Sort, Time will make manifest: To this thy supposed reasoning, from the Lord Jesus, I answer, if thou *Oliver Cromwell* dost as really understand and believe with thy Heart that there is a Creator, as thou confesst it with thy Tongue, then by this infallible Rule thou shalt one Day believe the Truth of this Epistle from all imaginary Voices, Visions, Revelations, Dreams, or high-flown Fancies whatsoever in this confused Age. Mark what I say, both thou and thy Council, yea and all Men which truly confess a Personal Divine Majesty; Whether I live or die, if the God of eternal Glory from his immortal Throne, do not own this Writing, and utterly disown those Men and their Writings which are left to despise it, then it was not from the Spirit of the true God, but meer imaginary Flashes from mine own Spirit.

[1719 pp. 64–65, omitted from 1661 p. 61.] Again, whoever thou art which art offended at the present Government, under what Pretence soever, if Health, Wealth, Honour, Friendship with Mortals, or long Life be thy esteemed chief Good, or if thou confess an Eternal Being of all timely Beings, besides their perishing Delights; yet if thou say'st there is no other God but what is within thee, be thou never so seemingly Pure at present, it shall be manifested one Day in the Presence of God, Elect men, and Angels; and in thine own Conscience, that thou art so far from any Spiritual purity, that thou never truly knewest what Rational Purity was, nor where it is. Again, seeing all Created Beings thro' their Finiteness, are naturally Subject to Change, or to be changed in their Resolutions, and that nothing comes to pass by Man's Will, nor Angel's Wills, but by the Will of the Unchangeable God of all Infinite Power, Wisdom, and Glory: who then is that Spiritual or Rational wise Man, but he that is made truly to understand, that to contend with a Sword of Steel against a Head-Magistrate exalted upon the Throne, thro' so many marvellous Difficulties as this present Power hath been possessed withal; is to Call in question the Wisdom and Power of God in all the Transactions of Foreign or Civil Wars since this World began? Thus thou which art Spiritually Rational may'st know, that it is neither Chance, nor Fortune, nor natural Endowments, nor deep Subtility, nor Valour, not

Silver, not carnal Weapons, nor any Power in Men, nor Angels, is the Cause of exalting *Oliver Cromwell* in a Place of so great Concernment: But the mighty God of *Jacob* hath brought it to pass, to manifest his Prerogative will on Earth, as it is in Heaven; that his Natural Wonders may be as visible unto Men in this World, as his Spiritual Wonders are visible, I say unto Angels, *Moses* and *Elias*, in that World to come: Therefore whoever thou art, after the Knowledge or Perusal of this Epistle, whether Emperour, King, or Beggar, that shall be left to thy own fleshly Wisdom to endeavour the Ruin of this present Power of *England, Scotland*, and *Ireland;* thou shalt be possessed with Fear of natural Destruction in this Life, and with a secret Fear of eternal Damnation in the life to come. And now as an eternal Memento of Glory, or Shame in this Life, and that to come, from the Spirit of the Divine Majesty himself, suffer me to speak a few Words unto thee, which possesseth the Title of a Lord Protector's Highness: If thou hast Ears to hear, I humbly beseech thee with a meek and patient Spirit deeply to consider what I shall say, If thou shalt be left unto thy own Natural Wisdom, only to pretend Liberty of Conscience, and Temporal Equity between Man and Man, that *Alexander* like thou mightest conquer the whole World, and through great Victories shalt say in thy Heart, There is no other God, or Glory, but what thou injoyest already: Then after the Divine Majesty hath delivered his innocent people by thy hand out of their Spiritual and Natural Tyranny in many places; as sure as the Lord liveth, thou may'st justly expect that he will discover thy exceeding Hypocrasy in the Sight of Men and Angels. Remember what befel *Herod*, when the People said, it was the Voice of God, and not of Man; though I am made thus to write, there is a Secret hope in me of better Things concerning thee: Again, if thou hast any true Light in thee, concerning an Eternal Glory in the Life to come, thou knowest then that Truth cannot flatter; but it will be a righteous Judge in all our Consciences in the great and dreadful Day of our Lord Jesus Christ. Lastly, Be it known unto thee, most noble *Cromwell*, though this Epistle was written by the hand of a poor sinful Man, if it be not owned by the Eternal Spirit, as proceeding from the Divine Majesty himself, then I neither can desire, hope, or expect from the Lord any Mercy upon my Soul and Body to all Eternity: So much concerning a Rational Discourse in a Divine Ballance between the present Civil Powers, and those which ingaged with them or against them, in the late unnatural Wars. O Blessed are all Spiritual Warriors, for their Crowns are Immotal and Eternal.

[1719 pp. 66–67, omitted from 1661 p. 61.] Again, in the next Place, according to former Thoughts, I shall write of the Language of a despairing Reprobate, which after great literal or notional Light, is not only fallen under the Guilt of many natural and unnatural Evils, but is also guilty of despising the holy Spirit of all divine Purity, either because it did not prevent him from his Uncleanness, or because it will not justify him in his Filthiness. Again, if a Friend shall visit him and inquire him of his Condition, instead of receiving any Hopes concerning Deliverance from his present unspeakable Misery, you shall hear him utter these or such like Words: My Sins are greater tnen can be forgiven, what are God, Men, or Angels unto me seeing I am eternally damned; or else he will say, I did not care if they were eternally cut off, or in my Condition, so that I were delivered: Again, he doth not only abhor all Expressions of Hope concerning a spiritual Deliverance, but he also hateth to hear the very Name of God, Mercy, Salvation, or the like. Again, instead of a Spiritual yielding unto the divine Pleasure of the Creator, through a longing after his glorious Presence, his dark Spirit is full of all secret Envy and blasphemous Cursings against his holy Spirit; yea, it is become so natural unto him, through the absenting of Motions of the Holy Spirit, that nothing is so suitable unto him as the language of fiery Wrath, or burning Death, or Blackness of utter Darkness, or cursed Devil, Hell and Damnation, and such like doleful Expressions as these are, so that instead of having any desire of having Hopes of Mercy from its Creator, it rather is pleased with a language of condemning its God of Unjustice or merciless Cruelty. Again, all the Love or Mercy remaining in such an outcast Condition as this, is but hypocritical Hellishness at the best; for in the midst of his unspeakable Torment, if he seemeth unwilling that his familiar Friends should possess the like Misery, it is because he thinks it will increase his own Torments: Again, a Man in this desperate Condition is full of Torment, at the visible Sight of any living Creature whatsoever, with bloody Thoughts or Desires to it; especially if he thinks that that Creature possesseth any kind of Joy or Peace in it self in the least. Again, a despairing Reprobate is very ready to hear an experimental Man, that can speak of a more dreadful Damnation, answerable to his present Condition; but if any man speaks unto him that is ignorant of his Condition, it doth so enrage him that he would tear him in Pieces if he could. Again, you shall seldom or never hear a despairing Castaway complain of Cold; truly he hath small Cause for it; Why, because his Spirit being close Prisoner in the Flesh, it burneth oftentimes more terrible through the whole Man than natural Fire, through want not only of cooling divine Motions from above, but also for want of motioning forth upon natural Comfort beneath as formerly.

Notes

PREFACE

Place of publication is London unless otherwise noted. I have retained Old Style dates but begun the year on 1 January. I have also maintained original spelling, capitalization, and punctuation as much as possible, making alterations only when necessary for meaning.

1. *World*, p. 19.

2. See for example, Juleen Eichinger, "Muggletonians: A People Apart." (Ph.D. diss., Western Michigan University, 1999).

INTRODUCTION

1. John Smyth, *The Character of the Beast* (1609), 1. For these Baptist groups and their beginnings, see B. R. White, *The English Baptists of the Seventeenth Century* (Baptist Historical Society, 1983); Stephen Brachlow, "Puritan Theology and General Baptist Origins," *Baptist Quarterly* 31 (1985): 179–94; B. R. White, "Baptist Beginnings and the Kiffin Manuscript," *Baptist History and Heritage* 2 (1967): 27–37; T. L. Underwood, Introduction, *The Miscellaneous Works of John Bunyan*, ed. Roger Sharrock, 13 vols. (Oxford: Clarendon Press, 1976–94), 4 (1989): xlv–lii; Bryan W. Ball, *The Seventh-Day Men: Sabbatarians and Sabbatarianism in England and Wales, 1600–1800* (Oxford: Oxford University Press, 1994).

2. W. T. Whitley, "Baptist Churches till 1660," Baptist Historical Society *Transactions* 2 (1911): 232–34; Alfred C. Underwood, *A History of the English*

Baptists (London: Kingsgate Press, 1947), 85. I have used the admittedly anachronistic term "radical," for the defense of which see Richard L. Greaves, *Enemies Under His Feet: Radicals and Nonconformists in Britain, 1664–1677* (Stanford: Stanford University Press, 1990), 7–8.

3. J. F. McGregor and Barry Reay, eds., *Radical Religion in the English Revolution* (Oxford: Oxford University Press, 1984), vii; J. F. McGregor, "Seekers and Ranters," in ibid., 121–39, (129 quoted; emphasis added); Thomas Edwards, *Grangraena* (1646), 73, 77–78; *The Second Part of Gangraena* (1646), 21; *The Third Part of Gangraena* (1646), 75, 89–90; William Erbery, *The Testimony* (1658); William Walwyn, *A Whisper in the Eare of Mr. Thomas Edwards* (1645); John Saltmarsh, *Sparkles of Glory* (1647); Laurence Claxton, *The Lost Sheep Found* (1660), 19; John Jackson, *A Sober Word* (1651), 34–35; Richard Baxter, *A Key for Catholicks* (1659), 331–34 (332 quoted); John Tomkins, *Piety Promoted*, 2d ed., 3 pts. (1703–6), pt. 3 (1706): 119; Thomas Taylor, *Truth's Innocency* (1697), sigs. B2ʳ, C2ʳ; Burrough to Fell, 1654, Library of the Religious Society of Friends, London, Swarthmore Manuscripts 3/83; Caton to Fell, 19 January 1656, Swarthmore Manuscripts 1/314; *DNB*; and *BDBR*. See also Douglas Gwyn's study in progress, "Seekers Found: Saints Errant in Seventeenth-Century England."

4. J. C. Davis, *Fear, Myth and History* (Cambridge: Cambridge University Press, 1986); idem, "Fear, Myth and Furore: Reappraising the Ranters," *Past and Present* 129 (1990): 98–103; Jerome Friedman, *Blasphemy, Immorality, and Anarchy: The Ranters and the English Revolution* (Athens: Ohio University Press, 1987), 236–49; Abiezer Coppe, *A Second Fiery Flying Roll* (1649), sig. B3ʳ (faulty pagination); Ariel Hessayon, " 'Gold Tried in the Fire': The Prophet Theaurau John Tany and the Puritan Revolution" (Ph.D. diss., Cambridge University, 1996). Reeve and Muggleton referred to him as John Tany. John Taylor, *Ranters of Both Sexes* (1651), 2; Nigel Smith, ed., *A Collection of Ranter Writings from the 17th Century* (Junction Books, 1983), 10. Richard Baxter, *Reliquiae Baxterianae* (1696), pt. 1: 76; *BDBR*. See also A. L. Morton, *The World of the Ranters* (Lawrence and Wishart, 1970); J. F. McGregor, "Ranterism and the Development of Early Quakerism," *Journal of Religious History* 9 (1977): 349–63; Nigel Smith, *Perfection Proclaimed: Language and Literature in English Radical Religion, 1640–1660* (Oxford: Clarendon Press, 1989).

5. Geoffrey F. Nuttall, *The Holy Spirit in Puritan Faith and Experience* (Oxford: Blackwell, 1946; reprint, Chicago: University of Chicago Press, 1992), 91–92; T. L. Underwood, *Primitivism, Radicalism, and the Lamb's War: The Baptist-Quaker Conflict in Seventeenth-Century England* (New York: Oxford University Press, 1997); H. Larry Ingle, "From Mysticism to Radicalism: Recent Historiography of Quaker Beginnings," *Quaker History* 76 (1987): 79–94. Kenneth L. Carroll, "Early Quakers and Going Naked as a Sign," *Quaker History* 67 (1978): 69–87. William G. Bittle, *James Nayler 1618–1660: The Quaker Indicted by Parliament* (York: William Sessions, 1986), 103–4; Bonnelyn Young Kunze, *Margaret Fell and the Rise of Quakerism* (Stanford: Stanford University Press, 1994); H. Larry Ingle, *First Among Friends: George Fox and the Creation of Quakerism* (New York: Oxford University Press, 1994), 150–52.

6. John Bunyan, *Some Gospel-Truths Opened* (1657), in *The Miscellaneous Works of John Bunyan*, vol. 1 (1980), 45; George Fox, *The Great Mistery of the Great Whore Unfolded* (1659), 8; Margaret Fell, *A Testimonie of the Touch-Stone* (1656), 27; Abiezer Coppe, *A Fiery Flying Roll* (1649), 14. John Jackson,

Strength in Weakness (1655), 12–14; Edward Burrough, *A Trumpet of the Lord Sounded Out of Sion* (1656), 28–29; George Fox, *Something in Answer to Lodowick Muggleton's Book* (1667), 21; William Penn, *The New Witnesses Proved Old Hereticks* (1672), 65. For an indication of how numerous tracts of controversy had become, see Peter Milward, *Religious Controversies of the Jacobean Age: A Survey of Printed Sources* (Lincoln: University of Nebraska Press, 1978).

7. Christopher Hill, "Debate: The Muggletonians," *Past and Present* 104 (1984): 153–58 (158 quoted); *Mercurius Politicus*, 18–25 August 1653, 2685–86 (2685 quoted).

8. *Mercurius Politicus*, 11–18 August 1653, 2657–58; Alexander Ross, *A View of all the Religions in the World*, 2d ed. (1655), 379–80. I am using the Cambridge University Library copies of *A Remonstrance* and *Joyful News from Heaven*: F. 13. 5 (3.) and F. 13. 5 (5.). Lodowick Muggleton, *A True Interpretation of the Eleventh Chapter of the Revelation of St. John* (1662), sig. A4ʳ.

9. John Reeve and Lodowick Muggleton, "A General Epistle from the Holy Spirit" (1653), Add. Mss 60185/2; see also Wing: R678; and Joseph and Isaac Frost, eds., *The Works of John Reeve and Lodowick Muggleton*, 3 vols. (1832), 1 (hereafter *Works*). Keith Thomas, *Religion and the Decline of Magic: Studies in Popular Beliefs in Sixteenth and Seventeenth Century England* (Weidenfeld and Nicolson, 1971), 504–10; Alexander Gordon, "The Origin of the Muggletonians," *Proceedings of the Literary and Philosophical Society of Liverpool* 24 (1869–70): 272. *A Book of Letters, or Spiritual Epistles* [a variation of the title from the 1755 publication], 40, in *Works*, 3. For Fowke (d. 1662), who was Lord Mayor of London in 1652–53, see *DNB*. For the deaths of these two Quakers, see *Acts*, pt. 4, chap. 3, sec. 2, and chap. 4, sec. 5.

10. T. L. Underwood, Introduction, *The Miscellaneous Works of John Bunyan*, vol. 4 (1989), xix–xx; A. Neave Brayshaw, *The Quakers*, 3d ed. (New York: Macmillan, 1953), 75. See also H. Larry Ingle, *First Among Friends: George Fox and the Creation of Quakerism* (New York: Oxford University Press, 1994).

11. *Mercurius Politicus*, 11–18 August 1653, 2657–58. When the contributor to this publication made such a visit, it resulted in one member of his company being cursed.

12. *World*, frontis., 50–55. For Delamaine, Tomkinson, and Saddington see *DNB*.

13. The entire fine was not paid before his release, however.

14. See the alternative version of the epistle dedicatory in Appendix A, which, by making "Fellow-Witness" plural and omitting "both" from "there they are both to remain" in the final paragraph, eliminates the impression that the two prophets were buried side by side. Was this a reflection of hostility between "Reevonians" and Muggletonians?

15. Alexander Gordon, "Ancient and Modern Muggletonians" and "The Origin of the Muggletonians," *Proceedings of the Literary and Philosophical Society of Liverpool* 24 (1869–70): 186–244, 246–79; for the Bethlehem Churchyard, see 192; and for Walnut Tree Yard, see 240. The dinners were held on 14, 15, and 16 February and the celebrations of Muggleton's 19 July release from prison held on 30 July to reflect the change to the "new" calendar. *Chambers Encyclopedia* (1874), 6: 601–2; (1888–92), 7: 338. Thomas Robinson, "To the Editor of Chambers Journal," 9 August 1881, British Library Add. MSS 60170/47; see also Add. MSS 60170/48 and 60170/50. It is curious to note that

Merriam-Webster's Biographical Dictionary (1995), 741, describes Muggletonians as a sect only "lasting into the 18th century."

16. *Times Literary Supplement*, 29 November 1974, 7 March 1975 (quoted). The story of the "discovery" of Philip Noakes and the archive is told in *World*, 1–5; and E. P. Thompson, *Witness Against the Beast: William Blake and the Moral Law* (New York: New Press, 1993), 115–19.

17. Christopher Hill, "John Reeve and the Origins of Muggletonianism," in *Prophecy and Millenarianism: Essays in Honour of Marjorie Reeves*, ed. Ann Williams (Harlow, Essex: Longman, 1980), 305–33. See also the revised version of this article in *World*, 64–110. Such contextual connections are yet another area deserving further investigation.

18. Delno C. West and Sandra Zimdars-Swartz, *Joachim of Fiore: A Study in Spiritual Perception and History* (Bloomington: Indiana University Press, 1983), 1–29; Morton W. Bloomfield, "Recent Scholarship on Joachim of Fiore and His Influence," in *Prophecy and Millenarianism*, 21–52. Andrew Weeks, *Boehme: An Intellectual Biography of the Seventeenth-Century Philosopher and Mystic* (Albany: State University of New York Press, 1991), 1–10, 35–59, 194–208 (200, 57 quoted). In *Acts* Muggleton mentioned his discourse with "Beamonites" and others in Nottingham in the 1660s.

19. Rodney L. Petersen, *Preaching in the Last Days: The Theme of "Two Witnesses" in the Sixteenth and Seventeenth Centuries* (New York: Oxford University Press, 1993), 14, 202, 207.

20. Lodowick Muggleton, *A True Interpretation of the Eleventh Chapter of the Revelation of St. John* (1662), 6; Thomas Heywood, *False Prophets Discovered* (1642), title page, sig. A2^r. See also Thomas, *Religion and the Decline of Magic: Studies in Popular Beliefs in Sixteenth and Seventeenth Century England*, 135.

21. Reflecting this divine declaration to Reeve was Muggleton's later statement that no one had "the true interpretation of the Scriptures, but us two onely." *A True Interpretation of the Eleventh Chapter of the Revelation of St. John* (1662), 172. Penn, *The New Witnesses Proved Old Hereticks* (1672), sig. A3^r; Fox, *Something in Answer to Lodowick Muggleton's Book* (1667), 9; Lodowick Muggleton, *A Looking-Glass for George Fox* (1667), 1.

22. Claxton, *The Lost Sheep Found* (1662), 33–44. Letter 9 below. *Acts*, pt. 4, chap. 10. In "The White Divell Uncased" (1704), Tomkinson noted that it was the "infinite spirit" God of Quakers and others that could take notice of everything.

23. This differs from Lamont's interpretation of the letter in *World*, 128.

24. Although in his chapter on "Lodowick Muggleton and 'Immediate Notice' " William Lamont claimed that "all quotations from that work [*A Divine Looking-Glass*] are taken from the 1656 edition" (*World*, 157 n.20), it seems more likely that he used the 1719 or 1760 editions, or both, each of which claimed to be "reprints" of the first edition. The primary differences between the third and fourth editions lie in the placement of sections of materials. It should also be noted with respect to the 1661 revised edition that, quite understandably, library bibliographers have sometimes been misled by the title page notation "Printed in the year of our Lord 1656," neglecting the remainder of the statement that it was reprinted in 1661 and thus entering it incorrectly in catalogs as the 1656 edition. See also Lamont's *Puritanism and Historical Controversy* (Montreal and Kingston: McGill-Queen's University Press, 1996), 91,

204 n.61. For the Birch defection, see Gordon, "Ancient and Modern Muggle-tonians," *Proceedings of the Literary and Philosophical Society of Liverpool* 24 (1869–70): 234–369; and *DNB*. The University of Michigan also has a set of the three-volume *Works* edited by Joseph and Isaac Frost. For Lamont's argument see *World*, 128–34, 154–55. Frost also criticized the 1760 "editors" for using Muggleton's 1661 preface and chapter/versification scheme to mislead readers into thinking it was the second edition. Thomas Robinson to Joseph Frost, 22 July 1857, Add. MSS 60169/207.

25. Reeve and Muggleton, "A General Epistle from the Holy Spirit," [1653], Add. MSS 60185/2, folio 2. Reeve and Muggleton believed "the Man Christ glorified, to be Father, Son, and Holy Spirit in one distinct Person," according to their *A Divine Looking-Glass*, 2d ed. (1661), 36. Lodowick Muggleton, *A Discourse between John Reeve and Richard Leader* (1682), 7; idem *An Answer to Isaac Pennington* (1669), 16. Muggletonians believed God to be in the form of a moderately tall man; Heaven to be six miles above the earth; and the sun and moon actually to be about the size they appear to the human eye (see Muggleton's *A Discourse between John Reeve and Richard Leader*, 1682). This may have appealed especially to what Christopher Hill has described as the "no-damned-nonsense" approach of London artisans (*World*, 25, 102).

26. Penn, *The New Witnesses Proved Old Hereticks* (1672), 6–8, 10–11; Joseph Smith, *Bibliotheca Anti-Quakeriana* (1873), 300–333; Douglas G. Greene, "Muggletonians and Quakers: A Study in the Interaction of Seventeenth-Century Dissent," *Albion* 15 (1983): 102–22 (102 quoted); Kenneth Carroll, "Quakers and Muggletonians in Seventeenth-Century Ireland," in *A Quaker Miscellany for Edward H. Milligan*, ed. David Blamires, Jeremy Greenwood, and Alex Kerr (Manchester: David Blamires, 1985), 49–53. See also Richard L. Greaves, *God's Other Children: Protestant Nonconformists and the Emergence of Denominational Churches in Ireland, 1660–1700* (Stanford: Stanford University Press, 1997), 375. For such accusations of Ranterism, see Muggleton, *A Looking-Glass for George Fox* (1668), 85–86; Fox, *Something in Answer to Lodowick Muggleton's Book* (1667), 9; and Penn, *The New Witnesses Proved Old Hereticks* (1672), 65. Richard Baxter, *Reliquiae Baxterianae* (1696), pt. 1: 77. Muggleton, *An Answer to Isaac Penington* (1669), 20: "You Quakers have taken up the Doctrinal part of the Ranters, but left their Practice." Isaac Penington, *Observations on Some Passages of Lodowick Muggleton* (1668), 14; Muggleton, *An Answer to Isaac Penington* (1669), 20. For Penington see *DNB* and *BDBR*.

27. *World*, 77–78.

28. Reeve and Muggleton, *A Divine Looking-Glass*, 2d ed. (1661), 129–61.

29. *World*, 27, 28, 85; Peter White, *Predestination, Policy and Polemic: Conflict and Consensus in the English Church from the Reformation to the Civil War* (Cambridge: Cambridge University Press, 1992). For criticism of White's argument, see Nicholas Tyacke, "Anglican Attitudes: Some Recent Writings on English Religious History, from the Reformation to the Civil War," *Journal of British Studies* 35 (1996): 139–67. See also Patrick Collinson, *The Religion of Protestants: the Church in English Society, 1559–1625* (Oxford: Oxford University Press, 1982); and idem, *The Birthpangs of Protestant England: Religious and Cultural Change in the Sixteenth and Seventeenth Centuries* (Oxford: Oxford University Press, 1988); Nicholas Tyacke, *Anti-Calvinists: The Rise of English Arminianism c. 1590–1640* (Oxford: Oxford University Press, 1987); and

idem, "Debate: The Rise of Arminianism Reconsidered," *Past and Present* 115 (1987): 201–16; Peter White, "The Rise of Arminianism Reconsidered," *Past and Present* 101 (1983): 34–54; and idem, "Debate: The Rise of Arminianism Reconsidered," *Past and Present* 115 (1987): 217–29; William Lamont, "The Rise of Arminianism Reconsidered: A Comment," *Past and Present* 107 (1985): 227–31. Thompson, *Witness Against the Beast*, 74–75. See also Dewey D. Wallace, Jr., *Puritans and Predestination: Grace in English Protestant Theology* (Chapel Hill: University of North Carolina Press, 1982).

30. See, for example, in *Acts* Muggleton's answers to William Medgate's Nine Assertions and the cases of James Barker and Walter Bohanan; letters 9 and 11.

31. For example, it was reported on 3 June 1678: "They expound the scripture according to their pleasure. Sometimes they sung Divines' songs, then drank, for it is a kind of an alehouse." *Calendar of State Papers, Domestic: Charles II, 1678* (T. Fisher Unwin, 1913), 202; John Gratton, *A Journal of the Life of that Ancient servant of Christ, John Gratton* (1720), 24. For Gratton see *BDBR* and *DNB*. Gordon, "Ancient and Modern Muggletonians," *Proceedings of the Literary and Philosophical Society of Liverpool* 24 (1869–70): 214–17; *World*, 32–33, 36–38; T. L. Underwood, *Primitivism, Radicalism, and the Lamb's War*, 11, 13; Greene, "Muggletonians and Quakers: A Study in the Interaction of Seventeenth-Century Dissent," *Albion* 15 (1983): 102.

32. Gordon, "Ancient and Modern Muggletonians," *Proceedings of the Literary and Philosophical Society of Liverpool* 24 (1869–70): 219–20.

33. For additional portraits and photographs of Muggleton's death mask and the reading room at 7 New Street, see George Charles Williamson, *Lodowick Muggleton* (London Privately printed, 1919; British Library Department of Printed Books).

34. Horton Davies, *The Worship of the English Puritans* (Dacre Press, 1948), 172–73; Thomas Grantham, *Christianismus Primitivus* (1678), pt. 2: 112–16; William T. Whitley, ed., *Minutes of the General Assembly of the General Baptist Churches in England*, 2 vols. (Kingsgate Press, 1909–10), 1: 27–28; William J. McGlorhlin, ed., *Baptist Confessions of Faith* (Philadelphia: American Baptist Publication Society, 1911), Particular Baptist confession: 1677, chap. 22, sect. 5, p. 260; London, Maze Pond Minute Book, p. 3, Baptist Union Archives MSS 2, Regent's Park College Library, Oxford; Alfred C. Underwood, *A History of the English Baptists* (Kingsgste Press, 1947), 112; Kenneth L. Carroll, "Singing in the Spirit in Early Quakerism," *Quaker History* (Haverford, Pa., Friends Historical Association) 73 (1984): 1–13; McGregor, "Seekers and Ranters," 130; Friedman, *Blasphemy, Immorality, and Anarchy: The Ranters and the English Revolution*, 288, 296–97, 302–3. See also the illustrations on the cover page of Timothy Stubbs, *The Ranters Declaration* (1650).

THE ACTS OF THE WITNESSES

The First Part

1. William Cavendish (d. 1628) was created first Earl of Devonshire in 1618. His son William (1591?–1628) and grandson William (1617–84) were second and third Earls of Devonshire. *DNB*.

2. For the plague of 1625, see F. P. Wilson, *The Plague in Shakespeare's London* (Oxford: Oxford University Press, 1963), 129–75.

3. See letter 9 and note.

The Second Part

1. "A General Epistle from the Holy Spirit" [1653], Add. MSS 60185/2; *Works*, vol. 1. Wing: R678.

2. "And thou, Capernaum, which art exalted unto heaven, shalt be brought down to hell: . . ." (Matt. 11:23).

3. A John Gostlin (c. 1625–57) took his Master of arts in 1648 and was made a fellow at Caius in 1649. See John Venn and J. A. Venn, comp., *Alumni Cantabrigienses*, 4 vols. (1922–27), (hereafter *Alumni Cant*).

The Third Part

1. The mayor was John Fowke, mentioned in the introduction.

2. Such a pamphlet does not appear in Wing.

3. The Blasphemy Act of 1650 condemned, among other things, claims to be God or that God dwelled in a person and nowhere else, as well as sodomy, drunkenness, and the denial of the reality of sin, heaven, and hell. See McGregor, "Seekers and Ranters," in McGregor and Reay, *Radical Religion in the English Revolution*, 132–34.

4. The English groat was equal to four pence. *OED*.

5. William Steele was Recorder (1649–55) and Chancellor of Ireland (1656–60). Alfred B. Beavan, *The Aldermen of the City of London*, 2 vols. (Eden Fisher, 1908–13), 2:290 (hereafter *Aldermen*).

6. Wing: R680.

7. Wing: R682.

8. William Sedgwick (c. 1610–63), M.A. Oxford and preacher at Ely, was in contact with both John Reeve and the Quaker James Nayler. *BDBR*.

9. Philip Herbert (1619–69) was fifth Earl of Pembroke. *DNB*.

10. Of these Claxton works, only *A Wonder of Wonders* is not extant. *Look About You* (1659), Wing: C4579; *The Quakers Downfall* (1959), Wing: C4582; *A Paradisical Dialogue* (1660), Wing: C4581; *The Lost Sheep Found* (1660), Wing: C4580.

11. Wing: M3050.

12. Wing: M3048.

13. John Coup (Coope) became vicar at Chesterfield on 6 February 1663. He died in 1680. A. G. Matthews, ed., *Walker Revised* (Oxford: Clarendon Press, 1988), p. 249.

14. William Cavendish (1592–1677) was Earl of Newcastle-Upon-Tyne. *DNB*.

15. Wing: M3049.

16. Wing: M3044.

The Fourth Part

1. This was probably Roger Twysden (1597–1672) or his brother Thomas Twysden (1602–83). *DNB*.

2. There does not seem to be an appropriate entry for John Cowlye in *Alumni Cant.*

3. In response to Muggleton's *The Neck of the Quakers Broken* (1663), Fox wrote *Something in Answer to Lodowick Muggleton's Book* (1668), to which Muggleton replied with *A Looking-Glass for George Fox* (1667, 1668), Wing: M3046, M3047.

4. Thomas Loe (fl. 1654–68), known as "the apostle to Ireland," is also credited with having converted William Penn to Quaker principles. *BDBR.*

5. George Whitehead (1637–1724), writer of numerous tracts, was a prominent lobbyist for Quakerism at court and Parliament. Josiah Coale (or Cole; 1633–69) was a traveling evangelist in England and North America. *BDBR.*

6. Penn, *The New Witnesses Proved Old Hereticks* (1672).

7. For the Peal (Peel) meetinghouse, see William Beck and T. Frederick Ball, *The London Friends' Meetings* (Kitto, 1869), 192–213.

8. See Num. 16.

9. For William Smith (d. 1672), former minister in Nottinghamshire, see *DNB.* Samuel Hutton was probably the Samuel Hooten, son of Elizabeth Hooten (*BDBR*), to whom Muggleton addressed an answering letter in *The Neck of the Quakers Broken.* See *Dictionary of Quaker Biography* at the Library of the Religious Society of Friends, London. For Thomas Taylor (1618–82), noted in the introduction, see *DNB.* For Richard Farnworth (or Farnsworth; c. 1630–66), convert of Fox and writer of numerous tracts, see *DNB* and *BDBR.*

10. This is *An Answer to Isaac Penington* (1669), mentioned in the introduction.

11. *A True Interpretation of the Witch of Endor* (1669), Wing: M3051.

12. *The Prophet Muggleton's Epistle to the Believers* (1690?).

The Fifth Part

1. A John James, brewer, was elected Sheriff of London in 1666. *Aldermen* 2:74.

2. Henry Compton (1637–1713) became Bishop of London following the death of Humphrey Henchman (1592–1675). *DNB.*

3. Richard Rainsford (1605–80) became Lord Chief Justice on 12, April 1676. *DNB.*

4. Thomas Davis (or Davies, 1631–79) was Lord Mayor of London 1676–77. *DNB; Aldermen* 2:101.

5. For Dr. Edward Bourne (d. 1708) of Worcester, see Norman Penney, ed., *The Journal of George Fox*, 2 vols. (Cambridge: Cambridge University Press, 1911), 2:384.

6. On these pages Muggleton claimed to be "chief Judge in the world," Christ's "onely Ambassador," and that his words in the Six Principles and against the Quakers were "as true as any thing that ever was spoken by Prophet or Apostle." The title page of his *The Neck of the Quakers Broken* bore the date 1663 and "Amsterdam," the place sometimes inscribed on works actually printed in England in order to circumvent the Licensing Act of 1662. For that act and Charles II's Declarations of Indulgence (1662 and 1672), see N. H. Keeble, *The Literary Culture of Nonconformity in Later Seventeenth-Century England* (Athens: University of Georgia Press, 1987), 55–59, 93–126; Fredrick

Seaton Siebert, *Freedom of the Press in England 1476–1776* (Urbana: University of Illinois Press, 1952), 237–88.

7. Perhaps Edward Atkyns (1630–98), later Lord Chief Justice. *DNB*.

8. George Jeffreys (1648–89) is most remembered as judge in the "bloody assizes" following the 1685 Monmouth Rebellion. *DNB*.

9. John Peak(e) (d. 1688), mercer and Sheriff of London (1676–77), was also Lord Mayor (1686–87) and president of Christ's Hospital (1687–88). Thomas Stampe (d. 1711), draper, was also Sheriff of London (Muggleton says Middlesex) in 1676–77 and Lord Mayor in 1691–92. *Aldermen* 2:107, 216.

A TRANSCENDENT SPIRITUAL TREATISE

1. 2 Kings 2:1–13.
2. Matt. 27:46–50; Luke 23:46.
3. Jer. 19:5–6; Rev. 19:20–20:15.

"THE WHITE DIVELL UNCASED"

1. Tomkinson's title may reflect the Elizabethan proverb "The white devil is worse than the black" and some of the themes of John Webster's play *The White Devil* (performed first in 1612 and as late in the century as 1682): the contradictory nature of appearances illustrated by the character Vittoria (generally thought to be the white devil), the corruption of the church, and the issue of justice and reward. See M. P. Tilley, *A Dictionary of the Proverbs in England in the Sixteenth and Seventeenth Centuries* (Ann Arbor: University of Michigan Press, 1950), D310; the Methuen edition of the play (1986) with commentary by Simon Trussler and notes by Jacqui Russell; M. C. Bradbrook, *John Webster, Citizen and Dramatist* (New York: Columbia University Press, 1980); Frederick O. Waage, *The White Devil Discover'd: Backgrounds and Foregrounds to Webster's Tragedy* (New York: Peter Lang, 1984); Samuel Schuman, *John Webster: A Reference Guide* (Boston, Mass.: G. K. Hall, 1985); and *DNB*.

2. In fact, Augustine had two concubines, one who bore his son Adeodatus and another who served him between the dismissal of the first and his subsequent marriage to a young heiress. He admitted that sex was his great compulson. See Augustine's *Confessions*, book 6:15, trans. R. S. Fine-Coffin (New York: Penguin Books, 1961), 131. See also Everett Ferguson, ed., *Encyclopedia of Early Christianity* (New York: Garland Publishing, 1990) (hereafter *EED*); F. van der Meer, *Augustine the Bishop*, trans. Brian Battershaw and G. R. Lamb (New York: Sheed and Word, 1961), 180–82; Elizabeth A. Clark, ed., *St. Augustine on Marriage and Sexuality* (Washington: Catholic University Press of America, 1996).

3. Clement V (1304–14) was the first of the Avignon popes, but Tomkinson may have confused him with Clement VI (1342–52), who was accused by Petrarch of having illicit love affairs. See Guillaume Mullat, *The Popes at Avignon 1305–1378* (New York: Harper and Row, 1965), 42–43; and J. N. D. Kelly, ed., *The Oxford Dictionary of Popes* (Oxford: Oxford University Press, 1986) (hereafter *ODP*).

4. See F. van der Meer, *Augustine the Bishop*, 440–42.

5. For Pliny the Elder (A.D. 23–79), Pliny the Younger (A.D. c. 61–c. 112),

Thales (c. 640–c.547 B.C.), and Plato (c. 429–347 B.C.), see Simon Hornblower and Antony Spawforth, eds., *Oxford Classical Dictionary*, 3d ed. (New York: Oxford University Press, 1996).

6. To glid was to look awry, squint. *OED*.

7. Athanasius (c. 300–73) was secretary to Bishop Alexander at the Council of Nicaea in 325 and was himself Bishop of Alexandria (328–73). See *EEC*.

8. Bishop Hosius of Cordova (c. 257–c. 357), adviser to Emperor Constantine, was instrumental in making the arrangements for the Council of Nicaea to meet in 325.

9. For Pope Silvester I (314–35), see *ODP*.

10. Tertullian (fl. 200), as a Montanist, emphasized the "Church of the Spirit" and challenged the authority of the hierarchical "Church of the Bishops" (*De Pudicitia* 21). See *ECC; T. D. Barnes, *Tertullian: A Historical and Literary Study* (Oxford: Clarendon Press, 1985), 82–85; and *The New Catholic Encyclopedia* (New York: McGraw Hill, 1967).

11. The conflicting traditions over whether Clement or Linus (2 Tim. 4:21) immediately succeeded Peter were based on, among others, Tertullian and Irenaeus, respectively. See *EEC*

12. Marcellinus, Bishop of Rome (296–304?), was said to have obeyed a directive of Diocletian by surrendering sacred books and offering incense to the gods. See *ODP*.

13. For Sixtus II see *ODP*.

14. For Thomas Aquinas (c. 1225–74), see Thomas Gilby, ed., *St. Thomas Aquinas, Theological Texts* (Durham, N.C.: Labyrinth, 1982), 399–400.

15. The notion of cursing with "bell, book, and candle" arose from a form of excommunication ending with the words "Do to (close) the book, quench the candle, ring the bell!" See Tilley, *A Dictionary of the Proverbs in England in the Sixteenth and Seventeenth Centuries*, B276.

16. For Archbishop William Laud's (1573–1645) arraignment and trial and John Pym (1584–1643) and Harbottle Grimston (1603–85), see Charles Carlton, *Archbishop William Laud* (New York: Routledge and Kegan Paul, 1987), 197–226; and *DNB*.

17. Matthew Wren (1585–1667), Bishop of Ely, was one of the twelve bishops imprisoned in the Tower as they faced impeachment. Thomas Widdrington (d. 1664), the Member of Parliament who drew up the articles against Wren, declared that as Bishop of Norwich Wren began "to dresse out Gods Worship, according to his owne fancy, this he expresseth in Instructions and directions . . . stiled *Regales Injunctions Domini Episcopis;* a title too sacred, to baptise his brats withal; I shall be bold to call them *Tyrannicus Injunctiones Do. Episcopis*." *S. Tho. Widdringtons Speech at a Conference betweene Both Houses, on Tuesday the 20. of July, 1641* (1641), sig. A2ᵛ. According to Gardiner, Wren's ceremonial practices "aroused even greater opposition than those which had been advocated by Laud." Samuel R. Gardiner, *History of England 1603–42*, 10 vols. (New York: Longmans, Green, 1883–84), 9:407. See also *DNB*.

18. A mountebank was a person who performed from an elevated platform and used tricks, stories, juggling, and the like to entertain the audience. *OED*.

19. For the Cambridge Platonist Henry More (1614–87), see *DNB*; and A. Rupert Hall, *Henry More and the Scientific Revolution* (Cambridge: Cambridge University Press, 1996), 107–45.

20. Pope John XXII (1316–24) argued that it would not be until after the

final judgment that the souls of saints would be in paradise enjoying the full vision of God. His view was condemned by the University of Paris in 1333. See *ODP*.

21. See William J. Bouwsma, *John Calvin: A Sixteenth-Century Portrait* (New York: Oxford University Press, 1988), 78–81; and Calvin's commentary on 1 Cor. 13, *Commentary on the Epistles of Paul the Apostle to the Corinthians*, trans. John Pringle, Publication no. 10, 2 vols. (Edinburgh: Calvin Translation Society, 1848–49), 1:418–33.

22. Irenaeus (c. 115–c. 202) was Bishop of Lyons. See Walter H. Wagner, *After the Apostles: Christianity in the Second Century* (Minneapolis: Augsburg Fortress, 1994), 205–22; Johannes Quasten, *Patrology*, 2 vols. (Utrecht-Antwerp: Spectrum, 1966), 1:287–313; and F. R. Montgomery Hitchcock, *Irenaeus of Lugdunum: A Study of His Teaching* (Cambridge: Cambridge University Press, 1914), 283–97.

23. For St. Bernard of Clairvaux (1090–1153), see M. B. Pranger, *Bernard of Clairvaux and the Shape of Monastic Thought: Broken Dreams* (Leiden: E. J. Brill, 1994), 163–206.

LETTERS

1. Among the six principles, this one eventually would be replaced by that of the mortality of the soul, and other variations would also occur. See *World*, 77–78.

2. For the conspiracy and resulting deaths of Ananias and Sapphira, see Acts 5:7–10.

3. Gehazi was cursed with leprosy because of his greed and lies (2 Kings 5: 20–27).

4. This letter appears to be by the same hand as a fragment identified by John Nichols in 1724 as Muggleton's own (Add. MSS 60168/44). The few words lost at the damaged bottom of the sheet have been replaced by those from a copy transcribed in 1682 by Tobiah Terry (Add. MSS 60171/44–49) and have been placed within brackets.

5. Martain was probably the John Martin who took degrees at Cambridge in the 1660s and who also may have been the vicar of Orwell, where he was buried in 1693. *Alumni Cant.*

6. William Meadgate's nine assertions and Muggleton's answers to them are included in *Acts*, pt. 4, chaps. 7–9.

7. See 1 Sam. 15.

8. In Tudor-Stuart London, "foreigners" referred to London inhabitants who were born in England but were not citizens, and "aliens" were inhabitants born in other countries. Such persons were sometimes resented because they were thought to produce substandard goods, employ too many apprentices, and in other ways provide an economic threat. The 1563 Statute of Apprentices (Artificers) and subsequent legislation attempted to regulate and restrict the movement of people within the kingdom, especially the nonfree, and to punish vagabonds severely. Apparently, Bohanan had not achieved free status in Ware or elsewhere and thus was "not free borne nor free by redemption," as Muggleton puts it. Muggleton's animosity toward the Scots reflected the general English attitude of superiority, perhaps heightened by the perception that the Scots had "changed sides" during the Civil War. See Steve Rappaport, *Worlds Within*

Worlds: Structures of Life in Sixteenth-Century London (Cambridge: Cambridge University Press, 1989), 29–36, 42–47; Ian W. Archer, *The Pursuit of Stability: Social Relations in Elizabethan London* (Cambridge: Cambridge University Press, 1991), 58–63, 131–40; Keith M. Brown, *Kingdom or Province? Scotland and the Regal Union, 1603–1715* (New York: St. Martin's Press, 1992).

9. See Num. 16.

10. Robert Sidney (1595–1677) was second Earl of Leicester. See George Edward Cokayne, *The Complete Peerage*, 6 vols. (Gloucester: Alan Sutton, 1982); *DNB*.

APPENDIX B

1. For this episode see M. A. Gibb, *John Lilburne the Leveller: A Christian Democrat* (Linday Drummond, 1947), 278–94; Pauline Gregg, *Free-born John: A Biography of John Lilburne* (J. M. Dent, 1986), 285–302.

Index of Persons

Aaron, 7–9, 13, 53–54, 75, 108, 113, 116
Abel, 29, 40, 144, 153, 165, 180
Abiram, 11, 120, 207
Abraham, 28–29, 40, 45–46, 56, 156, 159
Adam, 12, 16–17, 29, 44, 94, 105, 107, 140, 144, 152, 158–59, 172–73, 189, 196
Adam Melchisadick (Melchizedek). *See* Melchisadick, Adam
Alexander the Great, 240
Allwood, John, mayor of Chesterfield, 82
Ananias, 198
Aquinas, Thomas, 187, 252 n.14
Athanasius, 185–86, 252 n.7
Atkins (Judge), (Edward Atkyns), 129, 131, 133–34, 251 n.7
Atkinson (Mr.), Muggletonian, 227
Atkinson (Mis.), Muggletonian, 227
Augustine, St., 12, 179, 182, 251 n.2

Balaam, 167
Baptists, 3–4, 6, 10, 14, 23
Barker, James, astrologer, 59–62
Barker, Mary, Muggletonian, 81. *See also* Parker, Mary
Baxter, Richard, 4–5, 16
Beamonists (Beamonites), 79
Benet (Mr.), disputant, 89, 91
Benjamin, 40
Bernard of Clairvaux, 190, 253 n.23
Birch, John, Muggletonian, 4
Bishop of London (Henry Compton), 124, 250 n.2
Boehme, Jacob, 12. *See also* Beamonists
Bohanan, Walter, schismatic Muggletonian, 10, 14, 113, 202–3
Boner (Mrs.), Muggletonian, 77

Boose, Dorcas, Muggletonian, 55
Bosor, 167
Brightman, Thomas, 13
Brocke (Mr.), Muggletonian, 227
Brooks, Lidiah, Muggletonian, 109
Brunte (Brante), John, Muggletonian, 76, 85
Brunt, Deborah, Muggletonian(?) widow, 123–24, 135
Bull, John, 13
Bullinger, Heinrich, 13
Bunyan, John, 6, 9
Burne (Bourne), Edward, Quaker, 127, 250 n.5
Burrell (Mr.), Muggletonian, 227
Burrough, Edward, Quaker, 5–6
Burton, Thomas, Muggletonian, 113

Cain, 17, 144–46, 153, 156, 165, 173, 180, 183, 191, 201, 204, 208
Calvin, John, 17, 190
Canaanites, 169, 234
Carroll, Kenneth, 16
Carter, Dorothy, Muggletonian, 79–80, 82, 85, 92–93, 110
Carter, Elizabeth, daughter of Dorothy Carter, 110
Casseel, G. V., 19
Caton, William, Quaker, 5
Chandler (Mr.), persecutor, 69
Chapman, Muggletonian, 184
Charles I, 5, 236, 238
Clark (Captain), Muggletonian, 59, 61
Clarke (Mr.), alderman of Chesterfield, 83
Clark, Richard, warden, 20, 125–26
Claxton, Laurence, (Lawrence Clarkson), Muggletonian, 4, 10, 14, 77–79, 118, 198

255

Index of Places